2008 | THE LITTLE DATA BOOK ON PRIVATE SECTOR DEVELOPMENT

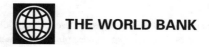

THE WORLD BANK

ISBN: 978-0-8213-7430-6
E-ISBN: 978-0-8213-7431-3
DOI: 10.1596/978-0-8213-7430-6

The Little Data Book on Private Sector Development 2008 is a product
of the Development Data Group of the Development Economics
Vice Presidency and the Investment Climate Department of the Financial
and Private Sector Development Vice Presidency of the World Bank Group.

Editing, design, and layout by Communications Development Incorporated,
Washington, D.C. Cover design by Peter Grundy Art & Design, London, U.K.

Contents

Acknowledgments

The Little Data Book on Private Sector Development 2008 is based on *World Development Indicators 2008* and its accompanying CD-ROM, with a focus on the private sector in development. *The Little Data Book on Private Sector Development 2008* is the result of close collaboration between the staff of the World Bank's Development Data Group of the Development Economics Vice Presidency and the Investment Climate Department of the Financial and Private Sector Development Vice Presidency. The Development Data Group team included David Cieslikowski, Richard Fix, Buyant Erdene Khaltarkhuu, Raymond Muhula, Beatriz Prieto-Oramas, and William Prince. The Investment Climate Department's project coordinator was Shokraneh Minovi. This effort benefited from input by Leora Klapper, Anjali Kumar, Veselin Kuntchev, and Jorge Luis Rodriquez Meza. The work was carried out under the management of Shaida Badiee, director of the Development Data Group, and Pierre Guislain, director of the Investment Climate Department. Meta de Coquereaumont, Christopher Trott, and Elaine Wilson of Communications Development Incorporated provided design, editing, and layout. Staff from External Affairs oversaw publication and dissemination of the book.

Preface

Publication of this edition of *The Little Data Book on Private Sector Development* coincides with continued rising interest in private sector development and growing understanding of the links between private sector development and economic growth. Well functioning finance markets and a robust private sector play critical roles in increasing productivity and growth and in spreading equality of opportunity. The availability of cross-country data on the business environment has expanded rapidly in recent years, including data from the World Bank's Doing Business project and Enterprise Surveys. These data sources report on the scope and types of regulations that enhance—and constrain—business activity and provide information on business owners' assessments of the business environment. The data have led to new research, enabled benchmarking, and informed the reform process in many developing countries.

Included in this guide are indicators on the economic and social context, the business environment, private sector investment, finance and banking, and infrastructure. Though not all relevant variables can be included in a pocket guide, the indicators that are included provide users with a general understanding of the private sector in each country. Indicators displayed in the tables are defined in the *Glossary,* which also lists data sources.

We welcome your suggestions for how to improve future editions and make them more useful.

Data notes

The data in this book are for 2000 and 2006 or the most recent year unless otherwise noted in the *Glossary*.

- Growth rates are proportional changes from the previous year unless otherwise noted.

- Regional aggregates include data for low- and middle-income economies only.

- Figures in italics indicate data for years or periods other than those specified.

Symbols used:

..	indicates that data are not available or that aggregates cannot be calculated because of missing data.
0 or 0.0	indicates zero or small enough that the number would round to zero at the displayed number of decimal places.
$	indicates current U.S. dollars.

Data are shown for economies with populations greater than 30,000 or for smaller economies if they are members of the World Bank. The term *country* (used interchangeably with *economy*) does not imply political independence or official recognition by the World Bank but refers to any economy for which the authorities report separate social or economic statistics.

In keeping with *World Development Indicators 2008*, this edition of *The Little Data Book on Private Sector Development* uses terminology in line with the 1993 System of National Accounts (SNA).

Regional tables

The country composition of regions is based on the World Bank's analytical regions and may differ from common geographic usage.

East Asia and Pacific

    American Samoa, Cambodia, China, Fiji, Indonesia, Kiribati, Democratic Republic of Korea, Lao People's Democratic Republic, Malaysia, Marshall Islands, Federated States of Micronesia, Mongolia, Myanmar, Northern Mariana Islands, Palau, Papua New Guinea, Philippines, Samoa, Solomon Islands, Thailand, Timor-Leste, Tonga, Vanuatu, Vietnam

Europe and Central Asia

    Albania, Armenia, Azerbaijan, Belarus, Bosnia and Herzegovina, Bulgaria, Croatia, Georgia, Hungary, Kazakhstan, Kyrgyz Republic, Latvia, Lithuania, Former Yugoslav Republic of Macedonia, Moldova, Montenegro, Poland, Romania, Russian Federation, Serbia, Slovak Republic, Tajikistan, Turkey, Turkmenistan, Ukraine, Uzbekistan

Latin America and the Caribbean

    Argentina, Belize, Bolivia, Brazil, Chile, Colombia, Costa Rica, Cuba, Dominica, Dominican Republic, Ecuador, El Salvador, Grenada, Guatemala, Guyana, Haiti, Honduras, Jamaica, Mexico, Nicaragua, Panama, Paraguay, Peru, St. Kitts and Nevis, St. Lucia, St. Vincent and the Grenadines, Suriname, Uruguay, Bolivarian Republic of Venezuela

Middle East and North Africa

    Algeria, Djibouti, Arab Republic of Egypt, Islamic Republic of Iran, Iraq, Jordan, Lebanon, Libya, Morocco, Oman, Syrian Arab Republic, Tunisia, West Bank and Gaza, Republic of Yemen

South Asia

    Afghanistan, Bangladesh, Bhutan, India, Maldives, Nepal, Pakistan, Sri Lanka

Sub-Saharan Africa

    Angola, Benin, Botswana, Burkina Faso, Burundi, Cameroon, Cape Verde, Central African Republic, Chad, Comoros, Democratic Republic of the Congo, Republic of Congo, Côte d'Ivoire, Equatorial Guinea, Eritrea, Ethiopia, Gabon, The Gambia, Ghana, Guinea, Guinea-Bissau, Kenya, Lesotho, Liberia, Madagascar, Malawi, Mali, Mauritania, Mauritius, Mayotte, Mozambique, Namibia, Niger, Nigeria, Rwanda, São Tomé and Principe, Senegal, Seychelles, Sierra Leone, Somalia, South Africa, Sudan, Swaziland, Tanzania, Togo, Uganda, Zambia, Zimbabwe

World

	2000	2006
Economic and social context		
Population (millions)	6,076.7	6,538.1
Labor force (millions)	2,801.1	3,081.8
Unemployment rate (% of labor force)	5.4	6.7
GNI per capita, *World Bank Atlas* method ($)	5,252	7,448
GDP growth, 1995–2000 and 2000–06 (average annual %)	3.2	3.0
Agriculture value added (% of GDP)	3.7	*3.2*
Industry value added (% of GDP)	29.2	27.9
Manufacturing value added (% of GDP)	19.3	*17.7*
Services value added (% of GDP)	67.1	69.0
Inflation (annual % change in consumer price index)		
Exchange rate (local currency units per $)		
Exports of goods and services (% of GDP)	24.6	*27.1*
Imports of goods and services (% of GDP)	24.7	*27.3*
Business environment		
Ease of doing business (ranking 1-178; 1=best)		
Time to start a business (days)	..	44
Procedures to start a business (number)	..	9
Firing cost (weeks of wages)	..	48.3
Closing a business (years to resolve insolvency)	..	3.0
Total tax rate (% of profit)	..	50.7
Highest marginal tax rate, corporate (%)		
Business entry rate (new registrations as % of total)	*7.9*	*8.6*
Enterprise surveys		
Time dealing with gov't officials (% of management time)		
Firms expected to give gifts in meetings w/tax officials (%)		
Firms using banks to finance investments (% of firms)		
Delay in obtaining an electrical connection (days)		
ISO certification ownership (% of firms)		
Private sector investment		
Invest. in infrastructure w/private participation ($ millions)	93,044	114,658
Private foreign direct investment, net (% of GDP)	4.9	2.8
Gross fixed capital formation (% of GDP)	21.6	*21.2*
Gross fixed private capital formation (% of GDP)	..	..
Finance and banking		
Government cash surplus or deficit (% of GDP)	*–0.1*	*–1.2*
Government debt (% of GDP)	..	
Deposit money banks' assets (% of GDP)	99.2	90.9
Total financial system deposits (% of GDP)	92.9	*84.9*
Bank capital to asset ratio (%)	8.7	8.9
Bank nonperforming loans to total gross loans ratio (%)	9.5	3.0
Domestic credit to the private sector (% of GDP)	131.1	136.7
Real interest rate (%)		
Interest rate spread (percentage points)	7.4	6.6
Infrastructure		
Paved roads (% of total roads)	35.9	..
Electric power consumption (kWh per capita)	2,389	*2,678*
Power outages in a typical month (number)		
Fixed line and mobile subscribers (per 100 people)	28	59
Internet users (per 100 people)	6.5	21.4
Cost of telephone call to U.S. ($ per 3 minutes)	3.01	*1.42*

East Asia & Pacific

	2000	2006
Economic and social context		
Population (millions)	1,804.0	1,898.9
Labor force (millions)	997.0	1,074.1
Unemployment rate (% of labor force)	3.6	4.9
GNI per capita, *World Bank Atlas* method ($)	908	1,856
GDP growth, 1995–2000 and 2000–06 (average annual %)	6.0	8.6
Agriculture value added (% of GDP)	14.9	12.0
Industry value added (% of GDP)	44.5	46.9
Manufacturing value added (% of GDP)	30.7	32.0
Services value added (% of GDP)	40.6	41.1
Inflation (annual % change in consumer price index)		
Exchange rate (local currency units per $)		
Exports of goods and services (% of GDP)	36.1	47.3
Imports of goods and services (% of GDP)	31.8	40.2
Business environment		
Ease of doing business (ranking 1-178; 1=best)		
Time to start a business (days)	..	47
Procedures to start a business (number)	..	9
Firing cost (weeks of wages)	..	37.2
Closing a business (years to resolve insolvency)	..	3.1
Total tax rate (% of profit)	..	39.9
Highest marginal tax rate, corporate (%)		
Business entry rate (new registrations as % of total)	3.0	7.6
Enterprise surveys		
Time dealing with gov't officials (% of management time)		
Firms expected to give gifts in meetings w/tax officials (%)		
Firms using banks to finance investments (% of firms)		
Delay in obtaining an electrical connection (days)		
ISO certification ownership (% of firms)		
Private sector investment		
Invest. in infrastructure w/private participation ($ millions)	18,027	18,472
Private foreign direct investment, net (% of GDP)	2.6	2.9
Gross fixed capital formation (% of GDP)	30.7	37.2
Gross fixed private capital formation (% of GDP)	11.3	8.4
Finance and banking		
Government cash surplus or deficit (% of GDP)	-2.6	-1.3
Government debt (% of GDP)	..	
Deposit money banks' assets (% of GDP)	104.9	99.6
Total financial system deposits (% of GDP)	45.8	46.4
Bank capital to asset ratio (%)	..	..
Bank nonperforming loans to total gross loans ratio (%)	..	..
Domestic credit to the private sector (% of GDP)	101.3	98.7
Real interest rate (%)		
Interest rate spread (percentage points)	6.9	6.5
Infrastructure		
Paved roads (% of total roads)	11.4	..
Electric power consumption (kWh per capita)	886	1,492
Power outages in a typical month (number)		
Fixed line and mobile subscribers (per 100 people)	15	58
Internet users (per 100 people)	1.9	11.1
Cost of telephone call to U.S. ($ per 3 minutes)	4.32	1.16

Europe & Central Asia

	2000	2006
Economic and social context		
Population (millions)	460.0	460.5
Labor force (millions)	207.1	214.6
Unemployment rate (% of labor force)	10.6	10.0
GNI per capita, *World Bank Atlas* method ($)	1,965	4,815
GDP growth, 1995–2000 and 2000–06 (average annual %)	2.8	5.8
Agriculture value added (% of GDP)	9.9	7.0
Industry value added (% of GDP)	32.2	33.4
Manufacturing value added (% of GDP)	19.1	20.1
Services value added (% of GDP)	57.9	59.6
Inflation (annual % change in consumer price index)		
Exchange rate (local currency units per $)		
Exports of goods and services (% of GDP)	38.9	40.1
Imports of goods and services (% of GDP)	37.4	40.0
Business environment		
Ease of doing business (ranking 1-178; 1=best)		
Time to start a business (days)	..	26
Procedures to start a business (number)	..	9
Firing cost (weeks of wages)	..	25.4
Closing a business (years to resolve insolvency)	..	3.2
Total tax rate (% of profit)	..	51.4
Highest marginal tax rate, corporate (%)		
Business entry rate (new registrations as % of total)	6.7	8.3
Enterprise surveys		
Time dealing with gov't officials (% of management time)		
Firms expected to give gifts in meetings w/tax officials (%)		
Firms using banks to finance investments (% of firms)		
Delay in obtaining an electrical connection (days)		
ISO certification ownership (% of firms)		
Private sector investment		
Invest. in infrastructure w/private participation ($ millions)	24,117	22,772
Private foreign direct investment, net (% of GDP)	2.8	5.0
Gross fixed capital formation (% of GDP)	20.7	21.1
Gross fixed private capital formation (% of GDP)	17.1	17.3
Finance and banking		
Government cash surplus or deficit (% of GDP)	..	1.8
Government debt (% of GDP)	..	..
Deposit money banks' assets (% of GDP)	30.4	..
Total financial system deposits (% of GDP)	28.1	..
Bank capital to asset ratio (%)	11.1	10.3
Bank nonperforming loans to total gross loans ratio (%)	11.1	3.2
Domestic credit to the private sector (% of GDP)	20.7	35.1
Real interest rate (%)		
Interest rate spread (percentage points)	8.6	6.8
Infrastructure		
Paved roads (% of total roads)	74.3	..
Electric power consumption (kWh per capita)	3,276	3,633
Power outages in a typical month (number)		
Fixed line and mobile subscribers (per 100 people)	31	88
Internet users (per 100 people)	2.8	19.2
Cost of telephone call to U.S. ($ per 3 minutes)	3.03	1.55

Latin America & Caribbean

	2000	2006
Economic and social context		
Population (millions)	513.9	556.1
Labor force (millions)	227.2	257.4
Unemployment rate (% of labor force)	9.2	8.9
GNI per capita, *World Bank Atlas* method ($)	3,766	4,785
GDP growth, 1995–2000 and 2000–06 (average annual %)	3.0	3.1
Agriculture value added (% of GDP)	6.1	6.2
Industry value added (% of GDP)	29.6	31.3
Manufacturing value added (% of GDP)	18.1	18.3
Services value added (% of GDP)	64.3	62.4
Inflation (annual % change in consumer price index)		
Exchange rate (local currency units per $)		
Exports of goods and services (% of GDP)	20.4	25.7
Imports of goods and services (% of GDP)	21.4	23.3
Business environment		
Ease of doing business (ranking 1-178; 1=best)		
Time to start a business (days)	..	73
Procedures to start a business (number)	..	10
Firing cost (weeks of wages)	..	58.1
Closing a business (years to resolve insolvency)	..	3.2
Total tax rate (% of profit)	..	48.7
Highest marginal tax rate, corporate (%)		
Business entry rate (new registrations as % of total)	7.2	8.4
Enterprise surveys		
Time dealing with gov't officials (% of management time)		
Firms expected to give gifts in meetings w/tax officials (%)		
Firms using banks to finance investments (% of firms)		
Delay in obtaining an electrical connection (days)		
ISO certification ownership (% of firms)		
Private sector investment		
Invest. in infrastructure w/private participation ($ millions)	39,377	27,653
Private foreign direct investment, net (% of GDP)	4.0	2.4
Gross fixed capital formation (% of GDP)	18.4	19.8
Gross fixed private capital formation (% of GDP)	..	..
Finance and banking		
Government cash surplus or deficit (% of GDP)	–1.3	..
Government debt (% of GDP)	..	..
Deposit money banks' assets (% of GDP)	42.7	48.9
Total financial system deposits (% of GDP)	31.1	36.0
Bank capital to asset ratio (%)	9.6	10.1
Bank nonperforming loans to total gross loans ratio (%)	7.5	2.6
Domestic credit to the private sector (% of GDP)	27.9	30.9
Real interest rate (%)		
Interest rate spread (percentage points)	8.6	7.4
Infrastructure		
Paved roads (% of total roads)	24.3	..
Electric power consumption (kWh per capita)	1,580	*1,715*
Power outages in a typical month (number)		
Fixed line and mobile subscribers (per 100 people)	27	73
Internet users (per 100 people)	3.8	18.4
Cost of telephone call to U.S. ($ per 3 minutes)	2.46	*1.21*

Middle East & North Africa

	2000	2006
Economic and social context		
Population (millions)	278.8	310.7
Labor force (millions)	90.6	111.8
Unemployment rate (% of labor force)	12.1	13.8
GNI per capita, *World Bank Atlas* method ($)	1,684	2,507
GDP growth, 1995–2000 and 2000–06 (average annual %)	4.5	4.2
Agriculture value added (% of GDP)	12.1	11.8
Industry value added (% of GDP)	43.8	40.2
Manufacturing value added (% of GDP)	12.3	13.4
Services value added (% of GDP)	44.0	48.0
Inflation (annual % change in consumer price index)		
Exchange rate (local currency units per $)		
Exports of goods and services (% of GDP)	28.1	37.8
Imports of goods and services (% of GDP)	25.8	34.9
Business environment		
Ease of doing business (ranking 1-178; 1=best)		
Time to start a business (days)	..	39
Procedures to start a business (number)	..	10
Firing cost (weeks of wages)	..	47.0
Closing a business (years to resolve insolvency)	..	3.5
Total tax rate (% of profit)	..	41.4
Highest marginal tax rate, corporate (%)		
Business entry rate (new registrations as % of total)	9.8	7.9
Enterprise surveys		
Time dealing with gov't officials (% of management time)		
Firms expected to give gifts in meetings w/tax officials (%)		
Firms using banks to finance investments (% of firms)		
Delay in obtaining an electrical connection (days)		
ISO certification ownership (% of firms)		
Private sector investment		
Invest. in infrastructure w/private participation ($ millions)	4,115	10,954
Private foreign direct investment, net (% of GDP)	1.2	4.2
Gross fixed capital formation (% of GDP)	21.5	23.1
Gross fixed private capital formation (% of GDP)	13.5	15.1
Finance and banking		
Government cash surplus or deficit (% of GDP)	-0.4	1.0
Government debt (% of GDP)	..	..
Deposit money banks' assets (% of GDP)	47.6	46.6
Total financial system deposits (% of GDP)	45.3	49.9
Bank capital to asset ratio (%)		
Bank nonperforming loans to total gross loans ratio (%)	..	..
Domestic credit to the private sector (% of GDP)	38.3	41.3
Real interest rate (%)		
Interest rate spread (percentage points)	4.8	4.3
Infrastructure		
Paved roads (% of total roads)	62.8	70.2
Electric power consumption (kWh per capita)	1,077	1,358
Power outages in a typical month (number)		
Fixed line and mobile subscribers (per 100 people)	11	53
Internet users (per 100 people)	0.9	13.8
Cost of telephone call to U.S. ($ per 3 minutes)	4.06	1.66

South Asia

	2000	2006
Economic and social context		
Population (millions)	1,358.8	1,499.4
Labor force (millions)	524.8	597.1
Unemployment rate (% of labor force)	4.5	5.3
GNI per capita, *World Bank Atlas* method ($)	443	768
GDP growth, 1995–2000 and 2000–06 (average annual %)	5.4	7.0
Agriculture value added (% of GDP)	23.9	18.0
Industry value added (% of GDP)	25.8	27.7
Manufacturing value added (% of GDP)	15.4	16.6
Services value added (% of GDP)	50.3	54.3
Inflation (annual % change in consumer price index)		
Exchange rate (local currency units per $)		
Exports of goods and services (% of GDP)	14.2	22.0
Imports of goods and services (% of GDP)	15.9	26.0
Business environment		
Ease of doing business (ranking 1-178; 1=best)		
Time to start a business (days)	..	33
Procedures to start a business (number)	..	8
Firing cost (weeks of wages)	..	66.0
Closing a business (years to resolve insolvency)	..	5.0
Total tax rate (% of profit)	..	41.4
Highest marginal tax rate, corporate (%)		
Business entry rate (new registrations as % of total)	5.0	7.7
Enterprise surveys		
Time dealing with gov't officials (% of management time)		
Firms expected to give gifts in meetings w/tax officials (%)		
Firms using banks to finance investments (% of firms)		
Delay in obtaining an electrical connection (days)		
ISO certification ownership (% of firms)		
Private sector investment		
Invest. in infrastructure w/private participation ($ millions)	3,451	21,793
Private foreign direct investment, net (% of GDP)	0.7	2.0
Gross fixed capital formation (% of GDP)	22.2	28.0
Gross fixed private capital formation (% of GDP)	15.8	21.2
Finance and banking		
Government cash surplus or deficit (% of GDP)	–4.0	–3.1
Government debt (% of GDP)	69.3	55.1
Deposit money banks' assets (% of GDP)	38.6	54.7
Total financial system deposits (% of GDP)	39.0	50.7
Bank capital to asset ratio (%)	4.9	6.6
Bank nonperforming loans to total gross loans ratio (%)	19.5	7.7
Domestic credit to the private sector (% of GDP)	27.7	42.6
Real interest rate (%)		
Interest rate spread (percentage points)	6.9	6.7
Infrastructure		
Paved roads (% of total roads)	30.8	56.9
Electric power consumption (kWh per capita)	359	432
Power outages in a typical month (number)		
Fixed line and mobile subscribers (per 100 people)	3	19
Internet users (per 100 people)	0.5	4.9
Cost of telephone call to U.S. ($ per 3 minutes)	3.48	2.02

Sub-Saharan Africa

	2000	2006
Economic and social context		
Population (millions)	673.3	781.8
Labor force (millions)	276.2	323.0
Unemployment rate (% of labor force)	..	..
GNI per capita, *World Bank Atlas* method ($)	483	829
GDP growth, 1995–2000 and 2000–06 (average annual %)	3.2	4.7
Agriculture value added (% of GDP)	17.7	14.5
Industry value added (% of GDP)	31.9	30.3
Manufacturing value added (% of GDP)	13.7	14.3
Services value added (% of GDP)	50.4	55.1
Inflation (annual % change in consumer price index)		
Exchange rate (local currency units per $)		
Exports of goods and services (% of GDP)	32.6	35.5
Imports of goods and services (% of GDP)	30.9	36.3
Business environment		
Ease of doing business (ranking 1-178; 1=best)		
Time to start a business (days)	..	56
Procedures to start a business (number)	..	11
Firing cost (weeks of wages)	..	68.3
Closing a business (years to resolve insolvency)	..	3.4
Total tax rate (% of profit)	..	68.0
Highest marginal tax rate, corporate (%)		
Business entry rate (new registrations as % of total)	*6.1*	*6.6*
Enterprise surveys		
Time dealing with gov't officials (% of management time)		
Firms expected to give gifts in meetings w/tax officials (%)		
Firms using banks to finance investments (% of firms)		
Delay in obtaining an electrical connection (days)		
ISO certification ownership (% of firms)		
Private sector investment		
Invest. in infrastructure w/private participation ($ millions)	2,166	12,165
Private foreign direct investment, net (% of GDP)	2.0	2.4
Gross fixed capital formation (% of GDP)	16.8	19.8
Gross fixed private capital formation (% of GDP)	12.0	14.2
Finance and banking		
Government cash surplus or deficit (% of GDP)	..	..
Government debt (% of GDP)	..	..
Deposit money banks' assets (% of GDP)	39.9	*40.6*
Total financial system deposits (% of GDP)	31.1	*32.7*
Bank capital to asset ratio (%)	..	..
Bank nonperforming loans to total gross loans ratio (%)	..	..
Domestic credit to the private sector (% of GDP)	61.2	78.1
Real interest rate (%)		
Interest rate spread (percentage points)	13.1	9.6
Infrastructure		
Paved roads (% of total roads)	11.9	..
Electric power consumption (kWh per capita)	490	*542*
Power outages in a typical month (number)		
Fixed line and mobile subscribers (per 100 people)	3	15
Internet users (per 100 people)	0.5	3.8
Cost of telephone call to U.S. ($ per 3 minutes)	5.88	*2.43*

Income group tables

For operational and analytical purposes the World Bank's main criterion for classifying economies is gross national income (GNI) per capita. Every economy in *The Little Data Book on Private Sector Development* is classified as low income, middle income, or high income. Low- and middle-income economies are sometimes referred to as developing economies. The use of the term is convenient; it is not intended to imply that all economies in the group are experiencing similar development or that other economies have reached a preferred or final stage of development. Classification by income does not necessarily reflect development status.

Low-income economies are those with a GNI per capita of $905 or less in 2006.

Middle-income economies are those with a GNI per capita of more than $905 but less than $11,116. Lower-middle-income and upper-middle-income economies are separated at a GNI per capita of $3,595.

High-income economies are those with a GNI per capita of $11,116 or more.

Euro area includes the member states of the Economic and Monetary Union of the European Union that have adopted the euro as their currency: Austria, Belgium, Cyprus, Finland, France, Germany, Greece, Ireland, Italy, Luxembourg, Malta, Netherlands, Portugal, Slovenia, and Spain.

Low income

	2000	2006
Economic and social context		
Population (millions)	2,160.9	2,419.7
Labor force (millions)	865.2	995.4
Unemployment rate (% of labor force)	..	..
GNI per capita, *World Bank Atlas* method ($)	381	649
GDP growth, 1995–2000 and 2000–06 (average annual %)	5.0	6.5
Agriculture value added (% of GDP)	26.4	20.4
Industry value added (% of GDP)	26.4	27.7
Manufacturing value added (% of GDP)	14.0	15.8
Services value added (% of GDP)	47.2	51.9
Inflation (annual % change in consumer price index)		
Exchange rate (local currency units per $)		
Exports of goods and services (% of GDP)	19.4	26.7
Imports of goods and services (% of GDP)	20.8	30.1
Business environment		
Ease of doing business (ranking 1-178; 1=best)		
Time to start a business (days)	..	54
Procedures to start a business (number)	..	10
Firing cost (weeks of wages)	..	62.6
Closing a business (years to resolve insolvency)	..	3.8
Total tax rate (% of profit)	..	67.4
Highest marginal tax rate, corporate (%)		
Business entry rate (new registrations as % of total)	*4.2*	*6.4*
Enterprise surveys		
Time dealing with gov't officials (% of management time)		
Firms expected to give gifts in meetings w/tax officials (%)		
Firms using banks to finance investments (% of firms)		
Delay in obtaining an electrical connection (days)		
ISO certification ownership (% of firms)		
Private sector investment		
Invest. in infrastructure w/private participation ($ millions)	4,907	29,785
Private foreign direct investment, net (% of GDP)	1.2	2.6
Gross fixed capital formation (% of GDP)	21.3	26.7
Gross fixed private capital formation (% of GDP)	14.5	19.6
Finance and banking		
Government cash surplus or deficit (% of GDP)	-3.7	-2.6
Government debt (% of GDP)	..	
Deposit money banks' assets (% of GDP)	34.2	50.5
Total financial system deposits (% of GDP)	33.5	44.6
Bank capital to asset ratio (%)	..	..
Bank nonperforming loans to total gross loans ratio (%)	..	..
Domestic credit to the private sector (% of GDP)	24.5	38.3
Real interest rate (%)		
Interest rate spread (percentage points)	13.1	*11.3*
Infrastructure		
Paved roads (% of total roads)	12.1	..
Electric power consumption (kWh per capita)	325	*391*
Power outages in a typical month (number)		
Fixed line and mobile subscribers (per 100 people)	2	17
Internet users (per 100 people)	0.3	*4.2*
Cost of telephone call to U.S. ($ per 3 minutes)	5.93	*1.99*

Middle income

	2000	2006
Economic and social context		
Population (millions)	2,927.8	3,087.7
Labor force (millions)	1,457.7	1,582.6
Unemployment rate (% of labor force)	5.7	6.4
GNI per capita, *World Bank Atlas* method ($)	1,725	3,053
GDP growth, 1995–2000 and 2000–06 (average annual %)	4.0	5.6
Agriculture value added (% of GDP)	9.7	8.4
Industry value added (% of GDP)	36.3	37.3
Manufacturing value added (% of GDP)	22.0	19.6
Services value added (% of GDP)	54.1	54.3
Inflation (annual % change in consumer price index)		
Exchange rate (local currency units per $)		
Exports of goods and services (% of GDP)	29.7	36.0
Imports of goods and services (% of GDP)	28.1	32.9
Business environment		
Ease of doing business (ranking 1-178; 1=best)		
Time to start a business (days)	..	48
Procedures to start a business (number)	..	9
Firing cost (weeks of wages)	..	45.9
Closing a business (years to resolve insolvency)	..	3.1
Total tax rate (% of profit)	..	45.3
Highest marginal tax rate, corporate (%)		
Business entry rate (new registrations as % of total)	7.6	8.3
Enterprise surveys		
Time dealing with gov't officials (% of management time)		
Firms expected to give gifts in meetings w/tax officials (%)		
Firms using banks to finance investments (% of firms)		
Delay in obtaining an electrical connection (days)		
ISO certification ownership (% of firms)		
Private sector investment		
Invest. in infrastructure w/private participation ($ millions)	86,346	84,023
Private foreign direct investment, net (% of GDP)	3.0	3.3
Gross fixed capital formation (% of GDP)	22.8	25.7
Gross fixed private capital formation (% of GDP)	14.4	13.9
Finance and banking		
Government cash surplus or deficit (% of GDP)	..	..
Government debt (% of GDP)	..	..
Deposit money banks' assets (% of GDP)	64.3	70.8
Total financial system deposits (% of GDP)	37.6	42.3
Bank capital to asset ratio (%)	9.6	10.0
Bank nonperforming loans to total gross loans ratio (%)	10.9	3.4
Domestic credit to the private sector (% of GDP)	54.4	60.1
Real interest rate (%)		
Interest rate spread (percentage points)	7.8	6.6
Infrastructure		
Paved roads (% of total roads)	44.0	..
Electric power consumption (kWh per capita)	1,464	*1,928*
Power outages in a typical month (number)		
Fixed line and mobile subscribers (per 100 people)	20	66
Internet users (per 100 people)	2.4	14.1
Cost of telephone call to U.S. ($ per 3 minutes)	3.05	*1.65*

Lower middle income

	2000	2006
Economic and social context		
Population (millions)	2,153.1	2,276.5
Labor force (millions)	1,111.9	1,208.6
Unemployment rate (% of labor force)	4.6	5.7
GNI per capita, *World Bank Atlas* method ($)	1,055	2,038
GDP growth, 1995–2000 and 2000–06 (average annual %)	5.3	7.6
Agriculture value added (% of GDP)	14.1	11.9
Industry value added (% of GDP)	42.5	43.5
Manufacturing value added (% of GDP)	25.5	26.7
Services value added (% of GDP)	43.4	44.6
Inflation (annual % change in consumer price index)		
Exchange rate (local currency units per $)		
Exports of goods and services (% of GDP)	30.5	40.4
Imports of goods and services (% of GDP)	28.5	36.4
Business environment		
Ease of doing business (ranking 1-178; 1=best)		
Time to start a business (days)	..	53
Procedures to start a business (number)	..	10
Firing cost (weeks of wages)	..	50.2
Closing a business (years to resolve insolvency)	..	3.3
Total tax rate (% of profit)	..	45.8
Highest marginal tax rate, corporate (%)		
Business entry rate (new registrations as % of total)	8.0	7.6
Enterprise surveys		
Time dealing with gov't officials (% of management time)		
Firms expected to give gifts in meetings w/tax officials (%)		
Firms using banks to finance investments (% of firms)		
Delay in obtaining an electrical connection (days)		
ISO certification ownership (% of firms)		
Private sector investment		
Invest. in infrastructure w/private participation ($ millions)	21,801	38,154
Private foreign direct investment, net (% of GDP)	2.4	3.0
Gross fixed capital formation (% of GDP)	27.7	33.5
Gross fixed private capital formation (% of GDP)	12.5	10.9
Finance and banking		
Government cash surplus or deficit (% of GDP)	-2.6	-0.9
Government debt (% of GDP)	..	..
Deposit money banks' assets (% of GDP)	84.9	87.8
Total financial system deposits (% of GDP)	40.5	43.1
Bank capital to asset ratio (%)	9.5	10.7
Bank nonperforming loans to total gross loans ratio (%)	13.4	4.0
Domestic credit to the private sector (% of GDP)	77.9	81.3
Real interest rate (%)		
Interest rate spread (percentage points)	8.0	7.2
Infrastructure		
Paved roads (% of total roads)	49.2	65.8
Electric power consumption (kWh per capita)	968	1,502
Power outages in a typical month (number)		
Fixed line and mobile subscribers (per 100 people)	15	60
Internet users (per 100 people)	1.6	11.4
Cost of telephone call to U.S. ($ per 3 minutes)	3.33	2.08

Upper middle income

	2000	2006
Economic and social context		
Population (millions)	774.8	811.3
Labor force (millions)	345.8	374.0
Unemployment rate (% of labor force)	10.4	9.8
GNI per capita, *World Bank Atlas* method ($)	3,588	5,913
GDP growth, 1995–2000 and 2000–06 (average annual %)	3.0	3.9
Agriculture value added (% of GDP)	6.2	5.7
Industry value added (% of GDP)	31.3	32.4
Manufacturing value added (% of GDP)	19.0	19.4
Services value added (% of GDP)	62.5	62.0
Inflation (annual % change in consumer price index)		
Exchange rate (local currency units per $)		
Exports of goods and services (% of GDP)	29.1	32.7
Imports of goods and services (% of GDP)	27.7	30.3
Business environment		
Ease of doing business (ranking 1-178; 1=best)		
Time to start a business (days)	..	41
Procedures to start a business (number)	..	9
Firing cost (weeks of wages)	..	39.7
Closing a business (years to resolve insolvency)	..	2.9
Total tax rate (% of profit)	..	44.5
Highest marginal tax rate, corporate (%)		
Business entry rate (new registrations as % of total)	7.1	9.1
Enterprise surveys		
Time dealing with gov't officials (% of management time)		
Firms expected to give gifts in meetings w/tax officials (%)		
Firms using banks to finance investments (% of firms)		
Delay in obtaining an electrical connection (days)		
ISO certification ownership (% of firms)		
Private sector investment		
Invest. in infrastructure w/private participation ($ millions)	64,545	45,869
Private foreign direct investment, net (% of GDP)	3.6	3.5
Gross fixed capital formation (% of GDP)	19.1	19.9
Gross fixed private capital formation (% of GDP)	..	..
Finance and banking		
Government cash surplus or deficit (% of GDP)	..	..
Government debt (% of GDP)	..	..
Deposit money banks' assets (% of GDP)	46.2	52.9
Total financial system deposits (% of GDP)	35.1	41.4
Bank capital to asset ratio (%)	9.6	9.8
Bank nonperforming loans to total gross loans ratio (%)	7.8	3.2
Domestic credit to the private sector (% of GDP)	35.9	41.4
Real interest rate (%)		
Interest rate spread (percentage points)	7.4	5.9
Infrastructure		
Paved roads (% of total roads)	34.1	..
Electric power consumption (kWh per capita)	2,855	3,131
Power outages in a typical month (number)		
Fixed line and mobile subscribers (per 100 people)	33	88
Internet users (per 100 people)	4.7	22.2
Cost of telephone call to U.S. ($ per 3 minutes)	2.55	1.06

Low and middle income

	2000	2006
Economic and social context		
Population (millions)	5,088.8	5,507.4
Labor force (millions)	2,322.9	2,578.0
Unemployment rate (% of labor force)	5.3	6.8
GNI per capita, *World Bank Atlas* method ($)	1,154	1,997
GDP growth, 1995–2000 and 2000–06 (average annual %)	4.1	5.7
Agriculture value added (% of GDP)	12.0	10.1
Industry value added (% of GDP)	34.9	36.0
Manufacturing value added (% of GDP)	20.8	19.0
Services value added (% of GDP)	53.1	54.0
Inflation (annual % change in consumer price index)		
Exchange rate (local currency units per $)		
Exports of goods and services (% of GDP)	28.2	34.7
Imports of goods and services (% of GDP)	27.0	32.5
Business environment		
Ease of doing business (ranking 1-178; 1=best)		
Time to start a business (days)	..	50
Procedures to start a business (number)	..	10
Firing cost (weeks of wages)	..	51.9
Closing a business (years to resolve insolvency)	..	3.3
Total tax rate (% of profit)	..	53.2
Highest marginal tax rate, corporate (%)		
Business entry rate (new registrations as % of total)	6.8	7.9
Enterprise surveys		
Time dealing with gov't officials (% of management time)		
Firms expected to give gifts in meetings w/tax officials (%)		
Firms using banks to finance investments (% of firms)		
Delay in obtaining an electrical connection (days)		
ISO certification ownership (% of firms)		
Private sector investment		
Invest. in infrastructure w/private participation ($ millions)	91,253	113,808
Private foreign direct investment, net (% of GDP)	2.8	3.2
Gross fixed capital formation (% of GDP)	22.6	25.9
Gross fixed private capital formation (% of GDP)	14.4	14.9
Finance and banking		
Government cash surplus or deficit (% of GDP)	..	..
Government debt (% of GDP)		
Deposit money banks' assets (% of GDP)	60.1	68.1
Total financial system deposits (% of GDP)	37.0	42.6
Bank capital to asset ratio (%)	9.5	9.4
Bank nonperforming loans to total gross loans ratio (%)	11.5	5.3
Domestic credit to the private sector (% of GDP)	50.4	57.3
Real interest rate (%)		
Interest rate spread (percentage points)	8.6	7.3
Infrastructure		
Paved roads (% of total roads)	26.8	..
Electric power consumption (kWh per capita)	1,004	*1,290*
Power outages in a typical month (number)		
Fixed line and mobile subscribers (per 100 people)	13	44
Internet users (per 100 people)	1.6	8.0
Cost of telephone call to U.S. ($ per 3 minutes)	3.97	*1.81*

Euro area

	2000	2006
Economic and social context		
Population (millions)	306.1	316.7
Labor force (millions)	140.9	148.8
Unemployment rate (% of labor force)	8.9	9.0
GNI per capita, *World Bank Atlas* method ($)	22,314	34,307
GDP growth, 1995–2000 and 2000–06 (average annual %)	2.8	1.5
Agriculture value added (% of GDP)	2.5	1.8
Industry value added (% of GDP)	27.8	26.5
Manufacturing value added (% of GDP)	19.9	18.1
Services value added (% of GDP)	69.7	71.7
Inflation (annual % change in consumer price index)		
Exchange rate (local currency units per $)		
Exports of goods and services (% of GDP)	36.6	39.8
Imports of goods and services (% of GDP)	35.9	38.5
Business environment		
Ease of doing business (ranking 1-178; 1=best)		
Time to start a business (days)	..	22
Procedures to start a business (number)	..	7
Firing cost (weeks of wages)	..	34.0
Closing a business (years to resolve insolvency)	..	1.4
Total tax rate (% of profit)	..	50.9
Highest marginal tax rate, corporate (%)		
Business entry rate (new registrations as % of total)	8.4	8.4
Enterprise surveys		
Time dealing with gov't officials (% of management time)		
Firms expected to give gifts in meetings w/tax officials (%)		
Firms using banks to finance investments (% of firms)		
Delay in obtaining an electrical connection (days)		
ISO certification ownership (% of firms)		
Private sector investment		
Invest. in infrastructure w/private participation ($ millions)	..	..
Private foreign direct investment, net (% of GDP)	10.2	3.8
Gross fixed capital formation (% of GDP)	21.4	20.7
Gross fixed private capital formation (% of GDP)	..	..
Finance and banking		
Government cash surplus or deficit (% of GDP)	0.1	-1.3
Government debt (% of GDP)	60.0	63.4
Deposit money banks' assets (% of GDP)	..	..
Total financial system deposits (% of GDP)	..	..
Bank capital to asset ratio (%)	6.4	5.2
Bank nonperforming loans to total gross loans ratio (%)	2.6	1.6
Domestic credit to the private sector (% of GDP)	97.7	115.9
Real interest rate (%)		
Interest rate spread (percentage points)	4.2	3.9
Infrastructure		
Paved roads (% of total roads)	99.0	100.0
Electric power consumption (kWh per capita)	6,410	6,926
Power outages in a typical month (number)		
Fixed line and mobile subscribers (per 100 people)	115	153
Internet users (per 100 people)	23.0	47.9
Cost of telephone call to U.S. ($ per 3 minutes)	0.81	0.73

High income

	2000	2006
Economic and social context		
Population (millions)	987.9	1,030.7
Labor force (millions)	478.2	503.8
Unemployment rate (% of labor force)	6.0	6.2
GNI per capita, *World Bank Atlas* method ($)	26,365	36,608
GDP growth, 1995–2000 and 2000–06 (average annual %)	3.0	2.3
Agriculture value added (% of GDP)	1.8	1.5
Industry value added (% of GDP)	28.0	26.2
Manufacturing value added (% of GDP)	18.9	16.8
Services value added (% of GDP)	70.2	72.3
Inflation (annual % change in consumer price index)		
Exchange rate (local currency units per $)		
Exports of goods and services (% of GDP)	23.8	25.6
Imports of goods and services (% of GDP)	24.2	26.3
Business environment		
Ease of doing business (ranking 1-178; 1=best)		
Time to start a business (days)	..	22
Procedures to start a business (number)	..	7
Firing cost (weeks of wages)	..	34.9
Closing a business (years to resolve insolvency)	..	2.0
Total tax rate (% of profit)	..	41.5
Highest marginal tax rate, corporate (%)		
Business entry rate (new registrations as % of total)	9.6	10.1
Enterprise surveys		
Time dealing with gov't officials (% of management time)		
Firms expected to give gifts in meetings w/tax officials (%)		
Firms using banks to finance investments (% of firms)		
Delay in obtaining an electrical connection (days)		
ISO certification ownership (% of firms)		
Private sector investment		
Invest. in infrastructure w/private participation ($ millions)	1,792	849
Private foreign direct investment, net (% of GDP)	5.3	2.7
Gross fixed capital formation (% of GDP)	21.4	20.4
Gross fixed private capital formation (% of GDP)	..	..
Finance and banking		
Government cash surplus or deficit (% of GDP)	0.2	-1.3
Government debt (% of GDP)	52.3	47.6
Deposit money banks' assets (% of GDP)	110.8	99.7
Total financial system deposits (% of GDP)	92.0	..
Bank capital to asset ratio (%)	6.8	6.2
Bank nonperforming loans to total gross loans ratio (%)	3.4	1.1
Domestic credit to the private sector (% of GDP)	149.9	162.0
Real interest rate (%)		
Interest rate spread (percentage points)	4.2	4.4
Infrastructure		
Paved roads (% of total roads)	92.9	90.9
Electric power consumption (kWh per capita)	9,265	9,760
Power outages in a typical month (number)		
Fixed line and mobile subscribers (per 100 people)	109	143
Internet users (per 100 people)	31.6	59.3
Cost of telephone call to U.S. ($ per 3 minutes)	0.96	0.77

Country tables

China

Unless otherwise noted, data for China do not include data for Hong Kong, China; Macao, China; or Taiwan, China.

Montenegro

Montenegro declared independence from Serbia and Montenegro on June 3, 2006. Where available, data for each country are shown separately.

Serbia

Some indicators for Serbia prior to 2006 include data for Montenegro. Moreover, data for most indicators from 1999 onward for Serbia exclude data for Kosovo, a territory within Serbia that is currently under international administration pursuant to UN Security Council Resolution 1244 (1999).

Afghanistan

	Country data		Low-income group
	2000	2006	2006
Economic and social context			
Population (millions)	..	..	2,420
Labor force (millions)	..	..	995
Unemployment rate (% of labor force)	..	8.5	..
GNI per capita, *World Bank Atlas* method ($)	..	..	649
GDP growth, 1995–2000 and 2000–06 (average annual %)	..	10.7	6.5
Agriculture value added (% of GDP)	49.8	36.1	20.4
Industry value added (% of GDP)	20.1	24.5	27.7
Manufacturing value added (% of GDP)	15.1	14.9	15.8
Services value added (% of GDP)	30.1	39.4	51.9
Inflation (annual % change in consumer price index)	..	..	
Exchange rate (local currency units per $)	61.6	49.5	
Exports of goods and services (% of GDP)	32.9	12.4	26.7
Imports of goods and services (% of GDP)	66.2	55.7	30.1
Business environment			
Ease of doing business (ranking 1-178; 1=best)	..	159	
Time to start a business (days)	..	9	54
Procedures to start a business (number)	..	4	10
Firing cost (weeks of wages)	..	4.3	62.6
Closing a business (years to resolve insolvency)	..	..	3.8
Total tax rate (% of profit)	..	35.5	67.4
Highest marginal tax rate, corporate (%)	..	..	
Business entry rate (new registrations as % of total)			6.4
Enterprise surveys			
Time dealing with gov't officials (% of management time)	..	..	
Firms expected to give gifts in meetings w/tax officials (%)	..	..	
Firms using banks to finance investments (% of firms)	..	..	
Delay in obtaining an electrical connection (days)	..	..	
ISO certification ownership (% of firms)	..	..	
Private sector investment			
Invest. in infrastructure w/private participation ($ millions)	70	463	29,785
Private foreign direct investment, net (% of GDP)	..	..	2.6
Gross fixed capital formation (% of GDP)	28.3	24.3	26.7
Gross fixed private capital formation (% of GDP)	1.2	8.1	19.6
Finance and banking			
Government cash surplus or deficit (% of GDP)	..	-1.7	-2.6
Government debt (% of GDP)	..	9.3	..
Deposit money banks' assets (% of GDP)	..	..	50.5
Total financial system deposits (% of GDP)	..	..	44.6
Bank capital to asset ratio (%)	..	..	..
Bank nonperforming loans to total gross loans ratio (%)	..	..	..
Domestic credit to the private sector (% of GDP)	..	..	38.3
Real interest rate (%)	..	..	
Interest rate spread (percentage points)	..	..	11.3
Infrastructure			
Paved roads (% of total roads)	13.3	23.7	..
Electric power consumption (kWh per capita)	..	..	391
Power outages in a typical month (number)	..	..	
Fixed line and mobile subscribers (per 100 people)	0	10	17
Internet users (per 100 people)	0.0	2.1	4.2
Cost of telephone call to U.S. ($ per 3 minutes)	..	0.39	1.99

Albania

	Country data		Lower middle-income group
	2000	2006	2006
Economic and social context			
Population (millions)	3.1	3.2	2,276
Labor force (millions)	1.3	1.4	1,209
Unemployment rate (% of labor force)	22.7	14.4	5.7
GNI per capita, World Bank Atlas method ($)	1,170	2,930	2,038
GDP growth, 1995–2000 and 2000–06 (average annual %)	5.2	5.3	7.6
Agriculture value added (% of GDP)	29.1	22.8	11.9
Industry value added (% of GDP)	19.0	21.5	43.5
Manufacturing value added (% of GDP)	11.4	12.3	26.7
Services value added (% of GDP)	51.9	55.7	44.6
Inflation (annual % change in consumer price index)	0.1	2.4	
Exchange rate (local currency units per $)	143.7	98.1	
Exports of goods and services (% of GDP)	19.1	25.1	40.4
Imports of goods and services (% of GDP)	37.5	49.2	36.4
Business environment			
Ease of doing business (ranking 1-178; 1=best)	..	136	
Time to start a business (days)	..	36	53
Procedures to start a business (number)	..	10	10
Firing cost (weeks of wages)	..	56.0	50.2
Closing a business (years to resolve insolvency)	..	4.0	3.3
Total tax rate (% of profit)	..	46.8	45.8
Highest marginal tax rate, corporate (%)	..	20	
Business entry rate (new registrations as % of total)	7.5	14.5	7.6
Enterprise surveys			
Time dealing with gov't officials (% of management time)	..	10.4	
Firms expected to give gifts in meetings w/tax officials (%)	78.5	76.7	
Firms using banks to finance investments (% of firms)	8.8	27.9	
Delay in obtaining an electrical connection (days)	26.1	26.6	
ISO certification ownership (% of firms)	..	16.7	
Private sector investment			
Invest. in infrastructure w/private participation ($ millions)	102	1,094	38,154
Private foreign direct investment, net (% of GDP)	3.9	3.6	3.0
Gross fixed capital formation (% of GDP)	24.7	25.0	33.5
Gross fixed private capital formation (% of GDP)	18.1	19.4	10.9
Finance and banking			
Government cash surplus or deficit (% of GDP)	-6.7	-3.0	-0.9
Government debt (% of GDP)	51.9	..	
Deposit money banks' assets (% of GDP)	32.4	43.3	87.8
Total financial system deposits (% of GDP)	40.9	51.5	43.1
Bank capital to asset ratio (%)	..	6.2	10.7
Bank nonperforming loans to total gross loans ratio (%)	..	3.1	4.0
Domestic credit to the private sector (% of GDP)	4.7	21.8	81.3
Real interest rate (%)	17.0	10.8	
Interest rate spread (percentage points)	13.8	7.7	7.2
Infrastructure			
Paved roads (% of total roads)	39.0	..	65.8
Electric power consumption (kWh per capita)	1,191	1,167	1,502
Power outages in a typical month (number)	..	..	
Fixed line and mobile subscribers (per 100 people)	6	60	60
Internet users (per 100 people)	0.1	14.9	11.4
Cost of telephone call to U.S. ($ per 3 minutes)	4.59	1.34	2.08

Algeria

Middle East & North Africa			Lower middle income

	Country data		Lower middle-income group
	2000	2006	2006
Economic and social context			
Population (millions)	30.5	33.4	2,276
Labor force (millions)	11.1	13.9	1,209
Unemployment rate (% of labor force)	27.3	15.3	5.7
GNI per capita, World Bank Atlas method ($)	1,610	3,030	2,038
GDP growth, 1995–2000 and 2000–06 (average annual %)	3.2	5.0	7.6
Agriculture value added (% of GDP)	8.9	8.5	11.9
Industry value added (% of GDP)	58.6	61.5	43.5
Manufacturing value added (% of GDP)	7.5	5.6	26.7
Services value added (% of GDP)	32.5	30.1	44.6
Inflation (annual % change in consumer price index)	0.3	2.5	
Exchange rate (local currency units per $)	75.3	72.6	
Exports of goods and services (% of GDP)	41.2	47.8	40.4
Imports of goods and services (% of GDP)	21.4	23.6	36.4
Business environment			
Ease of doing business (ranking 1-178; 1=best)	..	125	
Time to start a business (days)	..	24	53
Procedures to start a business (number)	..	14	10
Firing cost (weeks of wages)	..	17.0	50.2
Closing a business (years to resolve insolvency)	..	2.5	3.3
Total tax rate (% of profit)	..	72.6	45.8
Highest marginal tax rate, corporate (%)	..	..	
Business entry rate (new registrations as % of total)	19.8	11.8	7.6
Enterprise surveys			
Time dealing with gov't officials (% of management time)	..	..	
Firms expected to give gifts in meetings w/tax officials (%)	..	15.0	
Firms using banks to finance investments (% of firms)	16.9	8.9	
Delay in obtaining an electrical connection (days)	124.9	49.1	
ISO certification ownership (% of firms)	..	..	
Private sector investment			
Invest. in infrastructure w/private participation ($ millions)	472	3,022	38,154
Private foreign direct investment, net (% of GDP)	0.8	1.6	3.0
Gross fixed capital formation (% of GDP)	20.7	23.9	33.5
Gross fixed private capital formation (% of GDP)	12.9	14.1	10.9
Finance and banking			
Government cash surplus or deficit (% of GDP)	9.7	13.8	–0.9
Government debt (% of GDP)	62.1	..	
Deposit money banks' assets (% of GDP)	33.1	33.6	87.8
Total financial system deposits (% of GDP)	24.0	37.3	43.1
Bank capital to asset ratio (%)	..	..	10.7
Bank nonperforming loans to total gross loans ratio (%)	..	..	4.0
Domestic credit to the private sector (% of GDP)	6.0	12.5	81.3
Real interest rate (%)	–11.7	–1.0	
Interest rate spread (percentage points)	2.5	6.3	7.2
Infrastructure			
Paved roads (% of total roads)	68.9	70.2	65.8
Electric power consumption (kWh per capita)	695	899	1,502
Power outages in a typical month (number)	..	5.1	
Fixed line and mobile subscribers (per 100 people)	6	71	60
Internet users (per 100 people)	0.5	7.4	11.4
Cost of telephone call to U.S. ($ per 3 minutes)	3.67	2.08	2.08

American Samoa

Upper middle income

	Country data		Upper middle-income group
	2000	2006	2006
Economic and social context			
Population (millions)	..	0.06	811
Labor force (millions)	..	..	374
Unemployment rate (% of labor force)	..	..	9.8
GNI per capita, *World Bank Atlas* method ($)	..	..	5,913
GDP growth, 1995–2000 and 2000–06 (average annual %)	..	..	3.9
Agriculture value added (% of GDP)	..	..	5.7
Industry value added (% of GDP)	..	..	32.4
Manufacturing value added (% of GDP)	..	..	19.4
Services value added (% of GDP)	..	..	62.0
Inflation (annual % change in consumer price index)	..	..	
Exchange rate (local currency units per $)	..	..	
Exports of goods and services (% of GDP)	..	..	32.7
Imports of goods and services (% of GDP)	..	..	30.3
Business environment			
Ease of doing business (ranking 1-178; 1=best)	..	..	
Time to start a business (days)	..	..	41
Procedures to start a business (number)	..	..	9
Firing cost (weeks of wages)	..	..	39.7
Closing a business (years to resolve insolvency)	..	..	2.9
Total tax rate (% of profit)	..	..	44.5
Highest marginal tax rate, corporate (%)	..	..	
Business entry rate (new registrations as % of total)	..	..	9.1
Enterprise surveys			
Time dealing with gov't officials (% of management time)	..	..	
Firms expected to give gifts in meetings w/tax officials (%)	..	..	
Firms using banks to finance investments (% of firms)	..	..	
Delay in obtaining an electrical connection (days)	..	..	
ISO certification ownership (% of firms)	..	..	
Private sector investment			
Invest. in infrastructure w/private participation ($ millions)	..	..	45,869
Private foreign direct investment, net (% of GDP)	..	..	3.5
Gross fixed capital formation (% of GDP)	..	..	19.9
Gross fixed private capital formation (% of GDP)	..	..	..
Finance and banking			
Government cash surplus or deficit (% of GDP)	..	..	..
Government debt (% of GDP)	..	..	
Deposit money banks' assets (% of GDP)	..	..	52.9
Total financial system deposits (% of GDP)	..	..	41.4
Bank capital to asset ratio (%)	..	..	9.8
Bank nonperforming loans to total gross loans ratio (%)	..	..	3.2
Domestic credit to the private sector (% of GDP)	..	..	41.4
Real interest rate (%)	..	..	
Interest rate spread (percentage points)	..	..	5.9
Infrastructure			
Paved roads (% of total roads)	..	..	..
Electric power consumption (kWh per capita)	..	..	3,131
Power outages in a typical month (number)	..	..	
Fixed line and mobile subscribers (per 100 people)	..	22	88
Internet users (per 100 people)	..	..	22.2
Cost of telephone call to U.S. ($ per 3 minutes)	..	..	1.06

Andorra

	Country data		High-income group
	2000	2006	2006
Economic and social context			
Population (millions)	..	0.07	1,031
Labor force (millions)	..	..	504
Unemployment rate (% of labor force)	..	..	6.2
GNI per capita, *World Bank Atlas* method ($)	..	..	36,608
GDP growth, 1995–2000 and 2000–06 (average annual %)	..	..	2.3
Agriculture value added (% of GDP)	..	..	1.5
Industry value added (% of GDP)	..	..	26.2
Manufacturing value added (% of GDP)	..	..	16.8
Services value added (% of GDP)	..	..	72.3
Inflation (annual % change in consumer price index)	..	..	
Exchange rate (local currency units per $)	..	..	
Exports of goods and services (% of GDP)	..	..	25.6
Imports of goods and services (% of GDP)	..	..	26.3
Business environment			
Ease of doing business (ranking 1-178; 1=best)	..	..	
Time to start a business (days)	..	..	22
Procedures to start a business (number)	..	..	7
Firing cost (weeks of wages)	..	..	34.9
Closing a business (years to resolve insolvency)	..	..	2.0
Total tax rate (% of profit)	..	..	41.5
Highest marginal tax rate, corporate (%)	..	..	
Business entry rate (new registrations as % of total)	..	..	10.1
Enterprise surveys			
Time dealing with gov't officials (% of management time)	..	..	
Firms expected to give gifts in meetings w/tax officials (%)	..	..	
Firms using banks to finance investments (% of firms)	..	..	
Delay in obtaining an electrical connection (days)	..	..	
ISO certification ownership (% of firms)	..	..	
Private sector investment			
Invest. in infrastructure w/private participation ($ millions)	..	..	849
Private foreign direct investment, net (% of GDP)	..	..	2.7
Gross fixed capital formation (% of GDP)	..	..	20.4
Gross fixed private capital formation (% of GDP)	..	..	..
Finance and banking			
Government cash surplus or deficit (% of GDP)	..	..	-1.3
Government debt (% of GDP)	..	..	47.6
Deposit money banks' assets (% of GDP)	..	..	99.7
Total financial system deposits (% of GDP)	..	..	..
Bank capital to asset ratio (%)	..	..	6.2
Bank nonperforming loans to total gross loans ratio (%)	..	..	1.1
Domestic credit to the private sector (% of GDP)	..	..	162.0
Real interest rate (%)	..	..	
Interest rate spread (percentage points)	..	..	4.4
Infrastructure			
Paved roads (% of total roads)	..	..	90.9
Electric power consumption (kWh per capita)	..	..	9,760
Power outages in a typical month (number)	..	..	
Fixed line and mobile subscribers (per 100 people)	..	151	143
Internet users (per 100 people)	..	33.1	59.3
Cost of telephone call to U.S. ($ per 3 minutes)	2.30	..	0.77

Angola

Lower middle income

	Country data		Lower middle-income group
	2000	2006	2006
Economic and social context			
Population (millions)	13.9	16.6	2,276
Labor force (millions)	6.1	7.3	1,209
Unemployment rate (% of labor force)	..	..	5.7
GNI per capita, *World Bank Atlas* method ($)	420	1,970	2,038
GDP growth, 1995–2000 and 2000–06 (average annual %)	6.3	11.5	7.6
Agriculture value added (% of GDP)	5.7	8.9	11.9
Industry value added (% of GDP)	72.1	69.7	43.5
Manufacturing value added (% of GDP)	2.9	4.3	26.7
Services value added (% of GDP)	22.2	21.4	44.6
Inflation (annual % change in consumer price index)	325.0	11.7	
Exchange rate (local currency units per $)	10.0	80.4	
Exports of goods and services (% of GDP)	89.6	73.8	40.4
Imports of goods and services (% of GDP)	62.8	37.9	36.4
Business environment			
Ease of doing business (ranking 1-178; 1=best)	..	167	
Time to start a business (days)	..	119	53
Procedures to start a business (number)	..	12	10
Firing cost (weeks of wages)	..	58.0	50.2
Closing a business (years to resolve insolvency)	..	6.2	3.3
Total tax rate (% of profit)	..	53.2	45.8
Highest marginal tax rate, corporate (%)	..	..	
Business entry rate (new registrations as % of total)	..	..	7.6
Enterprise surveys			
Time dealing with gov't officials (% of management time)	..	7.1	
Firms expected to give gifts in meetings w/tax officials (%)	..	14.8	
Firms using banks to finance investments (% of firms)	..	2.1	
Delay in obtaining an electrical connection (days)	..	60.2	
ISO certification ownership (% of firms)	..	5.1	
Private sector investment			
Invest. in infrastructure w/private participation ($ millions)	68	259	38,154
Private foreign direct investment, net (% of GDP)	9.6	-0.1	3.0
Gross fixed capital formation (% of GDP)	15.1	13.7	33.5
Gross fixed private capital formation (% of GDP)	8.9	2.4	10.9
Finance and banking			
Government cash surplus or deficit (% of GDP)	..	..	-0.9
Government debt (% of GDP)	..	..	..
Deposit money banks' assets (% of GDP)	1.3	7.7	87.8
Total financial system deposits (% of GDP)	8.3	10.5	43.1
Bank capital to asset ratio (%)	10.6	11.3	10.7
Bank nonperforming loans to total gross loans ratio (%)	10.4	13.3	4.0
Domestic credit to the private sector (% of GDP)	2.0	7.5	81.3
Real interest rate (%)	-60.8	4.2	
Interest rate spread (percentage points)	63.6	15.0	7.2
Infrastructure			
Paved roads (% of total roads)	10.4	..	65.8
Electric power consumption (kWh per capita)	89	141	1,502
Power outages in a typical month (number)	..	7.8	
Fixed line and mobile subscribers (per 100 people)	1	14	60
Internet users (per 100 people)	0.1	0.5	11.4
Cost of telephone call to U.S. ($ per 3 minutes)	9.32	3.23	2.08

Antigua and Barbuda

High income

	Country data		High-income group
	2000	2006	2006
Economic and social context			
Population (millions)	0.08	0.08	1,031
Labor force (millions)	..	..	504
Unemployment rate (% of labor force)	..	..	6.2
GNI per capita, *World Bank Atlas* method ($)	8,100	11,050	36,608
GDP growth, 1995–2000 and 2000–06 (average annual %)	4.6	5.1	2.3
Agriculture value added (% of GDP)	3.9	3.6	1.5
Industry value added (% of GDP)	19.8	22.9	26.2
Manufacturing value added (% of GDP)	2.3	2.0	16.8
Services value added (% of GDP)	76.3	73.5	72.3
Inflation (annual % change in consumer price index)	..	..	
Exchange rate (local currency units per $)	2.7	2.7	
Exports of goods and services (% of GDP)	70.2	59.6	25.6
Imports of goods and services (% of GDP)	74.9	71.3	26.3
Business environment			
Ease of doing business (ranking 1-178; 1=best)	..	41	
Time to start a business (days)	..	21	22
Procedures to start a business (number)	..	7	7
Firing cost (weeks of wages)	..	52.0	34.9
Closing a business (years to resolve insolvency)	..	3.0	2.0
Total tax rate (% of profit)	..	46.8	41.5
Highest marginal tax rate, corporate (%)	40	30	
Business entry rate (new registrations as % of total)	..	..	10.1
Enterprise surveys			
Time dealing with gov't officials (% of management time)	..	..	
Firms expected to give gifts in meetings w/tax officials (%)	..	..	
Firms using banks to finance investments (% of firms)	..	..	
Delay in obtaining an electrical connection (days)	..	..	
ISO certification ownership (% of firms)	..	..	
Private sector investment			
Invest. in infrastructure w/private participation ($ millions)	..	..	849
Private foreign direct investment, net (% of GDP)	6.5	13.4	2.7
Gross fixed capital formation (% of GDP)	48.0	58.9	20.4
Gross fixed private capital formation (% of GDP)	23.5	..	..
Finance and banking			
Government cash surplus or deficit (% of GDP)	..	..	-1.3
Government debt (% of GDP)	..	..	47.6
Deposit money banks' assets (% of GDP)	..	..	99.7
Total financial system deposits (% of GDP)	..	..	
Bank capital to asset ratio (%)	..	..	6.2
Bank nonperforming loans to total gross loans ratio (%)	..	..	1.1
Domestic credit to the private sector (% of GDP)	72.8	74.4	162.0
Real interest rate (%)	13.5	7.8	
Interest rate spread (percentage points)	7.0	7.2	4.4
Infrastructure			
Paved roads (% of total roads)	33.0	..	90.9
Electric power consumption (kWh per capita)	..	..	9,760
Power outages in a typical month (number)	..	..	
Fixed line and mobile subscribers (per 100 people)	79	169	143
Internet users (per 100 people)	6.5	38.1	59.3
Cost of telephone call to U.S. ($ per 3 minutes)	5.90	..	0.77

Argentina

	Country data		Upper middle-income group
	2000	2006	2006
Economic and social context			
Population (millions)	36.9	39.1	811
Labor force (millions)	16.2	18.8	374
Unemployment rate (% of labor force)	14.7	10.2	*9.8*
GNI per capita, *World Bank Atlas* method ($)	7,470	5,150	5,913
GDP growth, 1995–2000 and 2000–06 (average annual %)	2.7	3.6	3.9
Agriculture value added (% of GDP)	5.0	8.4	5.7
Industry value added (% of GDP)	27.6	35.6	32.4
Manufacturing value added (% of GDP)	17.5	22.3	19.4
Services value added (% of GDP)	67.4	56.0	62.0
Inflation (annual % change in consumer price index)	-0.9	10.9	
Exchange rate (local currency units per $)	1.0	3.1	
Exports of goods and services (% of GDP)	10.9	24.7	32.7
Imports of goods and services (% of GDP)	11.5	19.2	30.3
Business environment			
Ease of doing business (ranking 1-178; 1=best)	..	109	
Time to start a business (days)	..	31	41
Procedures to start a business (number)	..	14	9
Firing cost (weeks of wages)	..	139.0	39.7
Closing a business (years to resolve insolvency)	..	2.8	2.9
Total tax rate (% of profit)	..	112.9	44.5
Highest marginal tax rate, corporate (%)	35	35	
Business entry rate (new registrations as % of total)	*6.1*	*11.8*	*9.1*
Enterprise surveys			
Time dealing with gov't officials (% of management time)	..	14.1	
Firms expected to give gifts in meetings w/tax officials (%)	..	4.3	
Firms using banks to finance investments (% of firms)	..	6.9	
Delay in obtaining an electrical connection (days)	..	46.2	
ISO certification ownership (% of firms)	..	26.9	
Private sector investment			
Invest. in infrastructure w/private participation ($ millions)	4,863	3,160	45,869
Private foreign direct investment, net (% of GDP)	3.7	2.3	3.5
Gross fixed capital formation (% of GDP)	16.2	23.5	19.9
Gross fixed private capital formation (% of GDP)	15.2	20.9	..
Finance and banking			
Government cash surplus or deficit (% of GDP)	-5.7	-0.5	..
Government debt (% of GDP)	..	..	..
Deposit money banks' assets (% of GDP)	33.7	25.5	52.9
Total financial system deposits (% of GDP)	27.2	20.7	41.4
Bank capital to asset ratio (%)	..	13.6	9.8
Bank nonperforming loans to total gross loans ratio (%)	16.0	3.4	3.2
Domestic credit to the private sector (% of GDP)	23.9	13.0	41.4
Real interest rate (%)	9.9	-4.3	
Interest rate spread (percentage points)	2.7	2.2	5.9
Infrastructure			
Paved roads (% of total roads)	29.4	*30.0*	..
Electric power consumption (kWh per capita)	2,087	*2,418*	*3,131*
Power outages in a typical month (number)	..	1.3	
Fixed line and mobile subscribers (per 100 people)	39	105	88
Internet users (per 100 people)	7.0	20.9	22.2
Cost of telephone call to U.S. ($ per 3 minutes)	2.77	..	*1.06*

Armenia

Europe & Central Asia			Lower middle income

	Country data		Lower middle-income group
	2000	2006	2006

Economic and social context

Population (millions)	3.1	3.0	2,276
Labor force (millions)	1.3	1.3	1,209
Unemployment rate (% of labor force)	36.4	..	5.7
GNI per capita, World Bank Atlas method ($)	660	1,920	2,038
GDP growth, 1995–2000 and 2000–06 (average annual %)	5.1	12.5	7.6
Agriculture value added (% of GDP)	25.5	19.6	11.9
Industry value added (% of GDP)	35.4	43.6	43.5
Manufacturing value added (% of GDP)	24.1	16.8	26.7
Services value added (% of GDP)	39.0	36.8	44.6
Inflation (annual % change in consumer price index)	-0.8	2.9	
Exchange rate (local currency units per $)	539.5	416.0	
Exports of goods and services (% of GDP)	23.4	22.0	40.4
Imports of goods and services (% of GDP)	50.5	36.5	36.4

Business environment

Ease of doing business (ranking 1-178; 1=best)	..	39	
Time to start a business (days)	..	18	53
Procedures to start a business (number)	..	9	10
Firing cost (weeks of wages)	..	13.0	50.2
Closing a business (years to resolve insolvency)	..	1.9	3.3
Total tax rate (% of profit)	..	36.6	45.8
Highest marginal tax rate, corporate (%)	..	..	
Business entry rate (new registrations as % of total)	7.6	7.8	7.6
Enterprise surveys			
Time dealing with gov't officials (% of management time)	..	3.0	
Firms expected to give gifts in meetings w/tax officials (%)	27.2	67.8	
Firms using banks to finance investments (% of firms)	4.7	35.0	
Delay in obtaining an electrical connection (days)	5.0	3.0	
ISO certification ownership (% of firms)	..	5.7	

Private sector investment

Invest. in infrastructure w/private participation ($ millions)	33	20	38,154
Private foreign direct investment, net (% of GDP)	5.5	5.4	3.0
Gross fixed capital formation (% of GDP)	18.4	33.3	33.5
Gross fixed private capital formation (% of GDP)	15.9	27.6	10.9

Finance and banking

Government cash surplus or deficit (% of GDP)	..	-0.3	-0.9
Government debt (% of GDP)	..	..	..
Deposit money banks' assets (% of GDP)	10.5	9.5	87.8
Total financial system deposits (% of GDP)	7.6	9.3	43.1
Bank capital to asset ratio (%)	14.3	22.9	10.7
Bank nonperforming loans to total gross loans ratio (%)	17.5	2.5	4.0
Domestic credit to the private sector (% of GDP)	9.9	8.8	81.3
Real interest rate (%)	33.4	11.4	
Interest rate spread (percentage points)	13.5	10.7	7.2

Infrastructure

Paved roads (% of total roads)	96.8	90.0	65.8
Electric power consumption (kWh per capita)	1,292	1,503	1,502
Power outages in a typical month (number)	..	..	
Fixed line and mobile subscribers (per 100 people)	18	30	60
Internet users (per 100 people)	1.3	5.7	11.4
Cost of telephone call to U.S. ($ per 3 minutes)	5.34	2.42	2.08

Aruba

High income

	Country data		High-income group
	2000	2006	2006
Economic and social context			
Population (millions)	..	0.10	1,031
Labor force (millions)	..	..	504
Unemployment rate (% of labor force)	7.5	..	6.2
GNI per capita, *World Bank Atlas* method ($)	..	..	36,608
GDP growth, 1995–2000 and 2000–06 (average annual %)	4.4	−0.8	2.3
Agriculture value added (% of GDP)	..	..	1.5
Industry value added (% of GDP)	..	..	26.2
Manufacturing value added (% of GDP)	..	..	16.8
Services value added (% of GDP)	..	..	72.3
Inflation (annual % change in consumer price index)	4.0	3.6	
Exchange rate (local currency units per $)	1.8	1.8	
Exports of goods and services (% of GDP)	69.9	..	25.6
Imports of goods and services (% of GDP)	91.2	..	26.3
Business environment			
Ease of doing business (ranking 1-178; 1=best)	..	..	
Time to start a business (days)	..	..	22
Procedures to start a business (number)	..	..	7
Firing cost (weeks of wages)	..	..	34.9
Closing a business (years to resolve insolvency)	..	..	2.0
Total tax rate (% of profit)	..	..	41.5
Highest marginal tax rate, corporate (%)	..	..	
Business entry rate (new registrations as % of total)	..	..	10.1
Enterprise surveys			
Time dealing with gov't officials (% of management time)	..	..	
Firms expected to give gifts in meetings w/tax officials (%)	..	..	
Firms using banks to finance investments (% of firms)	..	..	
Delay in obtaining an electrical connection (days)	..	..	
ISO certification ownership (% of firms)	..	..	
Private sector investment			
Invest. in infrastructure w/private participation ($ millions)	..	..	849
Private foreign direct investment, net (% of GDP)	−6.4	..	2.7
Gross fixed capital formation (% of GDP)	..	..	20.4
Gross fixed private capital formation (% of GDP)	..	..	..
Finance and banking			
Government cash surplus or deficit (% of GDP)	..	..	−1.3
Government debt (% of GDP)	..	..	47.6
Deposit money banks' assets (% of GDP)	44.9	56.2	99.7
Total financial system deposits (% of GDP)	47.7	55.6	..
Bank capital to asset ratio (%)	..	..	6.2
Bank nonperforming loans to total gross loans ratio (%)	..	..	1.1
Domestic credit to the private sector (% of GDP)	45.2	57.0	162.0
Real interest rate (%)	7.7	9.8	
Interest rate spread (percentage points)	5.9	7.4	4.4
Infrastructure			
Paved roads (% of total roads)	..	..	90.9
Electric power consumption (kWh per capita)	..	..	9,760
Power outages in a typical month (number)	..	..	
Fixed line and mobile subscribers (per 100 people)	..	146	143
Internet users (per 100 people)	..	23.9	59.3
Cost of telephone call to U.S. ($ per 3 minutes)	2.90	..	0.77

Australia

	Country data		High-income group
	2000	2006	2006
Economic and social context			
Population (millions)	19.2	20.7	1,031
Labor force (millions)	9.6	10.5	504
Unemployment rate (% of labor force)	6.3	5.1	6.2
GNI per capita, *World Bank Atlas* method ($)	20,720	35,860	36,608
GDP growth, 1995–2000 and 2000–06 (average annual %)	4.1	3.2	2.3
Agriculture value added (% of GDP)	4.0	3.1	1.5
Industry value added (% of GDP)	26.1	28.0	26.2
Manufacturing value added (% of GDP)	12.7	11.0	16.8
Services value added (% of GDP)	69.9	69.0	72.3
Inflation (annual % change in consumer price index)	4.5	3.5	
Exchange rate (local currency units per $)	1.7	1.3	
Exports of goods and services (% of GDP)	22.7	20.3	25.6
Imports of goods and services (% of GDP)	22.4	21.8	26.3
Business environment			
Ease of doing business (ranking 1-178; 1=best)	..	9	
Time to start a business (days)	..	2	22
Procedures to start a business (number)	..	2	7
Firing cost (weeks of wages)		4.0	34.9
Closing a business (years to resolve insolvency)	..	1.0	2.0
Total tax rate (% of profit)	..	50.6	41.5
Highest marginal tax rate, corporate (%)	34	30	
Business entry rate (new registrations as % of total)	9.6	8.7	10.1
Enterprise surveys			
Time dealing with gov't officials (% of management time)	..	..	
Firms expected to give gifts in meetings w/tax officials (%)	..	..	
Firms using banks to finance investments (% of firms)	..	..	
Delay in obtaining an electrical connection (days)	..	..	
ISO certification ownership (% of firms)	..	..	
Private sector investment			
Invest. in infrastructure w/private participation ($ millions)	..	..	849
Private foreign direct investment, net (% of GDP)	3.4	3.4	2.7
Gross fixed capital formation (% of GDP)	22.0	26.5	20.4
Gross fixed private capital formation (% of GDP)	..	..	..
Finance and banking			
Government cash surplus or deficit (% of GDP)	1.9	1.7	-1.3
Government debt (% of GDP)	28.4	20.5	47.6
Deposit money banks' assets (% of GDP)	..	..	99.7
Total financial system deposits (% of GDP)	..	..	..
Bank capital to asset ratio (%)	6.9	4.9	6.2
Bank nonperforming loans to total gross loans ratio (%)	0.5	0.2	1.1
Domestic credit to the private sector (% of GDP)	84.2	109.6	162.0
Real interest rate (%)	4.2	4.6	
Interest rate spread (percentage points)	5.1	5.5	4.4
Infrastructure			
Paved roads (% of total roads)	38.7	..	90.9
Electric power consumption (kWh per capita)	10,055	11,481	9,760
Power outages in a typical month (number)	..	..	
Fixed line and mobile subscribers (per 100 people)	97	143	143
Internet users (per 100 people)	34.5	73.9	59.3
Cost of telephone call to U.S. ($ per 3 minutes)	0.67	..	0.77

Austria

High income

	Country data		High-income group
	2000	2006	2006
Economic and social context			
Population (millions)	8.0	8.3	1,031
Labor force (millions)	3.9	4.0	504
Unemployment rate (% of labor force)	3.6	5.2	6.2
GNI per capita, *World Bank Atlas* method ($)	26,010	39,750	36,608
GDP growth, 1995–2000 and 2000–06 (average annual %)	2.9	1.7	2.3
Agriculture value added (% of GDP)	2.1	1.7	1.5
Industry value added (% of GDP)	30.9	30.9	26.2
Manufacturing value added (% of GDP)	20.3	19.4	16.8
Services value added (% of GDP)	67.0	67.4	72.3
Inflation (annual % change in consumer price index)	2.4	1.5	
Exchange rate (local currency units per $)	1.1	0.8	
Exports of goods and services (% of GDP)	45.4	57.7	25.6
Imports of goods and services (% of GDP)	44.1	52.0	26.3
Business environment			
Ease of doing business (ranking 1-178; 1=best)	..	25	
Time to start a business (days)	..	28	22
Procedures to start a business (number)	..	8	7
Firing cost (weeks of wages)	..	2.0	34.9
Closing a business (years to resolve insolvency)	..	1.1	2.0
Total tax rate (% of profit)	..	54.6	41.5
Highest marginal tax rate, corporate (%)	34	25	
Business entry rate (new registrations as % of total)	7.9	8.5	10.1
Enterprise surveys			
Time dealing with gov't officials (% of management time)	..	..	
Firms expected to give gifts in meetings w/tax officials (%)	..	..	
Firms using banks to finance investments (% of firms)	..	..	
Delay in obtaining an electrical connection (days)	..	..	
ISO certification ownership (% of firms)	..	..	
Private sector investment			
Invest. in infrastructure w/private participation ($ millions)	..	..	849
Private foreign direct investment, net (% of GDP)	4.4	0.0	2.7
Gross fixed capital formation (% of GDP)	22.8	20.8	20.4
Gross fixed private capital formation (% of GDP)	..	..	..
Finance and banking			
Government cash surplus or deficit (% of GDP)	–1.9	–1.6	–1.3
Government debt (% of GDP)	64.4	63.4	47.6
Deposit money banks' assets (% of GDP)	..	..	99.7
Total financial system deposits (% of GDP)	..	..	..
Bank capital to asset ratio (%)	5.2	5.2	6.2
Bank nonperforming loans to total gross loans ratio (%)	2.4	2.6	1.1
Domestic credit to the private sector (% of GDP)	101.7	114.9	162.0
Real interest rate (%)	5.0	..	
Interest rate spread (percentage points)*	3.4	..	4.4
Infrastructure			
Paved roads (% of total roads)	100.0	100.0	90.9
Electric power consumption (kWh per capita)	7,107	7,889	9,760
Power outages in a typical month (number)	..	..	
Fixed line and mobile subscribers (per 100 people)	126	155	143
Internet users (per 100 people)	33.7	50.7	59.3
Cost of telephone call to U.S. ($ per 3 minutes)	1.19	0.71	0.77

Azerbaijan

Europe & Central Asia

Lower middle income

	Country data		Lower middle-income group
	2000	2006	2006
Economic and social context			
Population (millions)	8.0	8.5	2,276
Labor force (millions)	3.7	4.3	1,209
Unemployment rate (% of labor force)	..	8.6	5.7
GNI per capita, *World Bank Atlas* method ($)	610	1,840	2,038
GDP growth, 1995–2000 and 2000–06 (average annual %)	7.3	15.6	7.6
Agriculture value added (% of GDP)	17.1	7.4	11.9
Industry value added (% of GDP)	45.3	70.1	43.5
Manufacturing value added (% of GDP)	5.6	5.6	26.7
Services value added (% of GDP)	37.5	22.5	44.6
Inflation (annual % change in consumer price index)	1.9	8.3	
Exchange rate (local currency units per $)	0.9	0.9	
Exports of goods and services (% of GDP)	39.0	70.3	40.4
Imports of goods and services (% of GDP)	38.4	41.0	36.4
Business environment			
Ease of doing business (ranking 1-178; 1=best)	..	96	
Time to start a business (days)	..	30	53
Procedures to start a business (number)	..	13	10
Firing cost (weeks of wages)	..	22.0	50.2
Closing a business (years to resolve insolvency)	..	2.7	3.3
Total tax rate (% of profit)	..	40.9	45.8
Highest marginal tax rate, corporate (%)	27	22	
Business entry rate (new registrations as % of total)	..	..	7.6
Enterprise surveys			
Time dealing with gov't officials (% of management time)	..	5.2	
Firms expected to give gifts in meetings w/tax officials (%)	53.2	66.7	
Firms using banks to finance investments (% of firms)	2.9	0.6	
Delay in obtaining an electrical connection (days)	18.0	2.0	
ISO certification ownership (% of firms)	..	10.3	
Private sector investment			
Invest. in infrastructure w/private participation ($ millions)	61	414	38,154
Private foreign direct investment, net (% of GDP)	2.5	-2.9	3.0
Gross fixed capital formation (% of GDP)	23.1	31.4	33.5
Gross fixed private capital formation (% of GDP)	20.1	22.8	10.9
Finance and banking			
Government cash surplus or deficit (% of GDP)	-4.7	..	-0.9
Government debt (% of GDP)	..	..	..
Deposit money banks' assets (% of GDP)	10.3	11.0	87.8
Total financial system deposits (% of GDP)	7.5	9.2	43.1
Bank capital to asset ratio (%)	..	14.2	10.7
Bank nonperforming loans to total gross loans ratio (%)	28.0	7.2	4.0
Domestic credit to the private sector (% of GDP)	5.9	12.4	81.3
Real interest rate (%)	6.4	11.9	
Interest rate spread (percentage points)	6.8	7.3	7.2
Infrastructure			
Paved roads (% of total roads)	92.3	49.4	65.8
Electric power consumption (kWh per capita)	2,040	2,407	1,502
Power outages in a typical month (number)	..	..	
Fixed line and mobile subscribers (per 100 people)	15	53	60
Internet users (per 100 people)	0.1	9.8	11.4
Cost of telephone call to U.S. ($ per 3 minutes)	7.10	4.18	2.08

Bahamas, The

High income

	Country data		High-income group
	2000	2006	2006
Economic and social context			
Population (millions)	0.30	0.33	1,031
Labor force (millions)	0.15	0.16	504
Unemployment rate (% of labor force)	6.9	10.2	6.2
GNI per capita, *World Bank Atlas* method ($)	15,290	..	36,608
GDP growth, 1995–2000 and 2000–06 (average annual %)	4.2	..	2.3
Agriculture value added (% of GDP)	..	..	1.5
Industry value added (% of GDP)	..	..	26.2
Manufacturing value added (% of GDP)	..	..	16.8
Services value added (% of GDP)	..	..	72.3
Inflation (annual % change in consumer price index)	1.0	2.4	
Exchange rate (local currency units per $)	1.0	1.0	
Exports of goods and services (% of GDP)	..	..	25.6
Imports of goods and services (% of GDP)	..	..	26.3
Business environment			
Ease of doing business (ranking 1-178; 1=best)	..	..	
Time to start a business (days)	..	..	22
Procedures to start a business (number)	..	..	7
Firing cost (weeks of wages)	..	..	34.9
Closing a business (years to resolve insolvency)	..	..	2.0
Total tax rate (% of profit)	..	..	41.5
Highest marginal tax rate, corporate (%)	..	..	
Business entry rate (new registrations as % of total)	..	..	10.1
Enterprise surveys			
Time dealing with gov't officials (% of management time)	..	..	
Firms expected to give gifts in meetings w/tax officials (%)	..	..	
Firms using banks to finance investments (% of firms)	..	..	
Delay in obtaining an electrical connection (days)	..	..	
ISO certification ownership (% of firms)	..	..	
Private sector investment			
Invest. in infrastructure w/private participation ($ millions)	..	..	849
Private foreign direct investment, net (% of GDP)	5.0	3.5	2.7
Gross fixed capital formation (% of GDP)	..	..	20.4
Gross fixed private capital formation (% of GDP)	..	..	..
Finance and banking			
Government cash surplus or deficit (% of GDP)	0.4	-1.8	-1.3
Government debt (% of GDP)	30.3	..	47.6
Deposit money banks' assets (% of GDP)	..	..	99.7
Total financial system deposits (% of GDP)	..	..	..
Bank capital to asset ratio (%)	..	..	6.2
Bank nonperforming loans to total gross loans ratio (%)	..	..	1.1
Domestic credit to the private sector (% of GDP)	72.3	82.2	162.0
Real interest rate (%)	1.8	..	
Interest rate spread (percentage points)	1.9	2.1	4.4
Infrastructure			
Paved roads (% of total roads)	57.4	..	90.9
Electric power consumption (kWh per capita)	..	..	9,760
Power outages in a typical month (number)	..	..	
Fixed line and mobile subscribers (per 100 people)	48	112	143
Internet users (per 100 people)	4.3	31.9	59.3
Cost of telephone call to U.S. ($ per 3 minutes)	2.40	..	0.77

Bahrain

	Country data		High-income group
	2000	2006	2006
Economic and social context			
Population (millions)	0.65	0.74	1,031
Labor force (millions)	0.30	0.35	504
Unemployment rate (% of labor force)	5.2	..	6.2
GNI per capita, *World Bank Atlas* method ($)	10,740	*19,350*	36,608
GDP growth, 1995–2000 and 2000–06 (average annual %)	4.3	6.1	2.3
Agriculture value added (% of GDP)	..	..	1.5
Industry value added (% of GDP)	..	..	26.2
Manufacturing value added (% of GDP)	..	..	16.8
Services value added (% of GDP)	..	..	72.3
Inflation (annual % change in consumer price index)	-0.7	2.0	
Exchange rate (local currency units per $)	0.4	0.4	
Exports of goods and services (% of GDP)	89.4	*72.9*	25.6
Imports of goods and services (% of GDP)	64.4	*54.2*	26.3
Business environment			
Ease of doing business (ranking 1-178; 1=best)	..	..	
Time to start a business (days)	..	..	22
Procedures to start a business (number)	..	..	7
Firing cost (weeks of wages)	..	..	34.9
Closing a business (years to resolve insolvency)	..	..	2.0
Total tax rate (% of profit)	..	..	41.5
Highest marginal tax rate, corporate (%)	..	..	
Business entry rate (new registrations as % of total)	..	..	*10.1*
Enterprise surveys			
Time dealing with gov't officials (% of management time)	..	..	
Firms expected to give gifts in meetings w/tax officials (%)	..	..	
Firms using banks to finance investments (% of firms)	..	..	
Delay in obtaining an electrical connection (days)	..	..	
ISO certification ownership (% of firms)	..	..	
Private sector investment			
Invest. in infrastructure w/private participation ($ millions)	..	..	849
Private foreign direct investment, net (% of GDP)	4.6	6.5	2.7
Gross fixed capital formation (% of GDP)	13.5	*14.8*	20.4
Gross fixed private capital formation (% of GDP)	..	..	..
Finance and banking			
Government cash surplus or deficit (% of GDP)	8.5	6.3	-1.3
Government debt (% of GDP)	29.3	*24.1*	47.6
Deposit money banks' assets (% of GDP)	55.6	..	99.7
Total financial system deposits (% of GDP)	63.6	..	..
Bank capital to asset ratio (%)	..	..	6.2
Bank nonperforming loans to total gross loans ratio (%)	..	..	1.1
Domestic credit to the private sector (% of GDP)	54.8	52.4	162.0
Real interest rate (%)	-2.3	-18.9	
Interest rate spread (percentage points)	5.9	4.8	4.4
Infrastructure			
Paved roads (% of total roads)	77.6	*79.1*	90.9
Electric power consumption (kWh per capita)	8,830	*11,401*	9,760
Power outages in a typical month (number)	..	..	
Fixed line and mobile subscribers (per 100 people)	58	148	143
Internet users (per 100 people)	6.2	21.3	59.3
Cost of telephone call to U.S. ($ per 3 minutes)	3.39	*1.74*	0.77

Bangladesh

	Country data		Low-income group
	2000	2006	2006
Economic and social context			
Population (millions)	139.4	156.0	2,420
Labor force (millions)	62.3	71.0	995
Unemployment rate (% of labor force)	3.3	4.3	..
GNI per capita, *World Bank Atlas* method ($)	360	450	649
GDP growth, 1995–2000 and 2000–06 (average annual %)	5.2	5.6	6.5
Agriculture value added (% of GDP)	25.5	19.6	20.4
Industry value added (% of GDP)	25.3	27.9	27.7
Manufacturing value added (% of GDP)	15.2	17.2	15.8
Services value added (% of GDP)	49.2	52.5	51.9
Inflation (annual % change in consumer price index)	2.2	6.8	
Exchange rate (local currency units per $)	52.1	68.9	
Exports of goods and services (% of GDP)	14.0	19.0	26.7
Imports of goods and services (% of GDP)	19.2	25.2	30.1
Business environment			
Ease of doing business (ranking 1-178; 1=best)	..	107	
Time to start a business (days)	..	74	54
Procedures to start a business (number)	..	8	10
Firing cost (weeks of wages)	..	104.0	62.6
Closing a business (years to resolve insolvency)	..	4.0	3.8
Total tax rate (% of profit)	..	39.5	67.4
Highest marginal tax rate, corporate (%)	..	..	
Business entry rate (new registrations as % of total)	5.7	7.9	6.4
Enterprise surveys			
Time dealing with gov't officials (% of management time)	..	3.2	
Firms expected to give gifts in meetings w/tax officials (%)	85.8	54.4	
Firms using banks to finance investments (% of firms)	50.5	24.7	
Delay in obtaining an electrical connection (days)	79.6	50.3	
ISO certification ownership (% of firms)	..	7.8	
Private sector investment			
Invest. in infrastructure w/private participation ($ millions)	93	893	29,785
Private foreign direct investment, net (% of GDP)	0.6	1.1	2.6
Gross fixed capital formation (% of GDP)	23.0	24.7	26.7
Gross fixed private capital formation (% of GDP)	15.6	18.7	19.6
Finance and banking			
Government cash surplus or deficit (% of GDP)	-0.7	-0.7	-2.6
Government debt (% of GDP)	36.2	36.2	..
Deposit money banks' assets (% of GDP)	30.0	49.4	50.5
Total financial system deposits (% of GDP)	27.2	47.0	44.6
Bank capital to asset ratio (%)	3.5	4.0	..
Bank nonperforming loans to total gross loans ratio (%)	34.9	13.2	..
Domestic credit to the private sector (% of GDP)	24.7	36.2	38.3
Real interest rate (%)	13.4	9.7	
Interest rate spread (percentage points)	6.9	6.2	11.3
Infrastructure			
Paved roads (% of total roads)	9.5	9.5	..
Electric power consumption (kWh per capita)	96	136	391
Power outages in a typical month (number)	..	101.6	
Fixed line and mobile subscribers (per 100 people)	1	13	17
Internet users (per 100 people)	0.1	0.3	4.2
Cost of telephone call to U.S. ($ per 3 minutes)	4.14	2.02	1.99

Barbados

High income

	Country data		High-income group
	2000	**2006**	**2006**
Economic and social context			
Population (millions)	0.29	0.29	1,031
Labor force (millions)	0.16	0.17	504
Unemployment rate (% of labor force)	9.4	9.8	6.2
GNI per capita, *World Bank Atlas* method ($)	8,480	..	36,608
GDP growth, 1995–2000 and 2000–06 (average annual %)	3.7	..	2.3
Agriculture value added (% of GDP)	4.3	3.7	1.5
Industry value added (% of GDP)	16.3	18.0	26.2
Manufacturing value added (% of GDP)	6.4	7.1	16.8
Services value added (% of GDP)	79.4	78.3	72.3
Inflation (annual % change in consumer price index)	2.4	7.3	
Exchange rate (local currency units per $)	2.0	2.0	
Exports of goods and services (% of GDP)	50.5	54.3	25.6
Imports of goods and services (% of GDP)	57.0	63.5	26.3
Business environment			
Ease of doing business (ranking 1-178; 1=best)	..	..	
Time to start a business (days)	..	..	22
Procedures to start a business (number)	..	..	7
Firing cost (weeks of wages)	..	..	34.9
Closing a business (years to resolve insolvency)	..	..	2.0
Total tax rate (% of profit)	..	..	41.5
Highest marginal tax rate, corporate (%)	40	36	
Business entry rate (new registrations as % of total)	..	..	10.1
Enterprise surveys			
Time dealing with gov't officials (% of management time)	..	..	
Firms expected to give gifts in meetings w/tax officials (%)	..	..	
Firms using banks to finance investments (% of firms)	..	..	
Delay in obtaining an electrical connection (days)	..	..	
ISO certification ownership (% of firms)	..	..	
Private sector investment			
Invest. in infrastructure w/private participation ($ millions)	38	13	849
Private foreign direct investment, net (% of GDP)	0.8	2.0	2.7
Gross fixed capital formation (% of GDP)	18.4	24.4	20.4
Gross fixed private capital formation (% of GDP)	16.2	23.5	..
Finance and banking			
Government cash surplus or deficit (% of GDP)	..	3.7	-1.3
Government debt (% of GDP)	..	..	47.6
Deposit money banks' assets (% of GDP)	74.3	86.1	99.7
Total financial system deposits (% of GDP)	67.6	88.8	..
Bank capital to asset ratio (%)	..	..	6.2
Bank nonperforming loans to total gross loans ratio (%)	..	..	1.1
Domestic credit to the private sector (% of GDP)	57.3	66.7	162.0
Real interest rate (%)	9.4	..	
Interest rate spread (percentage points)	5.2	5.7	4.4
Infrastructure			
Paved roads (% of total roads)	98.6	100.0	90.9
Electric power consumption (kWh per capita)	..	..	9,760
Power outages in a typical month (number)	..	..	
Fixed line and mobile subscribers (per 100 people)	53	117	143
Internet users (per 100 people)	3.5	54.8	59.3
Cost of telephone call to U.S. ($ per 3 minutes)	4.05	1.95	0.77

Belarus

Europe & Central Asia   **Lower middle income**

	Country data		Lower middle-income group
	2000	2006	2006
Economic and social context			
Population (millions)	10.0	9.7	2,276
Labor force (millions)	4.8	4.8	1,209
Unemployment rate (% of labor force)	..	..	5.7
GNI per capita, *World Bank Atlas* method ($)	1,380	3,470	2,038
GDP growth, 1995–2000 and 2000–06 (average annual %)	6.7	8.1	7.6
Agriculture value added (% of GDP)	14.2	9.3	11.9
Industry value added (% of GDP)	39.2	42.0	43.5
Manufacturing value added (% of GDP)	31.6	32.8	26.7
Services value added (% of GDP)	46.7	48.7	44.6
Inflation (annual % change in consumer price index)	168.6	7.0	
Exchange rate (local currency units per $)	876.8	2,144.6	
Exports of goods and services (% of GDP)	69.2	59.9	40.4
Imports of goods and services (% of GDP)	72.4	64.2	36.4
Business environment			
Ease of doing business (ranking 1-178; 1=best)	..	110	
Time to start a business (days)	..	48	53
Procedures to start a business (number)	..	10	10
Firing cost (weeks of wages)	..	22.0	50.2
Closing a business (years to resolve insolvency)	..	5.8	3.3
Total tax rate (% of profit)	..	144.4	45.8
Highest marginal tax rate, corporate (%)	..	..	
Business entry rate (new registrations as % of total)	..	..	7.6
Enterprise surveys			
Time dealing with gov't officials (% of management time)	..	3.6	
Firms expected to give gifts in meetings w/tax officials (%)	33.2	28.3	
Firms using banks to finance investments (% of firms)	4.8	10.5	
Delay in obtaining an electrical connection (days)	13.7	18.8	
ISO certification ownership (% of firms)	..	8.9	
Private sector investment			
Invest. in infrastructure w/private participation ($ millions)	39	220	38,154
Private foreign direct investment, net (% of GDP)	0.9	1.0	3.0
Gross fixed capital formation (% of GDP)	25.2	28.3	33.5
Gross fixed private capital formation (% of GDP)	22.7	24.9	10.9
Finance and banking			
Government cash surplus or deficit (% of GDP)	0.1	1.4	-0.9
Government debt (% of GDP)	15.0	..	..
Deposit money banks' assets (% of GDP)	11.3	24.6	87.8
Total financial system deposits (% of GDP)	9.3	15.7	43.1
Bank capital to asset ratio (%)	15.1	17.8	10.7
Bank nonperforming loans to total gross loans ratio (%)	10.8	1.2	4.0
Domestic credit to the private sector (% of GDP)	8.9	20.2	81.3
Real interest rate (%)	-41.2	-1.7	
Interest rate spread (percentage points)	30.1	1.2	7.2
Infrastructure			
Paved roads (% of total roads)	95.6	88.6	65.8
Electric power consumption (kWh per capita)	2,989	3,209	1,502
Power outages in a typical month (number)	..	..	
Fixed line and mobile subscribers (per 100 people)	28	96	60
Internet users (per 100 people)	1.9	56.3	11.4
Cost of telephone call to U.S. ($ per 3 minutes)	3.28	1.90	2.08

Belgium

High income

	Country data		High-income group
	2000	**2006**	**2006**
Economic and social context			
Population (millions)	10.3	10.5	1,031
Labor force (millions)	4.4	4.5	504
Unemployment rate (% of labor force)	6.6	8.1	6.2
GNI per capita, *World Bank Atlas* method ($)	25,360	38,460	36,608
GDP growth, 1995-2000 and 2000-06 (average annual %)	2.7	1.7	2.3
Agriculture value added (% of GDP)	1.4	1.0	1.5
Industry value added (% of GDP)	27.0	24.3	26.2
Manufacturing value added (% of GDP)	19.3	17.1	16.8
Services value added (% of GDP)	71.6	74.7	72.3
Inflation (annual % change in consumer price index)	2.5	1.8	
Exchange rate (local currency units per $)	1.1	0.8	
Exports of goods and services (% of GDP)	84.6	87.7	25.6
Imports of goods and services (% of GDP)	81.7	85.1	26.3
Business environment			
Ease of doing business (ranking 1-178; 1=best)	..	19	
Time to start a business (days)	..	4	22
Procedures to start a business (number)	..	3	7
Firing cost (weeks of wages)	..	16.0	34.9
Closing a business (years to resolve insolvency)	..	0.9	2.0
Total tax rate (% of profit)	..	64.3	41.5
Highest marginal tax rate, corporate (%)	39	34	
Business entry rate (new registrations as % of total)	6.7	7.4	10.1
Enterprise surveys			
Time dealing with gov't officials (% of management time)	..	..	
Firms expected to give gifts in meetings w/tax officials (%)	..	..	
Firms using banks to finance investments (% of firms)	..	..	
Delay in obtaining an electrical connection (days)	..	..	
ISO certification ownership (% of firms)	..	..	
Private sector investment			
Invest. in infrastructure w/private participation ($ millions)	..	..	849
Private foreign direct investment, net (% of GDP)	92.7	15.7	2.7
Gross fixed capital formation (% of GDP)	20.8	20.4	20.4
Gross fixed private capital formation (% of GDP)	..	..	..
Finance and banking			
Government cash surplus or deficit (% of GDP)	0.1	0.3	-1.3
Government debt (% of GDP)	106.5	84.8	47.6
Deposit money banks' assets (% of GDP)	..	..	99.7
Total financial system deposits (% of GDP)	..	..	..
Bank capital to asset ratio (%)	2.8	3.7	6.2
Bank nonperforming loans to total gross loans ratio (%)	2.8	1.8	1.1
Domestic credit to the private sector (% of GDP)	78.1	83.3	162.0
Real interest rate (%)	6.0	5.4	
Interest rate spread (percentage points)	4.4	5.2	4.4
Infrastructure			
Paved roads (% of total roads)	78.2	78.0	90.9
Electric power consumption (kWh per capita)	8,247	8,510	9,760
Power outages in a typical month (number)	..	..	
Fixed line and mobile subscribers (per 100 people)	104	136	143
Internet users (per 100 people)	29.3	45.8	59.3
Cost of telephone call to U.S. ($ per 3 minutes)	1.67	0.75	0.77

Belize

Latin America & Caribbean **Upper middle income**

	Country data		Upper middle-income group
	2000	2006	2006
Economic and social context			
Population (millions)	0.25	0.30	811
Labor force (millions)	0.09	0.12	374
Unemployment rate (% of labor force)	9.1	11.0	9.8
GNI per capita, *World Bank Atlas* method ($)	3,090	3,740	5,913
GDP growth, 1995–2000 and 2000–06 (average annual %)	5.6	5.6	3.9
Agriculture value added (% of GDP)	17.0	14.0	5.7
Industry value added (% of GDP)	21.1	21.0	32.4
Manufacturing value added (% of GDP)	10.9	12.3	19.4
Services value added (% of GDP)	61.8	65.0	62.0
Inflation (annual % change in consumer price index)	0.6	4.3	
Exchange rate (local currency units per $)	2.0	2.0	
Exports of goods and services (% of GDP)	53.0	63.5	32.7
Imports of goods and services (% of GDP)	73.3	61.8	30.3
Business environment			
Ease of doing business (ranking 1-178; 1=best)	..	59	
Time to start a business (days)	..	44	41
Procedures to start a business (number)	..	9	9
Firing cost (weeks of wages)	..	24.0	39.7
Closing a business (years to resolve insolvency)	..	1.0	2.9
Total tax rate (% of profit)	..	30.8	44.5
Highest marginal tax rate, corporate (%)	..	..	
Business entry rate (new registrations as % of total)	..	..	9.1
Enterprise surveys			
Time dealing with gov't officials (% of management time)	..	..	
Firms expected to give gifts in meetings w/tax officials (%)	..	..	
Firms using banks to finance investments (% of firms)	..	..	
Delay in obtaining an electrical connection (days)	..	..	
ISO certification ownership (% of firms)	..	..	
Private sector investment			
Invest. in infrastructure w/private participation ($ millions)	50	16	45,869
Private foreign direct investment, net (% of GDP)	2.8	6.0	3.5
Gross fixed capital formation (% of GDP)	28.7	19.0	19.9
Gross fixed private capital formation (% of GDP)	11.6	..	..
Finance and banking			
Government cash surplus or deficit (% of GDP)	-2.9	..	..
Government debt (% of GDP)	..	..	..
Deposit money banks' assets (% of GDP)	..	..	52.9
Total financial system deposits (% of GDP)	..	..	41.4
Bank capital to asset ratio (%)	..	..	9.8
Bank nonperforming loans to total gross loans ratio (%)	..	..	3.2
Domestic credit to the private sector (% of GDP)	52.8	55.3	41.4
Real interest rate (%)	14.6	10.7	
Interest rate spread (percentage points)	8.3	6.1	5.9
Infrastructure			
Paved roads (% of total roads)	17.0	..	..
Electric power consumption (kWh per capita)	..	..	3,131
Power outages in a typical month (number)	..	..	
Fixed line and mobile subscribers (per 100 people)	21	51	88
Internet users (per 100 people)	6.0	11.4	22.2
Cost of telephone call to U.S. ($ per 3 minutes)	4.45	2.59	1.06

Benin

Sub-Saharan Africa   **Low income**

	Country data		Low-income group
	2000	2006	2006
Economic and social context			
Population (millions)	7.2	8.8	2,420
Labor force (millions)	2.8	3.4	995
Unemployment rate (% of labor force)	..	..	..
GNI per capita, *World Bank Atlas* method ($)	340	530	649
GDP growth, 1995–2000 and 2000–06 (average annual %)	5.3	3.8	6.5
Agriculture value added (% of GDP)	36.5	32.2	20.4
Industry value added (% of GDP)	13.9	13.4	27.7
Manufacturing value added (% of GDP)	8.8	7.5	15.8
Services value added (% of GDP)	49.6	54.4	51.9
Inflation (annual % change in consumer price index)	4.2	3.8	
Exchange rate (local currency units per $)	712.0	522.9	
Exports of goods and services (% of GDP)	15.2	13.5	26.7
Imports of goods and services (% of GDP)	28.1	26.1	30.1
Business environment			
Ease of doing business (ranking 1-178; 1=best)	..	151	
Time to start a business (days)	..	31	54
Procedures to start a business (number)	..	7	10
Firing cost (weeks of wages)	..	36.0	62.6
Closing a business (years to resolve insolvency)	..	4.0	3.8
Total tax rate (% of profit)	..	73.3	67.4
Highest marginal tax rate, corporate (%)	..	38	
Business entry rate (new registrations as % of total)	..	..	6.4
Enterprise surveys			
Time dealing with gov't officials (% of management time)	..	6.5	
Firms expected to give gifts in meetings w/tax officials (%)	..	21.2	
Firms using banks to finance investments (% of firms)	..	20.8	
Delay in obtaining an electrical connection (days)	..	71.7	
ISO certification ownership (% of firms)	..	2.7	
Private sector investment			
Invest. in infrastructure w/private participation ($ millions)	90	17	29,785
Private foreign direct investment, net (% of GDP)	2.6	1.3	2.6
Gross fixed capital formation (% of GDP)	18.9	18.9	26.7
Gross fixed private capital formation (% of GDP)	11.3	12.2	19.6
Finance and banking			
Government cash surplus or deficit (% of GDP)	0.7	0.2	-2.6
Government debt (% of GDP)	..	..	..
Deposit money banks' assets (% of GDP)	12.2	17.3	50.5
Total financial system deposits (% of GDP)	14.2	17.8	44.6
Bank capital to asset ratio (%)	..	..	..
Bank nonperforming loans to total gross loans ratio (%)	..	..	..
Domestic credit to the private sector (% of GDP)	12.1	16.7	38.3
Real interest rate (%)	..	..	
Interest rate spread (percentage points)	..	..	11.3
Infrastructure			
Paved roads (% of total roads)	20.0	9.5	..
Electric power consumption (kWh per capita)	55	69	391
Power outages in a typical month (number)	..	..	
Fixed line and mobile subscribers (per 100 people)	1	13	17
Internet users (per 100 people)	0.2	8.0	4.2
Cost of telephone call to U.S. ($ per 3 minutes)	5.93	4.80	1.99

Bermuda

	Country data		High-income group
	2000	**2006**	**2006**
Economic and social context			
Population (millions)	0.06	0.06	1,031
Labor force (millions)	..	..	504
Unemployment rate (% of labor force)	..	..	6.2
GNI per capita, *World Bank Atlas* method ($)	35,990	..	36,608
GDP growth, 1995–2000 and 2000–06 (average annual %)	..	..	2.3
Agriculture value added (% of GDP)	..	..	1.5
Industry value added (% of GDP)	..	..	26.2
Manufacturing value added (% of GDP)	..	..	16.8
Services value added (% of GDP)	..	..	72.3
Inflation (annual % change in consumer price index)	..	..	
Exchange rate (local currency units per $)	1.0	1.0	
Exports of goods and services (% of GDP)	..	..	25.6
Imports of goods and services (% of GDP)	..	..	26.3
Business environment			
Ease of doing business (ranking 1-178; 1=best)	..	..	
Time to start a business (days)	..	..	22
Procedures to start a business (number)	..	..	7
Firing cost (weeks of wages)	..	..	34.9
Closing a business (years to resolve insolvency)	..	..	2.0
Total tax rate (% of profit)	..	..	41.5
Highest marginal tax rate, corporate (%)	..	..	
Business entry rate (new registrations as % of total)	..	..	10.1
Enterprise surveys			
Time dealing with gov't officials (% of management time)	..	..	
Firms expected to give gifts in meetings w/tax officials (%)	..	..	
Firms using banks to finance investments (% of firms)	..	..	
Delay in obtaining an electrical connection (days)	..	..	
ISO certification ownership (% of firms)	..	..	
Private sector investment			
Invest. in infrastructure w/private participation ($ millions)	..	..	849
Private foreign direct investment, net (% of GDP)	..	..	2.7
Gross fixed capital formation (% of GDP)	..	..	20.4
Gross fixed private capital formation (% of GDP)	..	..	..
Finance and banking			
Government cash surplus or deficit (% of GDP)	..	..	-1.3
Government debt (% of GDP)	..	..	47.6
Deposit money banks' assets (% of GDP)	..	..	99.7
Total financial system deposits (% of GDP)	..	..	..
Bank capital to asset ratio (%)	..	..	6.2
Bank nonperforming loans to total gross loans ratio (%)	..	..	1.1
Domestic credit to the private sector (% of GDP)	..	..	162.0
Real interest rate (%)	..	..	
Interest rate spread (percentage points)	..	..	4.4
Infrastructure			
Paved roads (% of total roads)	..	..	90.9
Electric power consumption (kWh per capita)	..	..	9,760
Power outages in a typical month (number)	..	..	
Fixed line and mobile subscribers (per 100 people)	111	185	143
Internet users (per 100 people)	43.5	66.1	59.3
Cost of telephone call to U.S. ($ per 3 minutes)	3.50	..	0.77

Bhutan

South Asia **Lower middle income**

	Country data		Lower middle-income group
	2000	2006	2006
Economic and social context			
Population (millions)	0.56	0.65	2,276
Labor force (millions)	0.20	0.29	1,209
Unemployment rate (% of labor force)	..	..	5.7
GNI per capita, World Bank Atlas method ($)	720	1,430	2,038
GDP growth, 1995–2000 and 2000–06 (average annual %)	6.3	7.8	7.6
Agriculture value added (% of GDP)	28.4	22.3	11.9
Industry value added (% of GDP)	35.5	37.9	43.5
Manufacturing value added (% of GDP)	8.3	7.4	26.7
Services value added (% of GDP)	36.2	39.8	44.6
Inflation (annual % change in consumer price index)	4.0	5.0	
Exchange rate (local currency units per $)	44.9	45.3	
Exports of goods and services (% of GDP)	29.4	31.6	40.4
Imports of goods and services (% of GDP)	46.9	45.2	36.4
Business environment			
Ease of doing business (ranking 1-178; 1=best)	..	119	
Time to start a business (days)	..	48	53
Procedures to start a business (number)	..	8	10
Firing cost (weeks of wages)	..	10.0	50.2
Closing a business (years to resolve insolvency)	..	..	3.3
Total tax rate (% of profit)	..	39.8	45.8
Highest marginal tax rate, corporate (%)	..	..	
Business entry rate (new registrations as % of total)	..	..	7.6
Enterprise surveys			
Time dealing with gov't officials (% of management time)	..	..	
Firms expected to give gifts in meetings w/tax officials (%)	..	..	
Firms using banks to finance investments (% of firms)	..	..	
Delay in obtaining an electrical connection (days)	..	..	
ISO certification ownership (% of firms)	..	..	
Private sector investment			
Invest. in infrastructure w/private participation ($ millions)	..	18	38,154
Private foreign direct investment, net (% of GDP)	0.0	0.6	3.0
Gross fixed capital formation (% of GDP)	49.1	51.6	33.5
Gross fixed private capital formation (% of GDP)	..	..	10.9
Finance and banking			
Government cash surplus or deficit (% of GDP)	-2.4	2.0	-0.9
Government debt (% of GDP)	38.4	74.1	..
Deposit money banks' assets (% of GDP)	9.4	..	87.8
Total financial system deposits (% of GDP)	37.5	..	43.1
Bank capital to asset ratio (%)	..	..	10.7
Bank nonperforming loans to total gross loans ratio (%)	..	..	4.0
Domestic credit to the private sector (% of GDP)	8.7	21.2	81.3
Real interest rate (%)	13.4	9.1	
Interest rate spread (percentage points)	7.8	9.5	7.2
Infrastructure			
Paved roads (% of total roads)	60.7	62.0	65.8
Electric power consumption (kWh per capita)	..	..	1,502
Power outages in a typical month (number)	..	..	
Fixed line and mobile subscribers (per 100 people)	3	18	60
Internet users (per 100 people)	0.4	4.6	11.4
Cost of telephone call to U.S. ($ per 3 minutes)	1.19	0.66	2.08

Bolivia

Latin America & Caribbean   **Lower middle income**

	Country data		Lower middle-income group
	2000	**2006**	**2006**
Economic and social context			
Population (millions)	8.3	9.4	2,276
Labor force (millions)	3.6	4.3	1,209
Unemployment rate (% of labor force)	4.5	..	5.7
GNI per capita, *World Bank Atlas* method ($)	1,000	1,100	2,038
GDP growth, 1995–2000 and 2000–06 (average annual %)	3.5	3.3	7.6
Agriculture value added (% of GDP)	15.0	14.0	11.9
Industry value added (% of GDP)	29.8	34.2	43.5
Manufacturing value added (% of GDP)	15.3	14.7	26.7
Services value added (% of GDP)	55.2	51.9	44.6
Inflation (annual % change in consumer price index)	4.6	4.3	
Exchange rate (local currency units per $)	6.2	8.0	
Exports of goods and services (% of GDP)	18.3	42.5	40.4
Imports of goods and services (% of GDP)	27.3	32.6	36.4
Business environment			
Ease of doing business (ranking 1-178; 1=best)	..	140	
Time to start a business (days)	..	50	53
Procedures to start a business (number)	..	15	10
Firing cost (weeks of wages)	..	99.5	50.2
Closing a business (years to resolve insolvency)	..	1.8	3.3
Total tax rate (% of profit)	..	78.1	45.8
Highest marginal tax rate, corporate (%)	25	25	
Business entry rate (new registrations as % of total)	9.1	6.6	7.6
Enterprise surveys			
Time dealing with gov't officials (% of management time)	..	13.5	
Firms expected to give gifts in meetings w/tax officials (%)	..	19.6	
Firms using banks to finance investments (% of firms)	..	22.2	
Delay in obtaining an electrical connection (days)	..	15.2	
ISO certification ownership (% of firms)	..	13.8	
Private sector investment			
Invest. in infrastructure w/private participation ($ millions)	323	122	38,154
Private foreign direct investment, net (% of GDP)	8.8	2.2	3.0
Gross fixed capital formation (% of GDP)	17.9	12.9	33.5
Gross fixed private capital formation (% of GDP)	12.8	6.1	10.9
Finance and banking			
Government cash surplus or deficit (% of GDP)	-8.7	12.5	-0.9
Government debt (% of GDP)	..	..	..
Deposit money banks' assets (% of GDP)	61.8	38.0	87.8
Total financial system deposits (% of GDP)	45.9	34.2	43.1
Bank capital to asset ratio (%)	9.8	10.0	10.7
Bank nonperforming loans to total gross loans ratio (%)	10.3	8.7	4.0
Domestic credit to the private sector (% of GDP)	58.7	36.1	81.3
Real interest rate (%)	27.9	-0.3	
Interest rate spread (percentage points)	23.6	7.9	7.2
Infrastructure			
Paved roads (% of total roads)	6.6	7.0	65.8
Electric power consumption (kWh per capita)	421	479	1,502
Power outages in a typical month (number)	..	1.0	
Fixed line and mobile subscribers (per 100 people)	13	36	60
Internet users (per 100 people)	1.4	6.2	11.4
Cost of telephone call to U.S. ($ per 3 minutes)	2.43	..	2.08

Bosnia and Herzegovina

Europe & Central Asia			Lower middle income

	Country data		Lower middle-income group
	2000	2006	2006
Economic and social context			
Population (millions)	3.8	3.9	2,276
Labor force (millions)	1.9	2.0	1,209
Unemployment rate (% of labor force)	..	..	5.7
GNI per capita, *World Bank Atlas* method ($)	1,520	3,230	2,038
GDP growth, 1995–2000 and 2000–06 (average annual %)	24.9	5.1	7.6
Agriculture value added (% of GDP)	11.0	10.4	11.9
Industry value added (% of GDP)	23.9	24.7	43.5
Manufacturing value added (% of GDP)	10.5	11.9	26.7
Services value added (% of GDP)	65.1	64.9	44.6
Inflation (annual % change in consumer price index)	..	..	
Exchange rate (local currency units per $)	2.1	1.6	
Exports of goods and services (% of GDP)	29.6	25.3	40.4
Imports of goods and services (% of GDP)	77.9	47.0	36.4
Business environment			
Ease of doing business (ranking 1-178; 1=best)	..	105	
Time to start a business (days)	..	54	53
Procedures to start a business (number)	..	12	10
Firing cost (weeks of wages)	..	31.0	50.2
Closing a business (years to resolve insolvency)	..	3.3	3.3
Total tax rate (% of profit)	..	44.1	45.8
Highest marginal tax rate, corporate (%)	..	30	
Business entry rate (new registrations as % of total)	..	4.1	7.6
Enterprise surveys			
Time dealing with gov't officials (% of management time)	..	4.3	
Firms expected to give gifts in meetings w/tax officials (%)	60.5	69.7	
Firms using banks to finance investments (% of firms)	14.3	17.5	
Delay in obtaining an electrical connection (days)	6.6	7.3	
ISO certification ownership (% of firms)	..	14.5	
Private sector investment			
Invest. in infrastructure w/private participation ($ millions)	..	861	38,154
Private foreign direct investment, net (% of GDP)	2.7	3.5	3.0
Gross fixed capital formation (% of GDP)	21.2	20.5	33.5
Gross fixed private capital formation (% of GDP)	10.0	14.6	10.9
Finance and banking			
Government cash surplus or deficit (% of GDP)	..	2.9	–0.9
Government debt (% of GDP)	..	..	
Deposit money banks' assets (% of GDP)	..	..	87.8
Total financial system deposits (% of GDP)	..	..	43.1
Bank capital to asset ratio (%)	20.1	13.8	10.7
Bank nonperforming loans to total gross loans ratio (%)	9.9	4.0	4.0
Domestic credit to the private sector (% of GDP)	38.5	48.4	81.3
Real interest rate (%)	10.5	1.4	
Interest rate spread (percentage points)	15.8	4.3	7.2
Infrastructure			
Paved roads (% of total roads)	52.3	52.3	65.8
Electric power consumption (kWh per capita)	2,011	2,316	1,502
Power outages in a typical month (number)	..	..	
Fixed line and mobile subscribers (per 100 people)	23	73	60
Internet users (per 100 people)	1.1	24.2	11.4
Cost of telephone call to U.S. ($ per 3 minutes)	2.96	3.62	2.08

Botswana

Sub-Saharan Africa   **Upper middle income**

	Country data		Upper middle-income group
	2000	**2006**	**2006**
Economic and social context			
Population (millions)	1.7	1.9	811
Labor force (millions)	0.63	0.69	374
Unemployment rate (% of labor force)	15.9	23.8	9.8
GNI per capita, *World Bank Atlas* method ($)	3,310	5,570	5,913
GDP growth, 1995–2000 and 2000–06 (average annual %)	8.7	5.1	3.9
Agriculture value added (% of GDP)	2.4	2.0	5.7
Industry value added (% of GDP)	58.9	53.1	32.4
Manufacturing value added (% of GDP)	4.4	3.6	19.4
Services value added (% of GDP)	38.6	44.9	62.0
Inflation (annual % change in consumer price index)	8.6	11.6	
Exchange rate (local currency units per $)	5.1	5.8	
Exports of goods and services (% of GDP)	52.6	55.2	32.7
Imports of goods and services (% of GDP)	33.7	28.6	30.3
Business environment			
Ease of doing business (ranking 1-178; 1=best)	..	51	
Time to start a business (days)	..	108	41
Procedures to start a business (number)	..	11	9
Firing cost (weeks of wages)	..	90.0	39.7
Closing a business (years to resolve insolvency)	..	1.7	2.9
Total tax rate (% of profit)	..	17.2	44.5
Highest marginal tax rate, corporate (%)	15	15	
Business entry rate (new registrations as % of total)	9.6	9.2	9.1
Enterprise surveys			
Time dealing with gov't officials (% of management time)	..	5.0	
Firms expected to give gifts in meetings w/tax officials (%)	..	4.5	
Firms using banks to finance investments (% of firms)	..	11.3	
Delay in obtaining an electrical connection (days)	..	25.5	
ISO certification ownership (% of firms)	..	12.7	
Private sector investment			
Invest. in infrastructure w/private participation ($ millions)	17	18	45,869
Private foreign direct investment, net (% of GDP)	0.9	4.6	3.5
Gross fixed capital formation (% of GDP)	21.7	17.8	19.9
Gross fixed private capital formation (% of GDP)	11.6	9.1	..
Finance and banking			
Government cash surplus or deficit (% of GDP)	..	..	..
Government debt (% of GDP)	..	..	..
Deposit money banks' assets (% of GDP)	15.8	20.4	52.9
Total financial system deposits (% of GDP)	23.9	33.2	41.4
Bank capital to asset ratio (%)	10.3	9.7	9.8
Bank nonperforming loans to total gross loans ratio (%)	1.7	2.8	3.2
Domestic credit to the private sector (% of GDP)	13.8	19.6	41.4
Real interest rate (%)	3.1	2.6	
Interest rate spread (percentage points)	6.1	7.6	5.9
Infrastructure			
Paved roads (% of total roads)	35.3	33.2	..
Electric power consumption (kWh per capita)	921	1,406	3,131
Power outages in a typical month (number)	..	1.7	
Fixed line and mobile subscribers (per 100 people)	21	60	88
Internet users (per 100 people)	2.9	3.3	22.2
Cost of telephone call to U.S. ($ per 3 minutes)	3.64	2.88	1.06

Brazil

| Latin America & Caribbean | | | Upper middle income |

	Country data		Upper middle-income group
	2000	2006	2006

Economic and social context
Population (millions)	174.2	189.3	811
Labor force (millions)	83.6	93.1	374
Unemployment rate (% of labor force)	9.3	8.9	9.8
GNI per capita, *World Bank Atlas* method ($)	3,870	4,710	5,913
GDP growth, 1995–2000 and 2000–06 (average annual %)	1.7	3.0	3.9
Agriculture value added (% of GDP)	5.6	5.1	5.7
Industry value added (% of GDP)	27.7	30.9	32.4
Manufacturing value added (% of GDP)	17.2	18.4	19.4
Services value added (% of GDP)	66.7	64.0	62.0
Inflation (annual % change in consumer price index)	7.0	4.2	
Exchange rate (local currency units per $)	1.8	2.2	
Exports of goods and services (% of GDP)	10.0	14.7	32.7
Imports of goods and services (% of GDP)	11.7	11.7	30.3

Business environment
Ease of doing business (ranking 1-178; 1=best)	..	122	
Time to start a business (days)	..	152	41
Procedures to start a business (number)	..	18	9
Firing cost (weeks of wages)	..	37.0	39.7
Closing a business (years to resolve insolvency)	..	4.0	2.9
Total tax rate (% of profit)	..	69.2	44.5
Highest marginal tax rate, corporate (%)	15	15	
Business entry rate (new registrations as % of total)	..	..	9.1
Enterprise surveys			
Time dealing with gov't officials (% of management time)	..	7.2	
Firms expected to give gifts in meetings w/tax officials (%)	..	9.9	
Firms using banks to finance investments (% of firms)	..	22.9	
Delay in obtaining an electrical connection (days)	..	23.9	
ISO certification ownership (% of firms)	..	19.1	

Private sector investment
Invest. in infrastructure w/private participation ($ millions)	21,075	9,835	45,869
Private foreign direct investment, net (% of GDP)	5.1	1.8	3.5
Gross fixed capital formation (% of GDP)	16.8	16.8	19.9
Gross fixed private capital formation (% of GDP)	..	..	..

Finance and banking
Government cash surplus or deficit (% of GDP)	–0.8	..	..
Government debt (% of GDP)	..	..	..
Deposit money banks' assets (% of GDP)	62.9	71.8	52.9
Total financial system deposits (% of GDP)	40.5	51.7	41.4
Bank capital to asset ratio (%)	12.1	9.9	9.8
Bank nonperforming loans to total gross loans ratio (%)	8.3	4.1	3.2
Domestic credit to the private sector (% of GDP)	33.0	36.5	41.4
Real interest rate (%)	47.7	44.6	
Interest rate spread (percentage points)	39.6	36.9	5.9

Infrastructure
Paved roads (% of total roads)	5.5	..	..
Electric power consumption (kWh per capita)	1,894	2,008	3,131
Power outages in a typical month (number)	..	..	
Fixed line and mobile subscribers (per 100 people)	31	73	88
Internet users (per 100 people)	2.9	22.5	22.2
Cost of telephone call to U.S. ($ per 3 minutes)	1.15	0.71	1.06

Brunei Darussalam

	Country data		High-income group
	2000	2006	2006
Economic and social context			
Population (millions)	0.33	0.38	1,031
Labor force (millions)	0.15	0.17	504
Unemployment rate (% of labor force)	..	..	6.2
GNI per capita, *World Bank Atlas* method ($)	14,670	26,930	36,608
GDP growth, 1995–2000 and 2000–06 (average annual %)	1.0	2.3	2.3
Agriculture value added (% of GDP)	1.0	0.7	1.5
Industry value added (% of GDP)	63.7	73.4	26.2
Manufacturing value added (% of GDP)	15.4	10.5	16.8
Services value added (% of GDP)	35.3	25.9	72.3
Inflation (annual % change in consumer price index)	1.6	0.1	
Exchange rate (local currency units per $)	1.7	1.6	
Exports of goods and services (% of GDP)	67.4	71.2	25.6
Imports of goods and services (% of GDP)	35.8	25.0	26.3
Business environment			
Ease of doing business (ranking 1-178; 1=best)	..	78	
Time to start a business (days)	..	116	22
Procedures to start a business (number)	..	18	7
Firing cost (weeks of wages)	..	4.0	34.9
Closing a business (years to resolve insolvency)	..	2.5	2.0
Total tax rate (% of profit)	..	37.4	41.5
Highest marginal tax rate, corporate (%)	30	30	
Business entry rate (new registrations as % of total)	..	..	10.1
Enterprise surveys			
Time dealing with gov't officials (% of management time)	..	..	
Firms expected to give gifts in meetings w/tax officials (%)	..	..	
Firms using banks to finance investments (% of firms)	..	..	
Delay in obtaining an electrical connection (days)	..	..	
ISO certification ownership (% of firms)	..	..	
Private sector investment			
Invest. in infrastructure w/private participation ($ millions)	..	..	849
Private foreign direct investment, net (% of GDP)	..	..	2.7
Gross fixed capital formation (% of GDP)	13.0	10.4	20.4
Gross fixed private capital formation (% of GDP)	..	..	..
Finance and banking			
Government cash surplus or deficit (% of GDP)	..	..	-1.3
Government debt (% of GDP)	..	..	47.6
Deposit money banks' assets (% of GDP)	73.4	60.2	99.7
Total financial system deposits (% of GDP)	105.4	82.5	..
Bank capital to asset ratio (%)	..	..	6.2
Bank nonperforming loans to total gross loans ratio (%)	..	..	1.1
Domestic credit to the private sector (% of GDP)	50.3	34.5	162.0
Real interest rate (%)	-18.2	-4.2	
Interest rate spread (percentage points)	..	4.5	4.4
Infrastructure			
Paved roads (% of total roads)	34.7	77.2	90.9
Electric power consumption (kWh per capita)	7,539	7,498	9,760
Power outages in a typical month (number)	..	..	
Fixed line and mobile subscribers (per 100 people)	53	87	143
Internet users (per 100 people)	9.0	43.3	59.3
Cost of telephone call to U.S. ($ per 3 minutes)	..	..	0.77

Bulgaria

Europe & Central Asia			Upper middle income

	Country data		Upper middle-income group
	2000	2006	2006
Economic and social context			
Population (millions)	8.1	7.7	811
Labor force (millions)	3.2	3.1	374
Unemployment rate (% of labor force)	17.1	10.1	9.8
GNI per capita, *World Bank Atlas* method ($)	1,600	3,990	5,913
GDP growth, 1995–2000 and 2000–06 (average annual %)	-0.4	5.5	3.9
Agriculture value added (% of GDP)	14.2	8.5	5.7
Industry value added (% of GDP)	30.7	31.4	32.4
Manufacturing value added (% of GDP)	18.1	18.6	19.4
Services value added (% of GDP)	55.1	60.0	62.0
Inflation (annual % change in consumer price index)	10.3	7.3	
Exchange rate (local currency units per $)	2.1	1.6	
Exports of goods and services (% of GDP)	55.7	64.0	32.7
Imports of goods and services (% of GDP)	61.1	83.0	30.3
Business environment			
Ease of doing business (ranking 1-178; 1=best)	..	46	
Time to start a business (days)	..	32	41
Procedures to start a business (number)	..	9	9
Firing cost (weeks of wages)	..	9.0	39.7
Closing a business (years to resolve insolvency)	..	3.3	2.9
Total tax rate (% of profit)	..	36.7	44.5
Highest marginal tax rate, corporate (%)	20	15	
Business entry rate (new registrations as % of total)	..	..	9.1
Enterprise surveys			
Time dealing with gov't officials (% of management time)	..	2.8	
Firms expected to give gifts in meetings w/tax officials (%)	51.5	6.2	
Firms using banks to finance investments (% of firms)	10.4	40.5	
Delay in obtaining an electrical connection (days)	..	85.6	
ISO certification ownership (% of firms)	..	11.0	
Private sector investment			
Invest. in infrastructure w/private participation ($ millions)	157	1,507	45,869
Private foreign direct investment, net (% of GDP)	7.9	16.4	3.5
Gross fixed capital formation (% of GDP)	15.7	26.2	19.9
Gross fixed private capital formation (% of GDP)	11.6	21.5	..
Finance and banking			
Government cash surplus or deficit (% of GDP)	-0.4	3.4	..
Government debt (% of GDP)	..	..	..
Deposit money banks' assets (% of GDP)	16.0	48.1	52.9
Total financial system deposits (% of GDP)	21.5	46.3	41.4
Bank capital to asset ratio (%)	15.3	10.4	9.8
Bank nonperforming loans to total gross loans ratio (%)	17.3	2.2	3.2
Domestic credit to the private sector (% of GDP)	12.6	47.4	41.4
Real interest rate (%)	4.4	0.7	
Interest rate spread (percentage points)	8.2	5.7	5.9
Infrastructure			
Paved roads (% of total roads)	92.1	99.0	..
Electric power consumption (kWh per capita)	3,724	4,121	3,131
Power outages in a typical month (number)	..	4.3	
Fixed line and mobile subscribers (per 100 people)	45	138	88
Internet users (per 100 people)	5.3	24.3	22.2
Cost of telephone call to U.S. ($ per 3 minutes)	2.55	0.57	1.06

Burkina Faso

	Country data		Low-income group
	2000	2006	2006
Economic and social context			
Population (millions)	11.9	14.4	2,420
Labor force (millions)	5.3	6.5	995
Unemployment rate (% of labor force)	2.4	..	
GNI per capita, *World Bank Atlas* method ($)	240	440	649
GDP growth, 1995–2000 and 2000–06 (average annual %)	6.8	6.2	6.5
Agriculture value added (% of GDP)	27.5	30.7	20.4
Industry value added (% of GDP)	23.1	20.6	27.7
Manufacturing value added (% of GDP)	15.3	12.6	15.8
Services value added (% of GDP)	44.1	40.9	51.9
Inflation (annual % change in consumer price index)	–0.3	2.3	
Exchange rate (local currency units per $)	712.0	522.9	
Exports of goods and services (% of GDP)	9.1	10.8	26.7
Imports of goods and services (% of GDP)	25.2	25.1	30.1
Business environment			
Ease of doing business (ranking 1-178; 1=best)	..	161	
Time to start a business (days)	..	18	54
Procedures to start a business (number)	..	6	10
Firing cost (weeks of wages)	..	34.0	62.6
Closing a business (years to resolve insolvency)	..	4.0	3.8
Total tax rate (% of profit)	..	48.9	67.4
Highest marginal tax rate, corporate (%)	..	..	
Business entry rate (new registrations as % of total)	..	..	6.4
Enterprise surveys			
Time dealing with gov't officials (% of management time)	..	9.5	
Firms expected to give gifts in meetings w/tax officials (%)	..	19.5	
Firms using banks to finance investments (% of firms)	..	23.1	
Delay in obtaining an electrical connection (days)	..	19.6	
ISO certification ownership (% of firms)	..	7.4	
Private sector investment			
Invest. in infrastructure w/private participation ($ millions)	27	290	29,785
Private foreign direct investment, net (% of GDP)	0.9	0.4	2.6
Gross fixed capital formation (% of GDP)	18.7	19.4	26.7
Gross fixed private capital formation (% of GDP)	11.0	11.1	19.6
Finance and banking			
Government cash surplus or deficit (% of GDP)	..	–5.7	–2.6
Government debt (% of GDP)	..	..	..
Deposit money banks' assets (% of GDP)	12.1	16.7	50.5
Total financial system deposits (% of GDP)	12.3	13.8	44.6
Bank capital to asset ratio (%)	..	..	..
Bank nonperforming loans to total gross loans ratio (%)	..	..	..
Domestic credit to the private sector (% of GDP)	11.7	16.7	38.3
Real interest rate (%)	..	..	
Interest rate spread (percentage points)	..	..	11.3
Infrastructure			
Paved roads (% of total roads)	16.0	4.2	..
Electric power consumption (kWh per capita)	..	..	391
Power outages in a typical month (number)	..	10.1	
Fixed line and mobile subscribers (per 100 people)	1	8	17
Internet users (per 100 people)	0.1	0.6	4.2
Cost of telephone call to U.S. ($ per 3 minutes)	3.16	1.14	1.99

Burundi

Sub-Saharan Africa **Low income**

	Country data		Low-income group
	2000	**2006**	**2006**
Economic and social context			
Population (millions)	6.7	8.2	2,420
Labor force (millions)	3.2	4.2	995
Unemployment rate (% of labor force)	..	..	
GNI per capita, *World Bank Atlas* method ($)	120	100	649
GDP growth, 1995–2000 and 2000–06 (average annual %)	−0.7	2.5	6.5
Agriculture value added (% of GDP)	40.4	34.8	20.4
Industry value added (% of GDP)	18.8	20.0	27.7
Manufacturing value added (% of GDP)	8.7	8.8	15.8
Services value added (% of GDP)	40.8	45.1	51.9
Inflation (annual % change in consumer price index)	24.3	2.8	
Exchange rate (local currency units per $)	720.7	1,028.4	
Exports of goods and services (% of GDP)	7.8	10.9	26.7
Imports of goods and services (% of GDP)	19.9	47.8	30.1
Business environment			
Ease of doing business (ranking 1-178; 1=best)	..	174	
Time to start a business (days)	..	43	54
Procedures to start a business (number)	..	11	10
Firing cost (weeks of wages)	..	26.0	62.6
Closing a business (years to resolve insolvency)	..	4.0	3.8
Total tax rate (% of profit)	..	278.7	67.4
Highest marginal tax rate, corporate (%)	..	..	
Business entry rate (new registrations as % of total)	..	..	6.4
Enterprise surveys			
Time dealing with gov't officials (% of management time)	..	5.7	
Firms expected to give gifts in meetings w/tax officials (%)	..	22.6	
Firms using banks to finance investments (% of firms)	..	12.3	
Delay in obtaining an electrical connection (days)	..	24.1	
ISO certification ownership (% of firms)	..	7.1	
Private sector investment			
Invest. in infrastructure w/private participation ($ millions)	36	6	29,785
Private foreign direct investment, net (% of GDP)	1.6	0.0	2.6
Gross fixed capital formation (% of GDP)	6.1	16.7	26.7
Gross fixed private capital formation (% of GDP)	0.8	1.7	19.6
Finance and banking			
Government cash surplus or deficit (% of GDP)	−2.4	..	−2.6
Government debt (% of GDP)	162.6	..	..
Deposit money banks' assets (% of GDP)	18.7	21.2	50.5
Total financial system deposits (% of GDP)	12.6	20.5	44.6
Bank capital to asset ratio (%)	..	..	
Bank nonperforming loans to total gross loans ratio (%)	..	..	..
Domestic credit to the private sector (% of GDP)	20.0	21.0	38.3
Real interest rate (%)	2.3	14.1	
Interest rate spread (percentage points)	..	..	11.3
Infrastructure			
Paved roads (% of total roads)	7.1	10.4	..
Electric power consumption (kWh per capita)	..	..	391
Power outages in a typical month (number)	..	12.0	
Fixed line and mobile subscribers (per 100 people)	1	2	17
Internet users (per 100 people)	0.1	0.7	4.2
Cost of telephone call to U.S. ($ per 3 minutes)	7.35	2.45	1.99

Cambodia

	Country data		Low-income group
	2000	2006	2006
Economic and social context			
Population (millions)	12.8	14.2	2,420
Labor force (millions)	5.8	6.9	995
Unemployment rate (% of labor force)	2.5	..	
GNI per capita, *World Bank Atlas* method ($)	280	490	649
GDP growth, 1995–2000 and 2000–06 (average annual %)	7.3	9.5	6.5
Agriculture value added (% of GDP)	35.9	30.1	20.4
Industry value added (% of GDP)	21.9	26.2	27.7
Manufacturing value added (% of GDP)	16.0	18.6	15.8
Services value added (% of GDP)	42.2	43.7	51.9
Inflation (annual % change in consumer price index)	–0.8	4.7	
Exchange rate (local currency units per $)	3,840.8	4,103.3	
Exports of goods and services (% of GDP)	49.8	68.8	26.7
Imports of goods and services (% of GDP)	61.8	75.8	30.1
Business environment			
Ease of doing business (ranking 1-178; 1=best)	..	145	
Time to start a business (days)	..	86	54
Procedures to start a business (number)	..	10	10
Firing cost (weeks of wages)	..	39.0	62.6
Closing a business (years to resolve insolvency)	..	..	3.8
Total tax rate (% of profit)	..	22.6	67.4
Highest marginal tax rate, corporate (%)	20	20	
Business entry rate (new registrations as % of total)	..	..	6.4
Enterprise surveys			
Time dealing with gov't officials (% of management time)	..	8.6	
Firms expected to give gifts in meetings w/tax officials (%)	..	42.0	
Firms using banks to finance investments (% of firms)	..	6.8	
Delay in obtaining an electrical connection (days)	..	7.6	
ISO certification ownership (% of firms)	..	2.8	
Private sector investment			
Invest. in infrastructure w/private participation ($ millions)	28	250	29,785
Private foreign direct investment, net (% of GDP)	4.1	6.7	2.6
Gross fixed capital formation (% of GDP)	18.3	19.5	26.7
Gross fixed private capital formation (% of GDP)	11.9	13.9	19.6
Finance and banking			
Government cash surplus or deficit (% of GDP)	–3.4	–1.7	–2.6
Government debt (% of GDP)	..	..	..
Deposit money banks' assets (% of GDP)	5.9	10.0	50.5
Total financial system deposits (% of GDP)	8.1	15.2	44.6
Bank capital to asset ratio (%)	..	..	..
Bank nonperforming loans to total gross loans ratio (%)	..	..	..
Domestic credit to the private sector (% of GDP)	6.4	12.0	38.3
Real interest rate (%)	21.2	11.2	
Interest rate spread (percentage points)	10.5	14.6	11.3
Infrastructure			
Paved roads (% of total roads)	16.2	6.3	..
Electric power consumption (kWh per capita)	..	..	391
Power outages in a typical month (number)	..	..	
Fixed line and mobile subscribers (per 100 people)	1	8	17
Internet users (per 100 people)	0.0	0.3	4.2
Cost of telephone call to U.S. ($ per 3 minutes)	6.00	2.94	1.99

Cameroon

Sub-Saharan Africa   **Lower middle income**

	Country data		Lower middle-income group
	2000	**2006**	**2006**
Economic and social context			
Population (millions)	15.9	18.2	2,276
Labor force (millions)	6.1	7.0	1,209
Unemployment rate (% of labor force)	7.5	..	5.7
GNI per capita, *World Bank Atlas* method ($)	620	990	2,038
GDP growth, 1995–2000 and 2000–06 (average annual %)	4.8	3.6	7.6
Agriculture value added (% of GDP)	22.1	19.9	11.9
Industry value added (% of GDP)	36.0	33.2	43.5
Manufacturing value added (% of GDP)	20.8	18.1	26.7
Services value added (% of GDP)	41.8	46.9	44.6
Inflation (annual % change in consumer price index)	1.2	5.1	
Exchange rate (local currency units per $)	712.0	522.9	
Exports of goods and services (% of GDP)	23.3	26.0	40.4
Imports of goods and services (% of GDP)	19.7	26.7	36.4
Business environment			
Ease of doing business (ranking 1-178; 1=best)	..	154	
Time to start a business (days)	..	37	53
Procedures to start a business (number)	..	13	10
Firing cost (weeks of wages)	..	33.0	50.2
Closing a business (years to resolve insolvency)	..	3.2	3.3
Total tax rate (% of profit)	..	51.9	45.8
Highest marginal tax rate, corporate (%)	39	..	
Business entry rate (new registrations as % of total)	..	..	7.6
Enterprise surveys			
Time dealing with gov't officials (% of management time)	..	12.8	
Firms expected to give gifts in meetings w/tax officials (%)	..	65.4	
Firms using banks to finance investments (% of firms)	..	19.5	
Delay in obtaining an electrical connection (days)	..	78.9	
ISO certification ownership (% of firms)	..	16.4	
Private sector investment			
Invest. in infrastructure w/private participation ($ millions)	95	503	38,154
Private foreign direct investment, net (% of GDP)	1.6	1.7	3.0
Gross fixed capital formation (% of GDP)	16.0	18.0	33.5
Gross fixed private capital formation (% of GDP)	13.9	15.1	10.9
Finance and banking			
Government cash surplus or deficit (% of GDP)	*0.1*	..	–0.9
Government debt (% of GDP)	*91.7*	..	..
Deposit money banks' assets (% of GDP)	11.4	11.5	87.8
Total financial system deposits (% of GDP)	10.1	14.0	43.1
Bank capital to asset ratio (%)	..	..	10.7
Bank nonperforming loans to total gross loans ratio (%)	..	..	4.0
Domestic credit to the private sector (% of GDP)	8.2	9.0	81.3
Real interest rate (%)	18.6	11.2	
Interest rate spread (percentage points)	17.0	11.0	7.2
Infrastructure			
Paved roads (% of total roads)	8.1	*10.0*	65.8
Electric power consumption (kWh per capita)	171	*196*	*1,502*
Power outages in a typical month (number)	..	12.7	
Fixed line and mobile subscribers (per 100 people)	1	*13*	60
Internet users (per 100 people)	0.3	2.0	11.4
Cost of telephone call to U.S. ($ per 3 minutes)	*3.25*	..	*2.08*

Canada

	Country data		High-income group
	2000	**2006**	**2006**
Economic and social context			
Population (millions)	30.8	32.6	1,031
Labor force (millions)	16.3	17.9	504
Unemployment rate (% of labor force)	6.8	6.8	6.2
GNI per capita, *World Bank Atlas* method ($)	22,130	36,650	36,608
GDP growth, 1995–2000 and 2000–06 (average annual %)	4.3	2.6	2.3
Agriculture value added (% of GDP)	2.3	2.1	1.5
Industry value added (% of GDP)	33.2	31.2	26.2
Manufacturing value added (% of GDP)	19.2	16.5	16.8
Services value added (% of GDP)	64.5	66.7	72.3
Inflation (annual % change in consumer price index)	2.7	2.0	
Exchange rate (local currency units per $)	1.5	1.1	
Exports of goods and services (% of GDP)	45.6	37.9	25.6
Imports of goods and services (% of GDP)	39.8	34.1	26.3
Business environment			
Ease of doing business (ranking 1-178; 1=best)	..	7	
Time to start a business (days)	..	3	22
Procedures to start a business (number)	..	2	7
Firing cost (weeks of wages)	..	28.0	34.9
Closing a business (years to resolve insolvency)	..	0.8	2.0
Total tax rate (% of profit)	..	45.9	41.5
Highest marginal tax rate, corporate (%)	38	22	
Business entry rate (new registrations as % of total)	6.3	6.3	10.1
Enterprise surveys			
Time dealing with gov't officials (% of management time)	..	..	
Firms expected to give gifts in meetings w/tax officials (%)	..	..	
Firms using banks to finance investments (% of firms)	..	..	
Delay in obtaining an electrical connection (days)	..	..	
ISO certification ownership (% of firms)	..	..	
Private sector investment			
Invest. in infrastructure w/private participation ($ millions)	..	..	849
Private foreign direct investment, net (% of GDP)	9.1	5.4	2.7
Gross fixed capital formation (% of GDP)	19.2	20.7	20.4
Gross fixed private capital formation (% of GDP)	..	..	..
Finance and banking			
Government cash surplus or deficit (% of GDP)	1.4	1.5	-1.3
Government debt (% of GDP)	59.9	48.6	47.6
Deposit money banks' assets (% of GDP)	83.6	141.8	99.7
Total financial system deposits (% of GDP)	67.8	152.0	..
Bank capital to asset ratio (%)	4.7	5.7	6.2
Bank nonperforming loans to total gross loans ratio (%)	1.3	0.4	1.1
Domestic credit to the private sector (% of GDP)	95.7	195.3	162.0
Real interest rate (%)	3.0	3.4	
Interest rate spread (percentage points)	3.8	4.0	4.4
Infrastructure			
Paved roads (% of total roads)	..	39.9	90.9
Electric power consumption (kWh per capita)	16,986	17,285	9,760
Power outages in a typical month (number)	..	..	
Fixed line and mobile subscribers (per 100 people)	96	117	143
Internet users (per 100 people)	42.2	68.1	59.3
Cost of telephone call to U.S. ($ per 3 minutes)	1.20	..	0.77

Cape Verde

Sub-Saharan Africa			Lower middle income

	Country data		Lower middle-income group
	2000	2006	2006

Economic and social context
Population (millions)	0.45	0.52	2,276
Labor force (millions)	0.14	0.17	1,209
Unemployment rate (% of labor force)	..	..	5.7
GNI per capita, *World Bank Atlas* method ($)	1,280	2,130	2,038
GDP growth, 1995-2000 and 2000-06 (average annual %)	6.6	5.1	7.6
Agriculture value added (% of GDP)	12.0	9.1	11.9
Industry value added (% of GDP)	17.9	16.9	43.5
Manufacturing value added (% of GDP)	9.3	4.8	26.7
Services value added (% of GDP)	70.2	74.1	44.6
Inflation (annual % change in consumer price index)	-2.5	5.4	
Exchange rate (local currency units per $)	119.7	87.9	
Exports of goods and services (% of GDP)	27.5	20.1	40.4
Imports of goods and services (% of GDP)	61.4	54.6	36.4

Business environment
Ease of doing business (ranking 1-178; 1=best)	..	132	
Time to start a business (days)	..	52	53
Procedures to start a business (number)	..	12	10
Firing cost (weeks of wages)	..	91.0	50.2
Closing a business (years to resolve insolvency)	..	..	3.3
Total tax rate (% of profit)	..	54.0	45.8
Highest marginal tax rate, corporate (%)	..	..	
Business entry rate (new registrations as % of total)	..	..	7.6
Enterprise surveys			
Time dealing with gov't officials (% of management time)	..	12.2	
Firms expected to give gifts in meetings w/tax officials (%)	..	10.4	
Firms using banks to finance investments (% of firms)	..	26.3	
Delay in obtaining an electrical connection (days)	..	7.8	
ISO certification ownership (% of firms)	..	12.2	

Private sector investment
Invest. in infrastructure w/private participation ($ millions)	48	..	38,154
Private foreign direct investment, net (% of GDP)	6.3	10.7	3.0
Gross fixed capital formation (% of GDP)	19.7	39.4	33.5
Gross fixed private capital formation (% of GDP)	7.2	30.3	10.9

Finance and banking
Government cash surplus or deficit (% of GDP)	..	..	-0.9
Government debt (% of GDP)	..	..	..
Deposit money banks' assets (% of GDP)	46.9	57.1	87.8
Total financial system deposits (% of GDP)	50.5	65.0	43.1
Bank capital to asset ratio (%)	..	..	10.7
Bank nonperforming loans to total gross loans ratio (%)	..	..	4.0
Domestic credit to the private sector (% of GDP)	40.7	50.0	81.3
Real interest rate (%)	13.3	2.7	
Interest rate spread (percentage points)	7.6	8.9	7.2

Infrastructure
Paved roads (% of total roads)	69.0	..	65.8
Electric power consumption (kWh per capita)	..	..	1,502
Power outages in a typical month (number)	..	12.5	
Fixed line and mobile subscribers (per 100 people)	17	35	60
Internet users (per 100 people)	1.8	5.7	11.4
Cost of telephone call to U.S. ($ per 3 minutes)	4.66	6.08	2.08

Cayman Islands

	Country data		High-income group
	2000	2006	2006
Economic and social context			
Population (millions)	..	0.05	1,031
Labor force (millions)	..	..	504
Unemployment rate (% of labor force)	4.1	..	6.2
GNI per capita, World Bank Atlas method ($)	..	..	36,608
GDP growth, 1995–2000 and 2000–06 (average annual %)	..	..	2.3
Agriculture value added (% of GDP)	..	..	1.5
Industry value added (% of GDP)	..	..	26.2
Manufacturing value added (% of GDP)	..	..	16.8
Services value added (% of GDP)	..	..	72.3
Inflation (annual % change in consumer price index)	..	..	
Exchange rate (local currency units per $)	0.8	0.8	
Exports of goods and services (% of GDP)	..	..	25.6
Imports of goods and services (% of GDP)	..	..	26.3
Business environment			
Ease of doing business (ranking 1-178; 1=best)	..	..	
Time to start a business (days)	..	..	22
Procedures to start a business (number)	..	..	7
Firing cost (weeks of wages)	..	..	34.9
Closing a business (years to resolve insolvency)	..	..	2.0
Total tax rate (% of profit)	..	..	41.5
Highest marginal tax rate, corporate (%)	..	..	
Business entry rate (new registrations as % of total)	..	..	10.1
Enterprise surveys			
Time dealing with gov't officials (% of management time)	..	..	
Firms expected to give gifts in meetings w/tax officials (%)	..	..	
Firms using banks to finance investments (% of firms)	..	..	
Delay in obtaining an electrical connection (days)	..	..	
ISO certification ownership (% of firms)	..	..	
Private sector investment			
Invest. in infrastructure w/private participation ($ millions)	..	..	849
Private foreign direct investment, net (% of GDP)	..	..	2.7
Gross fixed capital formation (% of GDP)	..	..	20.4
Gross fixed private capital formation (% of GDP)	..	..	..
Finance and banking			
Government cash surplus or deficit (% of GDP)	..	..	–1.3
Government debt (% of GDP)	..	..	47.6
Deposit money banks' assets (% of GDP)	..	..	99.7
Total financial system deposits (% of GDP)	..	..	..
Bank capital to asset ratio (%)	..	..	6.2
Bank nonperforming loans to total gross loans ratio (%)	..	..	1.1
Domestic credit to the private sector (% of GDP)	..	..	162.0
Real interest rate (%)	..	..	
Interest rate spread (percentage points)	..	..	4.4
Infrastructure			
Paved roads (% of total roads)	..	..	90.9
Electric power consumption (kWh per capita)	..	..	9,760
Power outages in a typical month (number)	..	..	
Fixed line and mobile subscribers (per 100 people)	..	..	143
Internet users (per 100 people)	..	45.7	59.3
Cost of telephone call to U.S. ($ per 3 minutes)	..	..	0.77

Central African Republic

	Country data		Low-income group
	2000	2006	2006
Economic and social context			
Population (millions)	3.9	4.3	2,420
Labor force (millions)	1.8	2.0	995
Unemployment rate (% of labor force)	..	..	..
GNI per capita, *World Bank Atlas* method ($)	270	350	649
GDP growth, 1995–2000 and 2000–06 (average annual %)	3.0	-0.7	6.5
Agriculture value added (% of GDP)	53.1	55.8	20.4
Industry value added (% of GDP)	15.8	15.5	27.7
Manufacturing value added (% of GDP)	7.0	7.5	15.8
Services value added (% of GDP)	31.0	28.7	51.9
Inflation (annual % change in consumer price index)	3.2	2.9	
Exchange rate (local currency units per $)	712.0	522.9	
Exports of goods and services (% of GDP)	19.8	13.9	26.7
Imports of goods and services (% of GDP)	24.1	21.7	30.1
Business environment			
Ease of doing business (ranking 1-178; 1=best)	..	177	
Time to start a business (days)	..	14	54
Procedures to start a business (number)	..	10	10
Firing cost (weeks of wages)	..	22.0	62.6
Closing a business (years to resolve insolvency)	..	4.8	3.8
Total tax rate (% of profit)	..	203.8	67.4
Highest marginal tax rate, corporate (%)	..	..	
Business entry rate (new registrations as % of total)	..	..	6.4
Enterprise surveys			
Time dealing with gov't officials (% of management time)	..	..	
Firms expected to give gifts in meetings w/tax officials (%)	..	..	
Firms using banks to finance investments (% of firms)	..	..	
Delay in obtaining an electrical connection (days)	..	..	
ISO certification ownership (% of firms)	..	..	
Private sector investment			
Invest. in infrastructure w/private participation ($ millions)	..	..	29,785
Private foreign direct investment, net (% of GDP)	0.1	1.6	2.6
Gross fixed capital formation (% of GDP)	9.5	8.8	26.7
Gross fixed private capital formation (% of GDP)	4.8	5.6	19.6
Finance and banking			
Government cash surplus or deficit (% of GDP)	..	-0.5	-2.6
Government debt (% of GDP)	..	..	..
Deposit money banks' assets (% of GDP)	7.6	8.8	50.5
Total financial system deposits (% of GDP)	3.9	4.7	44.6
Bank capital to asset ratio (%)	..	..	
Bank nonperforming loans to total gross loans ratio (%)	..	..	..
Domestic credit to the private sector (% of GDP)	4.5	6.6	38.3
Real interest rate (%)	18.3	11.1	
Interest rate spread (percentage points)	17.0	11.0	*11.3*
Infrastructure			
Paved roads (% of total roads)	2.7	..	..
Electric power consumption (kWh per capita)	..	..	*391*
Power outages in a typical month (number)	..	..	
Fixed line and mobile subscribers (per 100 people)	0	3	17
Internet users (per 100 people)	0.1	0.3	*4.2*
Cost of telephone call to U.S. ($ per 3 minutes)	13.31	*1.99*	*1.99*

Chad

	Country data		Low-income group
	2000	2006	2006
Economic and social context			
Population (millions)	8.5	10.5	2,420
Labor force (millions)	3.3	4.0	995
Unemployment rate (% of labor force)	..	..	..
GNI per capita, *World Bank Atlas* method ($)	180	450	649
GDP growth, 1995–2000 and 2000–06 (average annual %)	3.1	14.1	6.5
Agriculture value added (% of GDP)	42.3	20.5	20.4
Industry value added (% of GDP)	11.3	54.8	27.7
Manufacturing value added (% of GDP)	8.9	5.3	15.8
Services value added (% of GDP)	46.3	24.7	51.9
Inflation (annual % change in consumer price index)	3.8	8.0	
Exchange rate (local currency units per $)	712.0	522.9	
Exports of goods and services (% of GDP)	16.9	58.9	26.7
Imports of goods and services (% of GDP)	34.7	38.4	30.1
Business environment			
Ease of doing business (ranking 1-178; 1=best)	..	173	
Time to start a business (days)	..	75	54
Procedures to start a business (number)	..	19	10
Firing cost (weeks of wages)	..	36.0	62.6
Closing a business (years to resolve insolvency)	..	10.0	3.8
Total tax rate (% of profit)	..	63.7	67.4
Highest marginal tax rate, corporate (%)	..	..	
Business entry rate (new registrations as % of total)	..	..	6.4
Enterprise surveys			
Time dealing with gov't officials (% of management time)	..	..	
Firms expected to give gifts in meetings w/tax officials (%)	..	..	
Firms using banks to finance investments (% of firms)	..	..	
Delay in obtaining an electrical connection (days)	..	..	
ISO certification ownership (% of firms)	..	..	
Private sector investment			
Invest. in infrastructure w/private participation ($ millions)	5	26	29,785
Private foreign direct investment, net (% of GDP)	8.3	10.7	2.6
Gross fixed capital formation (% of GDP)	20.9	20.5	26.7
Gross fixed private capital formation (% of GDP)	10.5	12.7	19.6
Finance and banking			
Government cash surplus or deficit (% of GDP)	..	..	-2.6
Government debt (% of GDP)	..	..	..
Deposit money banks' assets (% of GDP)	5.3	4.8	50.5
Total financial system deposits (% of GDP)	3.6	3.9	44.6
Bank capital to asset ratio (%)	..	..	..
Bank nonperforming loans to total gross loans ratio (%)	..	..	
Domestic credit to the private sector (% of GDP)	3.5	2.5	38.3
Real interest rate (%)	15.9	5.2	
Interest rate spread (percentage points)	17.0	11.0	*11.3*
Infrastructure			
Paved roads (% of total roads)	0.8	..	..
Electric power consumption (kWh per capita)	..	..	*391*
Power outages in a typical month (number)	..	..	
Fixed line and mobile subscribers (per 100 people)	0	5	17
Internet users (per 100 people)	0.0	0.6	*4.2*
Cost of telephone call to U.S. ($ per 3 minutes)	12.50	..	*1.99*

Channel Islands

	Country data		High-income group
	2000	2006	2006
Economic and social context			
Population (millions)	0.15	0.15	1,031
Labor force (millions)	..	..	504
Unemployment rate (% of labor force)	..	..	6.2
GNI per capita, *World Bank Atlas* method ($)	..	..	36,608
GDP growth, 1995–2000 and 2000–06 (average annual %)	..	..	2.3
Agriculture value added (% of GDP)	..	..	1.5
Industry value added (% of GDP)	..	..	26.2
Manufacturing value added (% of GDP)	..	..	16.8
Services value added (% of GDP)	..	..	72.3
Inflation (annual % change in consumer price index)	..	..	
Exchange rate (local currency units per $)	..	..	
Exports of goods and services (% of GDP)	..	..	25.6
Imports of goods and services (% of GDP)	..	..	26.3
Business environment			
Ease of doing business (ranking 1-178; 1=best)	..	..	
Time to start a business (days)	..	..	22
Procedures to start a business (number)	..	..	7
Firing cost (weeks of wages)	..	..	34.9
Closing a business (years to resolve insolvency)	..	..	2.0
Total tax rate (% of profit)	..	..	41.5
Highest marginal tax rate, corporate (%)	20	20	
Business entry rate (new registrations as % of total)	..	..	10.1
Enterprise surveys			
Time dealing with gov't officials (% of management time)	..	..	
Firms expected to give gifts in meetings w/tax officials (%)	..	..	
Firms using banks to finance investments (% of firms)	..	..	
Delay in obtaining an electrical connection (days)	..	..	
ISO certification ownership (% of firms)	..	..	
Private sector investment			
Invest. in infrastructure w/private participation ($ millions)	..	..	849
Private foreign direct investment, net (% of GDP)	..	..	2.7
Gross fixed capital formation (% of GDP)	..	..	20.4
Gross fixed private capital formation (% of GDP)	..	..	..
Finance and banking			
Government cash surplus or deficit (% of GDP)	..	..	-1.3
Government debt (% of GDP)	..	..	47.6
Deposit money banks' assets (% of GDP)	..	..	99.7
Total financial system deposits (% of GDP)	..	..	..
Bank capital to asset ratio (%)	..	..	6.2
Bank nonperforming loans to total gross loans ratio (%)	..	..	1.1
Domestic credit to the private sector (% of GDP)	..	..	162.0
Real interest rate (%)	..	..	
Interest rate spread (percentage points)	..	..	4.4
Infrastructure			
Paved roads (% of total roads)	..	..	90.9
Electric power consumption (kWh per capita)	..	..	9,760
Power outages in a typical month (number)	..	..	
Fixed line and mobile subscribers (per 100 people)	..	..	143
Internet users (per 100 people)	..	..	59.3
Cost of telephone call to U.S. ($ per 3 minutes)	2.90	2.90	0.77

Chile

	Country data		Upper middle-income group
	2000	2006	2006
Economic and social context			
Population (millions)	15.4	16.4	811
Labor force (millions)	6.1	6.6	374
Unemployment rate (% of labor force)	8.3	6.9	9.8
GNI per capita, *World Bank Atlas* method ($)	4,850	6,810	5,913
GDP growth, 1995–2000 and 2000–06 (average annual %)	3.8	4.3	3.9
Agriculture value added (% of GDP)	6.1	4.1	5.7
Industry value added (% of GDP)	38.4	47.7	32.4
Manufacturing value added (% of GDP)	19.5	13.5	19.4
Services value added (% of GDP)	55.5	48.2	62.0
Inflation (annual % change in consumer price index)	3.8	3.4	
Exchange rate (local currency units per $)	539.6	530.3	
Exports of goods and services (% of GDP)	31.6	45.4	32.7
Imports of goods and services (% of GDP)	29.7	30.9	30.3
Business environment			
Ease of doing business (ranking 1-178; 1=best)	..	33	
Time to start a business (days)	..	27	41
Procedures to start a business (number)	..	9	9
Firing cost (weeks of wages)	..	52.0	39.7
Closing a business (years to resolve insolvency)	..	4.5	2.9
Total tax rate (% of profit)	..	25.9	44.5
Highest marginal tax rate, corporate (%)	15	17	
Business entry rate (new registrations as % of total)	16.6	18.2	9.1
Enterprise surveys			
Time dealing with gov't officials (% of management time)	..	9.0	
Firms expected to give gifts in meetings w/tax officials (%)	..	7.6	
Firms using banks to finance investments (% of firms)	..	29.1	
Delay in obtaining an electrical connection (days)	..	22.9	
ISO certification ownership (% of firms)	..	22.0	
Private sector investment			
Invest. in infrastructure w/private participation ($ millions)	1,605	484	45,869
Private foreign direct investment, net (% of GDP)	6.4	5.5	3.5
Gross fixed capital formation (% of GDP)	20.7	19.3	19.9
Gross fixed private capital formation (% of GDP)	..	..	..
Finance and banking			
Government cash surplus or deficit (% of GDP)	-0.7	7.7	..
Government debt (% of GDP)	..	..	..
Deposit money banks' assets (% of GDP)	60.5	63.0	52.9
Total financial system deposits (% of GDP)	48.7	46.6	41.4
Bank capital to asset ratio (%)	7.5	6.8	9.8
Bank nonperforming loans to total gross loans ratio (%)	1.7	0.8	3.2
Domestic credit to the private sector (% of GDP)	73.6	82.4	41.4
Real interest rate (%)	9.8	-3.3	
Interest rate spread (percentage points)	5.6	2.9	5.9
Infrastructure			
Paved roads (% of total roads)	18.4	..	..
Electric power consumption (kWh per capita)	2,488	3,074	3,131
Power outages in a typical month (number)	..	2.1	
Fixed line and mobile subscribers (per 100 people)	43	96	88
Internet users (per 100 people)	16.5	25.3	22.2
Cost of telephone call to U.S. ($ per 3 minutes)	2.45	..	1.06

China

East Asia & Pacific			Lower middle income

	Country data		Lower middle-income group
	2000	2006	2006

Economic and social context
Population (millions)	1,262.6	1,311.8	2,276
Labor force (millions)	738.3	780.5	1,209
Unemployment rate (% of labor force)	3.1	4.2	5.7
GNI per capita, *World Bank Atlas* method ($)	930	2,000	2,038
GDP growth, 1995-2000 and 2000-06 (average annual %)	8.5	9.8	7.6
Agriculture value added (% of GDP)	14.8	11.7	11.9
Industry value added (% of GDP)	45.9	48.4	43.5
Manufacturing value added (% of GDP)	32.1	33.5	26.7
Services value added (% of GDP)	39.3	39.9	44.6
Inflation (annual % change in consumer price index)	0.3	1.5	
Exchange rate (local currency units per $)	8.3	8.0	
Exports of goods and services (% of GDP)	23.3	40.1	40.4
Imports of goods and services (% of GDP)	20.9	32.2	36.4

Business environment
Ease of doing business (ranking 1-178; 1=best)	..	83	
Time to start a business (days)	..	35	53
Procedures to start a business (number)	..	13	10
Firing cost (weeks of wages)	..	91.0	50.2
Closing a business (years to resolve insolvency)	..	1.7	3.3
Total tax rate (% of profit)	..	73.9	45.8
Highest marginal tax rate, corporate (%)	30	..	
Business entry rate (new registrations as % of total)	..	..	7.6
Enterprise surveys			
Time dealing with gov't officials (% of management time)	..	18.3	
Firms expected to give gifts in meetings w/tax officials (%)	..	38.7	
Firms using banks to finance investments (% of firms)	..	9.8	
Delay in obtaining an electrical connection (days)	..	27.8	
ISO certification ownership (% of firms)	..	35.9	

Private sector investment
Invest. in infrastructure w/private participation ($ millions)	8,131	8,287	38,154
Private foreign direct investment, net (% of GDP)	3.2	3.0	3.0
Gross fixed capital formation (% of GDP)	34.1	42.8	33.5
Gross fixed private capital formation (% of GDP)	10.5	6.7	10.9

Finance and banking
Government cash surplus or deficit (% of GDP)	-2.6	-1.6	-0.9
Government debt (% of GDP)	11.6	..	..
Deposit money banks' assets (% of GDP)	114.7	111.9	87.8
Total financial system deposits (% of GDP)	36.2	41.4	43.1
Bank capital to asset ratio (%)	4.1	6.1	10.7
Bank nonperforming loans to total gross loans ratio (%)	22.4	7.5	4.0
Domestic credit to the private sector (% of GDP)	112.3	113.6	81.3
Real interest rate (%)	3.7	2.4	
Interest rate spread (percentage points)	3.6	3.6	7.2

Infrastructure
Paved roads (% of total roads)	78.3	81.6	65.8
Electric power consumption (kWh per capita)	993	1,781	1,502
Power outages in a typical month (number)	..	..	
Fixed line and mobile subscribers (per 100 people)	18	63	60
Internet users (per 100 people)	1.8	10.4	11.4
Cost of telephone call to U.S. ($ per 3 minutes)	6.67	2.90	2.08

Colombia

	Country data		Lower middle-income group
	2000	**2006**	**2006**
Economic and social context			
Population (millions)	41.7	45.6	2,276
Labor force (millions)	19.3	22.8	1,209
Unemployment rate (% of labor force)	20.5	9.5	5.7
GNI per capita, *World Bank Atlas* method ($)	2,080	3,120	2,038
GDP growth, 1995–2000 and 2000–06 (average annual %)	0.6	3.9	7.6
Agriculture value added (% of GDP)	12.9	12.0	11.9
Industry value added (% of GDP)	30.3	35.6	43.5
Manufacturing value added (% of GDP)	15.8	16.7	26.7
Services value added (% of GDP)	56.7	52.4	44.6
Inflation (annual % change in consumer price index)	9.2	4.3	
Exchange rate (local currency units per $)	2,087.9	2,361.1	
Exports of goods and services (% of GDP)	21.5	22.4	40.4
Imports of goods and services (% of GDP)	19.4	24.9	36.4
Business environment			
Ease of doing business (ranking 1-178; 1=best)	..	66	
Time to start a business (days)	..	42	53
Procedures to start a business (number)	..	11	10
Firing cost (weeks of wages)	..	59.0	50.2
Closing a business (years to resolve insolvency)	..	3.0	3.3
Total tax rate (% of profit)	..	82.4	45.8
Highest marginal tax rate, corporate (%)	35	39	
Business entry rate (new registrations as % of total)	6.0	4.9	7.6
Enterprise surveys			
Time dealing with gov't officials (% of management time)	..	14.3	
Firms expected to give gifts in meetings w/tax officials (%)	..	1.1	
Firms using banks to finance investments (% of firms)	..	30.6	
Delay in obtaining an electrical connection (days)	..	27.2	
ISO certification ownership (% of firms)	..	5.9	
Private sector investment			
Invest. in infrastructure w/private participation ($ millions)	1,032	2,808	38,154
Private foreign direct investment, net (% of GDP)	2.9	4.2	3.0
Gross fixed capital formation (% of GDP)	12.6	23.3	33.5
Gross fixed private capital formation (% of GDP)	..	..	10.9
Finance and banking			
Government cash surplus or deficit (% of GDP)	–7.0	–3.9	–0.9
Government debt (% of GDP)	..	68.0	..
Deposit money banks' assets (% of GDP)	33.3	41.0	87.8
Total financial system deposits (% of GDP)	27.1	19.3	43.1
Bank capital to asset ratio (%)	11.2	10.8	10.7
Bank nonperforming loans to total gross loans ratio (%)	11.0	2.6	4.0
Domestic credit to the private sector (% of GDP)	26.7	35.7	81.3
Real interest rate (%)	6.0	7.1	
Interest rate spread (percentage points)	6.6	6.6	7.2
Infrastructure			
Paved roads (% of total roads)	14.4	..	65.8
Electric power consumption (kWh per capita)	838	890	1,502
Power outages in a typical month (number)	..	1.0	
Fixed line and mobile subscribers (per 100 people)	23	83	60
Internet users (per 100 people)	2.1	14.7	11.4
Cost of telephone call to U.S. ($ per 3 minutes)	2.00	..	2.08

Comoros

Sub-Saharan Africa   **Low income**

	Country data		Low-income group
	2000	2006	2006
Economic and social context			
Population (millions)	0.54	0.61	2,420
Labor force (millions)	0.22	0.26	995
Unemployment rate (% of labor force)	..	..	..
GNI per capita, *World Bank Atlas* method ($)	400	660	649
GDP growth, 1995–2000 and 2000–06 (average annual %)	1.7	2.4	6.5
Agriculture value added (% of GDP)	48.6	45.2	20.4
Industry value added (% of GDP)	11.5	11.8	27.7
Manufacturing value added (% of GDP)	4.5	4.2	15.8
Services value added (% of GDP)	39.9	38.0	51.9
Inflation (annual % change in consumer price index)	..	..	
Exchange rate (local currency units per $)	534.0	392.2	
Exports of goods and services (% of GDP)	16.7	11.7	26.7
Imports of goods and services (% of GDP)	32.5	35.5	30.1
Business environment			
Ease of doing business (ranking 1-178; 1=best)	..	147	
Time to start a business (days)	..	23	54
Procedures to start a business (number)	..	11	10
Firing cost (weeks of wages)	..	100.0	62.6
Closing a business (years to resolve insolvency)	..	..	3.8
Total tax rate (% of profit)	..	48.8	67.4
Highest marginal tax rate, corporate (%)	..	..	
Business entry rate (new registrations as % of total)	..	..	6.4
Enterprise surveys			
Time dealing with gov't officials (% of management time)	..	..	
Firms expected to give gifts in meetings w/tax officials (%)	..	..	
Firms using banks to finance investments (% of firms)	..	..	
Delay in obtaining an electrical connection (days)	..	..	
ISO certification ownership (% of firms)	..	..	
Private sector investment			
Invest. in infrastructure w/private participation ($ millions)	..	0.5	29,785
Private foreign direct investment, net (% of GDP)	0.0	0.2	2.6
Gross fixed capital formation (% of GDP)	10.1	9.8	26.7
Gross fixed private capital formation (% of GDP)	6.2	4.9	19.6
Finance and banking			
Government cash surplus or deficit (% of GDP)	..	..	-2.6
Government debt (% of GDP)	..	..	..
Deposit money banks' assets (% of GDP)	..	..	50.5
Total financial system deposits (% of GDP)	..	..	44.6
Bank capital to asset ratio (%)	..	..	..
Bank nonperforming loans to total gross loans ratio (%)	..	..	..
Domestic credit to the private sector (% of GDP)	11.9	7.9	38.3
Real interest rate (%)	7.9	7.5	
Interest rate spread (percentage points)	9.0	8.0	11.3
Infrastructure			
Paved roads (% of total roads)	76.5	..	..
Electric power consumption (kWh per capita)	..	..	391
Power outages in a typical month (number)	..	..	
Fixed line and mobile subscribers (per 100 people)	1	5	17
Internet users (per 100 people)	0.3	3.4	4.2
Cost of telephone call to U.S. ($ per 3 minutes)	..	..	1.99

Congo, Dem. Rep.

Sub-Saharan Africa **Low income**

	Country data		Low-income group
	2000	**2006**	**2006**
Economic and social context			
Population (millions)	50.7	60.6	2,420
Labor force (millions)	20.2	24.2	995
Unemployment rate (% of labor force)	..	..	..
GNI per capita, *World Bank Atlas* method ($)	80	130	649
GDP growth, 1995–2000 and 2000–06 (average annual %)	-3.8	4.7	6.5
Agriculture value added (% of GDP)	50.0	45.7	20.4
Industry value added (% of GDP)	20.3	27.7	27.7
Manufacturing value added (% of GDP)	4.8	6.5	15.8
Services value added (% of GDP)	29.7	26.6	51.9
Inflation (annual % change in consumer price index)	550.0	21.3	
Exchange rate (local currency units per $)	21.8	468.3	
Exports of goods and services (% of GDP)	22.4	29.5	26.7
Imports of goods and services (% of GDP)	21.4	41.0	30.1
Business environment			
Ease of doing business (ranking 1-178; 1=best)	..	178	
Time to start a business (days)	..	155	54
Procedures to start a business (number)	..	13	10
Firing cost (weeks of wages)	..	31.0	62.6
Closing a business (years to resolve insolvency)	..	5.2	3.8
Total tax rate (% of profit)	..	229.8	67.4
Highest marginal tax rate, corporate (%)	40	40	
Business entry rate (new registrations as % of total)	..	..	6.4
Enterprise surveys			
Time dealing with gov't officials (% of management time)	..	6.3	
Firms expected to give gifts in meetings w/tax officials (%)	..	64.4	
Firms using banks to finance investments (% of firms)	..	3.3	
Delay in obtaining an electrical connection (days)	..	20.5	
ISO certification ownership (% of firms)	..	4.3	
Private sector investment			
Invest. in infrastructure w/private participation ($ millions)	41	74	29,785
Private foreign direct investment, net (% of GDP)	3.9	2.1	2.6
Gross fixed capital formation (% of GDP)	3.5	12.8	26.7
Gross fixed private capital formation (% of GDP)	3.0	10.0	19.6
Finance and banking			
Government cash surplus or deficit (% of GDP)	-4.0	..	-2.6
Government debt (% of GDP)	152.2	..	
Deposit money banks' assets (% of GDP)	0.6	1.7	50.5
Total financial system deposits (% of GDP)	1.7	3.1	44.6
Bank capital to asset ratio (%)	..	..	..
Bank nonperforming loans to total gross loans ratio (%)	..	..	..
Domestic credit to the private sector (% of GDP)	0.7	2.9	38.3
Real interest rate (%)	-57.0	..	
Interest rate spread (percentage points)	..	..	11.3
Infrastructure			
Paved roads (% of total roads)	..	1.8	..
Electric power consumption (kWh per capita)	89	91	391
Power outages in a typical month (number)	..	17.8	
Fixed line and mobile subscribers (per 100 people)	0	7	17
Internet users (per 100 people)	0.0	0.3	4.2
Cost of telephone call to U.S. ($ per 3 minutes)	..	..	1.99

Congo, Rep.

Sub-Saharan Africa　　　　　　　　　　**Lower middle income**

	Country data		Lower middle-income group
	2000	**2006**	**2006**
Economic and social context			
Population (millions)	3.2	3.7	2,276
Labor force (millions)	1.4	1.5	1,209
Unemployment rate (% of labor force)	..	..	5.7
GNI per capita, *World Bank Atlas* method ($)	550	*1,050*	2,038
GDP growth, 1995–2000 and 2000–06 (average annual %)	1.9	4.4	7.6
Agriculture value added (% of GDP)	5.3	4.2	11.9
Industry value added (% of GDP)	72.2	73.5	43.5
Manufacturing value added (% of GDP)	3.5	4.9	*26.7*
Services value added (% of GDP)	22.5	22.3	44.6
Inflation (annual % change in consumer price index)	-0.8	3.4	
Exchange rate (local currency units per $)	712.0	522.9	
Exports of goods and services (% of GDP)	80.3	91.0	40.4
Imports of goods and services (% of GDP)	43.6	46.0	36.4
Business environment			
Ease of doing business (ranking 1-178; 1=best)	..	175	
Time to start a business (days)	..	37	53
Procedures to start a business (number)	..	10	10
Firing cost (weeks of wages)	..	33.0	50.2
Closing a business (years to resolve insolvency)	..	3.0	3.3
Total tax rate (% of profit)	..	65.4	45.8
Highest marginal tax rate, corporate (%)	45	..	
Business entry rate (new registrations as % of total)	8.7	6.3	*7.6*
Enterprise surveys			
Time dealing with gov't officials (% of management time)	..	..	
Firms expected to give gifts in meetings w/tax officials (%)	..	..	
Firms using banks to finance investments (% of firms)	..	..	
Delay in obtaining an electrical connection (days)	..	..	
ISO certification ownership (% of firms)	..	..	
Private sector investment			
Invest. in infrastructure w/private participation ($ millions)	35	10	38,154
Private foreign direct investment, net (% of GDP)	5.2	4.7	3.0
Gross fixed capital formation (% of GDP)	20.9	23.5	33.5
Gross fixed private capital formation (% of GDP)	14.0	14.5	10.9
Finance and banking			
Government cash surplus or deficit (% of GDP)	*-1.3*	6.4	-0.9
Government debt (% of GDP)	..	0.2	
Deposit money banks' assets (% of GDP)	7.2	3.4	87.8
Total financial system deposits (% of GDP)	6.4	6.5	43.1
Bank capital to asset ratio (%)	..	..	10.7
Bank nonperforming loans to total gross loans ratio (%)	..	..	4.0
Domestic credit to the private sector (% of GDP)	4.8	2.2	81.3
Real interest rate (%)	-17.0	0.1	
Interest rate spread (percentage points)	17.0	11.0	7.2
Infrastructure			
Paved roads (% of total roads)	9.7	*5.0*	65.8
Electric power consumption (kWh per capita)	119	*160*	1,502
Power outages in a typical month (number)	..	..	
Fixed line and mobile subscribers (per 100 people)	3	14	60
Internet users (per 100 people)	0.0	1.9	11.4
Cost of telephone call to U.S. ($ per 3 minutes)	..	*5.39*	*2.08*

Costa Rica

Latin America & Caribbean　　　　　　　　**Upper middle income**

	Country data		Upper middle-income group
	2000	2006	2006
Economic and social context			
Population (millions)	3.9	4.4	811
Labor force (millions)	1.6	2.0	374
Unemployment rate (% of labor force)	5.1	6.6	9.8
GNI per capita, *World Bank Atlas* method ($)	3,710	4,980	5,913
GDP growth, 1995–2000 and 2000–06 (average annual %)	5.7	4.8	3.9
Agriculture value added (% of GDP)	9.5	8.8	5.7
Industry value added (% of GDP)	32.1	29.4	32.4
Manufacturing value added (% of GDP)	25.3	21.8	19.4
Services value added (% of GDP)	58.5	61.8	62.0
Inflation (annual % change in consumer price index)	11.0	11.5	
Exchange rate (local currency units per $)	308.2	511.3	
Exports of goods and services (% of GDP)	48.6	49.6	32.7
Imports of goods and services (% of GDP)	45.8	55.9	30.3
Business environment			
Ease of doing business (ranking 1-178; 1=best)	..	115	
Time to start a business (days)	..	77	41
Procedures to start a business (number)	..	12	9
Firing cost (weeks of wages)	..	35.0	39.7
Closing a business (years to resolve insolvency)	..	3.5	2.9
Total tax rate (% of profit)	..	55.7	44.5
Highest marginal tax rate, corporate (%)	30	30	
Business entry rate (new registrations as % of total)	..	*11.3*	*9.1*
Enterprise surveys			
Time dealing with gov't officials (% of management time)	..	*9.6*	
Firms expected to give gifts in meetings w/tax officials (%)	..	..	
Firms using banks to finance investments (% of firms)	..	*9.3*	
Delay in obtaining an electrical connection (days)	..	*48.6*	
ISO certification ownership (% of firms)	..	*10.5*	
Private sector investment			
Invest. in infrastructure w/private participation ($ millions)	161	123	45,869
Private foreign direct investment, net (% of GDP)	2.6	6.6	3.5
Gross fixed capital formation (% of GDP)	17.8	20.3	19.9
Gross fixed private capital formation (% of GDP)	16.3	19.3	..
Finance and banking			
Government cash surplus or deficit (% of GDP)	..	1.2	..
Government debt (% of GDP)	36.2	..	..
Deposit money banks' assets (% of GDP)	24.7	40.3	52.9
Total financial system deposits (% of GDP)	12.1	20.9	41.4
Bank capital to asset ratio (%)	10.8	10.2	9.8
Bank nonperforming loans to total gross loans ratio (%)	3.5	1.5	3.2
Domestic credit to the private sector (% of GDP)	24.0	39.1	41.4
Real interest rate (%)	16.7	11.0	
Interest rate spread (percentage points)	11.5	12.4	5.9
Infrastructure			
Paved roads (% of total roads)	22.0	*24.4*	..
Electric power consumption (kWh per capita)	1,518	*1,719*	*3,131*
Power outages in a typical month (number)	..	..	
Fixed line and mobile subscribers (per 100 people)	28	64	88
Internet users (per 100 people)	5.8	27.6	22.2
Cost of telephone call to U.S. ($ per 3 minutes)	1.93	..	*1.06*

Côte d'Ivoire

Sub-Saharan Africa   **Low income**

	Country data		Low-income group
	2000	2006	2006
Economic and social context			
Population (millions)	17.0	18.9	2,420
Labor force (millions)	6.3	7.1	995
Unemployment rate (% of labor force)	4.1	..	..
GNI per capita, World Bank Atlas method ($)	630	880	649
GDP growth, 1995–2000 and 2000–06 (average annual %)	3.4	0.1	6.5
Agriculture value added (% of GDP)	24.2	22.7	20.4
Industry value added (% of GDP)	24.9	26.3	27.7
Manufacturing value added (% of GDP)	21.7	18.3	15.8
Services value added (% of GDP)	50.9	51.0	51.9
Inflation (annual % change in consumer price index)	2.5	2.5	
Exchange rate (local currency units per $)	712.0	522.9	
Exports of goods and services (% of GDP)	40.4	51.3	26.7
Imports of goods and services (% of GDP)	33.3	41.0	30.1
Business environment			
Ease of doing business (ranking 1-178; 1=best)	..	155	
Time to start a business (days)	..	40	54
Procedures to start a business (number)	..	10	10
Firing cost (weeks of wages)	..	49.0	62.6
Closing a business (years to resolve insolvency)	..	2.2	3.8
Total tax rate (% of profit)	..	45.4	67.4
Highest marginal tax rate, corporate (%)	35	35	
Business entry rate (new registrations as % of total)	..	..	6.4
Enterprise surveys			
Time dealing with gov't officials (% of management time)	..	..	
Firms expected to give gifts in meetings w/tax officials (%)	..	..	
Firms using banks to finance investments (% of firms)	..	..	
Delay in obtaining an electrical connection (days)	..	..	
ISO certification ownership (% of firms)	..	..	
Private sector investment			
Invest. in infrastructure w/private participation ($ millions)	215	13	29,785
Private foreign direct investment, net (% of GDP)	2.3	1.8	2.6
Gross fixed capital formation (% of GDP)	11.2	9.7	26.7
Gross fixed private capital formation (% of GDP)	8.4	6.7	19.6
Finance and banking			
Government cash surplus or deficit (% of GDP)	2.8	-1.4	-2.6
Government debt (% of GDP)	105.2	107.9	..
Deposit money banks' assets (% of GDP)	19.7	16.8	50.5
Total financial system deposits (% of GDP)	13.9	15.2	44.6
Bank capital to asset ratio (%)	..	..	..
Bank nonperforming loans to total gross loans ratio (%)	..	..	..
Domestic credit to the private sector (% of GDP)	15.5	14.1	38.3
Real interest rate (%)	..	..	
Interest rate spread (percentage points)	..	..	11.3
Infrastructure			
Paved roads (% of total roads)	9.7	8.1	..
Electric power consumption (kWh per capita)	168	170	391
Power outages in a typical month (number)	..	..	
Fixed line and mobile subscribers (per 100 people)	4	23	17
Internet users (per 100 people)	0.2	1.6	4.2
Cost of telephone call to U.S. ($ per 3 minutes)	6.07	2.25	1.99

Croatia

Europe & Central Asia   **Upper middle income**

	Country data		Upper middle-income group
	2000	2006	2006
Economic and social context			
Population (millions)	4.5	4.4	811
Labor force (millions)	2.0	1.9	374
Unemployment rate (% of labor force)	16.1	11.2	9.8
GNI per capita, *World Bank Atlas* method ($)	4,360	9,310	5,913
GDP growth, 1995–2000 and 2000–06 (average annual %)	3.2	4.8	3.9
Agriculture value added (% of GDP)	9.1	7.4	5.7
Industry value added (% of GDP)	30.3	31.6	32.4
Manufacturing value added (% of GDP)	21.7	20.6	19.4
Services value added (% of GDP)	60.7	60.9	62.0
Inflation (annual % change in consumer price index)	4.6	3.2	
Exchange rate (local currency units per $)	8.3	5.8	
Exports of goods and services (% of GDP)	47.1	47.9	32.7
Imports of goods and services (% of GDP)	52.3	56.8	30.3
Business environment			
Ease of doing business (ranking 1-178; 1=best)	..	97	
Time to start a business (days)	..	40	41
Procedures to start a business (number)	..	8	9
Firing cost (weeks of wages)	..	39.0	39.7
Closing a business (years to resolve insolvency)	..	3.1	2.9
Total tax rate (% of profit)	..	32.5	44.5
Highest marginal tax rate, corporate (%)	35	20	
Business entry rate (new registrations as % of total)	5.5	7.7	9.1
Enterprise surveys			
Time dealing with gov't officials (% of management time)	..	2.7	
Firms expected to give gifts in meetings w/tax officials (%)	41.6	6.0	
Firms using banks to finance investments (% of firms)	19.8	60.0	
Delay in obtaining an electrical connection (days)	..	42.6	
ISO certification ownership (% of firms)	..	16.1	
Private sector investment			
Invest. in infrastructure w/private participation ($ millions)	746	396	45,869
Private foreign direct investment, net (% of GDP)	5.9	7.9	3.5
Gross fixed capital formation (% of GDP)	21.8	29.8	19.9
Gross fixed private capital formation (% of GDP)	18.6	23.8	..
Finance and banking			
Government cash surplus or deficit (% of GDP)	-6.2	-1.8	..
Government debt (% of GDP)	..	..	..
Deposit money banks' assets (% of GDP)	47.4	77.8	52.9
Total financial system deposits (% of GDP)	36.4	62.6	41.4
Bank capital to asset ratio (%)	11.9	10.3	9.8
Bank nonperforming loans to total gross loans ratio (%)	9.5	5.2	3.2
Domestic credit to the private sector (% of GDP)	37.4	68.7	41.4
Real interest rate (%)	7.0	6.3	
Interest rate spread (percentage points)	8.3	8.2	5.9
Infrastructure			
Paved roads (% of total roads)	85.4	89.0	..
Electric power consumption (kWh per capita)	2,792	3,475	3,131
Power outages in a typical month (number)	..	2.2	
Fixed line and mobile subscribers (per 100 people)	61	142	88
Internet users (per 100 people)	6.6	35.5	22.2
Cost of telephone call to U.S. ($ per 3 minutes)	..	..	1.06

Cuba

Latin America & Caribbean			Lower middle income

	Country data		Lower middle-income group
	2000	2006	2006

Economic and social context

Population (millions)	11.1	11.3	2,276
Labor force (millions)	5.2	5.3	1,209
Unemployment rate (% of labor force)	5.4	1.9	5.7
GNI per capita, *World Bank Atlas* method ($)	..	..	2,038
GDP growth, 1995–2000 and 2000–06 (average annual %)	4.2	3.4	7.6
Agriculture value added (% of GDP)	6.4	..	11.9
Industry value added (% of GDP)	47.5	..	43.5
Manufacturing value added (% of GDP)	38.7	..	26.7
Services value added (% of GDP)	46.1	..	44.6
Inflation (annual % change in consumer price index)	..	..	
Exchange rate (local currency units per $)	..		
Exports of goods and services (% of GDP)	16.0	..	40.4
Imports of goods and services (% of GDP)	18.7	..	36.4

Business environment

Ease of doing business (ranking 1-178; 1=best)	..	..	
Time to start a business (days)	..	..	53
Procedures to start a business (number)	..	..	10
Firing cost (weeks of wages)	..	..	50.2
Closing a business (years to resolve insolvency)	..	..	3.3
Total tax rate (% of profit)	..	..	45.8
Highest marginal tax rate, corporate (%)	..	..	
Business entry rate (new registrations as % of total)	..	..	7.6
Enterprise surveys			
Time dealing with gov't officials (% of management time)	..	..	
Firms expected to give gifts in meetings w/tax officials (%)	..	..	
Firms using banks to finance investments (% of firms)	..	..	
Delay in obtaining an electrical connection (days)	..	..	
ISO certification ownership (% of firms)	..	..	

Private sector investment

Invest. in infrastructure w/private participation ($ millions)	600	..	38,154
Private foreign direct investment, net (% of GDP)	..	..	3.0
Gross fixed capital formation (% of GDP)	10.4	..	33.5
Gross fixed private capital formation (% of GDP)	..	..	10.9

Finance and banking

Government cash surplus or deficit (% of GDP)	..	..	–0.9
Government debt (% of GDP)	..	..	
Deposit money banks' assets (% of GDP)	..	..	87.8
Total financial system deposits (% of GDP)	..	..	43.1
Bank capital to asset ratio (%)	..	..	10.7
Bank nonperforming loans to total gross loans ratio (%)	..	..	4.0
Domestic credit to the private sector (% of GDP)	..	..	81.3
Real interest rate (%)	..	..	
Interest rate spread (percentage points)	..	..	7.2

Infrastructure

Paved roads (% of total roads)	49.0	..	65.8
Electric power consumption (kWh per capita)	1,136	1,152	1,502
Power outages in a typical month (number)	..		
Fixed line and mobile subscribers (per 100 people)	4	10	60
Internet users (per 100 people)	0.5	2.1	11.4
Cost of telephone call to U.S. ($ per 3 minutes)	7.35	7.49	2.08

Cyprus

	Country data		High-income group
	2000	**2006**	**2006**
Economic and social context			
Population (millions)	0.69	0.77	1,031
Labor force (millions)	0.33	0.38	504
Unemployment rate (% of labor force)	4.8	5.3	6.2
GNI per capita, *World Bank Atlas* method ($)	13,440	23,270	36,608
GDP growth, 1995–2000 and 2000–06 (average annual %)	3.9	3.2	2.3
Agriculture value added (% of GDP)	..	..	1.5
Industry value added (% of GDP)	..	..	26.2
Manufacturing value added (% of GDP)	..	..	16.8
Services value added (% of GDP)	..	..	72.3
Inflation (annual % change in consumer price index)	4.1	2.5	
Exchange rate (local currency units per $)	0.6	0.5	
Exports of goods and services (% of GDP)	42.1	..	25.6
Imports of goods and services (% of GDP)	45.7	..	26.3
Business environment			
Ease of doing business (ranking 1-178; 1=best)	..	..	
Time to start a business (days)	..	..	22
Procedures to start a business (number)	..	..	7
Firing cost (weeks of wages)	..	..	34.9
Closing a business (years to resolve insolvency)	..	..	2.0
Total tax rate (% of profit)	..	..	41.5
Highest marginal tax rate, corporate (%)	25	10	
Business entry rate (new registrations as % of total)	7.8	10.5	10.1
Enterprise surveys			
Time dealing with gov't officials (% of management time)	..	..	
Firms expected to give gifts in meetings w/tax officials (%)	..	..	
Firms using banks to finance investments (% of firms)	..	..	
Delay in obtaining an electrical connection (days)	..	..	
ISO certification ownership (% of firms)	..	..	
Private sector investment			
Invest. in infrastructure w/private participation ($ millions)	..	..	849
Private foreign direct investment, net (% of GDP)	9.2	8.3	2.7
Gross fixed capital formation (% of GDP)	17.2	..	20.4
Gross fixed private capital formation (% of GDP)	..	..	..
Finance and banking			
Government cash surplus or deficit (% of GDP)	-2.2	-1.1	-1.3
Government debt (% of GDP)	91.4	100.4	47.6
Deposit money banks' assets (% of GDP)	170.3	188.2	99.7
Total financial system deposits (% of GDP)	153.3	176.7	..
Bank capital to asset ratio (%)	..	..	6.2
Bank nonperforming loans to total gross loans ratio (%)	..	..	1.1
Domestic credit to the private sector (% of GDP)	208.8	221.2	162.0
Real interest rate (%)	4.0	3.8	
Interest rate spread (percentage points)	1.5	3.3	4.4
Infrastructure			
Paved roads (% of total roads)	60.6	63.0	90.9
Electric power consumption (kWh per capita)	4,585	5,560	9,760
Power outages in a typical month (number)		..	
Fixed line and mobile subscribers (per 100 people)	95	154	143
Internet users (per 100 people)	17.3	46.2	59.3
Cost of telephone call to U.S. ($ per 3 minutes)	1.02	0.33	0.77

Czech Republic

	Country data		High-income group
	2000	2006	2006
Economic and social context			
Population (millions)	10.3	10.3	1,031
Labor force (millions)	5.2	5.2	504
Unemployment rate (% of labor force)	8.8	7.9	6.2
GNI per capita, World Bank Atlas method ($)	5,800	12,790	36,608
GDP growth, 1995–2000 and 2000–06 (average annual %)	1.0	4.1	2.3
Agriculture value added (% of GDP)	3.9	2.7	1.5
Industry value added (% of GDP)	38.1	39.0	26.2
Manufacturing value added (% of GDP)	26.8	27.1	16.8
Services value added (% of GDP)	58.0	58.3	72.3
Inflation (annual % change in consumer price index)	3.9	2.5	
Exchange rate (local currency units per $)	38.6	22.6	
Exports of goods and services (% of GDP)	63.4	75.8	25.6
Imports of goods and services (% of GDP)	66.4	72.6	26.3
Business environment			
Ease of doing business (ranking 1-178; 1=best)	..	56	
Time to start a business (days)	..	17	22
Procedures to start a business (number)	..	10	7
Firing cost (weeks of wages)	..	22.0	34.9
Closing a business (years to resolve insolvency)	..	6.5	2.0
Total tax rate (% of profit)	..	48.6	41.5
Highest marginal tax rate, corporate (%)	31	24	
Business entry rate (new registrations as % of total)	..	11.3	10.1
Enterprise surveys			
Time dealing with gov't officials (% of management time)	..	2.1	
Firms expected to give gifts in meetings w/tax officials (%)	32.9	37.3	
Firms using banks to finance investments (% of firms)	14.2	11.4	
Delay in obtaining an electrical connection (days)	..	5.0	
ISO certification ownership (% of firms)	..	12.5	
Private sector investment			
Invest. in infrastructure w/private participation ($ millions)	1,462	488	849
Private foreign direct investment, net (% of GDP)	8.8	4.2	2.7
Gross fixed capital formation (% of GDP)	28.0	25.2	20.4
Gross fixed private capital formation (% of GDP)	..	..	..
Finance and banking			
Government cash surplus or deficit (% of GDP)	-3.6	-4.3	-1.3
Government debt (% of GDP)	13.7	24.6	47.6
Deposit money banks' assets (% of GDP)	53.9	51.3	99.7
Total financial system deposits (% of GDP)	54.2	59.7	..
Bank capital to asset ratio (%)	5.4	6.2	6.2
Bank nonperforming loans to total gross loans ratio (%)	29.3	4.1	1.1
Domestic credit to the private sector (% of GDP)	49.0	40.9	162.0
Real interest rate (%)	5.6	3.5	
Interest rate spread (percentage points)	3.7	4.4	4.4
Infrastructure			
Paved roads (% of total roads)	100.0	100.0	90.9
Electric power consumption (kWh per capita)	5,694	6,343	9,760
Power outages in a typical month (number)	..	..	
Fixed line and mobile subscribers (per 100 people)	80	147	143
Internet users (per 100 people)	9.7	34.5	59.3
Cost of telephone call to U.S. ($ per 3 minutes)	0.97	1.06	0.77

Denmark

	Country data		High-income group
	2000	**2006**	**2006**
Economic and social context			
Population (millions)	5.3	5.4	1,031
Labor force (millions)	2.9	2.8	504
Unemployment rate (% of labor force)	4.5	4.8	6.2
GNI per capita, World Bank Atlas method ($)	31,850	52,110	36,608
GDP growth, 1995–2000 and 2000–06 (average annual %)	2.8	1.6	2.3
Agriculture value added (% of GDP)	2.6	1.6	1.5
Industry value added (% of GDP)	26.8	26.0	26.2
Manufacturing value added (% of GDP)	16.2	14.2	16.8
Services value added (% of GDP)	70.6	72.4	72.3
Inflation (annual % change in consumer price index)	2.9	1.9	
Exchange rate (local currency units per $)	8.1	5.9	
Exports of goods and services (% of GDP)	46.6	51.9	25.6
Imports of goods and services (% of GDP)	40.6	49.0	26.3
Business environment			
Ease of doing business (ranking 1-178; 1=best)	..	5	
Time to start a business (days)	..	6	22
Procedures to start a business (number)	..	4	7
Firing cost (weeks of wages)	..	10.0	34.9
Closing a business (years to resolve insolvency)	..	1.1	2.0
Total tax rate (% of profit)	..	33.3	41.5
Highest marginal tax rate, corporate (%)	30	28	
Business entry rate (new registrations as % of total)	8.1	14.1	10.1
Enterprise surveys			
Time dealing with gov't officials (% of management time)	..	..	
Firms expected to give gifts in meetings w/tax officials (%)	..	..	
Firms using banks to finance investments (% of firms)	..	..	
Delay in obtaining an electrical connection (days)	..	..	
ISO certification ownership (% of firms)	..	..	
Private sector investment			
Invest. in infrastructure w/private participation ($ millions)	..	..	849
Private foreign direct investment, net (% of GDP)	22.5	1.2	2.7
Gross fixed capital formation (% of GDP)	20.2	22.1	20.4
Gross fixed private capital formation (% of GDP)	..	..	..
Finance and banking			
Government cash surplus or deficit (% of GDP)	1.7	5.1	-1.3
Government debt (% of GDP)	50.1	29.0	47.6
Deposit money banks' assets (% of GDP)	91.8	183.0	99.7
Total financial system deposits (% of GDP)	48.1	58.0	..
Bank capital to asset ratio (%)	6.2	6.2	6.2
Bank nonperforming loans to total gross loans ratio (%)	0.7	0.4	1.1
Domestic credit to the private sector (% of GDP)	135.3	185.1	162.0
Real interest rate (%)	4.9	..	
Interest rate spread (percentage points)	4.9	..	4.4
Infrastructure			
Paved roads (% of total roads)	100.0	100.0	90.9
Electric power consumption (kWh per capita)	6,484	6,663	9,760
Power outages in a typical month (number)	..	..	
Fixed line and mobile subscribers (per 100 people)	135	164	143
Internet users (per 100 people)	39.2	58.3	59.3
Cost of telephone call to U.S. ($ per 3 minutes)	1.30	0.89	0.77

Djibouti

Middle East & North Africa			Lower middle income

	Country data		Lower middle-income group
	2000	2006	2006

Economic and social context
Population (millions)	0.73	0.82	2,276
Labor force (millions)	0.29	0.35	1,209
Unemployment rate (% of labor force)	..	..	5.7
GNI per capita, *World Bank Atlas* method ($)	760	1,060	2,038
GDP growth, 1995–2000 and 2000–06 (average annual %)	-0.2	3.3	7.6
Agriculture value added (% of GDP)	3.5	3.5	11.9
Industry value added (% of GDP)	15.4	16.4	43.5
Manufacturing value added (% of GDP)	2.6	2.5	26.7
Services value added (% of GDP)	81.1	80.1	44.6
Inflation (annual % change in consumer price index)	..	..	
Exchange rate (local currency units per $)	177.7	177.7	
Exports of goods and services (% of GDP)	35.1	39.9	40.4
Imports of goods and services (% of GDP)	50.4	57.3	36.4

Business environment
Ease of doing business (ranking 1-178; 1=best)	..	146	
Time to start a business (days)	..	37	53
Procedures to start a business (number)	..	11	10
Firing cost (weeks of wages)	..	56.0	50.2
Closing a business (years to resolve insolvency)	..	5.0	3.3
Total tax rate (% of profit)	..	38.7	45.8
Highest marginal tax rate, corporate (%)	..	..	
Business entry rate (new registrations as % of total)	..	..	7.6
Enterprise surveys			
Time dealing with gov't officials (% of management time)	..	..	
Firms expected to give gifts in meetings w/tax officials (%)	..	..	
Firms using banks to finance investments (% of firms)	..	..	
Delay in obtaining an electrical connection (days)	..	..	
ISO certification ownership (% of firms)	..	..	

Private sector investment
Invest. in infrastructure w/private participation ($ millions)	50	300	38,154
Private foreign direct investment, net (% of GDP)	0.6	14.1	3.0
Gross fixed capital formation (% of GDP)	8.8	29.6	33.5
Gross fixed private capital formation (% of GDP)	6.1	22.0	10.9

Finance and banking
Government cash surplus or deficit (% of GDP)	..	..	-0.9
Government debt (% of GDP)	..	..	
Deposit money banks' assets (% of GDP)	..	..	87.8
Total financial system deposits (% of GDP)	..	..	43.1
Bank capital to asset ratio (%)	..	..	10.7
Bank nonperforming loans to total gross loans ratio (%)	..	..	4.0
Domestic credit to the private sector (% of GDP)	32.1	20.1	81.3
Real interest rate (%)	9.5	7.8	
Interest rate spread (percentage points)	8.6	10.3	7.2

Infrastructure
Paved roads (% of total roads)	45.0	..	65.8
Electric power consumption (kWh per capita)	..	..	1,502
Power outages in a typical month (number)	..	..	
Fixed line and mobile subscribers (per 100 people)	1	7	60
Internet users (per 100 people)	0.2	1.3	11.4
Cost of telephone call to U.S. ($ per 3 minutes)	4.73	4.73	2.08

Dominica

Latin America & Caribbean   **Upper middle income**

	Country data		Upper middle-income group
	2000	2006	2006
Economic and social context			
Population (millions)	0.07	0.07	811
Labor force (millions)	..	..	374
Unemployment rate (% of labor force)	10.9	..	9.8
GNI per capita, *World Bank Atlas* method ($)	3,200	4,160	5,913
GDP growth, 1995–2000 and 2000–06 (average annual %)	2.2	5.3	3.9
Agriculture value added (% of GDP)	18.1	18.5	5.7
Industry value added (% of GDP)	23.4	23.8	32.4
Manufacturing value added (% of GDP)	8.8	8.1	19.4
Services value added (% of GDP)	58.4	57.7	62.0
Inflation (annual % change in consumer price index)	0.9	2.4	
Exchange rate (local currency units per $)	2.7	2.7	
Exports of goods and services (% of GDP)	53.3	41.9	32.7
Imports of goods and services (% of GDP)	67.5	65.2	30.3
Business environment			
Ease of doing business (ranking 1-178; 1=best)	..	77	
Time to start a business (days)	..	19	41
Procedures to start a business (number)	..	5	9
Firing cost (weeks of wages)	..	58.0	39.7
Closing a business (years to resolve insolvency)	..	..	2.9
Total tax rate (% of profit)	..	37.1	44.5
Highest marginal tax rate, corporate (%)	..	..	
Business entry rate (new registrations as % of total)	..	..	9.1
Enterprise surveys			
Time dealing with gov't officials (% of management time)	..	..	
Firms expected to give gifts in meetings w/tax officials (%)	..	..	
Firms using banks to finance investments (% of firms)	..	..	
Delay in obtaining an electrical connection (days)	..	..	
ISO certification ownership (% of firms)	..	..	
Private sector investment			
Invest. in infrastructure w/private participation ($ millions)	19	2	45,869
Private foreign direct investment, net (% of GDP)	6.5	10.5	3.5
Gross fixed capital formation (% of GDP)	28.1	28.5	19.9
Gross fixed private capital formation (% of GDP)	8.1	6.9	..
Finance and banking			
Government cash surplus or deficit (% of GDP)	..	..	..
Government debt (% of GDP)	..	..	..
Deposit money banks' assets (% of GDP)	76.6	67.9	52.9
Total financial system deposits (% of GDP)	69.8	86.2	41.4
Bank capital to asset ratio (%)	..	..	9.8
Bank nonperforming loans to total gross loans ratio (%)	..	..	3.2
Domestic credit to the private sector (% of GDP)	62.0	61.8	41.4
Real interest rate (%)	11.0	7.3	
Interest rate spread (percentage points)	7.8	6.2	5.9
Infrastructure			
Paved roads (% of total roads)	50.4	..	..
Electric power consumption (kWh per capita)	..	..	3,131
Power outages in a typical month (number)	..	..	
Fixed line and mobile subscribers (per 100 people)	34	88	88
Internet users (per 100 people)	8.4	36.1	22.2
Cost of telephone call to U.S. ($ per 3 minutes)	..	..	1.06

Dominican Republic

	Country data		Lower middle-income group
	2000	2006	2006
Economic and social context			
Population (millions)	8.7	9.6	2,276
Labor force (millions)	3.6	4.1	1,209
Unemployment rate (% of labor force)	13.9	17.9	5.7
GNI per capita, World Bank Atlas method ($)	2,050	2,910	2,038
GDP growth, 1995–2000 and 2000–06 (average annual %)	7.8	3.9	7.6
Agriculture value added (% of GDP)	11.1	12.1	11.9
Industry value added (% of GDP)	33.9	26.2	43.5
Manufacturing value added (% of GDP)	16.8	14.0	26.7
Services value added (% of GDP)	54.6	61.8	44.6
Inflation (annual % change in consumer price index)	7.7	7.6	
Exchange rate (local currency units per $)	16.4	33.4	
Exports of goods and services (% of GDP)	44.9	33.5	40.4
Imports of goods and services (% of GDP)	54.9	40.0	36.4
Business environment			
Ease of doing business (ranking 1-178; 1=best)	..	99	
Time to start a business (days)	..	22	53
Procedures to start a business (number)	..	9	10
Firing cost (weeks of wages)	..	88.0	50.2
Closing a business (years to resolve insolvency)	..	3.5	3.3
Total tax rate (% of profit)	..	40.2	45.8
Highest marginal tax rate, corporate (%)	25	30	
Business entry rate (new registrations as % of total)	..	..	7.6
Enterprise surveys			
Time dealing with gov't officials (% of management time)	..	8.8	
Firms expected to give gifts in meetings w/tax officials (%)	..	17.3	
Firms using banks to finance investments (% of firms)	..	3.6	
Delay in obtaining an electrical connection (days)	..	30.2	
ISO certification ownership (% of firms)	..	9.6	
Private sector investment			
Invest. in infrastructure w/private participation ($ millions)	1,076	281	38,154
Private foreign direct investment, net (% of GDP)	4.8	3.7	3.0
Gross fixed capital formation (% of GDP)	23.5	20.1	33.5
Gross fixed private capital formation (% of GDP)	19.2	15.0	10.9
Finance and banking			
Government cash surplus or deficit (% of GDP)	..	-1.2	-0.9
Government debt (% of GDP)	20.7	..	..
Deposit money banks' assets (% of GDP)	21.0	18.9	87.8
Total financial system deposits (% of GDP)	23.1	24.4	43.1
Bank capital to asset ratio (%)	9.4	10.0	10.7
Bank nonperforming loans to total gross loans ratio (%)	2.6	4.5	4.0
Domestic credit to the private sector (% of GDP)	34.7	25.8	81.3
Real interest rate (%)	17.7	11.1	
Interest rate spread (percentage points)	9.1	9.6	7.2
Infrastructure			
Paved roads (% of total roads)	49.4	..	65.8
Electric power consumption (kWh per capita)	716	1,000	1,502
Power outages in a typical month (number)	..	..	
Fixed line and mobile subscribers (per 100 people)	18	57	60
Internet users (per 100 people)	3.7	20.8	11.4
Cost of telephone call to U.S. ($ per 3 minutes)	3.90	0.22	2.08

Ecuador

Latin America & Caribbean   **Lower middle income**

	Country data		Lower middle-income group
	2000	2006	2006
Economic and social context			
Population (millions)	12.3	13.2	2,276
Labor force (millions)	5.6	6.4	1,209
Unemployment rate (% of labor force)	10.7	7.7	5.7
GNI per capita, *World Bank Atlas* method ($)	1,340	2,910	2,038
GDP growth, 1995–2000 and 2000–06 (average annual %)	0.7	5.3	7.6
Agriculture value added (% of GDP)	10.6	6.7	11.9
Industry value added (% of GDP)	34.7	34.6	43.5
Manufacturing value added (% of GDP)	13.6	9.0	26.7
Services value added (% of GDP)	54.6	58.7	44.6
Inflation (annual % change in consumer price index)	96.1	3.0	
Exchange rate (local currency units per $)	24,988.4	25,000.0	
Exports of goods and services (% of GDP)	37.1	34.3	40.4
Imports of goods and services (% of GDP)	31.0	33.2	36.4
Business environment			
Ease of doing business (ranking 1-178; 1=best)	..	128	
Time to start a business (days)	..	65	53
Procedures to start a business (number)	..	14	10
Firing cost (weeks of wages)	..	135.0	50.2
Closing a business (years to resolve insolvency)	..	5.3	3.3
Total tax rate (% of profit)	..	35.3	45.8
Highest marginal tax rate, corporate (%)	25	25	
Business entry rate (new registrations as % of total)	..	..	7.6
Enterprise surveys			
Time dealing with gov't officials (% of management time)	..	17.3	
Firms expected to give gifts in meetings w/tax officials (%)	..	11.3	
Firms using banks to finance investments (% of firms)	..	24.0	
Delay in obtaining an electrical connection (days)	..	24.8	
ISO certification ownership (% of firms)	..	18.2	
Private sector investment			
Invest. in infrastructure w/private participation ($ millions)	20	1,326	38,154
Private foreign direct investment, net (% of GDP)	4.5	0.7	3.0
Gross fixed capital formation (% of GDP)	20.5	21.6	33.5
Gross fixed private capital formation (% of GDP)	15.6	17.0	10.9
Finance and banking			
Government cash surplus or deficit (% of GDP)	..	..	-0.9
Government debt (% of GDP)	..	..	..
Deposit money banks' assets (% of GDP)	..	..	87.8
Total financial system deposits (% of GDP)	..	..	43.1
Bank capital to asset ratio (%)	12.9	13.7	10.7
Bank nonperforming loans to total gross loans ratio (%)	31.0	3.3	4.0
Domestic credit to the private sector (% of GDP)	32.6	24.0	81.3
Real interest rate (%)	25.1	2.2	
Interest rate spread (percentage points)	7.8	5.4	7.2
Infrastructure			
Paved roads (% of total roads)	18.9	15.0	65.8
Electric power consumption (kWh per capita)	654	714	1,502
Power outages in a typical month (number)	..	2.5	
Fixed line and mobile subscribers (per 100 people)	14	78	60
Internet users (per 100 people)	1.5	11.7	11.4
Cost of telephone call to U.S. ($ per 3 minutes)	2.48	..	2.08

Egypt, Arab Rep.

Middle East & North Africa   **Lower middle income**

	Country data		Lower middle-income group
	2000	**2006**	**2006**
Economic and social context			
Population (millions)	66.5	74.2	2,276
Labor force (millions)	19.8	23.1	1,209
Unemployment rate (% of labor force)	9.0	10.7	5.7
GNI per capita, World Bank Atlas method ($)	1,460	1,360	2,038
GDP growth, 1995–2000 and 2000–06 (average annual %)	5.2	4.0	7.6
Agriculture value added (% of GDP)	16.7	14.1	11.9
Industry value added (% of GDP)	33.1	38.4	43.5
Manufacturing value added (% of GDP)	19.4	16.6	26.7
Services value added (% of GDP)	50.1	47.5	44.6
Inflation (annual % change in consumer price index)	2.7	7.6	
Exchange rate (local currency units per $)	3.5	5.7	
Exports of goods and services (% of GDP)	16.2	29.9	40.4
Imports of goods and services (% of GDP)	22.8	31.6	36.4
Business environment			
Ease of doing business (ranking 1-178; 1=best)	..	126	
Time to start a business (days)	..	9	53
Procedures to start a business (number)	..	7	10
Firing cost (weeks of wages)	..	132.0	50.2
Closing a business (years to resolve insolvency)	..	4.2	3.3
Total tax rate (% of profit)	..	47.9	45.8
Highest marginal tax rate, corporate (%)	40	40	
Business entry rate (new registrations as % of total)	..	2.6	7.6
Enterprise surveys			
Time dealing with gov't officials (% of management time)	..	..	
Firms expected to give gifts in meetings w/tax officials (%)	..	23.0	
Firms using banks to finance investments (% of firms)	..	7.9	
Delay in obtaining an electrical connection (days)	..	167.4	
ISO certification ownership (% of firms)	..	12.0	
Private sector investment			
Invest. in infrastructure w/private participation ($ millions)	864	3,751	38,154
Private foreign direct investment, net (% of GDP)	1.2	9.3	3.0
Gross fixed capital formation (% of GDP)	18.9	18.7	33.5
Gross fixed private capital formation (% of GDP)	9.1	11.4	10.9
Finance and banking			
Government cash surplus or deficit (% of GDP)	–3.3	–5.8	–0.9
Government debt (% of GDP)	37.4	..	
Deposit money banks' assets (% of GDP)	74.3	75.4	87.8
Total financial system deposits (% of GDP)	63.9	82.4	43.1
Bank capital to asset ratio (%)	5.6	5.5	10.7
Bank nonperforming loans to total gross loans ratio (%)	13.6	24.7	4.0
Domestic credit to the private sector (% of GDP)	58.7	55.3	81.3
Real interest rate (%)	7.9	4.9	
Interest rate spread (percentage points)	3.8	6.6	7.2
Infrastructure			
Paved roads (% of total roads)	78.1	81.0	65.8
Electric power consumption (kWh per capita)	1,011	1,245	1,502
Power outages in a typical month (number)	..	..	
Fixed line and mobile subscribers (per 100 people)	10	39	60
Internet users (per 100 people)	0.7	8.1	11.4
Cost of telephone call to U.S. ($ per 3 minutes)	3.33	1.45	2.08

El Salvador

			Lower middle-income group
Latin America & Caribbean			**Lower middle income**
	Country data		
	2000	2006	2006
Economic and social context			
Population (millions)	6.2	6.8	2,276
Labor force (millions)	2.5	2.7	1,209
Unemployment rate (% of labor force)	6.8	6.6	5.7
GNI per capita, *World Bank Atlas* method ($)	2,030	2,680	2,038
GDP growth, 1995–2000 and 2000–06 (average annual %)	3.3	2.5	7.6
Agriculture value added (% of GDP)	10.5	10.9	11.9
Industry value added (% of GDP)	31.6	29.4	43.5
Manufacturing value added (% of GDP)	24.7	22.4	26.7
Services value added (% of GDP)	57.9	59.7	44.6
Inflation (annual % change in consumer price index)	2.3	4.0	
Exchange rate (local currency units per $)	8.8	8.8	
Exports of goods and services (% of GDP)	27.4	27.2	40.4
Imports of goods and services (% of GDP)	42.4	46.9	36.4
Business environment			
Ease of doing business (ranking 1-178; 1=best)	..	69	
Time to start a business (days)	..	26	53
Procedures to start a business (number)	..	9	10
Firing cost (weeks of wages)	..	86.0	50.2
Closing a business (years to resolve insolvency)	..	4.0	3.3
Total tax rate (% of profit)	..	33.8	45.8
Highest marginal tax rate, corporate (%)	25	..	
Business entry rate (new registrations as % of total)	..	3.8	7.6
Enterprise surveys			
Time dealing with gov't officials (% of management time)	..	9.2	
Firms expected to give gifts in meetings w/tax officials (%)	..	2.6	
Firms using banks to finance investments (% of firms)	..	17.3	
Delay in obtaining an electrical connection (days)	..	22.1	
ISO certification ownership (% of firms)	..	11.0	
Private sector investment			
Invest. in infrastructure w/private participation ($ millions)	277	172	38,154
Private foreign direct investment, net (% of GDP)	1.3	1.1	3.0
Gross fixed capital formation (% of GDP)	16.9	16.1	33.5
Gross fixed private capital formation (% of GDP)	14.2	14.0	10.9
Finance and banking			
Government cash surplus or deficit (% of GDP)	-4.7	-3.2	-0.9
Government debt (% of GDP)	55.3	43.3	..
Deposit money banks' assets (% of GDP)	5.2	5.0	87.8
Total financial system deposits (% of GDP)	4.8	4.1	43.1
Bank capital to asset ratio (%)	8.8	11.8	10.7
Bank nonperforming loans to total gross loans ratio (%)	4.3	1.9	4.0
Domestic credit to the private sector (% of GDP)	45.2	42.9	81.3
Real interest rate (%)	10.5	..	
Interest rate spread (percentage points)	4.6	..	7.2
Infrastructure			
Paved roads (% of total roads)	19.8	..	65.8
Electric power consumption (kWh per capita)	653	666	1,502
Power outages in a typical month (number)	..	2.8	
Fixed line and mobile subscribers (per 100 people)	22	72	60
Internet users (per 100 people)	1.1	9.6	11.4
Cost of telephone call to U.S. ($ per 3 minutes)	2.40	2.40	2.08

Equatorial Guinea

Sub-Saharan Africa   **Upper middle income**

	Country data		Upper middle-income group
	2000	2006	2006
Economic and social context			
Population (millions)	0.43	0.50	811
Labor force (millions)	0.17	0.20	374
Unemployment rate (% of labor force)	..	..	9.8
GNI per capita, *World Bank Atlas* method ($)	1,540	8,510	5,913
GDP growth, 1995–2000 and 2000–06 (average annual %)	36.0	19.4	3.9
Agriculture value added (% of GDP)	9.8	2.7	5.7
Industry value added (% of GDP)	85.9	94.3	32.4
Manufacturing value added (% of GDP)	1.4	8.6	19.4
Services value added (% of GDP)	4.2	3.0	62.0
Inflation (annual % change in consumer price index)	4.8	4.2	
Exchange rate (local currency units per $)	712.0	522.9	
Exports of goods and services (% of GDP)	98.6	94.5	32.7
Imports of goods and services (% of GDP)	85.4	50.1	30.3
Business environment			
Ease of doing business (ranking 1-178; 1=best)	..	165	
Time to start a business (days)	..	136	41
Procedures to start a business (number)	..	20	9
Firing cost (weeks of wages)	..	133.0	39.7
Closing a business (years to resolve insolvency)	..	..	2.9
Total tax rate (% of profit)	..	62.2	44.5
Highest marginal tax rate, corporate (%)	..	..	
Business entry rate (new registrations as % of total)	..	..	9.1
Enterprise surveys			
Time dealing with gov't officials (% of management time)	..	..	
Firms expected to give gifts in meetings w/tax officials (%)	..	..	
Firms using banks to finance investments (% of firms)	..	..	
Delay in obtaining an electrical connection (days)	..	..	
ISO certification ownership (% of firms)	..	..	
Private sector investment			
Invest. in infrastructure w/private participation ($ millions)	23	72	45,869
Private foreign direct investment, net (% of GDP)	8.6	19.3	3.5
Gross fixed capital formation (% of GDP)	61.3	41.6	19.9
Gross fixed private capital formation (% of GDP)	56.2	26.6	..
Finance and banking			
Government cash surplus or deficit (% of GDP)	..	..	..
Government debt (% of GDP)	..	..	..
Deposit money banks' assets (% of GDP)	2.9	2.6	52.9
Total financial system deposits (% of GDP)	3.2	5.9	41.4
Bank capital to asset ratio (%)	..	..	9.8
Bank nonperforming loans to total gross loans ratio (%)	..	..	3.2
Domestic credit to the private sector (% of GDP)	3.0	2.8	41.4
Real interest rate (%)	-16.8	-3.4	
Interest rate spread (percentage points)	17.0	11.0	5.9
Infrastructure			
Paved roads (% of total roads)	..	..	..
Electric power consumption (kWh per capita)	..	..	3,131
Power outages in a typical month (number)	..	..	
Fixed line and mobile subscribers (per 100 people)	3	22	88
Internet users (per 100 people)	0.2	1.6	22.2
Cost of telephone call to U.S. ($ per 3 minutes)	..	..	1.06

Eritrea

	Country data		Low-income group
	2000	**2006**	**2006**
Economic and social context			
Population (millions)	3.7	4.7	2,420
Labor force (millions)	1.5	2.0	995
Unemployment rate (% of labor force)	..	..	..
GNI per capita, *World Bank Atlas* method ($)	170	190	649
GDP growth, 1995–2000 and 2000–06 (average annual %)	1.5	2.7	6.5
Agriculture value added (% of GDP)	15.1	17.5	20.4
Industry value added (% of GDP)	23.0	23.0	27.7
Manufacturing value added (% of GDP)	11.2	8.7	15.8
Services value added (% of GDP)	61.9	59.5	51.9
Inflation (annual % change in consumer price index)	..	..	
Exchange rate (local currency units per $)	9.6	15.4	
Exports of goods and services (% of GDP)	15.1	8.0	26.7
Imports of goods and services (% of GDP)	81.8	50.0	30.1
Business environment			
Ease of doing business (ranking 1-178; 1=best)	..	171	
Time to start a business (days)	..	84	54
Procedures to start a business (number)	..	13	10
Firing cost (weeks of wages)	..	69.0	62.6
Closing a business (years to resolve insolvency)	..	1.7	3.8
Total tax rate (% of profit)	..	84.5	67.4
Highest marginal tax rate, corporate (%)	..	..	
Business entry rate (new registrations as % of total)	..	..	6.4
Enterprise surveys			
Time dealing with gov't officials (% of management time)	3.8	..	
Firms expected to give gifts in meetings w/tax officials (%)	..	..	
Firms using banks to finance investments (% of firms)	30.5	..	
Delay in obtaining an electrical connection (days)	..	..	
ISO certification ownership (% of firms)	6.6	..	
Private sector investment			
Invest. in infrastructure w/private participation ($ millions)	40	..	29,785
Private foreign direct investment, net (% of GDP)	4.4	0.3	2.6
Gross fixed capital formation (% of GDP)	31.9	18.7	26.7
Gross fixed private capital formation (% of GDP)	5.1	4.2	19.6
Finance and banking			
Government cash surplus or deficit (% of GDP)	..	..	-2.6
Government debt (% of GDP)	..	..	..
Deposit money banks' assets (% of GDP)	..	..	50.5
Total financial system deposits (% of GDP)	..	..	44.6
Bank capital to asset ratio (%)	..	..	..
Bank nonperforming loans to total gross loans ratio (%)	..	..	..
Domestic credit to the private sector (% of GDP)	32.5	29.0	38.3
Real interest rate (%)	..	..	
Interest rate spread (percentage points)	..	..	11.3
Infrastructure			
Paved roads (% of total roads)	21.8	..	..
Electric power consumption (kWh per capita)	..	..	391
Power outages in a typical month (number)	..	..	
Fixed line and mobile subscribers (per 100 people)	1	2	17
Internet users (per 100 people)	0.1	2.1	4.2
Cost of telephone call to U.S. ($ per 3 minutes)	5.83	3.59	1.99

Estonia

	Country data		High-income group
	2000	2006	2006
Economic and social context			
Population (millions)	1.4	1.3	1,031
Labor force (millions)	0.67	0.66	504
Unemployment rate (% of labor force)	12.7	7.9	6.2
GNI per capita, *World Bank Atlas* method ($)	4,120	11,400	36,608
GDP growth, 1995–2000 and 2000–06 (average annual %)	5.4	8.6	2.3
Agriculture value added (% of GDP)	4.9	3.2	1.5
Industry value added (% of GDP)	27.8	29.1	26.2
Manufacturing value added (% of GDP)	17.8	16.8	16.8
Services value added (% of GDP)	67.3	67.8	72.3
Inflation (annual % change in consumer price index)	4.0	4.4	
Exchange rate (local currency units per $)	17.0	12.5	
Exports of goods and services (% of GDP)	85.4	79.8	25.6
Imports of goods and services (% of GDP)	89.0	89.5	26.3
Business environment			
Ease of doing business (ranking 1-178; 1=best)	..	17	
Time to start a business (days)	..	7	22
Procedures to start a business (number)	..	5	7
Firing cost (weeks of wages)	..	35.0	34.9
Closing a business (years to resolve insolvency)	..	3.0	2.0
Total tax rate (% of profit)	..	49.2	41.5
Highest marginal tax rate, corporate (%)	35	23	
Business entry rate (new registrations as % of total)	11.1	13.4	10.1
Enterprise surveys			
Time dealing with gov't officials (% of management time)	..	2.3	
Firms expected to give gifts in meetings w/tax officials (%)	19.6	12.9	
Firms using banks to finance investments (% of firms)	16.5	17.8	
Delay in obtaining an electrical connection (days)	7.6	8.4	
ISO certification ownership (% of firms)	..	13.2	
Private sector investment			
Invest. in infrastructure w/private participation ($ millions)	172	132	849
Private foreign direct investment, net (% of GDP)	6.9	9.7	2.7
Gross fixed capital formation (% of GDP)	26.0	33.8	20.4
Gross fixed private capital formation (% of GDP)	20.6	..	..
Finance and banking			
Government cash surplus or deficit (% of GDP)	0.2	3.6	-1.3
Government debt (% of GDP)	6.9	7.0	47.6
Deposit money banks' assets (% of GDP)	23.6	64.3	99.7
Total financial system deposits (% of GDP)	24.7	41.1	..
Bank capital to asset ratio (%)	12.6	8.4	6.2
Bank nonperforming loans to total gross loans ratio (%)	1.0	0.2	1.1
Domestic credit to the private sector (% of GDP)	23.3	78.4	162.0
Real interest rate (%)	-0.8	-1.0	
Interest rate spread (percentage points)	3.7	2.2	4.4
Infrastructure			
Paved roads (% of total roads)	20.1	22.7	90.9
Electric power consumption (kWh per capita)	4,632	5,567	9,760
Power outages in a typical month (number)	..	..	
Fixed line and mobile subscribers (per 100 people)	79	164	143
Internet users (per 100 people)	28.6	56.6	59.3
Cost of telephone call to U.S. ($ per 3 minutes)	1.62	0.90	0.77

Ethiopia

Sub-Saharan Africa   **Low income**

	Country data		Low-income group
	2000	**2006**	**2006**
Economic and social context			
Population (millions)	65.8	77.2	2,420
Labor force (millions)	29.0	34.4	995
Unemployment rate (% of labor force)	..	5.4	..
GNI per capita, *World Bank Atlas* method ($)	120	170	649
GDP growth, 1995–2000 and 2000–06 (average annual %)	3.7	5.7	6.5
Agriculture value added (% of GDP)	47.4	47.3	20.4
Industry value added (% of GDP)	12.8	13.5	27.7
Manufacturing value added (% of GDP)	5.7	5.3	15.8
Services value added (% of GDP)	39.8	39.2	51.9
Inflation (annual % change in consumer price index)	0.7	13.6	
Exchange rate (local currency units per $)	8.2	8.7	
Exports of goods and services (% of GDP)	12.5	15.8	26.7
Imports of goods and services (% of GDP)	24.8	41.7	30.1
Business environment			
Ease of doing business (ranking 1-178; 1=best)	..	102	
Time to start a business (days)	..	16	54
Procedures to start a business (number)	..	7	10
Firing cost (weeks of wages)	..	40.0	62.6
Closing a business (years to resolve insolvency)	..	3.0	3.8
Total tax rate (% of profit)	..	31.1	67.4
Highest marginal tax rate, corporate (%)	30	30	
Business entry rate (new registrations as % of total)	..	..	6.4
Enterprise surveys			
Time dealing with gov't officials (% of management time)	..	3.8	
Firms expected to give gifts in meetings w/tax officials (%)	..	4.4	
Firms using banks to finance investments (% of firms)	13.6	11.0	
Delay in obtaining an electrical connection (days)	115.8	44.2	
ISO certification ownership (% of firms)	..	4.2	
Private sector investment			
Invest. in infrastructure w/private participation ($ millions)	..	..	29,785
Private foreign direct investment, net (% of GDP)	1.7	2.7	2.6
Gross fixed capital formation (% of GDP)	19.2	19.8	26.7
Gross fixed private capital formation (% of GDP)	11.8	11.4	19.6
Finance and banking			
Government cash surplus or deficit (% of GDP)	–7.9	..	–2.6
Government debt (% of GDP)	..	..	
Deposit money banks' assets (% of GDP)	35.9	28.8	50.5
Total financial system deposits (% of GDP)	35.6	37.3	44.6
Bank capital to asset ratio (%)	..	..	..
Bank nonperforming loans to total gross loans ratio (%)	..	..	..
Domestic credit to the private sector (% of GDP)	23.9	27.2	38.3
Real interest rate (%)	4.6	–0.7	
Interest rate spread (percentage points)	4.9	3.4	11.3
Infrastructure			
Paved roads (% of total roads)	12.0	12.7	..
Electric power consumption (kWh per capita)	23	34	391
Power outages in a typical month (number)	..	5.1	
Fixed line and mobile subscribers (per 100 people)	0	2	17
Internet users (per 100 people)	0.0	0.2	4.2
Cost of telephone call to U.S. ($ per 3 minutes)	7.35	4.01	1.99

Faeroe Islands

High income

	Country data		High-income group
	2000	2006	2006
Economic and social context			
Population (millions)	..	0.05	1,031
Labor force (millions)	..	..	504
Unemployment rate (% of labor force)	..	..	6.2
GNI per capita, *World Bank Atlas* method ($)	..	..	36,608
GDP growth, 1995–2000 and 2000–06 (average annual %)	..	..	2.3
Agriculture value added (% of GDP)	..	..	1.5
Industry value added (% of GDP)	..	..	26.2
Manufacturing value added (% of GDP)	..	..	16.8
Services value added (% of GDP)	..	..	72.3
Inflation (annual % change in consumer price index)	..	..	
Exchange rate (local currency units per $)	8.1	5.9	
Exports of goods and services (% of GDP)	..	..	25.6
Imports of goods and services (% of GDP)	..	..	26.3
Business environment			
Ease of doing business (ranking 1-178; 1=best)	..	..	
Time to start a business (days)	..	..	22
Procedures to start a business (number)	..	..	7
Firing cost (weeks of wages)	..	..	34.9
Closing a business (years to resolve insolvency)	..	..	2.0
Total tax rate (% of profit)	..	..	41.5
Highest marginal tax rate, corporate (%)	20	20	
Business entry rate (new registrations as % of total)	..	..	10.1
Enterprise surveys			
Time dealing with gov't officials (% of management time)	..	..	
Firms expected to give gifts in meetings w/tax officials (%)	..	..	
Firms using banks to finance investments (% of firms)	..	..	
Delay in obtaining an electrical connection (days)	..	..	
ISO certification ownership (% of firms)	..	..	
Private sector investment			
Invest. in infrastructure w/private participation ($ millions)	..	..	849
Private foreign direct investment, net (% of GDP)	..	..	2.7
Gross fixed capital formation (% of GDP)	..	..	20.4
Gross fixed private capital formation (% of GDP)	..	..	..
Finance and banking			
Government cash surplus or deficit (% of GDP)	..	..	-1.3
Government debt (% of GDP)	..	..	47.6
Deposit money banks' assets (% of GDP)	..	..	99.7
Total financial system deposits (% of GDP)	..	..	..
Bank capital to asset ratio (%)	..	..	6.2
Bank nonperforming loans to total gross loans ratio (%)	..	..	1.1
Domestic credit to the private sector (% of GDP)	..	..	162.0
Real interest rate (%)	..	..	
Interest rate spread (percentage points)	..	..	4.4
Infrastructure			
Paved roads (% of total roads)	..	..	90.9
Electric power consumption (kWh per capita)	..	..	9,760
Power outages in a typical month (number)	..	..	
Fixed line and mobile subscribers (per 100 people)	..	151	143
Internet users (per 100 people)	..	70.5	59.3
Cost of telephone call to U.S. ($ per 3 minutes)	..	..	0.77

Fiji

	Country data		Lower middle-income group
	2000	**2006**	**2006**
Economic and social context			
Population (millions)	0.80	0.83	2,276
Labor force (millions)	0.34	0.37	1,209
Unemployment rate (% of labor force)	..	..	5.7
GNI per capita, *World Bank Atlas* method ($)	2,250	3,720	2,038
GDP growth, 1995–2000 and 2000–06 (average annual %)	2.2	2.6	7.6
Agriculture value added (% of GDP)	17.0	15.0	11.9
Industry value added (% of GDP)	22.3	25.8	43.5
Manufacturing value added (% of GDP)	14.0	14.9	26.7
Services value added (% of GDP)	60.7	59.2	44.6
Inflation (annual % change in consumer price index)	1.1	2.5	
Exchange rate (local currency units per $)	2.1	1.7	
Exports of goods and services (% of GDP)	65.1	55.0	40.4
Imports of goods and services (% of GDP)	70.2	72.6	36.4
Business environment			
Ease of doing business (ranking 1-178; 1=best)	..	36	
Time to start a business (days)	..	46	53
Procedures to start a business (number)	..	8	10
Firing cost (weeks of wages)	..	2.0	50.2
Closing a business (years to resolve insolvency)	..	1.8	3.3
Total tax rate (% of profit)	..	38.5	45.8
Highest marginal tax rate, corporate (%)	32	31	
Business entry rate (new registrations as % of total)	..	..	7.6
Enterprise surveys			
Time dealing with gov't officials (% of management time)	..	..	
Firms expected to give gifts in meetings w/tax officials (%)	..	..	
Firms using banks to finance investments (% of firms)	..	..	
Delay in obtaining an electrical connection (days)	..	..	
ISO certification ownership (% of firms)	..	..	
Private sector investment			
Invest. in infrastructure w/private participation ($ millions)	3	50	38,154
Private foreign direct investment, net (% of GDP)	-0.1	5.0	3.0
Gross fixed capital formation (% of GDP)	15.4	18.3	33.5
Gross fixed private capital formation (% of GDP)	10.2	11.9	10.9
Finance and banking			
Government cash surplus or deficit (% of GDP)	..	-2.9	-0.9
Government debt (% of GDP)	..	..	..
Deposit money banks' assets (% of GDP)	36.4	41.0	87.8
Total financial system deposits (% of GDP)	36.7	40.2	43.1
Bank capital to asset ratio (%)	..	..	10.7
Bank nonperforming loans to total gross loans ratio (%)	..	..	4.0
Domestic credit to the private sector (% of GDP)	31.9	44.4	81.3
Real interest rate (%)	13.6	3.8	
Interest rate spread (percentage points)	7.5	6.6	7.2
Infrastructure			
Paved roads (% of total roads)	49.2	..	65.8
Electric power consumption (kWh per capita)	..	..	1,502
Power outages in a typical month (number)	..		
Fixed line and mobile subscribers (per 100 people)	18	38	60
Internet users (per 100 people)	1.5	9.6	11.4
Cost of telephone call to U.S. ($ per 3 minutes)	3.76	2.84	2.08

Finland

	Country data		High-income group
	2000	2006	2006
Economic and social context			
Population (millions)	5.2	5.3	1,031
Labor force (millions)	2.6	2.7	504
Unemployment rate (% of labor force)	9.8	8.4	6.2
GNI per capita, *World Bank Atlas* method ($)	25,400	41,360	36,608
GDP growth, 1995–2000 and 2000–06 (average annual %)	4.9	2.9	2.3
Agriculture value added (% of GDP)	3.5	2.6	1.5
Industry value added (% of GDP)	33.7	32.4	26.2
Manufacturing value added (% of GDP)	26.2	23.1	16.8
Services value added (% of GDP)	62.8	64.9	72.3
Inflation (annual % change in consumer price index)	3.4	1.6	
Exchange rate (local currency units per $)	1.1	0.8	
Exports of goods and services (% of GDP)	43.5	44.4	25.6
Imports of goods and services (% of GDP)	33.4	37.9	26.3
Business environment			
Ease of doing business (ranking 1-178; 1=best)	..	13	
Time to start a business (days)	..	14	22
Procedures to start a business (number)	..	3	7
Firing cost (weeks of wages)	..	26.0	34.9
Closing a business (years to resolve insolvency)	..	0.9	2.0
Total tax rate (% of profit)	..	47.8	41.5
Highest marginal tax rate, corporate (%)	29	26	
Business entry rate (new registrations as % of total)	6.4	6.8	10.1
Enterprise surveys			
Time dealing with gov't officials (% of management time)	..	..	
Firms expected to give gifts in meetings w/tax officials (%)	..	..	
Firms using banks to finance investments (% of firms)	..	..	
Delay in obtaining an electrical connection (days)	..	..	
ISO certification ownership (% of firms)	..	..	
Private sector investment			
Invest. in infrastructure w/private participation ($ millions)	..	..	849
Private foreign direct investment, net (% of GDP)	7.5	2.5	2.7
Gross fixed capital formation (% of GDP)	19.4	19.2	20.4
Gross fixed private capital formation (% of GDP)	..	..	..
Finance and banking			
Government cash surplus or deficit (% of GDP)	6.8	3.9	-1.3
Government debt (% of GDP)	46.9	39.7	47.6
Deposit money banks' assets (% of GDP)	55.8	..	99.7
Total financial system deposits (% of GDP)	22.1	..	..
Bank capital to asset ratio (%)	6.3	9.2	6.2
Bank nonperforming loans to total gross loans ratio (%)	0.6	0.3	1.1
Domestic credit to the private sector (% of GDP)	53.1	77.8	162.0
Real interest rate (%)	2.9	3.0	
Interest rate spread (percentage points)	4.0	2.7	4.4
Infrastructure			
Paved roads (% of total roads)	62.0	65.0	90.9
Electric power consumption (kWh per capita)	15,286	16,120	9,760
Power outages in a typical month (number)	..	..	
Fixed line and mobile subscribers (per 100 people)	127	144	143
Internet users (per 100 people)	37.2	55.5	59.3
Cost of telephone call to U.S. ($ per 3 minutes)	1.07	1.80	0.77

France

	Country data		High-income group
	2000	2006	2006
Economic and social context			
Population (millions)	58.9	61.3	1,031
Labor force (millions)	26.2	27.3	504
Unemployment rate (% of labor force)	10.0	9.8	6.2
GNI per capita, *World Bank Atlas* method ($)	24,450	36,560	36,608
GDP growth, 1995–2000 and 2000–06 (average annual %)	2.9	1.7	2.3
Agriculture value added (% of GDP)	2.8	2.0	1.5
Industry value added (% of GDP)	22.9	20.8	26.2
Manufacturing value added (% of GDP)	16.0	12.4	16.8
Services value added (% of GDP)	74.3	77.2	72.3
Inflation (annual % change in consumer price index)	1.7	1.6	
Exchange rate (local currency units per $)	1.1	0.8	
Exports of goods and services (% of GDP)	28.6	26.9	25.6
Imports of goods and services (% of GDP)	27.7	28.3	26.3
Business environment			
Ease of doing business (ranking 1-178; 1=best)	..	31	
Time to start a business (days)	..	7	22
Procedures to start a business (number)	..	5	7
Firing cost (weeks of wages)	..	32.0	34.9
Closing a business (years to resolve insolvency)	..	1.9	2.0
Total tax rate (% of profit)	..	66.3	41.5
Highest marginal tax rate, corporate (%)	33	33	
Business entry rate (new registrations as % of total)	10.0	11.8	10.1
Enterprise surveys			
Time dealing with gov't officials (% of management time)	..	..	
Firms expected to give gifts in meetings w/tax officials (%)	..	..	
Firms using banks to finance investments (% of firms)	..	..	
Delay in obtaining an electrical connection (days)	..	..	
ISO certification ownership (% of firms)	..	..	
Private sector investment			
Invest. in infrastructure w/private participation ($ millions)	..	..	849
Private foreign direct investment, net (% of GDP)	3.2	3.6	2.7
Gross fixed capital formation (% of GDP)	19.5	20.4	20.4
Gross fixed private capital formation (% of GDP)	..	..	..
Finance and banking			
Government cash surplus or deficit (% of GDP)	-1.7	-2.3	-1.3
Government debt (% of GDP)	60.0	67.4	47.6
Deposit money banks' assets (% of GDP)	..	..	99.7
Total financial system deposits (% of GDP)	..	..	
Bank capital to asset ratio (%)	6.7	5.8	6.2
Bank nonperforming loans to total gross loans ratio (%)	5.0	3.2	1.1
Domestic credit to the private sector (% of GDP)	85.0	98.7	162.0
Real interest rate (%)	5.2	4.9	
Interest rate spread (percentage points)	4.1	4.3	4.4
Infrastructure			
Paved roads (% of total roads)	100.0	100.0	90.9
Electric power consumption (kWh per capita)	7,486	7,938	9,760
Power outages in a typical month (number)	..	..	
Fixed line and mobile subscribers (per 100 people)	107	140	143
Internet users (per 100 people)	14.4	49.1	59.3
Cost of telephone call to U.S. ($ per 3 minutes)	0.82	0.84	0.77

French Polynesia

	Country data		High-income group
	2000	2006	2006
Economic and social context			
Population (millions)	0.24	0.26	1,031
Labor force (millions)	0.10	0.11	504
Unemployment rate (% of labor force)	..	..	6.2
GNI per capita, *World Bank Atlas* method ($)	16,070	..	36,608
GDP growth, 1995–2000 and 2000–06 (average annual %)	3.5	..	2.3
Agriculture value added (% of GDP)	4.7	..	1.5
Industry value added (% of GDP)	..	..	26.2
Manufacturing value added (% of GDP)	..	..	16.8
Services value added (% of GDP)	..	..	72.3
Inflation (annual % change in consumer price index)	..	..	
Exchange rate (local currency units per $)	129.5	95.1	
Exports of goods and services (% of GDP)	4.9	..	25.6
Imports of goods and services (% of GDP)	24.2	..	26.3
Business environment			
Ease of doing business (ranking 1-178; 1=best)	..	..	
Time to start a business (days)	..	..	22
Procedures to start a business (number)	..	..	7
Firing cost (weeks of wages)	..	..	34.9
Closing a business (years to resolve insolvency)	..	..	2.0
Total tax rate (% of profit)	..	..	41.5
Highest marginal tax rate, corporate (%)	..	..	
Business entry rate (new registrations as % of total)	..	..	10.1
Enterprise surveys			
Time dealing with gov't officials (% of management time)	..	..	
Firms expected to give gifts in meetings w/tax officials (%)	..	..	
Firms using banks to finance investments (% of firms)	..	..	
Delay in obtaining an electrical connection (days)	..	..	
ISO certification ownership (% of firms)	..	..	
Private sector investment			
Invest. in infrastructure w/private participation ($ millions)	..	..	849
Private foreign direct investment, net (% of GDP)	..	..	2.7
Gross fixed capital formation (% of GDP)	..	..	20.4
Gross fixed private capital formation (% of GDP)	..	..	..
Finance and banking			
Government cash surplus or deficit (% of GDP)	..	..	-1.3
Government debt (% of GDP)	..	..	47.6
Deposit money banks' assets (% of GDP)	..	..	99.7
Total financial system deposits (% of GDP)	..	..	
Bank capital to asset ratio (%)	..	..	6.2
Bank nonperforming loans to total gross loans ratio (%)	..	..	1.1
Domestic credit to the private sector (% of GDP)	..	..	162.0
Real interest rate (%)	..	..	
Interest rate spread (percentage points)	..	..	4.4
Infrastructure			
Paved roads (% of total roads)	..	..	90.9
Electric power consumption (kWh per capita)	..	..	9,760
Power outages in a typical month (number)	..	..	
Fixed line and mobile subscribers (per 100 people)	40	79	143
Internet users (per 100 people)	6.4	25.1	59.3
Cost of telephone call to U.S. ($ per 3 minutes)	3.67	..	0.77

Gabon

	Country data		Upper middle-income group
	2000	2006	2006
Economic and social context			
Population (millions)	1.2	1.3	811
Labor force (millions)	0.53	0.61	374
Unemployment rate (% of labor force)	..		9.8
GNI per capita, *World Bank Atlas* method ($)	3,220	5,360	5,913
GDP growth, 1995–2000 and 2000–06 (average annual %)	0.3	1.7	3.9
Agriculture value added (% of GDP)	6.2	4.9	5.7
Industry value added (% of GDP)	56.3	61.2	32.4
Manufacturing value added (% of GDP)	3.7	4.1	19.4
Services value added (% of GDP)	37.5	33.9	62.0
Inflation (annual % change in consumer price index)	0.5	4.1	
Exchange rate (local currency units per $)	712.0	522.9	
Exports of goods and services (% of GDP)	69.0	65.4	32.7
Imports of goods and services (% of GDP)	32.7	23.7	30.3
Business environment			
Ease of doing business (ranking 1-178; 1=best)	..	144	
Time to start a business (days)	..	58	41
Procedures to start a business (number)	..	9	9
Firing cost (weeks of wages)	..	43.0	39.7
Closing a business (years to resolve insolvency)	..	5.0	2.9
Total tax rate (% of profit)	..	44.2	44.5
Highest marginal tax rate, corporate (%)	35		..
Business entry rate (new registrations as % of total)	..	..	9.1
Enterprise surveys			
Time dealing with gov't officials (% of management time)	..	..	
Firms expected to give gifts in meetings w/tax officials (%)	..	..	
Firms using banks to finance investments (% of firms)	..	..	
Delay in obtaining an electrical connection (days)	..	..	
ISO certification ownership (% of firms)	..	..	
Private sector investment			
Invest. in infrastructure w/private participation ($ millions)	12	92	45,869
Private foreign direct investment, net (% of GDP)	–0.8	2.8	3.5
Gross fixed capital formation (% of GDP)	21.9	23.1	19.9
Gross fixed private capital formation (% of GDP)	19.0	18.3	..
Finance and banking			
Government cash surplus or deficit (% of GDP)	..	..	..
Government debt (% of GDP)	..	..	
Deposit money banks' assets (% of GDP)	12.1	9.8	52.9
Total financial system deposits (% of GDP)	10.4	13.2	41.4
Bank capital to asset ratio (%)	..	..	9.8
Bank nonperforming loans to total gross loans ratio (%)	6.6	11.1	3.2
Domestic credit to the private sector (% of GDP)	8.7	9.3	41.4
Real interest rate (%)	–4.8	6.9	
Interest rate spread (percentage points)	17.0	11.0	5.9
Infrastructure			
Paved roads (% of total roads)	9.9	*10.2*	..
Electric power consumption (kWh per capita)	914	*999*	*3,131*
Power outages in a typical month (number)	..	..	
Fixed line and mobile subscribers (per 100 people)	13	61	88
Internet users (per 100 people)	1.3	6.2	22.2
Cost of telephone call to U.S. ($ per 3 minutes)	*14.12*	*2.77*	*1.06*

Gambia, The

	Country data		Low-income group
	2000	2006	2006
Economic and social context			
Population (millions)	1.4	1.7	2,420
Labor force (millions)	0.59	0.71	995
Unemployment rate (% of labor force)	..	..	..
GNI per capita, *World Bank Atlas* method ($)	310	290	649
GDP growth, 1995–2000 and 2000–06 (average annual %)	4.6	3.9	6.5
Agriculture value added (% of GDP)	35.8	32.6	20.4
Industry value added (% of GDP)	13.1	13.1	27.7
Manufacturing value added (% of GDP)	5.4	5.2	15.8
Services value added (% of GDP)	51.1	54.2	51.9
Inflation (annual % change in consumer price index)	0.2	3.2	
Exchange rate (local currency units per $)	12.8	28.1	
Exports of goods and services (% of GDP)	48.0	44.8	26.7
Imports of goods and services (% of GDP)	56.8	65.4	30.1
Business environment			
Ease of doing business (ranking 1-178; 1=best)	..	131	
Time to start a business (days)	..	32	54
Procedures to start a business (number)	..	9	10
Firing cost (weeks of wages)	..	9.0	62.6
Closing a business (years to resolve insolvency)	..	3.0	3.8
Total tax rate (% of profit)	..	286.7	67.4
Highest marginal tax rate, corporate (%)	..	..	
Business entry rate (new registrations as % of total)	..	..	6.4
Enterprise surveys			
Time dealing with gov't officials (% of management time)	..	7.3	
Firms expected to give gifts in meetings w/tax officials (%)	..	13.6	
Firms using banks to finance investments (% of firms)	..	7.6	
Delay in obtaining an electrical connection (days)	..	63.9	
ISO certification ownership (% of firms)	..	22.2	
Private sector investment			
Invest. in infrastructure w/private participation ($ millions)	7	..	29,785
Private foreign direct investment, net (% of GDP)	10.3	16.1	2.6
Gross fixed capital formation (% of GDP)	17.4	24.8	26.7
Gross fixed private capital formation (% of GDP)	12.8	14.9	19.6
Finance and banking			
Government cash surplus or deficit (% of GDP)	..	..	-2.6
Government debt (% of GDP)	..	..	..
Deposit money banks' assets (% of GDP)	30.8	41.7	50.5
Total financial system deposits (% of GDP)	29.5	60.0	44.6
Bank capital to asset ratio (%)	..	..	..
Bank nonperforming loans to total gross loans ratio (%)	..	..	..
Domestic credit to the private sector (% of GDP)	12.5	15.6	38.3
Real interest rate (%)	19.6	24.7	
Interest rate spread (percentage points)	11.5	17.1	11.3
Infrastructure			
Paved roads (% of total roads)	35.4	19.3	..
Electric power consumption (kWh per capita)	..	..	391
Power outages in a typical month (number)	..	23.8	
Fixed line and mobile subscribers (per 100 people)	3	27	17
Internet users (per 100 people)	0.9	3.6	4.2
Cost of telephone call to U.S. ($ per 3 minutes)	5.39	1.81	1.99

Georgia

	Country data		Lower middle-income group
	2000	2006	2006
Economic and social context			
Population (millions)	4.7	4.4	2,276
Labor force (millions)	2.4	2.2	1,209
Unemployment rate (% of labor force)	10.8	13.8	5.7
GNI per capita, *World Bank Atlas* method ($)	700	1,580	2,038
GDP growth, 1995–2000 and 2000–06 (average annual %)	5.7	7.8	7.6
Agriculture value added (% of GDP)	21.9	13.0	11.9
Industry value added (% of GDP)	22.4	24.9	43.5
Manufacturing value added (% of GDP)	13.0	12.7	26.7
Services value added (% of GDP)	55.7	62.1	44.6
Inflation (annual % change in consumer price index)	4.1	8.2	
Exchange rate (local currency units per $)	2.0	1.8	
Exports of goods and services (% of GDP)	23.0	32.9	40.4
Imports of goods and services (% of GDP)	39.7	57.0	36.4
Business environment			
Ease of doing business (ranking 1-178; 1=best)	..	18	
Time to start a business (days)	..	11	53
Procedures to start a business (number)	..	5	10
Firing cost (weeks of wages)	..	4.0	50.2
Closing a business (years to resolve insolvency)	..	3.3	3.3
Total tax rate (% of profit)	..	38.6	45.8
Highest marginal tax rate, corporate (%)		20	
Business entry rate (new registrations as % of total)	6.2	8.9	7.6
Enterprise surveys			
Time dealing with gov't officials (% of management time)	..	3.1	
Firms expected to give gifts in meetings w/tax officials (%)	76.0	35.7	
Firms using banks to finance investments (% of firms)	9.2	12.5	
Delay in obtaining an electrical connection (days)	2.0	..	
ISO certification ownership (% of firms)	..	13.0	
Private sector investment			
Invest. in infrastructure w/private participation ($ millions)	49	583	38,154
Private foreign direct investment, net (% of GDP)	4.3	13.7	3.0
Gross fixed capital formation (% of GDP)	25.4	25.6	33.5
Gross fixed private capital formation (% of GDP)	24.5	20.2	10.9
Finance and banking			
Government cash surplus or deficit (% of GDP)	-1.6	1.6	-0.9
Government debt (% of GDP)	69.9	28.0	..
Deposit money banks' assets (% of GDP)	6.5	16.6	87.8
Total financial system deposits (% of GDP)	4.2	11.0	43.1
Bank capital to asset ratio (%)	30.5	18.8	10.7
Bank nonperforming loans to total gross loans ratio (%)	11.6	2.5	4.0
Domestic credit to the private sector (% of GDP)	8.7	19.5	81.3
Real interest rate (%)	26.8	9.5	
Interest rate spread (percentage points)	22.6	7.3	7.2
Infrastructure			
Paved roads (% of total roads)	93.4	39.4	65.8
Electric power consumption (kWh per capita)	1,360	1,672	1,502
Power outages in a typical month (number)	..	..	
Fixed line and mobile subscribers (per 100 people)	15	51	60
Internet users (per 100 people)	0.5	7.5	11.4
Cost of telephone call to U.S. ($ per 3 minutes)	2.88	..	2.08

Germany

	Country data		High-income group
	2000	2006	2006
Economic and social context			
Population (millions)	82.2	82.4	1,031
Labor force (millions)	40.4	41.0	504
Unemployment rate (% of labor force)	7.7	11.1	6.2
GNI per capita, *World Bank Atlas* method ($)	25,510	36,810	36,608
GDP growth, 1995–2000 and 2000–06 (average annual %)	2.0	0.8	2.3
Agriculture value added (% of GDP)	1.3	1.0	1.5
Industry value added (% of GDP)	30.3	30.0	26.2
Manufacturing value added (% of GDP)	22.9	23.2	16.8
Services value added (% of GDP)	68.5	69.1	72.3
Inflation (annual % change in consumer price index)	1.5	1.7	
Exchange rate (local currency units per $)	1.1	0.8	
Exports of goods and services (% of GDP)	33.4	45.1	25.6
Imports of goods and services (% of GDP)	33.0	39.6	26.3
Business environment			
Ease of doing business (ranking 1-178; 1=best)	..	20	
Time to start a business (days)	..	18	22
Procedures to start a business (number)	..	9	7
Firing cost (weeks of wages)	..	69.0	34.9
Closing a business (years to resolve insolvency)	..	1.2	2.0
Total tax rate (% of profit)	..	50.8	41.5
Highest marginal tax rate, corporate (%)	25	25	
Business entry rate (new registrations as % of total)	18.4	15.0	10.1
Enterprise surveys			
Time dealing with gov't officials (% of management time)	..	..	
Firms expected to give gifts in meetings w/tax officials (%)	..	..	
Firms using banks to finance investments (% of firms)	..	..	
Delay in obtaining an electrical connection (days)	..	..	
ISO certification ownership (% of firms)	..	..	
Private sector investment			
Invest. in infrastructure w/private participation ($ millions)	..	..	849
Private foreign direct investment, net (% of GDP)	11.1	1.5	2.7
Gross fixed capital formation (% of GDP)	21.5	17.8	20.4
Gross fixed private capital formation (% of GDP)	..	..	..
Finance and banking			
Government cash surplus or deficit (% of GDP)	1.4	–1.4	–1.3
Government debt (% of GDP)	37.8	43.5	47.6
Deposit money banks' assets (% of GDP)	144.5	..	99.7
Total financial system deposits (% of GDP)	63.1	..	
Bank capital to asset ratio (%)	4.2	4.7	6.2
Bank nonperforming loans to total gross loans ratio (%)	4.7	4.0	1.1
Domestic credit to the private sector (% of GDP)	118.6	109.8	162.0
Real interest rate (%)	10.4	..	
Interest rate spread (percentage points)	6.2	..	4.4
Infrastructure			
Paved roads (% of total roads)	..	100.0	90.9
Electric power consumption (kWh per capita)	6,680	7,111	9,760
Power outages in a typical month (number)	..	..	
Fixed line and mobile subscribers (per 100 people)	120	168	143
Internet users (per 100 people)	30.2	46.9	59.3
Cost of telephone call to U.S. ($ per 3 minutes)	0.34	0.43	0.77

Ghana

Low income

	Country data		Low-income group
	2000	2006	2006
Economic and social context			
Population (millions)	20.1	23.0	2,420
Labor force (millions)	8.8	10.3	995
Unemployment rate (% of labor force)	10.1	..	..
GNI per capita, *World Bank Atlas* method ($)	320	510	649
GDP growth, 1995–2000 and 2000–06 (average annual %)	4.4	5.3	6.5
Agriculture value added (% of GDP)	35.3	37.4	20.4
Industry value added (% of GDP)	25.4	25.4	27.7
Manufacturing value added (% of GDP)	9.0	8.5	15.8
Services value added (% of GDP)	39.3	37.2	51.9
Inflation (annual % change in consumer price index)	25.2	10.9	
Exchange rate (local currency units per $)	0.5	0.9	
Exports of goods and services (% of GDP)	48.8	39.2	26.7
Imports of goods and services (% of GDP)	67.2	63.8	30.1
Business environment			
Ease of doing business (ranking 1-178; 1=best)	..	87	
Time to start a business (days)	..	42	54
Procedures to start a business (number)	..	11	10
Firing cost (weeks of wages)	..	178.0	62.6
Closing a business (years to resolve insolvency)	..	1.9	3.8
Total tax rate (% of profit)	..	32.9	67.4
Highest marginal tax rate, corporate (%)	33	25	
Business entry rate (new registrations as % of total)	5.9	6.2	6.4
Enterprise surveys			
Time dealing with gov't officials (% of management time)	..	4.0	
Firms expected to give gifts in meetings w/tax officials (%)	..	18.1	
Firms using banks to finance investments (% of firms)	..	16.0	
Delay in obtaining an electrical connection (days)	..	24.4	
ISO certification ownership (% of firms)	..	6.8	
Private sector investment			
Invest. in infrastructure w/private participation ($ millions)	10	215	29,785
Private foreign direct investment, net (% of GDP)	3.3	3.4	2.6
Gross fixed capital formation (% of GDP)	23.1	32.4	26.7
Gross fixed private capital formation (% of GDP)	12.7	18.0	19.6
Finance and banking			
Government cash surplus or deficit (% of GDP)	–6.5	–2.9	–2.6
Government debt (% of GDP)	..	..	
Deposit money banks' assets (% of GDP)	..	..	50.5
Total financial system deposits (% of GDP)	..	..	44.6
Bank capital to asset ratio (%)	11.8	12.4	..
Bank nonperforming loans to total gross loans ratio (%)	11.9	7.9	..
Domestic credit to the private sector (% of GDP)	14.0	17.5	38.3
Real interest rate (%)	..	..	
Interest rate spread (percentage points)	..	..	11.3
Infrastructure			
Paved roads (% of total roads)	29.6	17.9	..
Electric power consumption (kWh per capita)	302	266	391
Power outages in a typical month (number)	..	9.7	
Fixed line and mobile subscribers (per 100 people)	2	24	17
Internet users (per 100 people)	0.1	2.7	4.2
Cost of telephone call to U.S. ($ per 3 minutes)	1.65	0.39	1.99

Greece

High income

	Country data		High-income group
	2000	2006	2006
Economic and social context			
Population (millions)	10.9	11.1	1,031
Labor force (millions)	4.9	5.2	504
Unemployment rate (% of labor force)	11.1	9.6	6.2
GNI per capita, *World Bank Atlas* method ($)	14,430	27,390	36,608
GDP growth, 1995–2000 and 2000–06 (average annual %)	3.5	4.4	2.3
Agriculture value added (% of GDP)	5.7	3.3	1.5
Industry value added (% of GDP)	21.2	20.8	26.2
Manufacturing value added (% of GDP)	10.3	9.5	16.8
Services value added (% of GDP)	73.1	75.9	72.3
Inflation (annual % change in consumer price index)	3.2	3.2	
Exchange rate (local currency units per $)	365.4	0.8	
Exports of goods and services (% of GDP)	21.6	18.6	25.6
Imports of goods and services (% of GDP)	32.7	27.0	26.3
Business environment			
Ease of doing business (ranking 1-178; 1=best)	..	100	
Time to start a business (days)	..	38	22
Procedures to start a business (number)	..	15	7
Firing cost (weeks of wages)	..	24.0	34.9
Closing a business (years to resolve insolvency)	..	2.0	2.0
Total tax rate (% of profit)	..	48.6	41.5
Highest marginal tax rate, corporate (%)	35	29	
Business entry rate (new registrations as % of total)	7.7	7.0	10.1
Enterprise surveys			
Time dealing with gov't officials (% of management time)	..	..	
Firms expected to give gifts in meetings w/tax officials (%)	..	..	
Firms using banks to finance investments (% of firms)	..	..	
Delay in obtaining an electrical connection (days)	..	..	
ISO certification ownership (% of firms)	..	..	
Private sector investment			
Invest. in infrastructure w/private participation ($ millions)	..	..	849
Private foreign direct investment, net (% of GDP)	0.8	1.8	2.7
Gross fixed capital formation (% of GDP)	23.2	25.7	20.4
Gross fixed private capital formation (% of GDP)	..	..	..
Finance and banking			
Government cash surplus or deficit (% of GDP)	-3.2	-4.5	-1.3
Government debt (% of GDP)	107.6	102.1	47.6
Deposit money banks' assets (% of GDP)	71.0	..	99.7
Total financial system deposits (% of GDP)	49.0	..	..
Bank capital to asset ratio (%)	8.9	5.2	6.2
Bank nonperforming loans to total gross loans ratio (%)	12.3	5.5	1.1
Domestic credit to the private sector (% of GDP)	40.9	72.3	162.0
Real interest rate (%)	8.7	3.1	
Interest rate spread (percentage points)	6.2	4.3	4.4
Infrastructure			
Paved roads (% of total roads)	91.8	..	90.9
Electric power consumption (kWh per capita)	4,539	5,242	9,760
Power outages in a typical month (number)	..	..	
Fixed line and mobile subscribers (per 100 people)	106	155	143
Internet users (per 100 people)	9.2	18.4	59.3
Cost of telephone call to U.S. ($ per 3 minutes)	0.69	1.09	0.77

Greenland

	Country data		High-income group
	2000	2006	2006
Economic and social context			
Population (millions)	0.06	0.06	1,031
Labor force (millions)	..	..	504
Unemployment rate (% of labor force)	11.0	9.3	6.2
GNI per capita, *World Bank Atlas* method ($)	..	..	36,608
GDP growth, 1995–2000 and 2000–06 (average annual %)	..	..	2.3
Agriculture value added (% of GDP)	..	..	1.5
Industry value added (% of GDP)	..	..	26.2
Manufacturing value added (% of GDP)	..	..	16.8
Services value added (% of GDP)	..	..	72.3
Inflation (annual % change in consumer price index)	..	..	
Exchange rate (local currency units per $)	8.1	5.9	
Exports of goods and services (% of GDP)	..	..	25.6
Imports of goods and services (% of GDP)	..	..	26.3
Business environment			
Ease of doing business (ranking 1-178; 1=best)	..	..	
Time to start a business (days)	..	..	22
Procedures to start a business (number)	..	..	7
Firing cost (weeks of wages)	..	..	34.9
Closing a business (years to resolve insolvency)	..	..	2.0
Total tax rate (% of profit)	..	..	41.5
Highest marginal tax rate, corporate (%)	..	..	
Business entry rate (new registrations as % of total)	..	..	10.1
Enterprise surveys			
Time dealing with gov't officials (% of management time)	..	..	
Firms expected to give gifts in meetings w/tax officials (%)	..	..	
Firms using banks to finance investments (% of firms)	..	..	
Delay in obtaining an electrical connection (days)	..	..	
ISO certification ownership (% of firms)	..	..	
Private sector investment			
Invest. in infrastructure w/private participation ($ millions)	..	..	849
Private foreign direct investment, net (% of GDP)	..	..	2.7
Gross fixed capital formation (% of GDP)	..	..	20.4
Gross fixed private capital formation (% of GDP)	..	..	..
Finance and banking			
Government cash surplus or deficit (% of GDP)	..	..	-1.3
Government debt (% of GDP)	..	..	47.6
Deposit money banks' assets (% of GDP)	..	..	99.7
Total financial system deposits (% of GDP)	..	..	..
Bank capital to asset ratio (%)	..	..	6.2
Bank nonperforming loans to total gross loans ratio (%)	..	..	1.1
Domestic credit to the private sector (% of GDP)	..	..	162.0
Real interest rate (%)	..	..	
Interest rate spread (percentage points)	..	..	4.4
Infrastructure			
Paved roads (% of total roads)	..	..	90.9
Electric power consumption (kWh per capita)	..	..	9,760
Power outages in a typical month (number)	..	..	
Fixed line and mobile subscribers (per 100 people)	75	..	143
Internet users (per 100 people)	31.7	66.8	59.3
Cost of telephone call to U.S. ($ per 3 minutes)	2.41	..	0.77

Grenada

Latin America & Caribbean			Upper middle income

	Country data		Upper middle-income group
	2000	2006	2006

Economic and social context
Population (millions)	0.10	0.11	811
Labor force (millions)	..	..	374
Unemployment rate (% of labor force)	*15.2*	..	*9.8*
GNI per capita, *World Bank Atlas* method ($)	3,670	4,650	5,913
GDP growth, 1995–2000 and 2000–06 (average annual %)	6.7	2.1	3.9
Agriculture value added (% of GDP)	7.7	6.7	5.7
Industry value added (% of GDP)	24.3	29.0	32.4
Manufacturing value added (% of GDP)	7.6	5.9	19.4
Services value added (% of GDP)	68.0	64.3	62.0
Inflation (annual % change in consumer price index)	2.1	3.8	
Exchange rate (local currency units per $)	2.7	2.7	
Exports of goods and services (% of GDP)	57.6	*32.9*	32.7
Imports of goods and services (% of GDP)	75.7	*76.1*	30.3

Business environment
Ease of doing business (ranking 1-178; 1=best)	..	70	
Time to start a business (days)	..	20	41
Procedures to start a business (number)	..	6	9
Firing cost (weeks of wages)	..	29.0	39.7
Closing a business (years to resolve insolvency)	..	..	2.9
Total tax rate (% of profit)	..	45.3	44.5
Highest marginal tax rate, corporate (%)	..	..	
Business entry rate (new registrations as % of total)	..	..	*9.1*
Enterprise surveys			
Time dealing with gov't officials (% of management time)	..	..	
Firms expected to give gifts in meetings w/tax officials (%)	..	..	
Firms using banks to finance investments (% of firms)	..	..	
Delay in obtaining an electrical connection (days)	..	..	
ISO certification ownership (% of firms)	..	..	

Private sector investment
Invest. in infrastructure w/private participation ($ millions)	..	*10*	45,869
Private foreign direct investment, net (% of GDP)	9.1	22.7	3.5
Gross fixed capital formation (% of GDP)	43.8	*63.2*	19.9
Gross fixed private capital formation (% of GDP)	36.8	*28.4*	..

Finance and banking
Government cash surplus or deficit (% of GDP)	..	..	..
Government debt (% of GDP)	..	..	..
Deposit money banks' assets (% of GDP)	83.7	86.5	52.9
Total financial system deposits (% of GDP)	86.2	*114.3*	41.4
Bank capital to asset ratio (%)	..	..	9.8
Bank nonperforming loans to total gross loans ratio (%)	..	..	3.2
Domestic credit to the private sector (% of GDP)	79.4	86.4	41.4
Real interest rate (%)	11.3	*7.1*	
Interest rate spread (percentage points)	7.4	6.9	5.9

Infrastructure
Paved roads (% of total roads)	61.0	..	..
Electric power consumption (kWh per capita)	..	..	*3,131*
Power outages in a typical month (number)	..	..	
Fixed line and mobile subscribers (per 100 people)	35	68	88
Internet users (per 100 people)	4.1	18.2	22.2
Cost of telephone call to U.S. ($ per 3 minutes)	*3.97*	..	*1.06*

Guam

	Country data		High-income group
	2000	2006	2006
Economic and social context			
Population (millions)	0.16	0.17	1,031
Labor force (millions)	0.07	0.08	504
Unemployment rate (% of labor force)	..	..	6.2
GNI per capita, *World Bank Atlas* method ($)	..	..	36,608
GDP growth, 1995–2000 and 2000–06 (average annual %)	..	..	2.3
Agriculture value added (% of GDP)	..	..	1.5
Industry value added (% of GDP)	..	..	26.2
Manufacturing value added (% of GDP)	..	..	16.8
Services value added (% of GDP)	..	..	72.3
Inflation (annual % change in consumer price index)	..	..	
Exchange rate (local currency units per $)	..	..	
Exports of goods and services (% of GDP)	..	..	25.6
Imports of goods and services (% of GDP)	..	..	26.3
Business environment			
Ease of doing business (ranking 1-178; 1=best)	..	..	
Time to start a business (days)	..	..	22
Procedures to start a business (number)	..	..	7
Firing cost (weeks of wages)	..	..	34.9
Closing a business (years to resolve insolvency)	..	..	2.0
Total tax rate (% of profit)	..	..	41.5
Highest marginal tax rate, corporate (%)	..	..	
Business entry rate (new registrations as % of total)	..	..	10.1
Enterprise surveys			
Time dealing with gov't officials (% of management time)	..	..	
Firms expected to give gifts in meetings w/tax officials (%)	..	..	
Firms using banks to finance investments (% of firms)	..	..	
Delay in obtaining an electrical connection (days)	..	..	
ISO certification ownership (% of firms)	..	..	
Private sector investment			
Invest. in infrastructure w/private participation ($ millions)	..	..	849
Private foreign direct investment, net (% of GDP)	..	..	2.7
Gross fixed capital formation (% of GDP)	..	..	20.4
Gross fixed private capital formation (% of GDP)	..	..	..
Finance and banking			
Government cash surplus or deficit (% of GDP)	..	..	-1.3
Government debt (% of GDP)	..	..	47.6
Deposit money banks' assets (% of GDP)	..	..	99.7
Total financial system deposits (% of GDP)	..	..	..
Bank capital to asset ratio (%)	..	..	6.2
Bank nonperforming loans to total gross loans ratio (%)	..	..	1.1
Domestic credit to the private sector (% of GDP)	..	..	162.0
Real interest rate (%)	..	..	
Interest rate spread (percentage points)	..	..	4.4
Infrastructure			
Paved roads (% of total roads)	..	..	90.9
Electric power consumption (kWh per capita)	..	..	9,760
Power outages in a typical month (number)	..	..	
Fixed line and mobile subscribers (per 100 people)	65	..	143
Internet users (per 100 people)	16.1	38.6	59.3
Cost of telephone call to U.S. ($ per 3 minutes)	..	..	0.77

Guatemala

Latin America & Caribbean   **Lower middle income**

	Country data		Lower middle-income group
	2000	**2006**	**2006**
Economic and social context			
Population (millions)	11.2	13.0	2,276
Labor force (millions)	3.6	4.2	1,209
Unemployment rate (% of labor force)	1.4	3.4	5.7
GNI per capita, *World Bank Atlas* method ($)	1,730	2,590	2,038
GDP growth, 1995-2000 and 2000-06 (average annual %)	4.1	2.7	7.6
Agriculture value added (% of GDP)	22.8	22.2	11.9
Industry value added (% of GDP)	19.8	19.1	43.5
Manufacturing value added (% of GDP)	13.2	12.5	26.7
Services value added (% of GDP)	57.4	58.7	44.6
Inflation (annual % change in consumer price index)	6.0	6.5	
Exchange rate (local currency units per $)	7.8	7.6	
Exports of goods and services (% of GDP)	20.2	15.7	40.4
Imports of goods and services (% of GDP)	29.0	30.6	36.4
Business environment			
Ease of doing business (ranking 1-178; 1=best)	..	114	
Time to start a business (days)	..	26	53
Procedures to start a business (number)	..	11	10
Firing cost (weeks of wages)	..	101.0	50.2
Closing a business (years to resolve insolvency)	..	3.0	3.3
Total tax rate (% of profit)	..	37.5	45.8
Highest marginal tax rate, corporate (%)	31	31	
Business entry rate (new registrations as % of total)	..	6.2	7.6
Enterprise surveys			
Time dealing with gov't officials (% of management time)	..	9.2	
Firms expected to give gifts in meetings w/tax officials (%)	..	3.8	
Firms using banks to finance investments (% of firms)	..	12.8	
Delay in obtaining an electrical connection (days)	..	35.3	
ISO certification ownership (% of firms)	..	8.0	
Private sector investment			
Invest. in infrastructure w/private participation ($ millions)	147	276	38,154
Private foreign direct investment, net (% of GDP)	1.2	1.0	3.0
Gross fixed capital formation (% of GDP)	16.1	16.9	33.5
Gross fixed private capital formation (% of GDP)	13.7	14.9	10.9
Finance and banking			
Government cash surplus or deficit (% of GDP)	-1.8	-1.7	-0.9
Government debt (% of GDP)	17.0	19.0	..
Deposit money banks' assets (% of GDP)	21.3	27.6	87.8
Total financial system deposits (% of GDP)	16.1	30.6	43.1
Bank capital to asset ratio (%)	8.9	8.2	10.7
Bank nonperforming loans to total gross loans ratio (%)	7.9	4.6	4.0
Domestic credit to the private sector (% of GDP)	19.8	26.8	81.3
Real interest rate (%)	13.2	6.1	
Interest rate spread (percentage points)	10.7	8.3	7.2
Infrastructure			
Paved roads (% of total roads)	34.5	..	65.8
Electric power consumption (kWh per capita)	343	522	*1,502*
Power outages in a typical month (number)	..	3.1	
Fixed line and mobile subscribers (per 100 people)	14	65	60
Internet users (per 100 people)	0.7	10.1	11.4
Cost of telephone call to U.S. ($ per 3 minutes)	*0.76*	*1.21*	*2.08*

Guinea

Low income

	Country data		Low-income group
	2000	2006	2006
Economic and social context			
Population (millions)	8.2	9.2	2,420
Labor force (millions)	3.9	4.4	995
Unemployment rate (% of labor force)	..	..	..
GNI per capita, *World Bank Atlas* method ($)	410	400	649
GDP growth, 1995–2000 and 2000–06 (average annual %)	4.4	2.9	6.5
Agriculture value added (% of GDP)	20.3	12.9	20.4
Industry value added (% of GDP)	32.5	37.5	27.7
Manufacturing value added (% of GDP)	4.0	3.7	15.8
Services value added (% of GDP)	47.2	49.6	51.9
Inflation (annual % change in consumer price index)	..	..	
Exchange rate (local currency units per $)	1,746.9	3,644.3	
Exports of goods and services (% of GDP)	23.6	32.4	26.7
Imports of goods and services (% of GDP)	27.9	35.1	30.1
Business environment			
Ease of doing business (ranking 1-178; 1=best)	..	166	
Time to start a business (days)	..	41	54
Procedures to start a business (number)	..	13	10
Firing cost (weeks of wages)	..	26.0	62.6
Closing a business (years to resolve insolvency)	..	3.8	3.8
Total tax rate (% of profit)	..	49.9	67.4
Highest marginal tax rate, corporate (%)	..	..	
Business entry rate (new registrations as % of total)	..	..	6.4
Enterprise surveys			
Time dealing with gov't officials (% of management time)	..	2.7	
Firms expected to give gifts in meetings w/tax officials (%)	..	57.3	
Firms using banks to finance investments (% of firms)	..	0.9	
Delay in obtaining an electrical connection (days)	..	16.1	
ISO certification ownership (% of firms)	..	5.2	
Private sector investment			
Invest. in infrastructure w/private participation ($ millions)	6	48	29,785
Private foreign direct investment, net (% of GDP)	0.3	3.3	2.6
Gross fixed capital formation (% of GDP)	18.9	12.9	26.7
Gross fixed private capital formation (% of GDP)	14.0	9.8	19.6
Finance and banking			
Government cash surplus or deficit (% of GDP)	–2.4	..	–2.6
Government debt (% of GDP)	..	..	..
Deposit money banks' assets (% of GDP)	..	..	50.5
Total financial system deposits (% of GDP)	..	..	44.6
Bank capital to asset ratio (%)	..	..	..
Bank nonperforming loans to total gross loans ratio (%)	..	..	..
Domestic credit to the private sector (% of GDP)	3.8	5.0	38.3
Real interest rate (%)	7.4	..	
Interest rate spread (percentage points)	11.9	..	11.3
Infrastructure			
Paved roads (% of total roads)	16.5	9.8	..
Electric power consumption (kWh per capita)	..	..	391
Power outages in a typical month (number)	..	33.9	
Fixed line and mobile subscribers (per 100 people)	1	2	17
Internet users (per 100 people)	0.1	0.5	4.2
Cost of telephone call to U.S. ($ per 3 minutes)	5.15	..	1.99

Guinea-Bissau

Sub-Saharan Africa   **Low income**

	Country data		Low-income group
	2000	2006	2006
Economic and social context			
Population (millions)	1.4	1.6	2,420
Labor force (millions)	0.56	0.66	995
Unemployment rate (% of labor force)	..	..	..
GNI per capita, *World Bank Atlas* method ($)	160	190	649
GDP growth, 1995–2000 and 2000–06 (average annual %)	-2.7	0.4	6.5
Agriculture value added (% of GDP)	56.4	61.8	20.4
Industry value added (% of GDP)	13.0	11.5	27.7
Manufacturing value added (% of GDP)	10.5	7.2	15.8
Services value added (% of GDP)	30.6	26.8	51.9
Inflation (annual % change in consumer price index)	8.6	2.0	
Exchange rate (local currency units per $)	712.0	522.9	
Exports of goods and services (% of GDP)	31.8	42.2	26.7
Imports of goods and services (% of GDP)	51.6	53.2	30.1
Business environment			
Ease of doing business (ranking 1-178; 1=best)	..	176	
Time to start a business (days)	..	233	54
Procedures to start a business (number)	..	17	10
Firing cost (weeks of wages)	..	87.0	62.6
Closing a business (years to resolve insolvency)	..	..	3.8
Total tax rate (% of profit)	..	45.9	67.4
Highest marginal tax rate, corporate (%)	..	..	
Business entry rate (new registrations as % of total)	..	..	6.4
Enterprise surveys			
Time dealing with gov't officials (% of management time)	..	2.9	
Firms expected to give gifts in meetings w/tax officials (%)	..	22.7	
Firms using banks to finance investments (% of firms)	..	0.7	
Delay in obtaining an electrical connection (days)	..	20.5	
ISO certification ownership (% of firms)	..	8.4	
Private sector investment			
Invest. in infrastructure w/private participation ($ millions)	..	0.6	29,785
Private foreign direct investment, net (% of GDP)	0.3	13.8	2.6
Gross fixed capital formation (% of GDP)	11.3	17.2	26.7
Gross fixed private capital formation (% of GDP)	1.3	4.8	19.6
Finance and banking			
Government cash surplus or deficit (% of GDP)	..	..	-2.6
Government debt (% of GDP)	..	..	
Deposit money banks' assets (% of GDP)	7.6	4.2	50.5
Total financial system deposits (% of GDP)	12.7	8.0	44.6
Bank capital to asset ratio (%)	..	..	..
Bank nonperforming loans to total gross loans ratio (%)	..	..	
Domestic credit to the private sector (% of GDP)	7.9	4.0	38.3
Real interest rate (%)	..	..	
Interest rate spread (percentage points)	..	..	11.3
Infrastructure			
Paved roads (% of total roads)	27.9	..	..
Electric power consumption (kWh per capita)	..	..	391
Power outages in a typical month (number)	..	9.2	
Fixed line and mobile subscribers (per 100 people)	1	7	17
Internet users (per 100 people)	0.2	2.2	4.2
Cost of telephone call to U.S. ($ per 3 minutes)	..	..	1.99

Guyana

Latin America & Caribbean   **Lower middle income**

	Country data		Lower middle-income group
	2000	2006	2006
Economic and social context			
Population (millions)	0.73	0.74	2,276
Labor force (millions)	0.31	0.32	1,209
Unemployment rate (% of labor force)	9.1	..	5.7
GNI per capita, *World Bank Atlas* method ($)	890	1,150	2,038
GDP growth, 1995–2000 and 2000–06 (average annual %)	2.5	1.0	7.6
Agriculture value added (% of GDP)	31.1	31.0	11.9
Industry value added (% of GDP)	29.0	24.5	43.5
Manufacturing value added (% of GDP)	8.2	8.0	26.7
Services value added (% of GDP)	39.9	44.5	44.6
Inflation (annual % change in consumer price index)	6.1	6.6	
Exchange rate (local currency units per $)	182.4	200.2	
Exports of goods and services (% of GDP)	96.1	87.9	40.4
Imports of goods and services (% of GDP)	110.7	123.9	36.4
Business environment			
Ease of doing business (ranking 1-178; 1=best)	..	104	
Time to start a business (days)	..	44	53
Procedures to start a business (number)	..	8	10
Firing cost (weeks of wages)	..	56.0	50.2
Closing a business (years to resolve insolvency)	..	3.0	3.3
Total tax rate (% of profit)	..	39.0	45.8
Highest marginal tax rate, corporate (%)	45	45	
Business entry rate (new registrations as % of total)	..	..	7.6
Enterprise surveys			
Time dealing with gov't officials (% of management time)	..	2.3	
Firms expected to give gifts in meetings w/tax officials (%)	..	5.4	
Firms using banks to finance investments (% of firms)	..	25.8	
Delay in obtaining an electrical connection (days)	..	93.4	
ISO certification ownership (% of firms)	..	17.8	
Private sector investment			
Invest. in infrastructure w/private participation ($ millions)	11	37	38,154
Private foreign direct investment, net (% of GDP)	9.4	11.4	3.0
Gross fixed capital formation (% of GDP)	23.8	25.8	33.5
Gross fixed private capital formation (% of GDP)	10.0	1.4	10.9
Finance and banking			
Government cash surplus or deficit (% of GDP)	..	..	–0.9
Government debt (% of GDP)	..	..	..
Deposit money banks' assets (% of GDP)	66.3	73.8	87.8
Total financial system deposits (% of GDP)	62.6	84.8	43.1
Bank capital to asset ratio (%)	..	..	10.7
Bank nonperforming loans to total gross loans ratio (%)	..	..	4.0
Domestic credit to the private sector (% of GDP)	57.1	60.2	81.3
Real interest rate (%)	10.0	6.1	
Interest rate spread (percentage points)	8.6	12.0	7.2
Infrastructure			
Paved roads (% of total roads)	7.4	..	65.8
Electric power consumption (kWh per capita)	..	..	1,502
Power outages in a typical month (number)			
Fixed line and mobile subscribers (per 100 people)	15	53	60
Internet users (per 100 people)	6.8	21.6	11.4
Cost of telephone call to U.S. ($ per 3 minutes)	3.89	..	2.08

Haiti

Latin America & Caribbean   **Low income**

	Country data		Low-income group
	2000	**2006**	**2006**
Economic and social context			
Population (millions)	8.6	9.4	2,420
Labor force (millions)	3.5	4.1	995
Unemployment rate (% of labor force)	7.2	..	..
GNI per capita, *World Bank Atlas* method ($)	470	430	649
GDP growth, 1995–2000 and 2000–06 (average annual %)	2.4	–0.3	6.5
Agriculture value added (% of GDP)	28.4	27.9	20.4
Industry value added (% of GDP)	16.6	17.0	27.7
Manufacturing value added (% of GDP)	9.0	8.4	15.8
Services value added (% of GDP)	55.0	55.1	51.9
Inflation (annual % change in consumer price index)	13.7	13.1	
Exchange rate (local currency units per $)	21.2	40.4	
Exports of goods and services (% of GDP)	12.1	14.1	26.7
Imports of goods and services (% of GDP)	31.8	43.2	30.1
Business environment			
Ease of doing business (ranking 1-178; 1=best)	..	148	
Time to start a business (days)	..	202	54
Procedures to start a business (number)	..	12	10
Firing cost (weeks of wages)	..	17.0	62.6
Closing a business (years to resolve insolvency)	..	5.7	3.8
Total tax rate (% of profit)	..	40.0	67.4
Highest marginal tax rate, corporate (%)	..	..	
Business entry rate (new registrations as % of total)	0.5	3.0	6.4
Enterprise surveys			
Time dealing with gov't officials (% of management time)	..	..	
Firms expected to give gifts in meetings w/tax officials (%)	..	..	
Firms using banks to finance investments (% of firms)	..	..	
Delay in obtaining an electrical connection (days)	..	..	
ISO certification ownership (% of firms)	..	..	
Private sector investment			
Invest. in infrastructure w/private participation ($ millions)	101	130	29,785
Private foreign direct investment, net (% of GDP)	0.3	3.2	2.6
Gross fixed capital formation (% of GDP)	26.0	28.8	26.7
Gross fixed private capital formation (% of GDP)	23.0	21.6	19.6
Finance and banking			
Government cash surplus or deficit (% of GDP)	..	..	–2.6
Government debt (% of GDP)	..	..	
Deposit money banks' assets (% of GDP)	15.6	15.1	50.5
Total financial system deposits (% of GDP)	27.2	30.1	44.6
Bank capital to asset ratio (%)	..	..	..
Bank nonperforming loans to total gross loans ratio (%)	..	..	..
Domestic credit to the private sector (% of GDP)	14.8	13.4	38.3
Real interest rate (%)	15.8	27.2	
Interest rate spread (percentage points)	19.6	37.1	11.3
Infrastructure			
Paved roads (% of total roads)	24.3	..	..
Electric power consumption (kWh per capita)	35	37	391
Power outages in a typical month (number)	..	..	
Fixed line and mobile subscribers (per 100 people)	1	7	17
Internet users (per 100 people)	0.2	6.9	4.2
Cost of telephone call to U.S. ($ per 3 minutes)	7.10	2.15	1.99

Honduras

	Country data		Lower middle-income group
	2000	2006	2006
Economic and social context			
Population (millions)	6.2	7.0	2,276
Labor force (millions)	2.3	3.0	1,209
Unemployment rate (% of labor force)	3.9	4.2	5.7
GNI per capita, World Bank Atlas method ($)	890	1,270	2,038
GDP growth, 1995–2000 and 2000–06 (average annual %)	2.8	4.0	7.6
Agriculture value added (% of GDP)	16.2	13.8	11.9
Industry value added (% of GDP)	31.6	31.1	43.5
Manufacturing value added (% of GDP)	19.6	19.7	26.7
Services value added (% of GDP)	52.2	55.1	44.6
Inflation (annual % change in consumer price index)	11.1	5.6	
Exchange rate (local currency units per $)	14.8	18.9	
Exports of goods and services (% of GDP)	41.3	40.8	40.4
Imports of goods and services (% of GDP)	55.2	66.5	36.4
Business environment			
Ease of doing business (ranking 1-178; 1=best)	..	121	
Time to start a business (days)	..	21	53
Procedures to start a business (number)	..	13	10
Firing cost (weeks of wages)	..	74.0	50.2
Closing a business (years to resolve insolvency)	..	3.8	3.3
Total tax rate (% of profit)	..	51.4	45.8
Highest marginal tax rate, corporate (%)	15	25	
Business entry rate (new registrations as % of total)	..	..	7.6
Enterprise surveys			
Time dealing with gov't officials (% of management time)	..	4.6	
Firms expected to give gifts in meetings w/tax officials (%)	..	6.1	
Firms using banks to finance investments (% of firms)	..	8.5	
Delay in obtaining an electrical connection (days)	..	27.6	
ISO certification ownership (% of firms)	..	16.5	
Private sector investment			
Invest. in infrastructure w/private participation ($ millions)	127	89	38,154
Private foreign direct investment, net (% of GDP)	4.7	4.2	3.0
Gross fixed capital formation (% of GDP)	26.1	24.9	33.5
Gross fixed private capital formation (% of GDP)	20.3	20.1	10.9
Finance and banking			
Government cash surplus or deficit (% of GDP)	..	-1.3	-0.9
Government debt (% of GDP)	..	..	..
Deposit money banks' assets (% of GDP)	39.1	47.9	87.8
Total financial system deposits (% of GDP)	38.8	49.2	43.1
Bank capital to asset ratio (%)	8.8	8.4	10.7
Bank nonperforming loans to total gross loans ratio (%)	10.6	6.6	4.0
Domestic credit to the private sector (% of GDP)	40.7	49.0	81.3
Real interest rate (%)	15.7	11.7	
Interest rate spread (percentage points)	10.9	8.1	7.2
Infrastructure			
Paved roads (% of total roads)	20.4	..	65.8
Electric power consumption (kWh per capita)	519	626	1,502
Power outages in a typical month (number)	..	3.0	
Fixed line and mobile subscribers (per 100 people)	7	42	60
Internet users (per 100 people)	1.2	4.8	11.4
Cost of telephone call to U.S. ($ per 3 minutes)	3.97	2.52	2.08

Hong Kong, China

High income

	Country data		High-income group
	2000	**2006**	**2006**
Economic and social context			
Population (millions)	6.7	6.9	1,031
Labor force (millions)	3.4	3.6	504
Unemployment rate (% of labor force)	4.9	5.6	6.2
GNI per capita, *World Bank Atlas* method ($)	27,000	29,040	36,608
GDP growth, 1995–2000 and 2000–06 (average annual %)	2.6	4.8	2.3
Agriculture value added (% of GDP)	0.1	0.1	1.5
Industry value added (% of GDP)	13.4	9.3	26.2
Manufacturing value added (% of GDP)	5.4	3.4	16.8
Services value added (% of GDP)	86.5	90.6	72.3
Inflation (annual % change in consumer price index)	-3.8	2.0	
Exchange rate (local currency units per $)	7.8	7.8	
Exports of goods and services (% of GDP)	143.3	205.4	25.6
Imports of goods and services (% of GDP)	138.8	194.0	26.3
Business environment			
Ease of doing business (ranking 1-178; 1=best)	..	4	
Time to start a business (days)	..	11	22
Procedures to start a business (number)	..	5	7
Firing cost (weeks of wages)	..	62.0	34.9
Closing a business (years to resolve insolvency)	..	1.1	2.0
Total tax rate (% of profit)	..	24.4	41.5
Highest marginal tax rate, corporate (%)	16	18	
Business entry rate (new registrations as % of total)	9.3	13.3	10.1
Enterprise surveys			
Time dealing with gov't officials (% of management time)	..	..	
Firms expected to give gifts in meetings w/tax officials (%)	..	..	
Firms using banks to finance investments (% of firms)	..	..	
Delay in obtaining an electrical connection (days)	..	..	
ISO certification ownership (% of firms)	..	..	
Private sector investment			
Invest. in infrastructure w/private participation ($ millions)	..	..	849
Private foreign direct investment, net (% of GDP)	36.6	22.6	2.7
Gross fixed capital formation (% of GDP)	26.4	21.5	20.4
Gross fixed private capital formation (% of GDP)	..	..	..
Finance and banking			
Government cash surplus or deficit (% of GDP)	..	..	-1.3
Government debt (% of GDP)	..	..	47.6
Deposit money banks' assets (% of GDP)	164.2	155.5	99.7
Total financial system deposits (% of GDP)	210.1	250.3	..
Bank capital to asset ratio (%)	9.0	11.8	6.2
Bank nonperforming loans to total gross loans ratio (%)	7.3	1.1	1.1
Domestic credit to the private sector (% of GDP)	152.6	139.5	162.0
Real interest rate (%)	16.0	7.9	
Interest rate spread (percentage points)	4.7	5.1	4.4
Infrastructure			
Paved roads (% of total roads)	100.0	100.0	90.9
Electric power consumption (kWh per capita)	5,447	5,878	9,760
Power outages in a typical month (number)	..	..	
Fixed line and mobile subscribers (per 100 people)	141	193	143
Internet users (per 100 people)	27.8	55.0	59.3
Cost of telephone call to U.S. ($ per 3 minutes)	2.62	0.77	0.77

Hungary

	Country data		Upper middle-income group
	2000	**2006**	**2006**
Economic and social context			
Population (millions)	10.2	10.1	811
Labor force (millions)	4.2	4.2	374
Unemployment rate (% of labor force)	6.4	7.2	9.8
GNI per capita, *World Bank Atlas* method ($)	4,620	10,870	5,913
GDP growth, 1995-2000 and 2000-06 (average annual %)	4.2	4.3	3.9
Agriculture value added (% of GDP)	5.4	4.2	5.7
Industry value added (% of GDP)	32.2	30.1	32.4
Manufacturing value added (% of GDP)	23.5	22.6	19.4
Services value added (% of GDP)	62.5	65.7	62.0
Inflation (annual % change in consumer price index)	9.8	3.9	
Exchange rate (local currency units per $)	282.2	210.4	
Exports of goods and services (% of GDP)	72.1	77.8	32.7
Imports of goods and services (% of GDP)	75.7	77.3	30.3
Business environment			
Ease of doing business (ranking 1-178; 1=best)	..	45	
Time to start a business (days)	..	16	41
Procedures to start a business (number)	..	6	9
Firing cost (weeks of wages)	..	35.0	39.7
Closing a business (years to resolve insolvency)	..	2.0	2.9
Total tax rate (% of profit)	..	55.1	44.5
Highest marginal tax rate, corporate (%)	18	16	
Business entry rate (new registrations as % of total)	10.0	9.2	9.1
Enterprise surveys			
Time dealing with gov't officials (% of management time)	..	4.0	
Firms expected to give gifts in meetings w/tax officials (%)	27.0	25.0	
Firms using banks to finance investments (% of firms)	15.2	22.3	
Delay in obtaining an electrical connection (days)	10.7	9.6	
ISO certification ownership (% of firms)	..	23.1	
Private sector investment			
Invest. in infrastructure w/private participation ($ millions)	1,168	1,987	45,869
Private foreign direct investment, net (% of GDP)	5.8	5.4	3.5
Gross fixed capital formation (% of GDP)	23.0	21.7	19.9
Gross fixed private capital formation (% of GDP)	..	..	..
Finance and banking			
Government cash surplus or deficit (% of GDP)	-2.7	-8.6	..
Government debt (% of GDP)	60.9	70.2	..
Deposit money banks' assets (% of GDP)	35.8	63.5	52.9
Total financial system deposits (% of GDP)	35.5	42.4	41.4
Bank capital to asset ratio (%)	8.3	8.7	9.8
Bank nonperforming loans to total gross loans ratio (%)	3.0	2.5	3.2
Domestic credit to the private sector (% of GDP)	31.4	55.4	41.4
Real interest rate (%)	-0.2	4.2	
Interest rate spread (percentage points)	3.1	0.6	5.9
Infrastructure			
Paved roads (% of total roads)	43.7	43.9	..
Electric power consumption (kWh per capita)	3,309	3,771	3,131
Power outages in a typical month (number)	..	..	
Fixed line and mobile subscribers (per 100 people)	67	132	88
Internet users (per 100 people)	7.0	34.8	22.2
Cost of telephone call to U.S. ($ per 3 minutes)	1.28	1.01	1.06

Iceland

High income

	Country data		High-income group
	2000	2006	2006
Economic and social context			
Population (millions)	0.28	0.30	1,031
Labor force (millions)	0.16	0.18	504
Unemployment rate (% of labor force)	2.3	2.6	6.2
GNI per capita, *World Bank Atlas* method ($)	30,750	49,960	36,608
GDP growth, 1995–2000 and 2000–06 (average annual %)	5.0	4.1	2.3
Agriculture value added (% of GDP)	8.6	5.8	1.5
Industry value added (% of GDP)	26.1	23.7	26.2
Manufacturing value added (% of GDP)	14.0	10.1	16.8
Services value added (% of GDP)	65.3	70.5	72.3
Inflation (annual % change in consumer price index)	5.2	6.7	
Exchange rate (local currency units per $)	78.6	70.2	
Exports of goods and services (% of GDP)	33.7	32.6	25.6
Imports of goods and services (% of GDP)	41.0	50.5	26.3
Business environment			
Ease of doing business (ranking 1-178; 1=best)	..	10	
Time to start a business (days)	..	5	22
Procedures to start a business (number)	..	5	7
Firing cost (weeks of wages)	..	13.0	34.9
Closing a business (years to resolve insolvency)	..	1.0	2.0
Total tax rate (% of profit)	..	27.2	41.5
Highest marginal tax rate, corporate (%)	..	..	
Business entry rate (new registrations as % of total)	16.8	11.6	10.1
Enterprise surveys			
Time dealing with gov't officials (% of management time)	..	..	
Firms expected to give gifts in meetings w/tax officials (%)	..	..	
Firms using banks to finance investments (% of firms)	..	..	
Delay in obtaining an electrical connection (days)	..	..	
ISO certification ownership (% of firms)	..	..	
Private sector investment			
Invest. in infrastructure w/private participation ($ millions)	..	..	849
Private foreign direct investment, net (% of GDP)	1.8	24.9	2.7
Gross fixed capital formation (% of GDP)	22.9	32.0	20.4
Gross fixed private capital formation (% of GDP)	..	..	..
Finance and banking			
Government cash surplus or deficit (% of GDP)	2.7	6.1	-1.3
Government debt (% of GDP)	60.6	45.4	47.6
Deposit money banks' assets (% of GDP)	83.1	270.4	99.7
Total financial system deposits (% of GDP)	40.6	78.1	..
Bank capital to asset ratio (%)	6.2	7.8	6.2
Bank nonperforming loans to total gross loans ratio (%)	1.5	0.9	1.1
Domestic credit to the private sector (% of GDP)	97.3	327.0	162.0
Real interest rate (%)	12.7	8.3	
Interest rate spread (percentage points)	6.2	7.2	4.4
Infrastructure			
Paved roads (% of total roads)	29.5	35.4	90.9
Electric power consumption (kWh per capita)	26,221	27,987	9,760
Power outages in a typical month (number)	..	..	
Fixed line and mobile subscribers (per 100 people)	146	173	143
Internet users (per 100 people)	44.5	64.3	59.3
Cost of telephone call to U.S. ($ per 3 minutes)	0.84	..	0.77

India

	Country data		Low-income group
	2000	**2006**	**2006**
Economic and social context			
Population (millions)	1,015.9	1,109.8	2,420
Labor force (millions)	391.7	438.0	995
Unemployment rate (% of labor force)	4.3	5.0	..
GNI per capita, *World Bank Atlas* method ($)	450	820	649
GDP growth, 1995–2000 and 2000–06 (average annual %)	5.9	7.4	6.5
Agriculture value added (% of GDP)	23.4	17.5	20.4
Industry value added (% of GDP)	26.2	27.9	27.7
Manufacturing value added (% of GDP)	15.6	16.3	15.8
Services value added (% of GDP)	50.5	54.6	51.9
Inflation (annual % change in consumer price index)	4.0	5.8	
Exchange rate (local currency units per $)	44.9	45.3	
Exports of goods and services (% of GDP)	13.2	23.0	26.7
Imports of goods and services (% of GDP)	14.2	25.8	30.1
Business environment			
Ease of doing business (ranking 1-178; 1=best)	..	120	
Time to start a business (days)	..	33	54
Procedures to start a business (number)	..	13	10
Firing cost (weeks of wages)	..	56.0	62.6
Closing a business (years to resolve insolvency)	..	10.0	3.8
Total tax rate (% of profit)	..	70.6	67.4
Highest marginal tax rate, corporate (%)	40	34	
Business entry rate (new registrations as % of total)	3.8	5.3	6.4
Enterprise surveys			
Time dealing with gov't officials (% of management time)	..	6.7	
Firms expected to give gifts in meetings w/tax officials (%)	..	52.3	
Firms using banks to finance investments (% of firms)	..	19.4	
Delay in obtaining an electrical connection (days)	72.6	29.5	
ISO certification ownership (% of firms)	..	22.5	
Private sector investment			
Invest. in infrastructure w/private participation ($ millions)	3,068	17,183	29,785
Private foreign direct investment, net (% of GDP)	0.8	1.9	2.6
Gross fixed capital formation (% of GDP)	22.8	29.5	26.7
Gross fixed private capital formation (% of GDP)	16.3	22.2	19.6
Finance and banking			
Government cash surplus or deficit (% of GDP)	-3.9	-2.8	-2.6
Government debt (% of GDP)	56.0	60.0	..
Deposit money banks' assets (% of GDP)	41.1	57.1	50.5
Total financial system deposits (% of GDP)	42.6	53.0	44.6
Bank capital to asset ratio (%)	5.7	6.6	..
Bank nonperforming loans to total gross loans ratio (%)	12.8	3.5	..
Domestic credit to the private sector (% of GDP)	28.8	45.0	38.3
Real interest rate (%)	8.5	5.0	
Interest rate spread (percentage points)	..	..	11.3
Infrastructure			
Paved roads (% of total roads)	47.5	..	..
Electric power consumption (kWh per capita)	402	480	391
Power outages in a typical month (number)	..	..	
Fixed line and mobile subscribers (per 100 people)	4	19	17
Internet users (per 100 people)	0.5	5.5	4.2
Cost of telephone call to U.S. ($ per 3 minutes)	3.36	1.19	1.99

Indonesia

East Asia & Pacific			Lower middle income

	Country data		Lower middle-income group
	2000	2006	2006

Economic and social context

Population (millions)	206.3	223.0	2,276
Labor force (millions)	97.1	109.2	1,209
Unemployment rate (% of labor force)	6.1	10.3	5.7
GNI per capita, World Bank Atlas method ($)	590	1,420	2,038
GDP growth, 1995-2000 and 2000-06 (average annual %)	-0.6	4.9	7.6
Agriculture value added (% of GDP)	15.6	12.9	11.9
Industry value added (% of GDP)	45.9	47.0	43.5
Manufacturing value added (% of GDP)	27.7	28.0	26.7
Services value added (% of GDP)	38.5	40.1	44.6
Inflation (annual % change in consumer price index)	3.7	13.1	
Exchange rate (local currency units per $)	8,421.8	9,159.3	
Exports of goods and services (% of GDP)	41.0	30.9	40.4
Imports of goods and services (% of GDP)	30.5	26.1	36.4

Business environment

Ease of doing business (ranking 1-178; 1=best)	..	123	
Time to start a business (days)	..	105	53
Procedures to start a business (number)	..	12	10
Firing cost (weeks of wages)	..	108.0	50.2
Closing a business (years to resolve insolvency)	..	5.5	3.3
Total tax rate (% of profit)	..	37.3	45.8
Highest marginal tax rate, corporate (%)	30	30	
Business entry rate (new registrations as % of total)	3.0	7.6	7.6
Enterprise surveys			
Time dealing with gov't officials (% of management time)	..	4.0	
Firms expected to give gifts in meetings w/tax officials (%)	..	11.2	
Firms using banks to finance investments (% of firms)	..	13.9	
Delay in obtaining an electrical connection (days)	..	14.6	
ISO certification ownership (% of firms)	..	22.1	

Private sector investment

Invest. in infrastructure w/private participation ($ millions)	642	4,622	38,154
Private foreign direct investment, net (% of GDP)	-2.8	1.5	3.0
Gross fixed capital formation (% of GDP)	19.9	24.0	33.5
Gross fixed private capital formation (% of GDP)	..	..	10.9

Finance and banking

Government cash surplus or deficit (% of GDP)	-2.5	-1.1	-0.9
Government debt (% of GDP)	45.2	28.8	..
Deposit money banks' assets (% of GDP)	43.7	32.7	87.8
Total financial system deposits (% of GDP)	44.7	34.5	43.1
Bank capital to asset ratio (%)	6.0	10.7	10.7
Bank nonperforming loans to total gross loans ratio (%)	34.4	13.1	4.0
Domestic credit to the private sector (% of GDP)	19.9	24.6	81.3
Real interest rate (%)	-1.7	2.1	
Interest rate spread (percentage points)	6.0	4.6	7.2

Infrastructure

Paved roads (% of total roads)	57.1	55.3	65.8
Electric power consumption (kWh per capita)	400	509	1,502
Power outages in a typical month (number)	..	..	
Fixed line and mobile subscribers (per 100 people)	5	35	60
Internet users (per 100 people)	0.9	7.3	11.4
Cost of telephone call to U.S. ($ per 3 minutes)	3.90	2.79	2.08

Iran, Islamic Rep.

Middle East & North Africa			Lower middle income

	Country data		Lower middle-income group
	2000	**2006**	**2006**

Economic and social context

Population (millions)	63.9	70.1	2,276
Labor force (millions)	22.0	29.1	1,209
Unemployment rate (% of labor force)	12.8	11.5	5.7
GNI per capita, *World Bank Atlas* method ($)	1,670	2,930	2,038
GDP growth, 1995–2000 and 2000–06 (average annual %)	3.7	5.6	7.6
Agriculture value added (% of GDP)	13.7	10.4	11.9
Industry value added (% of GDP)	36.7	44.6	43.5
Manufacturing value added (% of GDP)	13.2	11.8	26.7
Services value added (% of GDP)	49.5	45.0	44.6
Inflation (annual % change in consumer price index)	14.5	11.9	
Exchange rate (local currency units per $)	1,764.4	9,170.9	
Exports of goods and services (% of GDP)	22.7	41.6	40.4
Imports of goods and services (% of GDP)	17.4	33.6	36.4

Business environment

Ease of doing business (ranking 1-178; 1=best)	..	135	
Time to start a business (days)	..	47	53
Procedures to start a business (number)	..	8	10
Firing cost (weeks of wages)	..	91.0	50.2
Closing a business (years to resolve insolvency)	..	4.5	3.3
Total tax rate (% of profit)	..	47.4	45.8
Highest marginal tax rate, corporate (%)	54	25	
Business entry rate (new registrations as % of total)	..	..	7.6
Enterprise surveys			
Time dealing with gov't officials (% of management time)	..	..	
Firms expected to give gifts in meetings w/tax officials (%)	..	..	
Firms using banks to finance investments (% of firms)	..	..	
Delay in obtaining an electrical connection (days)	..	..	
ISO certification ownership (% of firms)	..	..	

Private sector investment

Invest. in infrastructure w/private participation ($ millions)	5	350	38,154
Private foreign direct investment, net (% of GDP)	0.0	0.4	3.0
Gross fixed capital formation (% of GDP)	26.4	27.3	33.5
Gross fixed private capital formation (% of GDP)	17.6	18.1	10.9

Finance and banking

Government cash surplus or deficit (% of GDP)	1.8	3.3	–0.9
Government debt (% of GDP)	..	..	..
Deposit money banks' assets (% of GDP)	18.3	26.2	87.8
Total financial system deposits (% of GDP)	31.4	34.6	43.1
Bank capital to asset ratio (%)	..	..	10.7
Bank nonperforming loans to total gross loans ratio (%)	..	..	4.0
Domestic credit to the private sector (% of GDP)	28.3	47.3	81.3
Real interest rate (%)	..	2.7	
Interest rate spread (percentage points)	..	4.2	7.2

Infrastructure

Paved roads (% of total roads)	64.8	67.4	65.8
Electric power consumption (kWh per capita)	1,586	2,117	1,502
Power outages in a typical month (number)	..	..	
Fixed line and mobile subscribers (per 100 people)	16	51	60
Internet users (per 100 people)	1.0	25.7	11.4
Cost of telephone call to U.S. ($ per 3 minutes)	7.65	0.55	2.08

Iraq

Middle East & North Africa			Lower middle income

	Country data		Lower middle-income group
	2000	2006	2006

Economic and social context			
Population (millions)	24.4	..	2,276
Labor force (millions)	6.7	..	1,209
Unemployment rate (% of labor force)		26.8	5.7
GNI per capita, *World Bank Atlas* method ($)	..	..	2,038
GDP growth, 1995–2000 and 2000–06 (average annual %)	17.9	-11.4	7.6
Agriculture value added (% of GDP)	5.4	8.6	11.9
Industry value added (% of GDP)	84.4	70.1	43.5
Manufacturing value added (% of GDP)	0.9	1.7	26.7
Services value added (% of GDP)	10.3	21.3	44.6
Inflation (annual % change in consumer price index)	..	..	
Exchange rate (local currency units per $)	0.3	1,467.4	
Exports of goods and services (% of GDP)	..	..	40.4
Imports of goods and services (% of GDP)	..	..	36.4

Business environment			
Ease of doing business (ranking 1-178; 1=best)	..	141	
Time to start a business (days)	..	77	53
Procedures to start a business (number)	..	11	10
Firing cost (weeks of wages)	..	4.0	50.2
Closing a business (years to resolve insolvency)	..	..	3.3
Total tax rate (% of profit)	..	24.7	45.8
Highest marginal tax rate, corporate (%)	..	..	
Business entry rate (new registrations as % of total)	..	..	7.6
Enterprise surveys			
Time dealing with gov't officials (% of management time)	..	..	
Firms expected to give gifts in meetings w/tax officials (%)	..	..	
Firms using banks to finance investments (% of firms)	..	..	
Delay in obtaining an electrical connection (days)	..	..	
ISO certification ownership (% of firms)	..	..	

Private sector investment			
Invest. in infrastructure w/private participation ($ millions)	..	90	38,154
Private foreign direct investment, net (% of GDP)	..	..	3.0
Gross fixed capital formation (% of GDP)	..	..	33.5
Gross fixed private capital formation (% of GDP)	..	..	10.9

Finance and banking			
Government cash surplus or deficit (% of GDP)	..	..	-0.9
Government debt (% of GDP)	..	..	
Deposit money banks' assets (% of GDP)	..	..	87.8
Total financial system deposits (% of GDP)	..	..	43.1
Bank capital to asset ratio (%)	..	..	10.7
Bank nonperforming loans to total gross loans ratio (%)	..	..	4.0
Domestic credit to the private sector (% of GDP)	..	..	81.3
Real interest rate (%)	..	..	
Interest rate spread (percentage points)	..	..	7.2

Infrastructure			
Paved roads (% of total roads)	84.3	..	65.8
Electric power consumption (kWh per capita)	1,195	..	1,502
Power outages in a typical month (number)	..	..	
Fixed line and mobile subscribers (per 100 people)	3	6	60
Internet users (per 100 people)	0.0	0.1	11.4
Cost of telephone call to U.S. ($ per 3 minutes)	..	..	2.08

Ireland

High income

	Country data		High-income group
	2000	**2006**	**2006**
Economic and social context			
Population (millions)	3.8	4.3	1,031
Labor force (millions)	1.8	2.1	504
Unemployment rate (% of labor force)	4.3	4.3	6.2
GNI per capita, *World Bank Atlas* method ($)	23,160	44,830	36,608
GDP growth, 1995-2000 and 2000-06 (average annual %)	9.8	5.1	2.3
Agriculture value added (% of GDP)	3.4	2.1	1.5
Industry value added (% of GDP)	42.7	36.1	26.2
Manufacturing value added (% of GDP)	33.7	24.5	16.8
Services value added (% of GDP)	53.9	61.9	72.3
Inflation (annual % change in consumer price index)	5.6	3.9	
Exchange rate (local currency units per $)	1.1	0.8	
Exports of goods and services (% of GDP)	98.4	81.3	25.6
Imports of goods and services (% of GDP)	84.8	68.6	26.3
Business environment			
Ease of doing business (ranking 1-178; 1=best)	..	8	
Time to start a business (days)	..	13	22
Procedures to start a business (number)	..	4	7
Firing cost (weeks of wages)	..	24.0	34.9
Closing a business (years to resolve insolvency)	..	0.4	2.0
Total tax rate (% of profit)	..	28.9	41.5
Highest marginal tax rate, corporate (%)	32	13	
Business entry rate (new registrations as % of total)	9.0	10.7	10.1
Enterprise surveys			
Time dealing with gov't officials (% of management time)	..	..	
Firms expected to give gifts in meetings w/tax officials (%)	..	..	
Firms using banks to finance investments (% of firms)	..	..	
Delay in obtaining an electrical connection (days)	..	..	
ISO certification ownership (% of firms)	..	..	
Private sector investment			
Invest. in infrastructure w/private participation ($ millions)	..	..	849
Private foreign direct investment, net (% of GDP)	26.5	-0.4	2.7
Gross fixed capital formation (% of GDP)	24.3	27.0	20.4
Gross fixed private capital formation (% of GDP)	..	..	..
Finance and banking			
Government cash surplus or deficit (% of GDP)	4.9	2.7	-1.3
Government debt (% of GDP)	40.2	28.2	47.6
Deposit money banks' assets (% of GDP)	88.6	..	99.7
Total financial system deposits (% of GDP)	68.7	..	..
Bank capital to asset ratio (%)	6.5	4.3	6.2
Bank nonperforming loans to total gross loans ratio (%)	1.0	0.7	1.1
Domestic credit to the private sector (% of GDP)	105.8	183.4	162.0
Real interest rate (%)	-0.7	-0.8	
Interest rate spread (percentage points)	4.7	2.6	4.4
Infrastructure			
Paved roads (% of total roads)	100.0	100.0	90.9
Electric power consumption (kWh per capita)	5,796	6,234	9,760
Power outages in a typical month (number)	..	..	
Fixed line and mobile subscribers (per 100 people)	113	159	143
Internet users (per 100 people)	17.8	33.7	59.3
Cost of telephone call to U.S. ($ per 3 minutes)	0.80	0.71	0.77

Isle of Man

	Country data		High-income group
	2000	2006	2006
Economic and social context			
Population (millions)	0.07	0.08	1,031
Labor force (millions)	..	..	504
Unemployment rate (% of labor force)	1.6	..	6.2
GNI per capita, World Bank Atlas method ($)	23,170	40,600	36,608
GDP growth, 1995–2000 and 2000–06 (average annual %)	10.4	5.8	2.3
Agriculture value added (% of GDP)	..	..	1.5
Industry value added (% of GDP)	..	..	26.2
Manufacturing value added (% of GDP)	..	..	16.8
Services value added (% of GDP)	..	..	72.3
Inflation (annual % change in consumer price index)	..	..	
Exchange rate (local currency units per $)	0.7	0.5	
Exports of goods and services (% of GDP)	..	..	25.6
Imports of goods and services (% of GDP)	..	..	26.3
Business environment			
Ease of doing business (ranking 1-178; 1=best)	..	..	
Time to start a business (days)	..	..	22
Procedures to start a business (number)	..	..	7
Firing cost (weeks of wages)	..	..	34.9
Closing a business (years to resolve insolvency)	..	..	2.0
Total tax rate (% of profit)	..	..	41.5
Highest marginal tax rate, corporate (%)	..	..	
Business entry rate (new registrations as % of total)	..	..	10.1
Enterprise surveys			
Time dealing with gov't officials (% of management time)	..	..	
Firms expected to give gifts in meetings w/tax officials (%)	..	..	
Firms using banks to finance investments (% of firms)	..	..	
Delay in obtaining an electrical connection (days)	..	..	
ISO certification ownership (% of firms)	..	..	
Private sector investment			
Invest. in infrastructure w/private participation ($ millions)	..	..	849
Private foreign direct investment, net (% of GDP)	..	..	2.7
Gross fixed capital formation (% of GDP)	..	..	20.4
Gross fixed private capital formation (% of GDP)	..	..	..
Finance and banking			
Government cash surplus or deficit (% of GDP)	..	..	-1.3
Government debt (% of GDP)	..	..	47.6
Deposit money banks' assets (% of GDP)	..	..	99.7
Total financial system deposits (% of GDP)	..	..	..
Bank capital to asset ratio (%)	..	..	6.2
Bank nonperforming loans to total gross loans ratio (%)	..	..	1.1
Domestic credit to the private sector (% of GDP)	..	..	162.0
Real interest rate (%)	..	..	
Interest rate spread (percentage points)	..	..	4.4
Infrastructure			
Paved roads (% of total roads)	..	..	90.9
Electric power consumption (kWh per capita)	..	..	9,760
Power outages in a typical month (number)	..	..	
Fixed line and mobile subscribers (per 100 people)	..	..	143
Internet users (per 100 people)	..	..	59.3
Cost of telephone call to U.S. ($ per 3 minutes)	..	..	0.77

Israel

	Country data		High-income group
	2000	**2006**	**2006**
Economic and social context			
Population (millions)	6.3	7.0	1,031
Labor force (millions)	2.5	2.8	504
Unemployment rate (% of labor force)	8.8	9.0	6.2
GNI per capita, *World Bank Atlas* method ($)	17,890	20,170	36,608
GDP growth, 1995–2000 and 2000–06 (average annual %)	4.4	2.6	2.3
Agriculture value added (% of GDP)	..	..	1.5
Industry value added (% of GDP)	..	..	26.2
Manufacturing value added (% of GDP)	..	..	16.8
Services value added (% of GDP)	..	..	72.3
Inflation (annual % change in consumer price index)	1.1	2.1	
Exchange rate (local currency units per $)	4.1	4.5	
Exports of goods and services (% of GDP)	38.2	44.5	25.6
Imports of goods and services (% of GDP)	38.5	43.8	26.3
Business environment			
Ease of doing business (ranking 1-178; 1=best)	..	29	
Time to start a business (days)	..	34	22
Procedures to start a business (number)	..	5	7
Firing cost (weeks of wages)	..	91.0	34.9
Closing a business (years to resolve insolvency)	..	4.0	2.0
Total tax rate (% of profit)	..	36.0	41.5
Highest marginal tax rate, corporate (%)	36	31	
Business entry rate (new registrations as % of total)	5.0	3.9	10.1
Enterprise surveys			
Time dealing with gov't officials (% of management time)	..	..	
Firms expected to give gifts in meetings w/tax officials (%)	..	..	
Firms using banks to finance investments (% of firms)	..	..	
Delay in obtaining an electrical connection (days)	..	..	
ISO certification ownership (% of firms)	..	..	
Private sector investment			
Invest. in infrastructure w/private participation ($ millions)	..	..	849
Private foreign direct investment, net (% of GDP)	4.2	10.2	2.7
Gross fixed capital formation (% of GDP)	19.1	17.3	20.4
Gross fixed private capital formation (% of GDP)	..	..	..
Finance and banking			
Government cash surplus or deficit (% of GDP)	-2.1	-1.6	-1.3
Government debt (% of GDP)	..	..	47.6
Deposit money banks' assets (% of GDP)	85.5	97.5	99.7
Total financial system deposits (% of GDP)	78.0	87.2	..
Bank capital to asset ratio (%)	7.3	5.9	6.2
Bank nonperforming loans to total gross loans ratio (%)	6.9	1.9	1.1
Domestic credit to the private sector (% of GDP)	79.2	89.6	162.0
Real interest rate (%)	11.5	5.0	
Interest rate spread (percentage points)	4.2	3.2	4.4
Infrastructure			
Paved roads (% of total roads)	100.0	100.0	90.9
Electric power consumption (kWh per capita)	6,372	6,759	9,760
Power outages in a typical month (number)	..	..	
Fixed line and mobile subscribers (per 100 people)	117	162	143
Internet users (per 100 people)	20.2	26.9	59.3
Cost of telephone call to U.S. ($ per 3 minutes)	3.30	0.59	0.77

Italy

	Country data		High-income group
	2000	2006	2006
Economic and social context			
Population (millions)	56.9	58.8	1,031
Labor force (millions)	23.5	24.8	504
Unemployment rate (% of labor force)	10.5	7.7	6.2
GNI per capita, *World Bank Atlas* method ($)	20,900	31,990	36,608
GDP growth, 1995–2000 and 2000–06 (average annual %)	1.9	0.7	2.3
Agriculture value added (% of GDP)	2.8	2.1	1.5
Industry value added (% of GDP)	28.4	26.6	26.2
Manufacturing value added (% of GDP)	21.0	18.1	16.8
Services value added (% of GDP)	68.8	71.4	72.3
Inflation (annual % change in consumer price index)	2.5	2.1	
Exchange rate (local currency units per $)	1.1	0.8	
Exports of goods and services (% of GDP)	27.1	27.8	25.6
Imports of goods and services (% of GDP)	26.1	28.7	26.3
Business environment			
Ease of doing business (ranking 1-178; 1=best)	..	53	
Time to start a business (days)	..	13	22
Procedures to start a business (number)	..	9	7
Firing cost (weeks of wages)	..	2.0	34.9
Closing a business (years to resolve insolvency)	..	1.8	2.0
Total tax rate (% of profit)	..	76.2	41.5
Highest marginal tax rate, corporate (%)	36	33	
Business entry rate (new registrations as % of total)	6.8	6.2	10.1
Enterprise surveys			
Time dealing with gov't officials (% of management time)	..	..	
Firms expected to give gifts in meetings w/tax officials (%)	..	..	
Firms using banks to finance investments (% of firms)	..	..	
Delay in obtaining an electrical connection (days)	..	..	
ISO certification ownership (% of firms)	..	..	
Private sector investment			
Invest. in infrastructure w/private participation ($ millions)	..	..	849
Private foreign direct investment, net (% of GDP)	1.2	2.1	2.7
Gross fixed capital formation (% of GDP)	20.3	20.8	20.4
Gross fixed private capital formation (% of GDP)	..	..	..
Finance and banking			
Government cash surplus or deficit (% of GDP)	-0.7	-3.3	-1.3
Government debt (% of GDP)	119.4	109.8	47.6
Deposit money banks' assets (% of GDP)	74.8	..	99.7
Total financial system deposits (% of GDP)	42.2	..	..
Bank capital to asset ratio (%)	7.0	7.1	6.2
Bank nonperforming loans to total gross loans ratio (%)	7.8	5.3	1.1
Domestic credit to the private sector (% of GDP)	76.0	95.6	162.0
Real interest rate (%)	4.9	3.8	
Interest rate spread (percentage points)	5.2	4.9	4.4
Infrastructure			
Paved roads (% of total roads)	100.0	100.0	90.9
Electric power consumption (kWh per capita)	5,299	5,669	9,760
Power outages in a typical month (number)		..	
Fixed line and mobile subscribers (per 100 people)	122	165	143
Internet users (per 100 people)	23.2	49.0	59.3
Cost of telephone call to U.S. ($ per 3 minutes)	0.81	0.79	0.77

Jamaica

Latin America & Caribbean			Lower middle income

	Country data		Lower middle-income group
	2000	2006	2006

Economic and social context
Population (millions)	2.6	2.7	2,276
Labor force (millions)	1.2	1.2	1,209
Unemployment rate (% of labor force)	15.5	10.9	5.7
GNI per capita, World Bank Atlas method ($)	2,930	3,560	2,038
GDP growth, 1995–2000 and 2000–06 (average annual %)	-0.1	1.8	7.6
Agriculture value added (% of GDP)	6.7	5.9	11.9
Industry value added (% of GDP)	31.3	32.8	43.5
Manufacturing value added (% of GDP)	13.7	12.7	26.7
Services value added (% of GDP)	62.0	61.3	44.6
Inflation (annual % change in consumer price index)	8.2	8.6	
Exchange rate (local currency units per $)	43.0	65.7	
Exports of goods and services (% of GDP)	42.6	45.8	40.4
Imports of goods and services (% of GDP)	53.9	63.0	36.4

Business environment
Ease of doing business (ranking 1-178; 1=best)	..	63	
Time to start a business (days)	..	8	53
Procedures to start a business (number)	..	6	10
Firing cost (weeks of wages)	..	61.0	50.2
Closing a business (years to resolve insolvency)	..	1.1	3.3
Total tax rate (% of profit)	..	51.3	45.8
Highest marginal tax rate, corporate (%)	33	33	
Business entry rate (new registrations as % of total)	..	..	7.6
Enterprise surveys			
Time dealing with gov't officials (% of management time)	..	6.3	
Firms expected to give gifts in meetings w/tax officials (%)	..	4.9	
Firms using banks to finance investments (% of firms)	..	10.6	
Delay in obtaining an electrical connection (days)	..	6.9	
ISO certification ownership (% of firms)	..	16.4	

Private sector investment
Invest. in infrastructure w/private participation ($ millions)	546	180	38,154
Private foreign direct investment, net (% of GDP)	5.8	8.8	3.0
Gross fixed capital formation (% of GDP)	26.4	33.0	33.5
Gross fixed private capital formation (% of GDP)	23.6	29.3	10.9

Finance and banking
Government cash surplus or deficit (% of GDP)	-2.6	0.3	-0.9
Government debt (% of GDP)	111.0	140.1	..
Deposit money banks' assets (% of GDP)	40.9	46.7	87.8
Total financial system deposits (% of GDP)	37.2	45.7	43.1
Bank capital to asset ratio (%)	9.2	8.7	10.7
Bank nonperforming loans to total gross loans ratio (%)	11.0	2.6	4.0
Domestic credit to the private sector (% of GDP)	28.9	27.9	81.3
Real interest rate (%)	10.7	10.7	
Interest rate spread (percentage points)	11.7	10.6	7.2

Infrastructure
Paved roads (% of total roads)	70.1	73.9	65.8
Electric power consumption (kWh per capita)	2,321	2,474	1,502
Power outages in a typical month (number)	..	..	
Fixed line and mobile subscribers (per 100 people)	33	118	60
Internet users (per 100 people)	3.1	46.4	11.4
Cost of telephone call to U.S. ($ per 3 minutes)	5.20	0.87	2.08

Japan

High income

	Country data		High-income group
	2000	**2006**	**2006**
Economic and social context			
Population (millions)	126.9	127.8	1,031
Labor force (millions)	67.6	66.2	504
Unemployment rate (% of labor force)	4.8	4.4	6.2
GNI per capita, World Bank Atlas method ($)	34,620	38,630	36,608
GDP growth, 1995–2000 and 2000–06 (average annual %)	0.6	1.5	2.3
Agriculture value added (% of GDP)	1.8	1.5	1.5
Industry value added (% of GDP)	32.4	29.9	26.2
Manufacturing value added (% of GDP)	22.2	21.0	16.8
Services value added (% of GDP)	65.8	68.6	72.3
Inflation (annual % change in consumer price index)	–0.7	0.2	
Exchange rate (local currency units per $)	107.8	116.3	
Exports of goods and services (% of GDP)	11.0	14.3	25.6
Imports of goods and services (% of GDP)	9.5	13.0	26.3
Business environment			
Ease of doing business (ranking 1-178; 1=best)	..	12	
Time to start a business (days)	..	23	22
Procedures to start a business (number)	..	8	7
Firing cost (weeks of wages)	..	4.0	34.9
Closing a business (years to resolve insolvency)	..	0.6	2.0
Total tax rate (% of profit)	..	52.0	41.5
Highest marginal tax rate, corporate (%)	30	30	
Business entry rate (new registrations as % of total)	..	4.4	10.1
Enterprise surveys			
Time dealing with gov't officials (% of management time)	..	..	
Firms expected to give gifts in meetings w/tax officials (%)	..	..	
Firms using banks to finance investments (% of firms)	..	..	
Delay in obtaining an electrical connection (days)	..	..	
ISO certification ownership (% of firms)	..	..	
Private sector investment			
Invest. in infrastructure w/private participation ($ millions)	..	..	849
Private foreign direct investment, net (% of GDP)	0.2	–0.2	2.7
Gross fixed capital formation (% of GDP)	25.2	23.1	20.4
Gross fixed private capital formation (% of GDP)	..	..	..
Finance and banking			
Government cash surplus or deficit (% of GDP)	..	..	–1.3
Government debt (% of GDP)	..	..	47.6
Deposit money banks' assets (% of GDP)	236.4	154.6	99.7
Total financial system deposits (% of GDP)	230.1	190.1	..
Bank capital to asset ratio (%)	4.6	5.3	6.2
Bank nonperforming loans to total gross loans ratio (%)	5.3	2.5	1.1
Domestic credit to the private sector (% of GDP)	222.3	182.0	162.0
Real interest rate (%)	3.9	2.5	
Interest rate spread (percentage points)	2.0	1.0	4.4
Infrastructure			
Paved roads (% of total roads)	76.6	..	90.9
Electric power consumption (kWh per capita)	7,992	8,233	9,760
Power outages in a typical month (number)	..	..	
Fixed line and mobile subscribers (per 100 people)	101	123	143
Internet users (per 100 people)	30.0	68.5	59.3
Cost of telephone call to U.S. ($ per 3 minutes)	1.67	1.63	0.77

Jordan

Middle East & North Africa   **Lower middle income**

	Country data		Lower middle-income group
	2000	**2006**	**2006**
Economic and social context			
Population (millions)	4.8	5.5	2,276
Labor force (millions)	1.5	1.9	1,209
Unemployment rate (% of labor force)	15.8	12.4	5.7
GNI per capita, *World Bank Atlas* method ($)	1,790	2,650	2,038
GDP growth, 1995–2000 and 2000–06 (average annual %)	3.2	6.1	7.6
Agriculture value added (% of GDP)	2.3	3.1	11.9
Industry value added (% of GDP)	25.5	29.5	43.5
Manufacturing value added (% of GDP)	15.7	19.2	26.7
Services value added (% of GDP)	72.1	67.4	44.6
Inflation (annual % change in consumer price index)	0.7	6.3	
Exchange rate (local currency units per $)	0.7	0.7	
Exports of goods and services (% of GDP)	41.8	54.6	40.4
Imports of goods and services (% of GDP)	68.5	92.0	36.4
Business environment			
Ease of doing business (ranking 1-178; 1=best)	..	80	
Time to start a business (days)	..	14	53
Procedures to start a business (number)	..	10	10
Firing cost (weeks of wages)	..	4.0	50.2
Closing a business (years to resolve insolvency)	..	4.3	3.3
Total tax rate (% of profit)	..	31.1	45.8
Highest marginal tax rate, corporate (%)	..	..	
Business entry rate (new registrations as % of total)	5.7	7.5	7.6
Enterprise surveys			
Time dealing with gov't officials (% of management time)	..	6.7	
Firms expected to give gifts in meetings w/tax officials (%)	..	0.9	
Firms using banks to finance investments (% of firms)	..	8.6	
Delay in obtaining an electrical connection (days)	..	47.1	
ISO certification ownership (% of firms)	..	15.5	
Private sector investment			
Invest. in infrastructure w/private participation ($ millions)	584	364	38,154
Private foreign direct investment, net (% of GDP)	9.6	22.8	3.0
Gross fixed capital formation (% of GDP)	21.1	26.8	33.5
Gross fixed private capital formation (% of GDP)	11.9	18.6	10.9
Finance and banking			
Government cash surplus or deficit (% of GDP)	–2.0	–3.9	–0.9
Government debt (% of GDP)	93.7	77.5	..
Deposit money banks' assets (% of GDP)	86.4	108.7	87.8
Total financial system deposits (% of GDP)	85.7	111.3	43.1
Bank capital to asset ratio (%)	7.0	10.7	10.7
Bank nonperforming loans to total gross loans ratio (%)	18.4	4.3	4.0
Domestic credit to the private sector (% of GDP)	77.8	98.0	81.3
Real interest rate (%)	12.2	2.3	
Interest rate spread (percentage points)	4.8	3.6	7.2
Infrastructure			
Paved roads (% of total roads)	100.0	100.0	65.8
Electric power consumption (kWh per capita)	1,377	1,676	1,502
Power outages in a typical month (number)	..	2.6	
Fixed line and mobile subscribers (per 100 people)	21	90	60
Internet users (per 100 people)	2.7	14.4	11.4
Cost of telephone call to U.S. ($ per 3 minutes)	2.86	1.44	2.08

Kazakhstan

Europe & Central Asia   **Upper middle income**

	Country data		Upper middle-income group
	2000	2006	2006
Economic and social context			
Population (millions)	14.9	15.3	811
Labor force (millions)	7.5	8.1	374
Unemployment rate (% of labor force)	12.8	7.8	9.8
GNI per capita, World Bank Atlas method ($)	1,270	3,870	5,913
GDP growth, 1995–2000 and 2000–06 (average annual %)	1.9	10.1	3.9
Agriculture value added (% of GDP)	8.7	5.9	5.7
Industry value added (% of GDP)	40.5	42.1	32.4
Manufacturing value added (% of GDP)	17.7	12.4	19.4
Services value added (% of GDP)	50.8	52.0	62.0
Inflation (annual % change in consumer price index)	13.2	8.6	
Exchange rate (local currency units per $)	142.1	126.1	
Exports of goods and services (% of GDP)	56.6	51.1	32.7
Imports of goods and services (% of GDP)	49.1	40.4	30.3
Business environment			
Ease of doing business (ranking 1-178; 1=best)	..	71	
Time to start a business (days)	..	21	41
Procedures to start a business (number)	..	8	9
Firing cost (weeks of wages)	..	9.0	39.7
Closing a business (years to resolve insolvency)	..	3.3	2.9
Total tax rate (% of profit)	..	36.7	44.5
Highest marginal tax rate, corporate (%)	30	30	
Business entry rate (new registrations as % of total)	..	10.3	9.1
Enterprise surveys			
Time dealing with gov't officials (% of management time)	..	3.1	
Firms expected to give gifts in meetings w/tax officials (%)	55.0	55.7	
Firms using banks to finance investments (% of firms)	6.4	15.4	
Delay in obtaining an electrical connection (days)	7.2	13.9	
ISO certification ownership (% of firms)		9.9	
Private sector investment			
Invest. in infrastructure w/private participation ($ millions)	475	635	45,869
Private foreign direct investment, net (% of GDP)	7.0	7.6	3.5
Gross fixed capital formation (% of GDP)	17.3	29.1	19.9
Gross fixed private capital formation (% of GDP)	16.5	24.6	..
Finance and banking			
Government cash surplus or deficit (% of GDP)	0.1	1.6	..
Government debt (% of GDP)	21.6	7.1	
Deposit money banks' assets (% of GDP)	10.2	39.0	52.9
Total financial system deposits (% of GDP)	8.7	23.1	41.4
Bank capital to asset ratio (%)	13.6	8.9	9.8
Bank nonperforming loans to total gross loans ratio (%)	..	4.8	3.2
Domestic credit to the private sector (% of GDP)	11.2	47.8	41.4
Real interest rate (%)	..	..	
Interest rate spread (percentage points)	..	..	5.9
Infrastructure			
Paved roads (% of total roads)	86.5	84.0	..
Electric power consumption (kWh per capita)	2,650	3,206	3,131
Power outages in a typical month (number)	..	..	
Fixed line and mobile subscribers (per 100 people)	14	70	88
Internet users (per 100 people)	0.7	8.1	22.2
Cost of telephone call to U.S. ($ per 3 minutes)	2.76	..	1.06

Kenya

Sub-Saharan Africa			Low income

	Country data		Low-income group
	2000	2006	2006
Economic and social context			
Population (millions)	31.3	36.6	2,420
Labor force (millions)	14.0	16.7	995
Unemployment rate (% of labor force)	9.8	..	..
GNI per capita, *World Bank Atlas* method ($)	420	580	649
GDP growth, 1995–2000 and 2000–06 (average annual %)	2.1	3.9	6.5
Agriculture value added (% of GDP)	32.4	27.1	20.4
Industry value added (% of GDP)	16.9	18.8	27.7
Manufacturing value added (% of GDP)	11.6	11.5	15.8
Services value added (% of GDP)	50.7	54.1	51.9
Inflation (annual % change in consumer price index)	10.0	14.5	
Exchange rate (local currency units per $)	76.2	72.1	
Exports of goods and services (% of GDP)	21.6	26.2	26.7
Imports of goods and services (% of GDP)	29.6	36.0	30.1
Business environment			
Ease of doing business (ranking 1-178; 1=best)	..	72	
Time to start a business (days)	..	44	54
Procedures to start a business (number)	..	12	10
Firing cost (weeks of wages)	..	47.0	62.6
Closing a business (years to resolve insolvency)	..	4.5	3.8
Total tax rate (% of profit)	..	50.9	67.4
Highest marginal tax rate, corporate (%)	30	30	
Business entry rate (new registrations as % of total)	4.7	5.9	6.4
Enterprise surveys			
Time dealing with gov't officials (% of management time)	..	11.7	
Firms expected to give gifts in meetings w/tax officials (%)	..	37.3	
Firms using banks to finance investments (% of firms)	..	25.7	
Delay in obtaining an electrical connection (days)	..	51.3	
ISO certification ownership (% of firms)	..	..	
Private sector investment			
Invest. in infrastructure w/private participation ($ millions)	130	1,140	29,785
Private foreign direct investment, net (% of GDP)	0.9	0.2	2.6
Gross fixed capital formation (% of GDP)	16.7	18.8	26.7
Gross fixed private capital formation (% of GDP)	12.2	14.0	19.6
Finance and banking			
Government cash surplus or deficit (% of GDP)	2.0	1.5	-2.6
Government debt (% of GDP)	52.6	..	..
Deposit money banks' assets (% of GDP)	33.7	33.9	50.5
Total financial system deposits (% of GDP)	31.8	34.0	44.6
Bank capital to asset ratio (%)	12.9	..	..
Bank nonperforming loans to total gross loans ratio (%)	33.3	5.2	..
Domestic credit to the private sector (% of GDP)	28.4	25.8	38.3
Real interest rate (%)	15.3	6.1	
Interest rate spread (percentage points)	14.2	8.5	11.3
Infrastructure			
Paved roads (% of total roads)	12.1	14.1	..
Electric power consumption (kWh per capita)	110	138	391
Power outages in a typical month (number)	..	..	
Fixed line and mobile subscribers (per 100 people)	1	19	17
Internet users (per 100 people)	0.3	7.6	4.2
Cost of telephone call to U.S. ($ per 3 minutes)	7.35	3.00	1.99

Kiribati

East Asia & Pacific			**Lower middle income**

	Country data		Lower middle-income group
	2000	**2006**	**2006**
Economic and social context			
Population (millions)	0.09	0.10	2,276
Labor force (millions)	..	..	1,209
Unemployment rate (% of labor force)	..	..	5.7
GNI per capita, *World Bank Atlas* method ($)	1,030	1,240	2,038
GDP growth, 1995–2000 and 2000–06 (average annual %)	6.4	1.4	7.6
Agriculture value added (% of GDP)	7.0	7.1	11.9
Industry value added (% of GDP)	9.7	6.6	43.5
Manufacturing value added (% of GDP)	0.9	0.9	26.7
Services value added (% of GDP)	83.3	86.4	44.6
Inflation (annual % change in consumer price index)	..	..	
Exchange rate (local currency units per $)	1.7	1.3	
Exports of goods and services (% of GDP)	9.6	14.6	40.4
Imports of goods and services (% of GDP)	65.2	118.7	36.4
Business environment			
Ease of doing business (ranking 1-178; 1=best)	..	73	
Time to start a business (days)	..	21	53
Procedures to start a business (number)	..	6	10
Firing cost (weeks of wages)	..	4.0	50.2
Closing a business (years to resolve insolvency)	..	..	3.3
Total tax rate (% of profit)	..	31.8	45.8
Highest marginal tax rate, corporate (%)	..	..	
Business entry rate (new registrations as % of total)	..	..	7.6
Enterprise surveys			
Time dealing with gov't officials (% of management time)	..	..	
Firms expected to give gifts in meetings w/tax officials (%)	..	..	
Firms using banks to finance investments (% of firms)	..	..	
Delay in obtaining an electrical connection (days)	..	..	
ISO certification ownership (% of firms)	..	..	
Private sector investment			
Invest. in infrastructure w/private participation ($ millions)	..	..	38,154
Private foreign direct investment, net (% of GDP)	..	..	3.0
Gross fixed capital formation (% of GDP)	..	..	33.5
Gross fixed private capital formation (% of GDP)	..	..	10.9
Finance and banking			
Government cash surplus or deficit (% of GDP)	..	..	–0.9
Government debt (% of GDP)	..	..	..
Deposit money banks' assets (% of GDP)	..	..	87.8
Total financial system deposits (% of GDP)	..	..	43.1
Bank capital to asset ratio (%)	..	..	10.7
Bank nonperforming loans to total gross loans ratio (%)	..	..	4.0
Domestic credit to the private sector (% of GDP)	..	..	81.3
Real interest rate (%)	..	..	
Interest rate spread (percentage points)	..	..	7.2
Infrastructure			
Paved roads (% of total roads)	..	..	65.8
Electric power consumption (kWh per capita)	..	..	1,502
Power outages in a typical month (number)	..	..	
Fixed line and mobile subscribers (per 100 people)	4	..	60
Internet users (per 100 people)	1.7	2.0	11.4
Cost of telephone call to U.S. ($ per 3 minutes)	6.98	8.82	2.08

Korea, Dem. Rep.

East Asia & Pacific　　　　　　　　　　　　　　　　　**Low income**

	Country data		Low-income group
	2000	**2006**	**2006**
Economic and social context			
Population (millions)	22.9	23.7	2,420
Labor force (millions)	10.8	11.4	995
Unemployment rate (% of labor force)	..	..	
GNI per capita, *World Bank Atlas* method ($)	..	..	649
GDP growth, 1995-2000 and 2000-06 (average annual %)	..	..	6.5
Agriculture value added (% of GDP)	..	..	20.4
Industry value added (% of GDP)	..	..	27.7
Manufacturing value added (% of GDP)	..	..	15.8
Services value added (% of GDP)	..	..	51.9
Inflation (annual % change in consumer price index)	..	..	
Exchange rate (local currency units per $)	..	..	
Exports of goods and services (% of GDP)	..	..	26.7
Imports of goods and services (% of GDP)	..	..	30.1
Business environment			
Ease of doing business (ranking 1-178; 1=best)	..	..	
Time to start a business (days)	..	..	54
Procedures to start a business (number)	..	..	10
Firing cost (weeks of wages)	..	..	62.6
Closing a business (years to resolve insolvency)	..	..	3.8
Total tax rate (% of profit)	..	..	67.4
Highest marginal tax rate, corporate (%)	..	..	
Business entry rate (new registrations as % of total)	..	..	*6.4*
Enterprise surveys			
Time dealing with gov't officials (% of management time)	..	*3.2*	
Firms expected to give gifts in meetings w/tax officials (%)	..	..	
Firms using banks to finance investments (% of firms)	..	..	
Delay in obtaining an electrical connection (days)	..	..	
ISO certification ownership (% of firms)	..	..	
Private sector investment			
Invest. in infrastructure w/private participation ($ millions)	..	..	29,785
Private foreign direct investment, net (% of GDP)	..	..	2.6
Gross fixed capital formation (% of GDP)	..	..	26.7
Gross fixed private capital formation (% of GDP)	..	..	19.6
Finance and banking			
Government cash surplus or deficit (% of GDP)	..	..	-2.6
Government debt (% of GDP)	..	..	..
Deposit money banks' assets (% of GDP)	..	..	50.5
Total financial system deposits (% of GDP)	..	..	44.6
Bank capital to asset ratio (%)	..	..	..
Bank nonperforming loans to total gross loans ratio (%)	..	..	..
Domestic credit to the private sector (% of GDP)	..	..	38.3
Real interest rate (%)	..	..	
Interest rate spread (percentage points)	..	..	*11.3*
Infrastructure			
Paved roads (% of total roads)	6.4	..	..
Electric power consumption (kWh per capita)	712	817	391
Power outages in a typical month (number)	..	..	
Fixed line and mobile subscribers (per 100 people)	2	..	17
Internet users (per 100 people)	..	..	*4.2*
Cost of telephone call to U.S. ($ per 3 minutes)	..	..	*1.99*

Korea, Rep.

High income

	Country data		High-income group
	2000	**2006**	**2006**
Economic and social context			
Population (millions)	47.0	48.4	1,031
Labor force (millions)	22.6	24.5	504
Unemployment rate (% of labor force)	4.4	3.7	6.2
GNI per capita, *World Bank Atlas* method ($)	9,800	17,690	36,608
GDP growth, 1995–2000 and 2000–06 (average annual %)	3.5	4.6	2.3
Agriculture value added (% of GDP)	4.9	3.2	1.5
Industry value added (% of GDP)	40.7	39.6	26.2
Manufacturing value added (% of GDP)	29.4	27.8	16.8
Services value added (% of GDP)	54.4	57.2	72.3
Inflation (annual % change in consumer price index)	2.3	2.2	
Exchange rate (local currency units per $)	1,131.0	954.8	
Exports of goods and services (% of GDP)	40.8	43.2	25.6
Imports of goods and services (% of GDP)	37.7	42.1	26.3
Business environment			
Ease of doing business (ranking 1-178; 1=best)	..	30	
Time to start a business (days)	..	17	22
Procedures to start a business (number)	..	10	7
Firing cost (weeks of wages)	..	91.0	34.9
Closing a business (years to resolve insolvency)	..	1.5	2.0
Total tax rate (% of profit)	..	34.9	41.5
Highest marginal tax rate, corporate (%)	28	25	
Business entry rate (new registrations as % of total)	..	..	10.1
Enterprise surveys			
Time dealing with gov't officials (% of management time)	..	3.2	
Firms expected to give gifts in meetings w/tax officials (%)	..	21.3	
Firms using banks to finance investments (% of firms)	..	11.5	
Delay in obtaining an electrical connection (days)	..	3.9	
ISO certification ownership (% of firms)	..	17.6	
Private sector investment			
Invest. in infrastructure w/private participation ($ millions)	..	..	849
Private foreign direct investment, net (% of GDP)	1.8	0.4	2.7
Gross fixed capital formation (% of GDP)	31.1	29.0	20.4
Gross fixed private capital formation (% of GDP)	..	..	..
Finance and banking			
Government cash surplus or deficit (% of GDP)	4.6	0.7	-1.3
Government debt (% of GDP)	9.6	..	47.6
Deposit money banks' assets (% of GDP)	76.5	101.5	99.7
Total financial system deposits (% of GDP)	60.8	66.1	..
Bank capital to asset ratio (%)	4.6	9.2	6.2
Bank nonperforming loans to total gross loans ratio (%)	8.9	0.8	1.1
Domestic credit to the private sector (% of GDP)	91.1	102.0	162.0
Real interest rate (%)	7.8	6.4	
Interest rate spread (percentage points)	0.6	1.5	4.4
Infrastructure			
Paved roads (% of total roads)	74.5	76.8	90.9
Electric power consumption (kWh per capita)	5,264	7,779	9,760
Power outages in a typical month (number)	..	..	
Fixed line and mobile subscribers (per 100 people)	112	139	143
Internet users (per 100 people)	40.5	70.5	59.3
Cost of telephone call to U.S. ($ per 3 minutes)	1.93	0.76	0.77

Kuwait

	Country data		High-income group
	2000	2006	2006
Economic and social context			
Population (millions)	2.2	2.6	1,031
Labor force (millions)	1.1	1.4	504
Unemployment rate (% of labor force)	0.8	1.7	6.2
GNI per capita, *World Bank Atlas* method ($)	16,790	30,630	36,608
GDP growth, 1995–2000 and 2000–06 (average annual %)	1.8	7.3	2.3
Agriculture value added (% of GDP)	0.4	0.5	1.5
Industry value added (% of GDP)	59.2	51.1	26.2
Manufacturing value added (% of GDP)	2.6	2.3	16.8
Services value added (% of GDP)	40.5	48.5	72.3
Inflation (annual % change in consumer price index)	2.5	3.1	
Exchange rate (local currency units per $)	0.3	0.3	
Exports of goods and services (% of GDP)	56.5	67.7	25.6
Imports of goods and services (% of GDP)	30.1	30.4	26.3
Business environment			
Ease of doing business (ranking 1-178; 1=best)	..	40	
Time to start a business (days)	..	35	22
Procedures to start a business (number)	..	13	7
Firing cost (weeks of wages)	..	78.0	34.9
Closing a business (years to resolve insolvency)	..	4.2	2.0
Total tax rate (% of profit)	..	14.4	41.5
Highest marginal tax rate, corporate (%)	6	..	
Business entry rate (new registrations as % of total)	..	..	10.1
Enterprise surveys			
Time dealing with gov't officials (% of management time)	..	..	
Firms expected to give gifts in meetings w/tax officials (%)	..	..	
Firms using banks to finance investments (% of firms)	..	..	
Delay in obtaining an electrical connection (days)	..	..	
ISO certification ownership (% of firms)	..	..	
Private sector investment			
Invest. in infrastructure w/private participation ($ millions)	..	..	849
Private foreign direct investment, net (% of GDP)	0.0	0.3	2.7
Gross fixed capital formation (% of GDP)	10.7	19.7	20.4
Gross fixed private capital formation (% of GDP)	..	..	..
Finance and banking			
Government cash surplus or deficit (% of GDP)	–9.4	8.2	–1.3
Government debt (% of GDP)	..	..	47.6
Deposit money banks' assets (% of GDP)	77.5	52.9	99.7
Total financial system deposits (% of GDP)	64.6	46.3	..
Bank capital to asset ratio (%)	11.5	12.0	6.2
Bank nonperforming loans to total gross loans ratio (%)	19.2	3.9	1.1
Domestic credit to the private sector (% of GDP)	52.0	63.1	162.0
Real interest rate (%)	–9.7	–13.6	
Interest rate spread (percentage points)	3.0	3.7	4.4
Infrastructure			
Paved roads (% of total roads)	80.6	85.0	90.9
Electric power consumption (kWh per capita)	13,378	15,345	9,760
Power outages in a typical month (number)	..	..	
Fixed line and mobile subscribers (per 100 people)	43	114	143
Internet users (per 100 people)	6.8	31.4	59.3
Cost of telephone call to U.S. ($ per 3 minutes)	1.94	1.51	0.77

Kyrgyz Republic

Europe & Central Asia   **Low income**

	Country data		Low-income group
	2000	2006	2006
Economic and social context			
Population (millions)	4.9	5.2	2,420
Labor force (millions)	2.1	2.3	995
Unemployment rate (% of labor force)	12.5	8.5	..
GNI per capita, *World Bank Atlas* method ($)	280	500	649
GDP growth, 1995–2000 and 2000–06 (average annual %)	5.4	3.8	6.5
Agriculture value added (% of GDP)	36.7	33.0	20.4
Industry value added (% of GDP)	31.4	20.1	27.7
Manufacturing value added (% of GDP)	19.5	12.9	15.8
Services value added (% of GDP)	31.9	46.9	51.9
Inflation (annual % change in consumer price index)	18.7	5.6	
Exchange rate (local currency units per $)	47.7	40.2	
Exports of goods and services (% of GDP)	41.8	39.3	26.7
Imports of goods and services (% of GDP)	47.6	76.5	30.1
Business environment			
Ease of doing business (ranking 1-178; 1=best)	..	94	
Time to start a business (days)	..	21	54
Procedures to start a business (number)	..	8	10
Firing cost (weeks of wages)	..	17.0	62.6
Closing a business (years to resolve insolvency)	..	4.0	3.8
Total tax rate (% of profit)	..	61.4	67.4
Highest marginal tax rate, corporate (%)	30	..	
Business entry rate (new registrations as % of total)	..	..	6.4
Enterprise surveys			
Time dealing with gov't officials (% of management time)	..	6.1	
Firms expected to give gifts in meetings w/tax officials (%)	75.8	85.0	
Firms using banks to finance investments (% of firms)	6.4	7.9	
Delay in obtaining an electrical connection (days)	10.5	13.8	
ISO certification ownership (% of firms)	..	11.9	
Private sector investment			
Invest. in infrastructure w/private participation ($ millions)	5	36	29,785
Private foreign direct investment, net (% of GDP)	-0.2	6.5	2.6
Gross fixed capital formation (% of GDP)	18.3	16.9	26.7
Gross fixed private capital formation (% of GDP)	10.5	12.3	19.6
Finance and banking			
Government cash surplus or deficit (% of GDP)	..	-0.6	-2.6
Government debt (% of GDP)	114.5	..	..
Deposit money banks' assets (% of GDP)	4.2	9.8	50.5
Total financial system deposits (% of GDP)	4.9	9.4	44.6
Bank capital to asset ratio (%)	..	..	..
Bank nonperforming loans to total gross loans ratio (%)	..	..	..
Domestic credit to the private sector (% of GDP)	4.2	10.5	38.3
Real interest rate (%)	19.5	12.8	
Interest rate spread (percentage points)	33.5	17.6	11.3
Infrastructure			
Paved roads (% of total roads)	91.1	..	..
Electric power consumption (kWh per capita)	1,904	1,842	391
Power outages in a typical month (number)	..	..	
Fixed line and mobile subscribers (per 100 people)	8	19	17
Internet users (per 100 people)	1.0	5.7	4.2
Cost of telephone call to U.S. ($ per 3 minutes)	9.84	5.40	1.99

Lao PDR

	Country data		Low-income group
	2000	**2006**	**2006**
Economic and social context			
Population (millions)	5.2	5.8	2,420
Labor force (millions)	2.0	2.4	995
Unemployment rate (% of labor force)	..	1.4	..
GNI per capita, *World Bank Atlas* method ($)	290	500	649
GDP growth, 1995–2000 and 2000–06 (average annual %)	6.1	6.4	6.5
Agriculture value added (% of GDP)	52.5	42.0	20.4
Industry value added (% of GDP)	22.9	32.5	27.7
Manufacturing value added (% of GDP)	17.0	20.9	15.8
Services value added (% of GDP)	24.6	25.5	51.9
Inflation (annual % change in consumer price index)	25.1	6.8	
Exchange rate (local currency units per $)	7,887.6	10,159.9	
Exports of goods and services (% of GDP)	30.1	36.0	26.7
Imports of goods and services (% of GDP)	34.4	42.3	30.1
Business environment			
Ease of doing business (ranking 1-178; 1=best)	..	164	
Time to start a business (days)	..	103	54
Procedures to start a business (number)	..	8	10
Firing cost (weeks of wages)	..	19.0	62.6
Closing a business (years to resolve insolvency)	..	5.0	3.8
Total tax rate (% of profit)	..	35.5	67.4
Highest marginal tax rate, corporate (%)	..		
Business entry rate (new registrations as % of total)	..	..	6.4
Enterprise surveys			
Time dealing with gov't officials (% of management time)	..	4.5	
Firms expected to give gifts in meetings w/tax officials (%)	..	34.7	
Firms using banks to finance investments (% of firms)	..	13.8	
Delay in obtaining an electrical connection (days)	..	58.8	
ISO certification ownership (% of firms)	..	3.3	
Private sector investment			
Invest. in infrastructure w/private participation ($ millions)	5	810	29,785
Private foreign direct investment, net (% of GDP)	2.0	5.5	2.6
Gross fixed capital formation (% of GDP)	20.9	32.5	26.7
Gross fixed private capital formation (% of GDP)	6.9	25.7	19.6
Finance and banking			
Government cash surplus or deficit (% of GDP)	..	..	-2.6
Government debt (% of GDP)	..	..	
Deposit money banks' assets (% of GDP)	8.8	8.4	50.5
Total financial system deposits (% of GDP)	13.6	14.9	44.6
Bank capital to asset ratio (%)	..	..	..
Bank nonperforming loans to total gross loans ratio (%)	..	..	..
Domestic credit to the private sector (% of GDP)	8.9	6.0	38.3
Real interest rate (%)	5.5	24.2	
Interest rate spread (percentage points)	20.0	25.0	11.3
Infrastructure			
Paved roads (% of total roads)	44.5	14.4	..
Electric power consumption (kWh per capita)	..	..	391
Power outages in a typical month (number)	..	..	
Fixed line and mobile subscribers (per 100 people)	1	13	17
Internet users (per 100 people)	0.1	0.4	4.2
Cost of telephone call to U.S. ($ per 3 minutes)	9.20	1.11	1.99

Latvia

Europe & Central Asia **Upper middle income**

	Country data		Upper middle-income group
	2000	2006	2006
Economic and social context			
Population (millions)	2.4	2.3	811
Labor force (millions)	1.1	1.1	374
Unemployment rate (% of labor force)	14.0	8.7	9.8
GNI per capita, *World Bank Atlas* method ($)	3,220	8,100	5,913
GDP growth, 1995–2000 and 2000–06 (average annual %)	5.7	8.6	3.9
Agriculture value added (% of GDP)	4.6	3.7	5.7
Industry value added (% of GDP)	23.6	21.5	32.4
Manufacturing value added (% of GDP)	13.7	11.8	19.4
Services value added (% of GDP)	71.8	74.8	62.0
Inflation (annual % change in consumer price index)	2.7	6.6	
Exchange rate (local currency units per $)	0.6	0.6	
Exports of goods and services (% of GDP)	41.6	44.2	32.7
Imports of goods and services (% of GDP)	48.7	64.4	30.3
Business environment			
Ease of doing business (ranking 1-178; 1=best)	..	22	
Time to start a business (days)	..	16	41
Procedures to start a business (number)	..	5	9
Firing cost (weeks of wages)	..	17.0	39.7
Closing a business (years to resolve insolvency)	..	3.0	2.9
Total tax rate (% of profit)	..	32.6	44.5
Highest marginal tax rate, corporate (%)	25	15	
Business entry rate (new registrations as % of total)	3.7	5.6	9.1
Enterprise surveys			
Time dealing with gov't officials (% of management time)	..	2.9	
Firms expected to give gifts in meetings w/tax officials (%)	33.3	24.3	
Firms using banks to finance investments (% of firms)	10.2	15.1	
Delay in obtaining an electrical connection (days)	8.6	31.0	
ISO certification ownership (% of firms)	..	9.3	
Private sector investment			
Invest. in infrastructure w/private participation ($ millions)	229	252	45,869
Private foreign direct investment, net (% of GDP)	5.3	8.3	3.5
Gross fixed capital formation (% of GDP)	24.2	34.4	19.9
Gross fixed private capital formation (% of GDP)	20.5	24.1	..
Finance and banking			
Government cash surplus or deficit (% of GDP)	-2.2	-0.5	..
Government debt (% of GDP)	12.0	..	..
Deposit money banks' assets (% of GDP)	20.8	74.6	52.9
Total financial system deposits (% of GDP)	16.3	35.1	41.4
Bank capital to asset ratio (%)	8.5	7.6	9.8
Bank nonperforming loans to total gross loans ratio (%)	4.6	0.4	3.2
Domestic credit to the private sector (% of GDP)	19.2	86.8	41.4
Real interest rate (%)	7.4	-3.4	
Interest rate spread (percentage points)	7.5	3.8	5.9
Infrastructure			
Paved roads (% of total roads)	100.0	100.0	..
Electric power consumption (kWh per capita)	2,078	2,702	3,131
Power outages in a typical month (number)	..	..	
Fixed line and mobile subscribers (per 100 people)	48	124	88
Internet users (per 100 people)	6.3	46.8	22.2
Cost of telephone call to U.S. ($ per 3 minutes)	2.05	1.63	1.06

Lebanon

	Country data		Upper middle-income group
	2000	2006	2006

Economic and social context
Population (millions)	3.8	4.1	811
Labor force (millions)	1.4	1.6	374
Unemployment rate (% of labor force)	..	..	9.8
GNI per capita, *World Bank Atlas* method ($)	4,580	5,580	5,913
GDP growth, 1995–2000 and 2000–06 (average annual %)	2.5	3.7	3.9
Agriculture value added (% of GDP)	7.3	6.7	5.7
Industry value added (% of GDP)	23.7	23.7	32.4
Manufacturing value added (% of GDP)	13.7	11.4	19.4
Services value added (% of GDP)	69.0	69.6	62.0
Inflation (annual % change in consumer price index)	..	..	
Exchange rate (local currency units per $)	1,507.5	1,507.5	
Exports of goods and services (% of GDP)	13.8	23.7	32.7
Imports of goods and services (% of GDP)	36.8	39.9	30.3

Business environment
Ease of doing business (ranking 1-178; 1=best)	..	85	
Time to start a business (days)	..	46	41
Procedures to start a business (number)	..	6	9
Firing cost (weeks of wages)	..	17.0	39.7
Closing a business (years to resolve insolvency)	..	4.0	2.9
Total tax rate (% of profit)	..	35.4	44.5
Highest marginal tax rate, corporate (%)	..	..	
Business entry rate (new registrations as % of total)	5.0	4.9	9.1
Enterprise surveys			
Time dealing with gov't officials (% of management time)	..	12.0	
Firms expected to give gifts in meetings w/tax officials (%)	..	23.7	
Firms using banks to finance investments (% of firms)	..	26.8	
Delay in obtaining an electrical connection (days)	..	71.6	
ISO certification ownership (% of firms)	..	20.9	

Private sector investment
Invest. in infrastructure w/private participation ($ millions)	196	3	45,869
Private foreign direct investment, net (% of GDP)	5.7	12.3	3.5
Gross fixed capital formation (% of GDP)	20.8	12.2	19.9
Gross fixed private capital formation (% of GDP)	15.9	9.7	..

Finance and banking
Government cash surplus or deficit (% of GDP)	-18.9	-8.5	..
Government debt (% of GDP)	..	..	..
Deposit money banks' assets (% of GDP)	..	..	52.9
Total financial system deposits (% of GDP)	..	..	41.4
Bank capital to asset ratio (%)	6.4	8.4	9.8
Bank nonperforming loans to total gross loans ratio (%)	7.8	13.5	3.2
Domestic credit to the private sector (% of GDP)	90.2	77.9	41.4
Real interest rate (%)	21.3	4.4	
Interest rate spread (percentage points)	6.9	2.3	5.9

Infrastructure
Paved roads (% of total roads)	84.9	..	..
Electric power consumption (kWh per capita)	2,081	2,242	3,131
Power outages in a typical month (number)	..	..	
Fixed line and mobile subscribers (per 100 people)	35	44	88
Internet users (per 100 people)	8.0	23.4	22.2
Cost of telephone call to U.S. ($ per 3 minutes)	4.48	2.19	1.06

Lesotho

Sub-Saharan Africa			Lower middle income

	Country data		Lower middle-income group
	2000	**2006**	**2006**
Economic and social context			
Population (millions)	1.9	2.0	2,276
Labor force (millions)	0.67	0.70	1,209
Unemployment rate (% of labor force)	39.3	..	5.7
GNI per capita, *World Bank Atlas* method ($)	590	980	2,038
GDP growth, 1995–2000 and 2000–06 (average annual %)	2.4	3.4	7.6
Agriculture value added (% of GDP)	17.9	16.3	11.9
Industry value added (% of GDP)	41.4	43.2	43.5
Manufacturing value added (% of GDP)	17.0	17.9	26.7
Services value added (% of GDP)	40.7	40.5	44.6
Inflation (annual % change in consumer price index)	6.1	6.0	
Exchange rate (local currency units per $)	6.9	6.8	
Exports of goods and services (% of GDP)	30.0	50.5	40.4
Imports of goods and services (% of GDP)	93.1	98.5	36.4
Business environment			
Ease of doing business (ranking 1-178; 1=best)	..	124	
Time to start a business (days)	..	73	53
Procedures to start a business (number)	..	8	10
Firing cost (weeks of wages)	..	44.0	50.2
Closing a business (years to resolve insolvency)	..	2.6	3.3
Total tax rate (% of profit)	..	20.8	45.8
Highest marginal tax rate, corporate (%)	..	..	
Business entry rate (new registrations as % of total)	..	..	7.6
Enterprise surveys			
Time dealing with gov't officials (% of management time)	..	19.8	
Firms expected to give gifts in meetings w/tax officials (%)	..	5.3	
Firms using banks to finance investments (% of firms)	..	6.7	
Delay in obtaining an electrical connection (days)	..	51.4	
ISO certification ownership (% of firms)	..	8.6	
Private sector investment			
Invest. in infrastructure w/private participation ($ millions)	3	6	38,154
Private foreign direct investment, net (% of GDP)	13.8	5.2	3.0
Gross fixed capital formation (% of GDP)	44.9	33.3	33.5
Gross fixed private capital formation (% of GDP)	36.9	26.1	10.9
Finance and banking			
Government cash surplus or deficit (% of GDP)	–2.6	4.1	–0.9
Government debt (% of GDP)	68.3	..	..
Deposit money banks' assets (% of GDP)	..	14.1	87.8
Total financial system deposits (% of GDP)	..	26.6	43.1
Bank capital to asset ratio (%)	..	..	10.7
Bank nonperforming loans to total gross loans ratio (%)	..	1.0	4.0
Domestic credit to the private sector (% of GDP)	14.3	8.9	81.3
Real interest rate (%)	12.1	7.7	
Interest rate spread (percentage points)	12.2	7.6	7.2
Infrastructure			
Paved roads (% of total roads)	18.3	..	65.8
Electric power consumption (kWh per capita)	..	..	1,502
Power outages in a typical month (number)	..	..	
Fixed line and mobile subscribers (per 100 people)	2	15	60
Internet users (per 100 people)	0.2	2.6	11.4
Cost of telephone call to U.S. ($ per 3 minutes)	2.31	3.28	2.08

Liberia

	Country data		Low-income group
	2000	2006	2006
Economic and social context			
Population (millions)	3.1	3.6	2,420
Labor force (millions)	1.1	1.3	995
Unemployment rate (% of labor force)	..	..	
GNI per capita, *World Bank Atlas* method ($)	130	130	649
GDP growth, 1995-2000 and 2000-06 (average annual %)	38.9	-4.7	6.5
Agriculture value added (% of GDP)	72.0	66.0	20.4
Industry value added (% of GDP)	11.6	15.8	27.7
Manufacturing value added (% of GDP)	9.4	12.4	15.8
Services value added (% of GDP)	16.4	18.2	51.9
Inflation (annual % change in consumer price index)	..	..	
Exchange rate (local currency units per $)	41.0	58.0	
Exports of goods and services (% of GDP)	21.5	27.8	26.7
Imports of goods and services (% of GDP)	26.0	71.9	30.1
Business environment			
Ease of doing business (ranking 1-178; 1=best)	..	170	
Time to start a business (days)	..	99	54
Procedures to start a business (number)	..	12	10
Firing cost (weeks of wages)	..	84.0	62.6
Closing a business (years to resolve insolvency)	..	3.0	3.8
Total tax rate (% of profit)	..	81.6	67.4
Highest marginal tax rate, corporate (%)	..	..	
Business entry rate (new registrations as % of total)	..	..	6.4
Enterprise surveys			
Time dealing with gov't officials (% of management time)	..	..	
Firms expected to give gifts in meetings w/tax officials (%)	..	..	
Firms using banks to finance investments (% of firms)	..	..	
Delay in obtaining an electrical connection (days)	..	..	
ISO certification ownership (% of firms)	..	..	
Private sector investment			
Invest. in infrastructure w/private participation ($ millions)	..	11	29,785
Private foreign direct investment, net (% of GDP)	3.7	-13.0	2.6
Gross fixed capital formation (% of GDP)	4.9	16.5	26.7
Gross fixed private capital formation (% of GDP)	2.0	4.3	19.6
Finance and banking			
Government cash surplus or deficit (% of GDP)	..	..	-2.6
Government debt (% of GDP)	..	..	..
Deposit money banks' assets (% of GDP)	..	..	50.5
Total financial system deposits (% of GDP)	..	..	44.6
Bank capital to asset ratio (%)	..	..	..
Bank nonperforming loans to total gross loans ratio (%)	..	..	..
Domestic credit to the private sector (% of GDP)	3.1	8.4	38.3
Real interest rate (%)	22.1	2.7	
Interest rate spread (percentage points)	14.3	13.6	11.3
Infrastructure			
Paved roads (% of total roads)	6.2	..	..
Electric power consumption (kWh per capita)	..	..	391
Power outages in a typical month (number)	..	..	
Fixed line and mobile subscribers (per 100 people)	0	..	17
Internet users (per 100 people)	0.0	..	4.2
Cost of telephone call to U.S. ($ per 3 minutes)	..	..	1.99

Libya

Middle East & North Africa			Upper middle income

	Country data		Upper middle-income group
	2000	2006	2006

Economic and social context
Population (millions)	5.3	6.0	811
Labor force (millions)	2.0	2.5	374
Unemployment rate (% of labor force)	..	..	9.8
GNI per capita, *World Bank Atlas* method ($)	..	7,290	5,913
GDP growth, 1995–2000 and 2000–06 (average annual %)	..	3.2	3.9
Agriculture value added (% of GDP)	..	..	5.7
Industry value added (% of GDP)	..	..	32.4
Manufacturing value added (% of GDP)	..	..	19.4
Services value added (% of GDP)	..	..	62.0
Inflation (annual % change in consumer price index)	-2.9	3.4	
Exchange rate (local currency units per $)	0.5	1.3	
Exports of goods and services (% of GDP)	35.0	..	32.7
Imports of goods and services (% of GDP)	15.2	..	30.3

Business environment
Ease of doing business (ranking 1-178; 1=best)	..	..	
Time to start a business (days)	..	..	41
Procedures to start a business (number)	..	..	9
Firing cost (weeks of wages)	..	..	39.7
Closing a business (years to resolve insolvency)	..	..	2.9
Total tax rate (% of profit)	..	..	44.5
Highest marginal tax rate, corporate (%)	..	..	
Business entry rate (new registrations as % of total)	..	..	9.1
Enterprise surveys			
Time dealing with gov't officials (% of management time)	..	..	
Firms expected to give gifts in meetings w/tax officials (%)	..	..	
Firms using banks to finance investments (% of firms)	..	..	
Delay in obtaining an electrical connection (days)	..	..	
ISO certification ownership (% of firms)	..	..	

Private sector investment
Invest. in infrastructure w/private participation ($ millions)	..	..	45,869
Private foreign direct investment, net (% of GDP)	..	..	3.5
Gross fixed capital formation (% of GDP)	12.9	..	19.9
Gross fixed private capital formation (% of GDP)	..	..	..

Finance and banking
Government cash surplus or deficit (% of GDP)	..	..	..
Government debt (% of GDP)	..	..	..
Deposit money banks' assets (% of GDP)	32.1	..	52.9
Total financial system deposits (% of GDP)	26.5	..	41.4
Bank capital to asset ratio (%)	..	..	9.8
Bank nonperforming loans to total gross loans ratio (%)	..	..	3.2
Domestic credit to the private sector (% of GDP)	27.0	15.5	41.4
Real interest rate (%)	-13.4	-7.4	
Interest rate spread (percentage points)	4.0	3.8	5.9

Infrastructure
Paved roads (% of total roads)	57.2	..	..
Electric power consumption (kWh per capita)	2,227	3,299	3,131
Power outages in a typical month (number)	..	..	
Fixed line and mobile subscribers (per 100 people)	12	73	88
Internet users (per 100 people)	0.2	3.9	22.2
Cost of telephone call to U.S. ($ per 3 minutes)	..	..	1.06

Liechtenstein

	Country data		High-income group
	2000	2006	2006
Economic and social context			
Population (millions)	..	0.03	1,031
Labor force (millions)	..	..	504
Unemployment rate (% of labor force)	..	..	6.2
GNI per capita, *World Bank Atlas* method ($)	..	..	36,608
GDP growth, 1995–2000 and 2000–06 (average annual %)	..	..	2.3
Agriculture value added (% of GDP)	..	..	1.5
Industry value added (% of GDP)	..	..	26.2
Manufacturing value added (% of GDP)	..	..	16.8
Services value added (% of GDP)	..	..	72.3
Inflation (annual % change in consumer price index)	..	..	
Exchange rate (local currency units per $)	..	..	
Exports of goods and services (% of GDP)	..	..	25.6
Imports of goods and services (% of GDP)	..	..	26.3
Business environment			
Ease of doing business (ranking 1-178; 1=best)	..	..	
Time to start a business (days)	..	..	22
Procedures to start a business (number)	..	..	7
Firing cost (weeks of wages)	..	..	34.9
Closing a business (years to resolve insolvency)	..	..	2.0
Total tax rate (% of profit)	..	..	41.5
Highest marginal tax rate, corporate (%)	15	15	
Business entry rate (new registrations as % of total)	..	..	10.1
Enterprise surveys			
Time dealing with gov't officials (% of management time)	..	..	
Firms expected to give gifts in meetings w/tax officials (%)	..	..	
Firms using banks to finance investments (% of firms)	..	..	
Delay in obtaining an electrical connection (days)	..	..	
ISO certification ownership (% of firms)	..	..	
Private sector investment			
Invest. in infrastructure w/private participation ($ millions)	..	..	849
Private foreign direct investment, net (% of GDP)	..	..	2.7
Gross fixed capital formation (% of GDP)	..	..	20.4
Gross fixed private capital formation (% of GDP)	..	..	..
Finance and banking			
Government cash surplus or deficit (% of GDP)	..	..	–1.3
Government debt (% of GDP)	..	..	47.6
Deposit money banks' assets (% of GDP)	..	..	99.7
Total financial system deposits (% of GDP)	..	..	..
Bank capital to asset ratio (%)	..	..	6.2
Bank nonperforming loans to total gross loans ratio (%)	..	..	1.1
Domestic credit to the private sector (% of GDP)	..	..	162.0
Real interest rate (%)	..	..	
Interest rate spread (percentage points)	..	..	4.4
Infrastructure			
Paved roads (% of total roads)	..	..	90.9
Electric power consumption (kWh per capita)	..	..	9,760
Power outages in a typical month (number)	..	..	
Fixed line and mobile subscribers (per 100 people)	..	140	143
Internet users (per 100 people)	..	63.0	59.3
Cost of telephone call to U.S. ($ per 3 minutes)	..	..	0.77

Lithuania

Europe & Central Asia   **Upper middle income**

	Country data		Upper middle-income group
	2000	2006	2006
Economic and social context			
Population (millions)	3.5	3.4	811
Labor force (millions)	1.7	1.6	374
Unemployment rate (% of labor force)	16.4	8.3	9.8
GNI per capita, World Bank Atlas method ($)	3,020	7,930	5,913
GDP growth, 1995–2000 and 2000–06 (average annual %)	4.3	8.0	3.9
Agriculture value added (% of GDP)	7.8	5.3	5.7
Industry value added (% of GDP)	29.8	35.3	32.4
Manufacturing value added (% of GDP)	19.4	17.6	19.4
Services value added (% of GDP)	62.4	59.4	62.0
Inflation (annual % change in consumer price index)	1.0	3.8	
Exchange rate (local currency units per $)	4.0	2.8	
Exports of goods and services (% of GDP)	44.8	59.7	32.7
Imports of goods and services (% of GDP)	51.1	70.1	30.3
Business environment			
Ease of doing business (ranking 1-178; 1=best)	..	26	
Time to start a business (days)	..	26	41
Procedures to start a business (number)	..	7	9
Firing cost (weeks of wages)	..	30.0	39.7
Closing a business (years to resolve insolvency)	..	1.7	2.9
Total tax rate (% of profit)	..	48.3	44.5
Highest marginal tax rate, corporate (%)	24	15	
Business entry rate (new registrations as % of total)	5.5	6.3	9.1
Enterprise surveys			
Time dealing with gov't officials (% of management time)	..	5.1	
Firms expected to give gifts in meetings w/tax officials (%)	26.3	31.9	
Firms using banks to finance investments (% of firms)	10.0	15.6	
Delay in obtaining an electrical connection (days)	4.3	30.2	
ISO certification ownership (% of firms)	..	15.1	
Private sector investment			
Invest. in infrastructure w/private participation ($ millions)	388	119	45,869
Private foreign direct investment, net (% of GDP)	3.3	6.1	3.5
Gross fixed capital formation (% of GDP)	18.8	24.8	19.9
Gross fixed private capital formation (% of GDP)	16.4	21.7	..
Finance and banking			
Government cash surplus or deficit (% of GDP)	-2.8	-0.2	..
Government debt (% of GDP)	..	20.0	..
Deposit money banks' assets (% of GDP)	18.2	47.4	52.9
Total financial system deposits (% of GDP)	15.4	32.1	41.4
Bank capital to asset ratio (%)	10.2	7.1	9.8
Bank nonperforming loans to total gross loans ratio (%)	11.3	1.0	3.2
Domestic credit to the private sector (% of GDP)	13.2	50.6	41.4
Real interest rate (%)	11.4	-1.4	
Interest rate spread (percentage points)	8.3	4.5	5.9
Infrastructure			
Paved roads (% of total roads)	91.3	78.2	..
Electric power consumption (kWh per capita)	2,517	3,104	3,131
Power outages in a typical month (number)	..	..	
Fixed line and mobile subscribers (per 100 people)	49	162	88
Internet users (per 100 people)	6.4	31.9	22.2
Cost of telephone call to U.S. ($ per 3 minutes)	3.10	1.55	1.06

Luxembourg

	Country data		High-income group
	2000	2006	2006
Economic and social context			
Population (millions)	0.44	0.46	1,031
Labor force (millions)	0.19	0.20	504
Unemployment rate (% of labor force)	2.3	4.5	6.2
GNI per capita, World Bank Atlas method ($)	43,490	71,240	36,608
GDP growth, 1995–2000 and 2000–06 (average annual %)	6.3	3.4	2.3
Agriculture value added (% of GDP)	0.7	0.4	1.5
Industry value added (% of GDP)	18.4	14.6	26.2
Manufacturing value added (% of GDP)	11.3	8.8	16.8
Services value added (% of GDP)	81.0	85.0	72.3
Inflation (annual % change in consumer price index)	3.1	2.7	
Exchange rate (local currency units per $)	1.1	0.8	
Exports of goods and services (% of GDP)	150.0	177.2	25.6
Imports of goods and services (% of GDP)	129.0	149.4	26.3
Business environment			
Ease of doing business (ranking 1-178; 1=best)	..	42	
Time to start a business (days)	..	26	22
Procedures to start a business (number)	..	6	7
Firing cost (weeks of wages)	..	39.0	34.9
Closing a business (years to resolve insolvency)	..	2.0	2.0
Total tax rate (% of profit)	..	35.3	41.5
Highest marginal tax rate, corporate (%)	30	23	
Business entry rate (new registrations as % of total)	11.9	10.7	10.1
Enterprise surveys			
Time dealing with gov't officials (% of management time)	..	..	
Firms expected to give gifts in meetings w/tax officials (%)	..	..	
Firms using banks to finance investments (% of firms)	..	..	
Delay in obtaining an electrical connection (days)	..	..	
ISO certification ownership (% of firms)	..	..	
Private sector investment			
Invest. in infrastructure w/private participation ($ millions)	..	..	849
Private foreign direct investment, net (% of GDP)	522.2	304.9	2.7
Gross fixed capital formation (% of GDP)	20.8	18.3	20.4
Gross fixed private capital formation (% of GDP)	..	..	..
Finance and banking			
Government cash surplus or deficit (% of GDP)	5.5	0.9	-1.3
Government debt (% of GDP)	4.9	4.6	47.6
Deposit money banks' assets (% of GDP)	..	..	99.7
Total financial system deposits (% of GDP)	..	..	..
Bank capital to asset ratio (%)	4.0	4.6	6.2
Bank nonperforming loans to total gross loans ratio (%)	0.5	0.2	1.1
Domestic credit to the private sector (% of GDP)	102.2	158.7	162.0
Real interest rate (%)	5.7	..	
Interest rate spread (percentage points)	2.0	..	4.4
Infrastructure			
Paved roads (% of total roads)	100.0	100.0	90.9
Electric power consumption (kWh per capita)	15,425	15,971	9,760
Power outages in a typical month (number)	..	..	
Fixed line and mobile subscribers (per 100 people)	126	208	143
Internet users (per 100 people)	22.8	73.4	59.3
Cost of telephone call to U.S. ($ per 3 minutes)	15.96	..	0.77

Macao, China

High income

	Country data		High-income group
	2000	**2006**	**2006**
Economic and social context			
Population (millions)	0.44	0.48	1,031
Labor force (millions)	0.22	0.28	504
Unemployment rate (% of labor force)	6.6	4.1	6.2
GNI per capita, *World Bank Atlas* method ($)	14,250	..	36,608
GDP growth, 1995–2000 and 2000–06 (average annual %)	–1.1	13.9	2.3
Agriculture value added (% of GDP)	..	..	1.5
Industry value added (% of GDP)	15.7	18.7	26.2
Manufacturing value added (% of GDP)	10.1	3.9	16.8
Services value added (% of GDP)	90.3	85.1	72.3
Inflation (annual % change in consumer price index)	–1.6	5.1	
Exchange rate (local currency units per $)	8.0	8.0	
Exports of goods and services (% of GDP)	104.3	92.2	25.6
Imports of goods and services (% of GDP)	67.1	58.3	26.3
Business environment			
Ease of doing business (ranking 1-178; 1=best)	..	..	
Time to start a business (days)	..	..	22
Procedures to start a business (number)	..	..	7
Firing cost (weeks of wages)	..	..	34.9
Closing a business (years to resolve insolvency)	..	..	2.0
Total tax rate (% of profit)	..	..	41.5
Highest marginal tax rate, corporate (%)	15	12	
Business entry rate (new registrations as % of total)	..	..	10.1
Enterprise surveys			
Time dealing with gov't officials (% of management time)	..	..	
Firms expected to give gifts in meetings w/tax officials (%)	..	..	
Firms using banks to finance investments (% of firms)	..	..	
Delay in obtaining an electrical connection (days)	..	..	
ISO certification ownership (% of firms)	..	..	
Private sector investment			
Invest. in infrastructure w/private participation ($ millions)	..	..	849
Private foreign direct investment, net (% of GDP)	6.2	18.7	2.7
Gross fixed capital formation (% of GDP)	11.9	33.8	20.4
Gross fixed private capital formation (% of GDP)	..	..	..
Finance and banking			
Government cash surplus or deficit (% of GDP)	1.7	10.2	–1.3
Government debt (% of GDP)			47.6
Deposit money banks' assets (% of GDP)	82.8	41.4	99.7
Total financial system deposits (% of GDP)	170.8	129.4	..
Bank capital to asset ratio (%)	..	..	6.2
Bank nonperforming loans to total gross loans ratio (%)	..	..	1.1
Domestic credit to the private sector (% of GDP)	83.0	42.8	162.0
Real interest rate (%)	11.0	2.6	
Interest rate spread (percentage points)	4.6	5.9	4.4
Infrastructure			
Paved roads (% of total roads)	100.0	100.0	90.9
Electric power consumption (kWh per capita)	..	..	9,760
Power outages in a typical month (number)	..	..	
Fixed line and mobile subscribers (per 100 people)	72	170	143
Internet users (per 100 people)	13.6	41.9	59.3
Cost of telephone call to U.S. ($ per 3 minutes)	1.12	1.12	0.77

Macedonia, FYR

Europe & Central Asia			Lower middle income

	Country data		Lower middle-income group
	2000	2006	2006
Economic and social context			
Population (millions)	2.0	2.0	2,276
Labor force (millions)	0.83	0.87	1,209
Unemployment rate (% of labor force)	32.2	37.3	5.7
GNI per capita, *World Bank Atlas* method ($)	1,850	3,070	2,038
GDP growth, 1995–2000 and 2000–06 (average annual %)	3.0	2.2	7.6
Agriculture value added (% of GDP)	12.0	13.0	11.9
Industry value added (% of GDP)	33.7	29.3	43.5
Manufacturing value added (% of GDP)	20.7	18.6	26.7
Services value added (% of GDP)	54.2	57.7	44.6
Inflation (annual % change in consumer price index)	6.6	3.3	
Exchange rate (local currency units per $)	65.9	48.8	
Exports of goods and services (% of GDP)	48.6	49.8	40.4
Imports of goods and services (% of GDP)	63.5	68.5	36.4
Business environment			
Ease of doing business (ranking 1-178; 1=best)	..	75	
Time to start a business (days)	..	15	53
Procedures to start a business (number)	..	9	10
Firing cost (weeks of wages)	..	26.0	50.2
Closing a business (years to resolve insolvency)	..	3.7	3.3
Total tax rate (% of profit)	..	49.8	45.8
Highest marginal tax rate, corporate (%)	..	15	
Business entry rate (new registrations as % of total)	7.3	6.8	7.6
Enterprise surveys			
Time dealing with gov't officials (% of management time)	..	8.2	
Firms expected to give gifts in meetings w/tax officials (%)	42.7	33.7	
Firms using banks to finance investments (% of firms)	4.7	9.0	
Delay in obtaining an electrical connection (days)	10.8	7.0	
ISO certification ownership (% of firms)	..	11.0	
Private sector investment			
Invest. in infrastructure w/private participation ($ millions)	429	493	38,154
Private foreign direct investment, net (% of GDP)	4.9	5.6	3.0
Gross fixed capital formation (% of GDP)	16.2	17.5	33.5
Gross fixed private capital formation (% of GDP)	11.5	11.5	10.9
Finance and banking			
Government cash surplus or deficit (% of GDP)	..	..	–0.9
Government debt (% of GDP)	..	..	..
Deposit money banks' assets (% of GDP)	..	..	87.8
Total financial system deposits (% of GDP)	..	..	43.1
Bank capital to asset ratio (%)	..	..	10.7
Bank nonperforming loans to total gross loans ratio (%)	23.1	11.2	4.0
Domestic credit to the private sector (% of GDP)	17.8	30.2	81.3
Real interest rate (%)	9.9	8.1	
Interest rate spread (percentage points)	7.7	5.5	7.2
Infrastructure			
Paved roads (% of total roads)	63.8	..	65.8
Electric power consumption (kWh per capita)	2,932	3,417	1,502
Power outages in a typical month (number)	..	..	
Fixed line and mobile subscribers (per 100 people)	31	94	60
Internet users (per 100 people)	2.5	13.2	11.4
Cost of telephone call to U.S. ($ per 3 minutes)	3.95	..	2.08

Madagascar

Sub-Saharan Africa   **Low income**

	Country data		Low-income group
	2000	2006	2006
Economic and social context			
Population (millions)	16.2	19.2	2,420
Labor force (millions)	7.3	8.9	995
Unemployment rate (% of labor force)	..	5.0	..
GNI per capita, *World Bank Atlas* method ($)	240	280	649
GDP growth, 1995–2000 and 2000–06 (average annual %)	3.9	2.7	6.5
Agriculture value added (% of GDP)	29.2	27.5	20.4
Industry value added (% of GDP)	14.2	15.3	27.7
Manufacturing value added (% of GDP)	12.2	13.4	15.8
Services value added (% of GDP)	56.6	57.2	51.9
Inflation (annual % change in consumer price index)	12.0	10.8	
Exchange rate (local currency units per $)	1,353.5	2,142.3	
Exports of goods and services (% of GDP)	30.7	29.7	26.7
Imports of goods and services (% of GDP)	38.0	40.9	30.1
Business environment			
Ease of doing business (ranking 1-178; 1=best)	..	149	
Time to start a business (days)	..	7	54
Procedures to start a business (number)	..	5	10
Firing cost (weeks of wages)	..	30.0	62.6
Closing a business (years to resolve insolvency)	..	..	3.8
Total tax rate (% of profit)	..	46.5	67.4
Highest marginal tax rate, corporate (%)	..	..	
Business entry rate (new registrations as % of total)	*4.2*	*6.4*	*6.4*
Enterprise surveys			
Time dealing with gov't officials (% of management time)	..	20.8	
Firms expected to give gifts in meetings w/tax officials (%)	..	12.7	
Firms using banks to finance investments (% of firms)	..	13.0	
Delay in obtaining an electrical connection (days)	..	58.0	
ISO certification ownership (% of firms)	..	6.6	
Private sector investment			
Invest. in infrastructure w/private participation ($ millions)	*10*	*13*	*29,785*
Private foreign direct investment, net (% of GDP)	2.1	4.2	2.6
Gross fixed capital formation (% of GDP)	15.0	24.8	26.7
Gross fixed private capital formation (% of GDP)	8.3	14.5	19.6
Finance and banking			
Government cash surplus or deficit (% of GDP)	–2.0	9.9	–2.6
Government debt (% of GDP)	111.9	..	
Deposit money banks' assets (% of GDP)	10.1	11.0	50.5
Total financial system deposits (% of GDP)	13.0	13.7	44.6
Bank capital to asset ratio (%)	7.1	6.2	..
Bank nonperforming loans to total gross loans ratio (%)	8.6	10.1	..
Domestic credit to the private sector (% of GDP)	9.2	10.2	38.3
Real interest rate (%)	18.0	16.4	
Interest rate spread (percentage points)	11.5	7.2	*11.3*
Infrastructure			
Paved roads (% of total roads)	11.6	..	..
Electric power consumption (kWh per capita)	..	..	391
Power outages in a typical month (number)	..	..	
Fixed line and mobile subscribers (per 100 people)	1	6	17
Internet users (per 100 people)	0.2	0.6	*4.2*
Cost of telephone call to U.S. ($ per 3 minutes)	8.98	0.59	*1.99*

Malawi

	Country data		Low-income group
	2000	**2006**	**2006**
Economic and social context			
Population (millions)	11.6	13.6	2,420
Labor force (millions)	5.4	6.3	995
Unemployment rate (% of labor force)	0.9	..	..
GNI per capita, *World Bank Atlas* method ($)	150	230	649
GDP growth, 1995–2000 and 2000–06 (average annual %)	3.8	2.4	6.5
Agriculture value added (% of GDP)	39.5	34.2	20.4
Industry value added (% of GDP)	17.9	19.7	27.7
Manufacturing value added (% of GDP)	12.9	13.6	15.8
Services value added (% of GDP)	42.5	46.1	51.9
Inflation (annual % change in consumer price index)	29.6	14.0	
Exchange rate (local currency units per $)	59.5	136.0	
Exports of goods and services (% of GDP)	25.6	17.0	26.7
Imports of goods and services (% of GDP)	35.3	29.4	30.1
Business environment			
Ease of doing business (ranking 1-178; 1=best)	..	127	
Time to start a business (days)	..	37	54
Procedures to start a business (number)	..	10	10
Firing cost (weeks of wages)	..	84.0	62.6
Closing a business (years to resolve insolvency)	..	2.6	3.8
Total tax rate (% of profit)	..	32.2	67.4
Highest marginal tax rate, corporate (%)	38	..	
Business entry rate (new registrations as % of total)	6.3	7.5	6.4
Enterprise surveys			
Time dealing with gov't officials (% of management time)	..	5.8	
Firms expected to give gifts in meetings w/tax officials (%)	..	15.3	
Firms using banks to finance investments (% of firms)	..	20.6	
Delay in obtaining an electrical connection (days)	..	98.5	
ISO certification ownership (% of firms)	..	17.2	
Private sector investment			
Invest. in infrastructure w/private participation ($ millions)	5	31	29,785
Private foreign direct investment, net (% of GDP)	1.5	0.9	2.6
Gross fixed capital formation (% of GDP)	12.3	21.8	26.7
Gross fixed private capital formation (% of GDP)	2.3	14.4	19.6
Finance and banking			
Government cash surplus or deficit (% of GDP)	..	..	-2.6
Government debt (% of GDP)	..	..	..
Deposit money banks' assets (% of GDP)	7.6	11.1	50.5
Total financial system deposits (% of GDP)	15.0	20.2	44.6
Bank capital to asset ratio (%)	..	..	..
Bank nonperforming loans to total gross loans ratio (%)	..	..	..
Domestic credit to the private sector (% of GDP)	9.1	8.7	38.3
Real interest rate (%)	17.3	11.6	
Interest rate spread (percentage points)	19.9	21.3	11.3
Infrastructure			
Paved roads (% of total roads)	19.0	45.0	..
Electric power consumption (kWh per capita)	..	..	391
Power outages in a typical month (number)	..	76.9	
Fixed line and mobile subscribers (per 100 people)	1	4	17
Internet users (per 100 people)	0.1	0.4	4.2
Cost of telephone call to U.S. ($ per 3 minutes)	4.32	..	1.99

Malaysia

East Asia & Pacific   **Upper middle income**

	Country data		Upper middle-income group
	2000	2006	2006
Economic and social context			
Population (millions)	23.3	26.1	811
Labor force (millions)	9.9	11.6	374
Unemployment rate (% of labor force)	3.0	3.5	9.8
GNI per capita, *World Bank Atlas* method ($)	3,390	5,620	5,913
GDP growth, 1995–2000 and 2000–06 (average annual %)	3.7	5.0	3.9
Agriculture value added (% of GDP)	8.8	8.7	5.7
Industry value added (% of GDP)	50.7	49.9	32.4
Manufacturing value added (% of GDP)	32.6	29.8	19.4
Services value added (% of GDP)	40.5	41.3	62.0
Inflation (annual % change in consumer price index)	1.5	3.6	
Exchange rate (local currency units per $)	3.8	3.7	
Exports of goods and services (% of GDP)	124.4	117.0	32.7
Imports of goods and services (% of GDP)	104.5	100.0	30.3
Business environment			
Ease of doing business (ranking 1-178; 1=best)	..	24	
Time to start a business (days)	..	24	41
Procedures to start a business (number)	..	9	9
Firing cost (weeks of wages)	..	75.0	39.7
Closing a business (years to resolve insolvency)	..	2.3	2.9
Total tax rate (% of profit)	..	36.0	44.5
Highest marginal tax rate, corporate (%)	28	28	
Business entry rate (new registrations as % of total)	..	..	9.1
Enterprise surveys			
Time dealing with gov't officials (% of management time)	7.3	..	
Firms expected to give gifts in meetings w/tax officials (%)	..	..	
Firms using banks to finance investments (% of firms)	23.8	..	
Delay in obtaining an electrical connection (days)	16.4	..	
ISO certification ownership (% of firms)	31.4	..	
Private sector investment			
Invest. in infrastructure w/private participation ($ millions)	5,519	1,230	45,869
Private foreign direct investment, net (% of GDP)	4.2	4.0	3.5
Gross fixed capital formation (% of GDP)	25.6	20.9	19.9
Gross fixed private capital formation (% of GDP)	31.8	..	..
Finance and banking			
Government cash surplus or deficit (% of GDP)	-3.1	-4.3	..
Government debt (% of GDP)	..	..	
Deposit money banks' assets (% of GDP)	131.0	111.8	52.9
Total financial system deposits (% of GDP)	107.6	110.4	41.4
Bank capital to asset ratio (%)	8.5	7.6	9.8
Bank nonperforming loans to total gross loans ratio (%)	15.4	8.5	3.2
Domestic credit to the private sector (% of GDP)	177.9	108.1	41.4
Real interest rate (%)	2.7	2.3	
Interest rate spread (percentage points)	4.3	3.3	5.9
Infrastructure			
Paved roads (% of total roads)	75.3	81.3	..
Electric power consumption (kWh per capita)	2,743	3,262	3,131
Power outages in a typical month (number)	..	..	
Fixed line and mobile subscribers (per 100 people)	42	91	88
Internet users (per 100 people)	21.4	43.2	22.2
Cost of telephone call to U.S. ($ per 3 minutes)	2.37	0.71	1.06

Maldives

<table>
<tr><td>South Asia</td><td colspan="3">Lower middle income</td></tr>
<tr><td></td><td colspan="2">Country data</td><td>Lower middle-income group</td></tr>
<tr><td></td><td>2000</td><td>2006</td><td>2006</td></tr>
<tr><td colspan="4">Economic and social context</td></tr>
<tr><td>Population (millions)</td><td>0.27</td><td>0.30</td><td>2,276</td></tr>
<tr><td>Labor force (millions)</td><td>0.09</td><td>0.12</td><td>1,209</td></tr>
<tr><td>Unemployment rate (% of labor force)</td><td>2.0</td><td>..</td><td>5.7</td></tr>
<tr><td>GNI per capita, World Bank Atlas method ($)</td><td>2,140</td><td>3,010</td><td>2,038</td></tr>
<tr><td>GDP growth, 1995–2000 and 2000–06 (average annual %)</td><td>8.7</td><td>7.2</td><td>7.6</td></tr>
<tr><td>Agriculture value added (% of GDP)</td><td>..</td><td>..</td><td>11.9</td></tr>
<tr><td>Industry value added (% of GDP)</td><td>..</td><td>..</td><td>43.5</td></tr>
<tr><td>Manufacturing value added (% of GDP)</td><td>..</td><td>..</td><td>26.7</td></tr>
<tr><td>Services value added (% of GDP)</td><td>..</td><td>..</td><td>44.6</td></tr>
<tr><td>Inflation (annual % change in consumer price index)</td><td></td><td>3.5</td><td></td></tr>
<tr><td>Exchange rate (local currency units per $)</td><td>11.8</td><td>12.8</td><td></td></tr>
<tr><td>Exports of goods and services (% of GDP)</td><td>89.5</td><td>94.8</td><td>40.4</td></tr>
<tr><td>Imports of goods and services (% of GDP)</td><td>71.6</td><td>83.3</td><td>36.4</td></tr>
<tr><td colspan="4">Business environment</td></tr>
<tr><td>Ease of doing business (ranking 1-178; 1=best)</td><td>..</td><td>60</td><td></td></tr>
<tr><td>Time to start a business (days)</td><td>..</td><td>9</td><td>53</td></tr>
<tr><td>Procedures to start a business (number)</td><td>..</td><td>5</td><td>10</td></tr>
<tr><td>Firing cost (weeks of wages)</td><td>..</td><td>9.0</td><td>50.2</td></tr>
<tr><td>Closing a business (years to resolve insolvency)</td><td>..</td><td>6.7</td><td>3.3</td></tr>
<tr><td>Total tax rate (% of profit)</td><td>..</td><td>9.1</td><td>45.8</td></tr>
<tr><td>Highest marginal tax rate, corporate (%)</td><td>..</td><td>..</td><td></td></tr>
<tr><td>Business entry rate (new registrations as % of total)</td><td>..</td><td>..</td><td>7.6</td></tr>
<tr><td>Enterprise surveys</td><td></td><td></td><td></td></tr>
<tr><td>Time dealing with gov't officials (% of management time)</td><td>..</td><td>..</td><td></td></tr>
<tr><td>Firms expected to give gifts in meetings w/tax officials (%)</td><td>..</td><td>..</td><td></td></tr>
<tr><td>Firms using banks to finance investments (% of firms)</td><td>..</td><td>..</td><td></td></tr>
<tr><td>Delay in obtaining an electrical connection (days)</td><td>..</td><td>..</td><td></td></tr>
<tr><td>ISO certification ownership (% of firms)</td><td>..</td><td>..</td><td></td></tr>
<tr><td colspan="4">Private sector investment</td></tr>
<tr><td>Invest. in infrastructure w/private participation ($ millions)</td><td>..</td><td>40</td><td>38,154</td></tr>
<tr><td>Private foreign direct investment, net (% of GDP)</td><td>2.1</td><td>1.5</td><td>3.0</td></tr>
<tr><td>Gross fixed capital formation (% of GDP)</td><td>26.3</td><td>36.1</td><td>33.5</td></tr>
<tr><td>Gross fixed private capital formation (% of GDP)</td><td>..</td><td>..</td><td>10.9</td></tr>
<tr><td colspan="4">Finance and banking</td></tr>
<tr><td>Government cash surplus or deficit (% of GDP)</td><td>–5.0</td><td>–7.7</td><td>–0.9</td></tr>
<tr><td>Government debt (% of GDP)</td><td>40.9</td><td>50.6</td><td>..</td></tr>
<tr><td>Deposit money banks' assets (% of GDP)</td><td>..</td><td>63.1</td><td>87.8</td></tr>
<tr><td>Total financial system deposits (% of GDP)</td><td>..</td><td>53.2</td><td>43.1</td></tr>
<tr><td>Bank capital to asset ratio (%)</td><td>..</td><td>..</td><td>10.7</td></tr>
<tr><td>Bank nonperforming loans to total gross loans ratio (%)</td><td>..</td><td>..</td><td>4.0</td></tr>
<tr><td>Domestic credit to the private sector (% of GDP)</td><td>19.1</td><td>69.0</td><td>81.3</td></tr>
<tr><td>Real interest rate (%)</td><td>11.3</td><td>12.9</td><td></td></tr>
<tr><td>Interest rate spread (percentage points)</td><td>6.1</td><td>6.5</td><td>7.2</td></tr>
<tr><td colspan="4">Infrastructure</td></tr>
<tr><td>Paved roads (% of total roads)</td><td>..</td><td>..</td><td>65.8</td></tr>
<tr><td>Electric power consumption (kWh per capita)</td><td>..</td><td>..</td><td>1,502</td></tr>
<tr><td>Power outages in a typical month (number)</td><td>..</td><td>..</td><td></td></tr>
<tr><td>Fixed line and mobile subscribers (per 100 people)</td><td>12</td><td>98</td><td>60</td></tr>
<tr><td>Internet users (per 100 people)</td><td>2.2</td><td>6.8</td><td>11.4</td></tr>
<tr><td>Cost of telephone call to U.S. ($ per 3 minutes)</td><td>11.72</td><td>5.86</td><td>2.08</td></tr>
</table>

Mali

Sub-Saharan Africa   **Low income**

	Country data		Low-income group
	2000	2006	2006
Economic and social context			
Population (millions)	10.0	12.0	2,420
Labor force (millions)	4.1	4.8	995
Unemployment rate (% of labor force)	3.3	8.8	..
GNI per capita, World Bank Atlas method ($)	260	460	649
GDP growth, 1995–2000 and 2000–06 (average annual %)	5.5	5.7	6.5
Agriculture value added (% of GDP)	41.6	36.9	20.4
Industry value added (% of GDP)	20.6	24.0	27.7
Manufacturing value added (% of GDP)	3.8	3.1	15.8
Services value added (% of GDP)	37.9	39.1	51.9
Inflation (annual % change in consumer price index)	-0.7	1.5	
Exchange rate (local currency units per $)	712.0	522.9	
Exports of goods and services (% of GDP)	26.8	32.1	26.7
Imports of goods and services (% of GDP)	39.4	40.2	30.1
Business environment			
Ease of doing business (ranking 1-178; 1=best)	..	158	
Time to start a business (days)	..	26	54
Procedures to start a business (number)	..	11	10
Firing cost (weeks of wages)	..	31.0	62.6
Closing a business (years to resolve insolvency)	..	3.6	3.8
Total tax rate (% of profit)	..	51.4	67.4
Highest marginal tax rate, corporate (%)	..	..	
Business entry rate (new registrations as % of total)	..	..	6.4
Enterprise surveys			
Time dealing with gov't officials (% of management time)	..	7.5	
Firms expected to give gifts in meetings w/tax officials (%)	..	30.2	
Firms using banks to finance investments (% of firms)	..	16.8	
Delay in obtaining an electrical connection (days)	..	35.6	
ISO certification ownership (% of firms)	..	6.5	
Private sector investment			
Invest. in infrastructure w/private participation ($ millions)	366	55	29,785
Private foreign direct investment, net (% of GDP)	3.4	3.2	2.6
Gross fixed capital formation (% of GDP)	24.6	22.9	26.7
Gross fixed private capital formation (% of GDP)	15.9	14.3	19.6
Finance and banking			
Government cash surplus or deficit (% of GDP)	-3.4	32.1	-2.6
Government debt (% of GDP)	..	..	
Deposit money banks' assets (% of GDP)	15.8	18.2	50.5
Total financial system deposits (% of GDP)	13.1	17.0	44.6
Bank capital to asset ratio (%)	..	..	..
Bank nonperforming loans to total gross loans ratio (%)	..	..	..
Domestic credit to the private sector (% of GDP)	16.6	17.2	38.3
Real interest rate (%)	..	..	
Interest rate spread (percentage points)	..	..	11.3
Infrastructure			
Paved roads (% of total roads)	12.1	18.0	..
Electric power consumption (kWh per capita)	..	..	391
Power outages in a typical month (number)	..	..	
Fixed line and mobile subscribers (per 100 people)	0	13	17
Internet users (per 100 people)	0.1	0.6	4.2
Cost of telephone call to U.S. ($ per 3 minutes)	12.64	..	1.99

Malta

High income

	Country data		High-income group
	2000	2006	2006
Economic and social context			
Population (millions)	0.39	0.41	1,031
Labor force (millions)	0.15	0.18	504
Unemployment rate (% of labor force)	6.7	7.5	6.2
GNI per capita, *World Bank Atlas* method ($)	9,670	15,310	36,608
GDP growth, 1995-2000 and 2000-06 (average annual %)	4.4	1.2	2.3
Agriculture value added (% of GDP)	..	..	1.5
Industry value added (% of GDP)	..	..	26.2
Manufacturing value added (% of GDP)	..	..	16.8
Services value added (% of GDP)	..	..	72.3
Inflation (annual % change in consumer price index)	2.4	2.8	
Exchange rate (local currency units per $)	0.4	0.3	
Exports of goods and services (% of GDP)	92.1	88.0	25.6
Imports of goods and services (% of GDP)	102.7	91.6	26.3
Business environment			
Ease of doing business (ranking 1-178; 1=best)	..	..	
Time to start a business (days)	..	..	22
Procedures to start a business (number)	..	..	7
Firing cost (weeks of wages)	..	..	34.9
Closing a business (years to resolve insolvency)	..	..	2.0
Total tax rate (% of profit)	..	..	41.5
Highest marginal tax rate, corporate (%)	35	35	
Business entry rate (new registrations as % of total)	5.4	6.3	10.1
Enterprise surveys			
Time dealing with gov't officials (% of management time)	..	..	
Firms expected to give gifts in meetings w/tax officials (%)	..	..	
Firms using banks to finance investments (% of firms)	..	..	
Delay in obtaining an electrical connection (days)	..	..	
ISO certification ownership (% of firms)	..	..	
Private sector investment			
Invest. in infrastructure w/private participation ($ millions)	..	..	849
Private foreign direct investment, net (% of GDP)	15.4	28.1	2.7
Gross fixed capital formation (% of GDP)	23.1	19.5	20.4
Gross fixed private capital formation (% of GDP)	..	..	..
Finance and banking			
Government cash surplus or deficit (% of GDP)	..	-2.5	-1.3
Government debt (% of GDP)	..	76.3	47.6
Deposit money banks' assets (% of GDP)	129.0	134.9	99.7
Total financial system deposits (% of GDP)	122.5	134.6	..
Bank capital to asset ratio (%)	..	8.6	6.2
Bank nonperforming loans to total gross loans ratio (%)	..	2.8	1.1
Domestic credit to the private sector (% of GDP)	106.9	115.7	162.0
Real interest rate (%)	-2.7	2.8	
Interest rate spread (percentage points)	2.4	2.6	4.4
Infrastructure			
Paved roads (% of total roads)	88.0	87.5	90.9
Electric power consumption (kWh per capita)	4,313	4,917	9,760
Power outages in a typical month (number)	..		
Fixed line and mobile subscribers (per 100 people)	82	135	143
Internet users (per 100 people)	13.1	31.5	59.3
Cost of telephone call to U.S. ($ per 3 minutes)	3.41	0.77	0.77

Marshall Islands

East Asia & Pacific   **Lower middle income**

	Country data		Lower middle-income group
	2000	2006	2006
Economic and social context			
Population (millions)	0.05	0.07	2,276
Labor force (millions)	..	..	1,209
Unemployment rate (% of labor force)	30.9	25.4	5.7
GNI per capita, *World Bank Atlas* method ($)	2,540	2,980	2,038
GDP growth, 1995–2000 and 2000–06 (average annual %)	–3.7	2.7	7.6
Agriculture value added (% of GDP)	9.4	..	11.9
Industry value added (% of GDP)	18.6	..	43.5
Manufacturing value added (% of GDP)	3.7	..	26.7
Services value added (% of GDP)	72.1	..	44.6
Inflation (annual % change in consumer price index)	..	..	
Exchange rate (local currency units per $)	..	..	
Exports of goods and services (% of GDP)	..	..	40.4
Imports of goods and services (% of GDP)	..	..	36.4
Business environment			
Ease of doing business (ranking 1-178; 1=best)	..	89	
Time to start a business (days)	..	17	53
Procedures to start a business (number)	..	5	10
Firing cost (weeks of wages)	..	..	50.2
Closing a business (years to resolve insolvency)	..	2.0	3.3
Total tax rate (% of profit)	..	64.9	45.8
Highest marginal tax rate, corporate (%)	..	..	
Business entry rate (new registrations as % of total)	..	..	7.6
Enterprise surveys			
Time dealing with gov't officials (% of management time)	..	..	
Firms expected to give gifts in meetings w/tax officials (%)	..	..	
Firms using banks to finance investments (% of firms)	..	..	
Delay in obtaining an electrical connection (days)	..	..	
ISO certification ownership (% of firms)	..	..	
Private sector investment			
Invest. in infrastructure w/private participation ($ millions)	..	..	38,154
Private foreign direct investment, net (% of GDP)	..	..	3.0
Gross fixed capital formation (% of GDP)	..	..	33.5
Gross fixed private capital formation (% of GDP)	..	..	10.9
Finance and banking			
Government cash surplus or deficit (% of GDP)	..	..	–0.9
Government debt (% of GDP)	..	..	..
Deposit money banks' assets (% of GDP)	..	..	87.8
Total financial system deposits (% of GDP)	..	..	43.1
Bank capital to asset ratio (%)	..	..	10.7
Bank nonperforming loans to total gross loans ratio (%)	..	..	4.0
Domestic credit to the private sector (% of GDP)	..	..	81.3
Real interest rate (%)	..	..	
Interest rate spread (percentage points)	..	..	7.2
Infrastructure			
Paved roads (% of total roads)	..	..	65.8
Electric power consumption (kWh per capita)	..	..	1,502
Power outages in a typical month (number)	..	..	
Fixed line and mobile subscribers (per 100 people)	8	9	60
Internet users (per 100 people)	1.5	3.4	11.4
Cost of telephone call to U.S. ($ per 3 minutes)	..	..	2.08

Mauritania

	Country data		Low-income group
	2000	**2006**	**2006**
Economic and social context			
Population (millions)	2.6	3.0	2,420
Labor force (millions)	1.0	1.3	995
Unemployment rate (% of labor force)	..	..	..
GNI per capita, *World Bank Atlas* method ($)	470	760	649
GDP growth, 1995–2000 and 2000–06 (average annual %)	2.3	5.0	6.5
Agriculture value added (% of GDP)	27.6	13.1	20.4
Industry value added (% of GDP)	29.7	47.8	27.7
Manufacturing value added (% of GDP)	9.0	5.0	15.8
Services value added (% of GDP)	42.6	39.1	51.9
Inflation (annual % change in consumer price index)	3.3	6.2	
Exchange rate (local currency units per $)	238.9	265.5	
Exports of goods and services (% of GDP)	46.2	54.6	26.7
Imports of goods and services (% of GDP)	74.2	59.1	30.1
Business environment			
Ease of doing business (ranking 1-178; 1=best)	..	157	
Time to start a business (days)	..	65	54
Procedures to start a business (number)	..	11	10
Firing cost (weeks of wages)	..	31.0	62.6
Closing a business (years to resolve insolvency)	..	8.0	3.8
Total tax rate (% of profit)	..	107.5	67.4
Highest marginal tax rate, corporate (%)	..	..	
Business entry rate (new registrations as % of total)	..	..	6.4
Enterprise surveys			
Time dealing with gov't officials (% of management time)	..	5.8	
Firms expected to give gifts in meetings w/tax officials (%)	..	48.2	
Firms using banks to finance investments (% of firms)	..	3.2	
Delay in obtaining an electrical connection (days)	..	7.5	
ISO certification ownership (% of firms)	..	5.9	
Private sector investment			
Invest. in infrastructure w/private participation ($ millions)	43	..	29,785
Private foreign direct investment, net (% of GDP)	3.7	-0.1	2.6
Gross fixed capital formation (% of GDP)	19.4	23.3	26.7
Gross fixed private capital formation (% of GDP)	14.8	17.7	19.6
Finance and banking			
Government cash surplus or deficit (% of GDP)	..	..	-2.6
Government debt (% of GDP)	..	..	..
Deposit money banks' assets (% of GDP)	22.0	27.5	50.5
Total financial system deposits (% of GDP)	9.5	11.2	44.6
Bank capital to asset ratio (%)	..	..	..
Bank nonperforming loans to total gross loans ratio (%)	..	..	..
Domestic credit to the private sector (% of GDP)	23.1	27.0	38.3
Real interest rate (%)	23.9	4.3	
Interest rate spread (percentage points)	16.2	15.1	11.3
Infrastructure			
Paved roads (% of total roads)	11.3	..	..
Electric power consumption (kWh per capita)	..	..	391
Power outages in a typical month (number)	..	3.7	
Fixed line and mobile subscribers (per 100 people)	1	36	17
Internet users (per 100 people)	0.2	3.3	4.2
Cost of telephone call to U.S. ($ per 3 minutes)	4.36	..	1.99

Mauritius

	Country data		Upper middle-income group
Sub-Saharan Africa			**Upper middle income**
	2000	2006	2006

Economic and social context

Population (millions)	1.2	1.3	811
Labor force (millions)	0.53	0.58	374
Unemployment rate (% of labor force)	8.8	9.6	9.8
GNI per capita, World Bank Atlas method ($)	3,740	5,430	5,913
GDP growth, 1995–2000 and 2000–06 (average annual %)	5.5	4.0	3.9
Agriculture value added (% of GDP)	5.9	5.6	5.7
Industry value added (% of GDP)	31.2	26.9	32.4
Manufacturing value added (% of GDP)	23.7	19.1	19.4
Services value added (% of GDP)	62.9	67.6	62.0
Inflation (annual % change in consumer price index)	4.2	8.9	
Exchange rate (local currency units per $)	26.2	31.7	
Exports of goods and services (% of GDP)	62.7	60.0	32.7
Imports of goods and services (% of GDP)	64.6	67.1	30.3

Business environment

Ease of doing business (ranking 1-178; 1=best)	..	27	
Time to start a business (days)	..	7	41
Procedures to start a business (number)	..	6	9
Firing cost (weeks of wages)	..	35.0	39.7
Closing a business (years to resolve insolvency)	..	1.7	2.9
Total tax rate (% of profit)	..	21.7	44.5
Highest marginal tax rate, corporate (%)	25	25	
Business entry rate (new registrations as % of total)	..	..	9.1
Enterprise surveys			
Time dealing with gov't officials (% of management time)	..	9.6	
Firms expected to give gifts in meetings w/tax officials (%)	..	1.4	
Firms using banks to finance investments (% of firms)	..	36.3	
Delay in obtaining an electrical connection (days)	..	23.2	
ISO certification ownership (% of firms)	..	28.4	

Private sector investment

Invest. in infrastructure w/private participation ($ millions)	338	26	45,869
Private foreign direct investment, net (% of GDP)	5.9	1.7	3.5
Gross fixed capital formation (% of GDP)	25.3	22.9	19.9
Gross fixed private capital formation (% of GDP)	17.5	15.9	..

Finance and banking

Government cash surplus or deficit (% of GDP)	–1.1	–3.0	..
Government debt (% of GDP)	34.5	43.2	
Deposit money banks' assets (% of GDP)	68.4	98.4	52.9
Total financial system deposits (% of GDP)	70.4	90.4	41.4
Bank capital to asset ratio (%)	..	..	9.8
Bank nonperforming loans to total gross loans ratio (%)	..	..	3.2
Domestic credit to the private sector (% of GDP)	60.7	78.0	41.4
Real interest rate (%)	16.5	16.3	
Interest rate spread (percentage points)	11.2	11.5	5.9

Infrastructure

Paved roads (% of total roads)	97.0	100.0	..
Electric power consumption (kWh per capita)	..	..	3,131
Power outages in a typical month (number)	..	..	
Fixed line and mobile subscribers (per 100 people)	39	90	88
Internet users (per 100 people)	7.3	14.5	22.2
Cost of telephone call to U.S. ($ per 3 minutes)	4.00	1.59	1.06

Mayotte

Upper middle income

	Country data		Upper middle-income group
	2000	**2006**	**2006**
Economic and social context			
Population (millions)	..	0.19	811
Labor force (millions)	..	..	374
Unemployment rate (% of labor force)	..	..	9.8
GNI per capita, *World Bank Atlas* method ($)	..	..	5,913
GDP growth, 1995–2000 and 2000–06 (average annual %)	..	..	3.9
Agriculture value added (% of GDP)	..	..	5.7
Industry value added (% of GDP)	..	..	32.4
Manufacturing value added (% of GDP)	..	..	19.4
Services value added (% of GDP)	..	..	62.0
Inflation (annual % change in consumer price index)	..	..	
Exchange rate (local currency units per $)	..	..	
Exports of goods and services (% of GDP)	..	..	32.7
Imports of goods and services (% of GDP)	..	..	30.3
Business environment			
Ease of doing business (ranking 1-178; 1=best)	..	..	
Time to start a business (days)	..	..	41
Procedures to start a business (number)	..	..	9
Firing cost (weeks of wages)	..	..	39.7
Closing a business (years to resolve insolvency)	..	..	2.9
Total tax rate (% of profit)	..	..	44.5
Highest marginal tax rate, corporate (%)	..	..	
Business entry rate (new registrations as % of total)	..	..	*9.1*
Enterprise surveys			
Time dealing with gov't officials (% of management time)	..	..	
Firms expected to give gifts in meetings w/tax officials (%)	..	..	
Firms using banks to finance investments (% of firms)	..	..	
Delay in obtaining an electrical connection (days)	..	..	
ISO certification ownership (% of firms)	..	..	
Private sector investment			
Invest. in infrastructure w/private participation ($ millions)	..	..	45,869
Private foreign direct investment, net (% of GDP)	..	..	3.5
Gross fixed capital formation (% of GDP)	..	..	19.9
Gross fixed private capital formation (% of GDP)	..	..	..
Finance and banking			
Government cash surplus or deficit (% of GDP)	..	..	..
Government debt (% of GDP)	..	..	..
Deposit money banks' assets (% of GDP)	..	..	52.9
Total financial system deposits (% of GDP)	..	..	41.4
Bank capital to asset ratio (%)	..	..	9.8
Bank nonperforming loans to total gross loans ratio (%)	..	..	3.2
Domestic credit to the private sector (% of GDP)	..	..	41.4
Real interest rate (%)	..	..	
Interest rate spread (percentage points)	..	..	5.9
Infrastructure			
Paved roads (% of total roads)	..	..	..
Electric power consumption (kWh per capita)	..	..	*3,131*
Power outages in a typical month (number)	..	..	
Fixed line and mobile subscribers (per 100 people)	..	..	88
Internet users (per 100 people)	..	..	22.2
Cost of telephone call to U.S. ($ per 3 minutes)	..	..	*1.06*

Mexico

Latin America & Caribbean			Upper middle income

	Country data		Upper middle-income group
	2000	2006	2006

Economic and social context

Population (millions)	98.0	104.2	811
Labor force (millions)	39.8	43.1	374
Unemployment rate (% of labor force)	2.2	3.5	9.8
GNI per capita, World Bank Atlas method ($)	5,110	7,830	5,913
GDP growth, 1995–2000 and 2000–06 (average annual %)	5.4	2.3	3.9
Agriculture value added (% of GDP)	4.2	3.9	5.7
Industry value added (% of GDP)	28.0	26.7	32.4
Manufacturing value added (% of GDP)	20.3	18.0	19.4
Services value added (% of GDP)	67.8	69.4	62.0
Inflation (annual % change in consumer price index)	9.5	3.6	
Exchange rate (local currency units per $)	9.5	10.9	
Exports of goods and services (% of GDP)	30.9	31.9	32.7
Imports of goods and services (% of GDP)	32.9	33.2	30.3

Business environment

Ease of doing business (ranking 1-178; 1=best)	..	44	
Time to start a business (days)	..	27	41
Procedures to start a business (number)	..	8	9
Firing cost (weeks of wages)	..	52.0	39.7
Closing a business (years to resolve insolvency)	..	1.8	2.9
Total tax rate (% of profit)	..	51.2	44.5
Highest marginal tax rate, corporate (%)	35	29	
Business entry rate (new registrations as % of total)	..	7.1	9.1
Enterprise surveys			
Time dealing with gov't officials (% of management time)	..	20.5	
Firms expected to give gifts in meetings w/tax officials (%)	..	9.6	
Firms using banks to finance investments (% of firms)	..	2.6	
Delay in obtaining an electrical connection (days)	..	11.8	
ISO certification ownership (% of firms)	..	20.3	

Private sector investment

Invest. in infrastructure w/private participation ($ millions)	5,277	5,696	45,869
Private foreign direct investment, net (% of GDP)	3.1	2.3	3.5
Gross fixed capital formation (% of GDP)	21.4	20.4	19.9
Gross fixed private capital formation (% of GDP)	17.8	16.0	..

Finance and banking

Government cash surplus or deficit (% of GDP)	–1.2	..	..
Government debt (% of GDP)	23.2	..	..
Deposit money banks' assets (% of GDP)	32.7	29.7	52.9
Total financial system deposits (% of GDP)	24.6	22.9	41.4
Bank capital to asset ratio (%)	9.6	13.2	9.8
Bank nonperforming loans to total gross loans ratio (%)	5.8	2.1	3.2
Domestic credit to the private sector (% of GDP)	18.3	22.1	41.4
Real interest rate (%)	4.3	2.9	
Interest rate spread (percentage points)	8.7	4.2	5.9

Infrastructure

Paved roads (% of total roads)	32.8	37.0	..
Electric power consumption (kWh per capita)	1,795	1,899	3,131
Power outages in a typical month (number)	..	2.6	
Fixed line and mobile subscribers (per 100 people)	27	74	88
Internet users (per 100 people)	5.2	17.5	22.2
Cost of telephone call to U.S. ($ per 3 minutes)	3.01	0.83	1.06

Micronesia, Fed. Sts.

East Asia & Pacific			Lower middle income

	Country data		Lower middle-income group
	2000	2006	2006

Economic and social context

Population (millions)	0.11	0.11	2,276
Labor force (millions)	..	..	1,209
Unemployment rate (% of labor force)	..	..	5.7
GNI per capita, *World Bank Atlas* method ($)	2,170	2,390	2,038
GDP growth, 1995–2000 and 2000–06 (average annual %)	-1.8	0.2	7.6
Agriculture value added (% of GDP)	..	..	11.9
Industry value added (% of GDP)	..	..	43.5
Manufacturing value added (% of GDP)	..	..	26.7
Services value added (% of GDP)	..	..	44.6
Inflation (annual % change in consumer price index)	..	..	
Exchange rate (local currency units per $)	1.0	1.0	
Exports of goods and services (% of GDP)	..	..	40.4
Imports of goods and services (% of GDP)	..	..	36.4

Business environment

Ease of doing business (ranking 1-178; 1=best)	..	112	
Time to start a business (days)	..	16	53
Procedures to start a business (number)	..	7	10
Firing cost (weeks of wages)	..	..	50.2
Closing a business (years to resolve insolvency)	..	5.3	3.3
Total tax rate (% of profit)	..	58.7	45.8
Highest marginal tax rate, corporate (%)	..	..	
Business entry rate (new registrations as % of total)	..	..	7.6
Enterprise surveys			
Time dealing with gov't officials (% of management time)	..	..	
Firms expected to give gifts in meetings w/tax officials (%)	..	..	
Firms using banks to finance investments (% of firms)	..	..	
Delay in obtaining an electrical connection (days)	..	..	
ISO certification ownership (% of firms)	..	..	

Private sector investment

Invest. in infrastructure w/private participation ($ millions)	..	..	38,154
Private foreign direct investment, net (% of GDP)	..	..	3.0
Gross fixed capital formation (% of GDP)	..	..	33.5
Gross fixed private capital formation (% of GDP)	..	..	10.9

Finance and banking

Government cash surplus or deficit (% of GDP)	..	..	-0.9
Government debt (% of GDP)	..	..	..
Deposit money banks' assets (% of GDP)	..	..	87.8
Total financial system deposits (% of GDP)	..	..	43.1
Bank capital to asset ratio (%)	..	..	10.7
Bank nonperforming loans to total gross loans ratio (%)	..	..	4.0
Domestic credit to the private sector (% of GDP)	33.2	21.4	81.3
Real interest rate (%)	13.0	11.2	
Interest rate spread (percentage points)	10.7	13.6	7.2

Infrastructure

Paved roads (% of total roads)	17.5	..	65.8
Electric power consumption (kWh per capita)	..	..	1,502
Power outages in a typical month (number)	..	..	
Fixed line and mobile subscribers (per 100 people)	9	24	60
Internet users (per 100 people)	3.7	14.5	11.4
Cost of telephone call to U.S. ($ per 3 minutes)	7.50	6.00	2.08

Moldova

Europe & Central Asia			Lower middle income

	Country data		Lower middle-income group
	2000	2006	2006
Economic and social context			
Population (millions)	4.1	3.8	2,276
Labor force (millions)	1.9	1.9	1,209
Unemployment rate (% of labor force)	8.5	7.3	5.7
GNI per capita, *World Bank Atlas* method ($)	370	1,080	2,038
GDP growth, 1995–2000 and 2000–06 (average annual %)	-2.6	6.8	7.6
Agriculture value added (% of GDP)	29.0	18.1	11.9
Industry value added (% of GDP)	21.7	15.1	43.5
Manufacturing value added (% of GDP)	16.3	14.5	26.7
Services value added (% of GDP)	49.2	66.8	44.6
Inflation (annual % change in consumer price index)	31.3	11.6	
Exchange rate (local currency units per $)	12.4	13.1	
Exports of goods and services (% of GDP)	49.8	45.9	40.4
Imports of goods and services (% of GDP)	75.4	93.2	36.4
Business environment			
Ease of doing business (ranking 1-178; 1=best)	..	92	
Time to start a business (days)	..	23	53
Procedures to start a business (number)	..	9	10
Firing cost (weeks of wages)	..	37.0	50.2
Closing a business (years to resolve insolvency)	..	2.8	3.3
Total tax rate (% of profit)	..	44.0	45.8
Highest marginal tax rate, corporate (%)	..	15	
Business entry rate (new registrations as % of total)	8.3	8.2	7.6
Enterprise surveys			
Time dealing with gov't officials (% of management time)	..	3.6	
Firms expected to give gifts in meetings w/tax officials (%)	68.0	43.2	
Firms using banks to finance investments (% of firms)	17.8	17.7	
Delay in obtaining an electrical connection (days)	18.0	28.8	
ISO certification ownership (% of firms)	..	6.9	
Private sector investment			
Invest. in infrastructure w/private participation ($ millions)	25	34	38,154
Private foreign direct investment, net (% of GDP)	9.9	7.2	3.0
Gross fixed capital formation (% of GDP)	15.4	27.9	33.5
Gross fixed private capital formation (% of GDP)	13.8	25.8	10.9
Finance and banking			
Government cash surplus or deficit (% of GDP)	-1.5	0.2	-0.9
Government debt (% of GDP)	73.0	29.6	..
Deposit money banks' assets (% of GDP)	14.1	28.2	87.8
Total financial system deposits (% of GDP)	11.0	29.2	43.1
Bank capital to asset ratio (%)	30.6	17.0	10.7
Bank nonperforming loans to total gross loans ratio (%)	20.6	4.3	4.0
Domestic credit to the private sector (% of GDP)	12.7	27.9	81.3
Real interest rate (%)	5.1	4.9	
Interest rate spread (percentage points)	8.9	6.2	7.2
Infrastructure			
Paved roads (% of total roads)	86.1	86.3	65.8
Electric power consumption (kWh per capita)	871	1,428	1,502
Power outages in a typical month (number)	..	..	
Fixed line and mobile subscribers (per 100 people)	17	62	60
Internet users (per 100 people)	1.3	19.0	11.4
Cost of telephone call to U.S. ($ per 3 minutes)	4.10	1.46	2.08

Monaco

	Country data		High-income group
	2000	**2006**	**2006**
Economic and social context			
Population (millions)	..	0.03	1,031
Labor force (millions)	..	..	504
Unemployment rate (% of labor force)	..	..	6.2
GNI per capita, *World Bank Atlas* method ($)	..	..	36,608
GDP growth, 1995–2000 and 2000–06 (average annual %)	..	..	2.3
Agriculture value added (% of GDP)	..	..	1.5
Industry value added (% of GDP)	..	..	26.2
Manufacturing value added (% of GDP)	..	..	16.8
Services value added (% of GDP)	..	..	72.3
Inflation (annual % change in consumer price index)	..	..	
Exchange rate (local currency units per $)	..	..	
Exports of goods and services (% of GDP)	..	..	25.6
Imports of goods and services (% of GDP)	..	..	26.3
Business environment			
Ease of doing business (ranking 1-178; 1=best)	..	..	
Time to start a business (days)	..	..	22
Procedures to start a business (number)	..	..	7
Firing cost (weeks of wages)	..	..	34.9
Closing a business (years to resolve insolvency)	..	..	2.0
Total tax rate (% of profit)	..	..	41.5
Highest marginal tax rate, corporate (%)	33	..	
Business entry rate (new registrations as % of total)	..	..	10.1
Enterprise surveys			
Time dealing with gov't officials (% of management time)	..	..	
Firms expected to give gifts in meetings w/tax officials (%)	..	..	
Firms using banks to finance investments (% of firms)	..	..	
Delay in obtaining an electrical connection (days)	..	..	
ISO certification ownership (% of firms)	..	..	
Private sector investment			
Invest. in infrastructure w/private participation ($ millions)	..	..	849
Private foreign direct investment, net (% of GDP)	..	..	2.7
Gross fixed capital formation (% of GDP)	..	..	20.4
Gross fixed private capital formation (% of GDP)	..	..	..
Finance and banking			
Government cash surplus or deficit (% of GDP)	..	..	-1.3
Government debt (% of GDP)	..	..	47.6
Deposit money banks' assets (% of GDP)	..	..	99.7
Total financial system deposits (% of GDP)	..	..	..
Bank capital to asset ratio (%)	..	..	6.2
Bank nonperforming loans to total gross loans ratio (%)	..	..	1.1
Domestic credit to the private sector (% of GDP)	..	..	162.0
Real interest rate (%)	..	..	
Interest rate spread (percentage points)	..	..	4.4
Infrastructure			
Paved roads (% of total roads)	100.0	..	90.9
Electric power consumption (kWh per capita)	..	..	9,760
Power outages in a typical month (number)	..	..	
Fixed line and mobile subscribers (per 100 people)	..	..	143
Internet users (per 100 people)	..	..	59.3
Cost of telephone call to U.S. ($ per 3 minutes)	..	..	0.77

Mongolia

	Country data		Low-income group
	2000	2006	2006
Economic and social context			
Population (millions)	2.4	2.6	2,420
Labor force (millions)	1.1	1.3	995
Unemployment rate (% of labor force)	17.5	14.2	..
GNI per capita, *World Bank Atlas* method ($)	410	1,000	649
GDP growth, 1995–2000 and 2000–06 (average annual %)	3.0	7.1	6.5
Agriculture value added (% of GDP)	32.7	21.9	20.4
Industry value added (% of GDP)	20.3	42.3	27.7
Manufacturing value added (% of GDP)	4.6	3.9	15.8
Services value added (% of GDP)	47.0	35.9	51.9
Inflation (annual % change in consumer price index)	11.6	5.1	
Exchange rate (local currency units per $)	1,076.7	1,165.4	
Exports of goods and services (% of GDP)	56.4	65.3	26.7
Imports of goods and services (% of GDP)	70.9	59.7	30.1
Business environment			
Ease of doing business (ranking 1-178; 1=best)	..	52	
Time to start a business (days)	..	20	54
Procedures to start a business (number)	..	8	10
Firing cost (weeks of wages)	..	9.0	62.6
Closing a business (years to resolve insolvency)	..	4.0	3.8
Total tax rate (% of profit)	..	38.4	67.4
Highest marginal tax rate, corporate (%)	..	..	
Business entry rate (new registrations as % of total)	..	..	6.4
Enterprise surveys			
Time dealing with gov't officials (% of management time)	..	6.0	
Firms expected to give gifts in meetings w/tax officials (%)	..	..	
Firms using banks to finance investments (% of firms)	..	32.8	
Delay in obtaining an electrical connection (days)	..	6.7	
ISO certification ownership (% of firms)	..	20.5	
Private sector investment			
Invest. in infrastructure w/private participation ($ millions)	11	2	29,785
Private foreign direct investment, net (% of GDP)	4.9	11.0	2.6
Gross fixed capital formation (% of GDP)	25.1	32.3	26.7
Gross fixed private capital formation (% of GDP)	22.0	27.9	19.6
Finance and banking			
Government cash surplus or deficit (% of GDP)	..	-0.4	-2.6
Government debt (% of GDP)	83.3	105.5	..
Deposit money banks' assets (% of GDP)	11.9	34.5	50.5
Total financial system deposits (% of GDP)	13.7	38.2	44.6
Bank capital to asset ratio (%)	..	..	
Bank nonperforming loans to total gross loans ratio (%)	..	..	..
Domestic credit to the private sector (% of GDP)	7.2	32.8	38.3
Real interest rate (%)	5.3	-1.4	
Interest rate spread (percentage points)	15.9	8.4	11.3
Infrastructure			
Paved roads (% of total roads)	3.5	..	..
Electric power consumption (kWh per capita)	..	..	391
Power outages in a typical month (number)	..	..	
Fixed line and mobile subscribers (per 100 people)	11	28	17
Internet users (per 100 people)	1.3	10.5	4.2
Cost of telephone call to U.S. ($ per 3 minutes)	4.92	..	1.99

Montenegro

Upper middle income

	Country data		Upper middle-income group
	2000	2006	2006
Economic and social context			
Population (millions)	0.67	0.60	811
Labor force (millions)	0.30	0.29	374
Unemployment rate (% of labor force)	..	..	9.8
GNI per capita, *World Bank Atlas* method ($)	1,630	4,130	5,913
GDP growth, 1995–2000 and 2000–06 (average annual %)	−1.6	4.0	3.9
Agriculture value added (% of GDP)	13.1	7.8	5.7
Industry value added (% of GDP)	24.6	17.6	32.4
Manufacturing value added (% of GDP)	12.3	12.6	19.4
Services value added (% of GDP)	62.4	74.6	62.0
Inflation (annual % change in consumer price index)	..	..	
Exchange rate (local currency units per $)	1.1	0.8	
Exports of goods and services (% of GDP)	38.4	48.0	32.7
Imports of goods and services (% of GDP)	53.3	80.9	30.3
Business environment			
Ease of doing business (ranking 1-178; 1=best)	..	81	
Time to start a business (days)	..	24	41
Procedures to start a business (number)	..	15	9
Firing cost (weeks of wages)	..	39.0	39.7
Closing a business (years to resolve insolvency)	..	2.0	2.9
Total tax rate (% of profit)	..	31.6	44.5
Highest marginal tax rate, corporate (%)	..	..	
Business entry rate (new registrations as % of total)	..	..	9.1
Enterprise surveys			
Time dealing with gov't officials (% of management time)	..	12.7	
Firms expected to give gifts in meetings w/tax officials (%)	..	..	
Firms using banks to finance investments (% of firms)	..	8.0	
Delay in obtaining an electrical connection (days)	..	..	
ISO certification ownership (% of firms)	..	12.0	
Private sector investment			
Invest. in infrastructure w/private participation ($ millions)	..	..	45,869
Private foreign direct investment, net (% of GDP)	..	..	3.5
Gross fixed capital formation (% of GDP)	17.6	31.7	19.9
Gross fixed private capital formation (% of GDP)	13.1	26.2	..
Finance and banking			
Government cash surplus or deficit (% of GDP)	..	..	..
Government debt (% of GDP)	..	..	..
Deposit money banks' assets (% of GDP)	..	..	52.9
Total financial system deposits (% of GDP)	..	..	41.4
Bank capital to asset ratio (%)	..	10.4	9.8
Bank nonperforming loans to total gross loans ratio (%)	..	2.9	3.2
Domestic credit to the private sector (% of GDP)	8.4	39.5	41.4
Real interest rate (%)	..	7.1	
Interest rate spread (percentage points)	..	4.5	5.9
Infrastructure			
Paved roads (% of total roads)	..	..	..
Electric power consumption (kWh per capita)	..	..	3,131
Power outages in a typical month (number)	..	..	
Fixed line and mobile subscribers (per 100 people)	..	..	88
Internet users (per 100 people)	..	..	22.2
Cost of telephone call to U.S. ($ per 3 minutes)	..	..	1.06

Morocco

Middle East & North Africa   **Lower middle income**

	Country data		Lower middle-income group
	2000	2006	2006
Economic and social context			
Population (millions)	28.5	30.5	2,276
Labor force (millions)	10.0	11.3	1,209
Unemployment rate (% of labor force)	13.6	9.7	5.7
GNI per capita, *World Bank Atlas* method ($)	1,340	2,160	2,038
GDP growth, 1995–2000 and 2000–06 (average annual %)	3.5	5.1	7.6
Agriculture value added (% of GDP)	14.9	15.7	11.9
Industry value added (% of GDP)	29.1	27.8	43.5
Manufacturing value added (% of GDP)	17.4	16.5	26.7
Services value added (% of GDP)	56.0	56.5	44.6
Inflation (annual % change in consumer price index)	1.9	3.3	
Exchange rate (local currency units per $)	10.6	8.8	
Exports of goods and services (% of GDP)	27.9	33.0	40.4
Imports of goods and services (% of GDP)	33.3	38.4	36.4
Business environment			
Ease of doing business (ranking 1-178; 1=best)	..	129	
Time to start a business (days)	..	12	53
Procedures to start a business (number)	..	6	10
Firing cost (weeks of wages)	..	85.0	50.2
Closing a business (years to resolve insolvency)	..	1.8	3.3
Total tax rate (% of profit)	..	53.1	45.8
Highest marginal tax rate, corporate (%)	35	35	
Business entry rate (new registrations as % of total)	7.8	8.6	7.6
Enterprise surveys			
Time dealing with gov't officials (% of management time)	..	9.2	
Firms expected to give gifts in meetings w/tax officials (%)	..	10.7	
Firms using banks to finance investments (% of firms)	..	12.3	
Delay in obtaining an electrical connection (days)	..	18.8	
ISO certification ownership (% of firms)	..	22.3	
Private sector investment			
Invest. in infrastructure w/private participation ($ millions)	2,135	716	38,154
Private foreign direct investment, net (% of GDP)	0.6	4.1	3.0
Gross fixed capital formation (% of GDP)	26.0	28.7	33.5
Gross fixed private capital formation (% of GDP)	21.3	24.9	10.9
Finance and banking			
Government cash surplus or deficit (% of GDP)	–4.9	–1.8	–0.9
Government debt (% of GDP)	56.4	43.7	..
Deposit money banks' assets (% of GDP)	70.7	75.9	87.8
Total financial system deposits (% of GDP)	62.6	82.5	43.1
Bank capital to asset ratio (%)	9.8	7.4	10.7
Bank nonperforming loans to total gross loans ratio (%)	17.5	10.9	4.0
Domestic credit to the private sector (% of GDP)	51.0	58.1	81.3
Real interest rate (%)	14.2	11.9	
Interest rate spread (percentage points)	8.2	7.9	7.2
Infrastructure			
Paved roads (% of total roads)	56.4	61.9	65.8
Electric power consumption (kWh per capita)	489	644	1,502
Power outages in a typical month (number)	..	2.5	
Fixed line and mobile subscribers (per 100 people)	13	57	60
Internet users (per 100 people)	0.7	20.0	11.4
Cost of telephone call to U.S. ($ per 3 minutes)	2.03	1.69	2.08

Mozambique

	Country data		Low-income group
	2000	2006	2006
Economic and social context			
Population (millions)	18.2	21.0	2,420
Labor force (millions)	8.8	9.8	995
Unemployment rate (% of labor force)	..	..	..
GNI per capita, *World Bank Atlas* method ($)	230	310	649
GDP growth, 1995–2000 and 2000–06 (average annual %)	8.1	8.2	6.5
Agriculture value added (% of GDP)	22.9	28.3	20.4
Industry value added (% of GDP)	23.4	25.9	27.7
Manufacturing value added (% of GDP)	11.7	15.5*	15.8
Services value added (% of GDP)	53.7	45.8	51.9
Inflation (annual % change in consumer price index)	12.7	13.2	
Exchange rate (local currency units per $)	5,550.7	25.4	
Exports of goods and services (% of GDP)	17.5	41.4	26.7
Imports of goods and services (% of GDP)	37.0	47.5	30.1
Business environment			
Ease of doing business (ranking 1-178; 1=best)	..	134	
Time to start a business (days)	..	29	54
Procedures to start a business (number)	..	10	10
Firing cost (weeks of wages)	..	143.0	62.6
Closing a business (years to resolve insolvency)	..	5.0	3.8
Total tax rate (% of profit)	..	34.3	67.4
Highest marginal tax rate, corporate (%)	35	32	
Business entry rate (new registrations as % of total)	..	..	6.4
Enterprise surveys			
Time dealing with gov't officials (% of management time)	..	..	
Firms expected to give gifts in meetings w/tax officials (%)	..	..	
Firms using banks to finance investments (% of firms)	..	..	
Delay in obtaining an electrical connection (days)	..	..	
ISO certification ownership (% of firms)	..	..	
Private sector investment			
Invest. in infrastructure w/private participation ($ millions)	45	16	29,785
Private foreign direct investment, net (% of GDP)	3.3	2.2	2.6
Gross fixed capital formation (% of GDP)	31.0	19.3	26.7
Gross fixed private capital formation (% of GDP)	21.7	7.1	19.6
Finance and banking			
Government cash surplus or deficit (% of GDP)	..	..	-2.6
Government debt (% of GDP)	..	..	
Deposit money banks' assets (% of GDP)	17.0	20.6	50.5
Total financial system deposits (% of GDP)	20.3	23.0	44.6
Bank capital to asset ratio (%)	8.2	6.4	..
Bank nonperforming loans to total gross loans ratio (%)	17.8	3.7	..
Domestic credit to the private sector (% of GDP)	16.7	13.8	38.3
Real interest rate (%)	6.3	11.9	
Interest rate spread (percentage points)	9.3	8.2	11.3
Infrastructure			
Paved roads (% of total roads)	18.7	..	..
Electric power consumption (kWh per capita)	122	450	391
Power outages in a typical month (number)	..	..	
Fixed line and mobile subscribers (per 100 people)	1	11	17
Internet users (per 100 people)	0.1	0.9	4.2
Cost of telephone call to U.S. ($ per 3 minutes)	6.21	1.17	1.99

Myanmar

East Asia & Pacific   **Low income**

	Country data		Low-income group
	2000	2006	2006
Economic and social context			
Population (millions)	45.9	48.4	2,420
Labor force (millions)	24.7	27.3	995
Unemployment rate (% of labor force)	..	..	..
GNI per capita, *World Bank Atlas* method ($)	..	..	649
GDP growth, 1995–2000 and 2000–06 (average annual %)	7.6	9.2	6.5
Agriculture value added (% of GDP)	57.2	..	20.4
Industry value added (% of GDP)	9.7	..	27.7
Manufacturing value added (% of GDP)	7.2	..	15.8
Services value added (% of GDP)	33.1	..	51.9
Inflation (annual % change in consumer price index)	-0.1	20.0	
Exchange rate (local currency units per $)	6.4	5.8	
Exports of goods and services (% of GDP)	0.4	..	26.7
Imports of goods and services (% of GDP)	1.1	..	30.1
Business environment			
Ease of doing business (ranking 1-178; 1=best)	..	..	
Time to start a business (days)	..	..	54
Procedures to start a business (number)	..	..	10
Firing cost (weeks of wages)	..	..	62.6
Closing a business (years to resolve insolvency)	..	..	3.8
Total tax rate (% of profit)	..	..	67.4
Highest marginal tax rate, corporate (%)	30	..	
Business entry rate (new registrations as % of total)	..	..	6.4
Enterprise surveys			
Time dealing with gov't officials (% of management time)	..	..	
Firms expected to give gifts in meetings w/tax officials (%)	..	..	
Firms using banks to finance investments (% of firms)	..	..	
Delay in obtaining an electrical connection (days)	..	..	
ISO certification ownership (% of firms)	..	..	
Private sector investment			
Invest. in infrastructure w/private participation ($ millions)	325	..	29,785
Private foreign direct investment, net (% of GDP)	..	..	2.6
Gross fixed capital formation (% of GDP)	12.0	..	26.7
Gross fixed private capital formation (% of GDP)	7.5	..	19.6
Finance and banking			
Government cash surplus or deficit (% of GDP)	..	-1.8	-2.6
Government debt (% of GDP)	..	..	
Deposit money banks' assets (% of GDP)	11.3	4.8	50.5
Total financial system deposits (% of GDP)	14.6	6.5	44.6
Bank capital to asset ratio (%)	..	..	..
Bank nonperforming loans to total gross loans ratio (%)	..	..	..
Domestic credit to the private sector (% of GDP)	10.4	5.6	38.3
Real interest rate (%)	8.6	-2.2	
Interest rate spread (percentage points)	5.5	5.5	11.3
Infrastructure			
Paved roads (% of total roads)	11.4	..	..
Electric power consumption (kWh per capita)	77	82	391
Power outages in a typical month (number)	..	..	
Fixed line and mobile subscribers (per 100 people)	1	1	17
Internet users (per 100 people)	0.0	0.2	4.2
Cost of telephone call to U.S. ($ per 3 minutes)	0.44	0.17	1.99

Namibia

	Country data		Lower middle-income group
	2000	2006	2006
Economic and social context			
Population (millions)	1.9	2.0	2,276
Labor force (millions)	0.61	0.69	1,209
Unemployment rate (% of labor force)	20.3	..	5.7
GNI per capita, *World Bank Atlas* method ($)	1,880	3,210	2,038
GDP growth, 1995–2000 and 2000–06 (average annual %)	3.5	4.8	7.6
Agriculture value added (% of GDP)	11.0	10.9	11.9
Industry value added (% of GDP)	28.4	30.6	43.5
Manufacturing value added (% of GDP)	11.1	13.9	26.7
Services value added (% of GDP)	60.7	58.5	44.6
Inflation (annual % change in consumer price index)	..	5.1	
Exchange rate (local currency units per $)	6.9	6.8	
Exports of goods and services (% of GDP)	45.6	54.5	40.4
Imports of goods and services (% of GDP)	51.2	55.5	36.4
Business environment			
Ease of doing business (ranking 1-178; 1=best)	..	43	
Time to start a business (days)	..	99	53
Procedures to start a business (number)	..	10	10
Firing cost (weeks of wages)	..	24.0	50.2
Closing a business (years to resolve insolvency)	..	1.5	3.3
Total tax rate (% of profit)	..	26.5	45.8
Highest marginal tax rate, corporate (%)	35	35	
Business entry rate (new registrations as % of total)	..	..	7.6
Enterprise surveys			
Time dealing with gov't officials (% of management time)	..	2.9	
Firms expected to give gifts in meetings w/tax officials (%)	..	2.6	
Firms using banks to finance investments (% of firms)	..	8.1	
Delay in obtaining an electrical connection (days)	..	9.2	
ISO certification ownership (% of firms)	..	17.6	
Private sector investment			
Invest. in infrastructure w/private participation ($ millions)	10	9	38,154
Private foreign direct investment, net (% of GDP)	..	..	3.0
Gross fixed capital formation (% of GDP)	18.8	28.2	33.5
Gross fixed private capital formation (% of GDP)	12.7	20.0	10.9
Finance and banking			
Government cash surplus or deficit (% of GDP)	-3.0	-6.8	-0.9
Government debt (% of GDP)	..	..	
Deposit money banks' assets (% of GDP)	46.5	56.3	87.8
Total financial system deposits (% of GDP)	35.2	38.8	43.1
Bank capital to asset ratio (%)	8.7	8.3	10.7
Bank nonperforming loans to total gross loans ratio (%)	3.4	2.9	4.0
Domestic credit to the private sector (% of GDP)	45.6	61.7	81.3
Real interest rate (%)	4.2	1.9	
Interest rate spread (percentage points)	7.9	4.9	7.2
Infrastructure			
Paved roads (% of total roads)	13.6	..	65.8
Electric power consumption (kWh per capita)	1,270	1,428	1,502
Power outages in a typical month (number)	..	1.7	
Fixed line and mobile subscribers (per 100 people)	10	31	60
Internet users (per 100 people)	1.6	4.0	11.4
Cost of telephone call to U.S. ($ per 3 minutes)	4.28	..	2.08

Nepal

	Country data		Low-income group
	2000	2006	2006
Economic and social context			
Population (millions)	24.4	27.6	2,420
Labor force (millions)	9.2	10.8	995
Unemployment rate (% of labor force)	8.8	..	..
GNI per capita, *World Bank Atlas* method ($)	220	320	649
GDP growth, 1995–2000 and 2000–06 (average annual %)	4.6	3.3	6.5
Agriculture value added (% of GDP)	40.8	34.4	20.4
Industry value added (% of GDP)	22.1	16.3	27.7
Manufacturing value added (% of GDP)	9.4	7.7	15.8
Services value added (% of GDP)	37.0	49.3	51.9
Inflation (annual % change in consumer price index)	2.5	7.6	
Exchange rate (local currency units per $)	71.1	72.8	
Exports of goods and services (% of GDP)	23.3	13.6	26.7
Imports of goods and services (% of GDP)	32.4	31.7	30.1
Business environment			
Ease of doing business (ranking 1-178; 1=best)	..	111	
Time to start a business (days)	..	31	54
Procedures to start a business (number)	..	7	10
Firing cost (weeks of wages)	..	90.0	62.6
Closing a business (years to resolve insolvency)	..	5.0	3.8
Total tax rate (% of profit)	..	32.5	67.4
Highest marginal tax rate, corporate (%)	..	..	
Business entry rate (new registrations as % of total)	..	..	6.4
Enterprise surveys			
Time dealing with gov't officials (% of management time)	..	..	
Firms expected to give gifts in meetings w/tax officials (%)	..	..	
Firms using banks to finance investments (% of firms)	..	..	
Delay in obtaining an electrical connection (days)	..	..	
ISO certification ownership (% of firms)	..	..	
Private sector investment			
Invest. in infrastructure w/private participation ($ millions)	54	34	29,785
Private foreign direct investment, net (% of GDP)	0.0	-0.1	2.6
Gross fixed capital formation (% of GDP)	19.3	20.9	26.7
Gross fixed private capital formation (% of GDP)	12.4	18.2	19.6
Finance and banking			
Government cash surplus or deficit (% of GDP)	..	-1.6	-2.6
Government debt (% of GDP)	64.6	50.3	
Deposit money banks' assets (% of GDP)	31.9	55.5	50.5
Total financial system deposits (% of GDP)	35.4	50.7	44.6
Bank capital to asset ratio (%)	..	..	..
Bank nonperforming loans to total gross loans ratio (%)	..	..	..
Domestic credit to the private sector (% of GDP)	30.7	37.7	38.3
Real interest rate (%)	4.7	1.2	
Interest rate spread (percentage points)	3.5	5.9	11.3
Infrastructure			
Paved roads (% of total roads)	30.8	56.9	..
Electric power consumption (kWh per capita)	58	70	391
Power outages in a typical month (number)	..	..	
Fixed line and mobile subscribers (per 100 people)	1	6	17
Internet users (per 100 people)	0.2	0.9	4.2
Cost of telephone call to U.S. ($ per 3 minutes)	5.28	2.04	1.99

Netherlands

High income

	Country data		High-income group
	2000	2006	2006
Economic and social context			
Population (millions)	15.9	16.3	1,031
Labor force (millions)	8.1	8.6	504
Unemployment rate (% of labor force)	2.9	5.2	6.2
GNI per capita, *World Bank Atlas* method ($)	26,580	43,050	36,608
GDP growth, 1995–2000 and 2000–06 (average annual %)	4.1	1.3	2.3
Agriculture value added (% of GDP)	2.6	2.3	1.5
Industry value added (% of GDP)	24.9	24.6	26.2
Manufacturing value added (% of GDP)	15.6	14.1	16.8
Services value added (% of GDP)	72.4	73.2	72.3
Inflation (annual % change in consumer price index)	2.5	1.1	
Exchange rate (local currency units per $)	1.1	0.8	
Exports of goods and services (% of GDP)	70.1	74.2	25.6
Imports of goods and services (% of GDP)	64.5	66.5	26.3
Business environment			
Ease of doing business (ranking 1-178; 1=best)	..	21	
Time to start a business (days)	..	10	22
Procedures to start a business (number)	..	6	7
Firing cost (weeks of wages)	..	17.0	34.9
Closing a business (years to resolve insolvency)	..	1.1	2.0
Total tax rate (% of profit)	..	43.4	41.5
Highest marginal tax rate, corporate (%)	35	30	
Business entry rate (new registrations as % of total)	9.4	11.3	10.1
Enterprise surveys			
Time dealing with gov't officials (% of management time)	..	..	
Firms expected to give gifts in meetings w/tax officials (%)	..	..	
Firms using banks to finance investments (% of firms)	..	..	
Delay in obtaining an electrical connection (days)	..	..	
ISO certification ownership (% of firms)	..	..	
Private sector investment			
Invest. in infrastructure w/private participation ($ millions)	..	..	849
Private foreign direct investment, net (% of GDP)	16.4	1.1	2.7
Gross fixed capital formation (% of GDP)	21.9	20.1	20.4
Gross fixed private capital formation (% of GDP)	..	..	..
Finance and banking			
Government cash surplus or deficit (% of GDP)	2.0	0.5	–1.3
Government debt (% of GDP)	54.5	49.0	47.6
Deposit money banks' assets (% of GDP)	..	..	99.7
Total financial system deposits (% of GDP)	..	..	..
Bank capital to asset ratio (%)	5.1	4.0	6.2
Bank nonperforming loans to total gross loans ratio (%)	1.8	1.0	1.1
Domestic credit to the private sector (% of GDP)	134.2	176.2	162.0
Real interest rate (%)	0.6	2.0	
Interest rate spread (percentage points)	1.9	0.6	4.4
Infrastructure			
Paved roads (% of total roads)	90.0	..	90.9
Electric power consumption (kWh per capita)	6,560	6,988	9,760
Power outages in a typical month (number)	..	..	
Fixed line and mobile subscribers (per 100 people)	130	144	143
Internet users (per 100 people)	44.0	89.0	59.3
Cost of telephone call to U.S. ($ per 3 minutes)	0.56	0.32	0.77

Netherlands Antilles

	Country data		High-income group
	2000	**2006**	**2006**
Economic and social context			
Population (millions)	0.18	0.19	1,031
Labor force (millions)	0.08	0.09	504
Unemployment rate (% of labor force)	14.0	15.1	6.2
GNI per capita, *World Bank Atlas* method ($)	..	..	36,608
GDP growth, 1995–2000 and 2000–06 (average annual %)	..	..	2.3
Agriculture value added (% of GDP)	..	..	1.5
Industry value added (% of GDP)	..	..	26.2
Manufacturing value added (% of GDP)	..	..	16.8
Services value added (% of GDP)	..	..	72.3
Inflation (annual % change in consumer price index)	5.8	3.1	
Exchange rate (local currency units per $)	1.8	1.8	
Exports of goods and services (% of GDP)	..	..	25.6
Imports of goods and services (% of GDP)	..	..	26.3
Business environment			
Ease of doing business (ranking 1-178; 1=best)	..	..	
Time to start a business (days)	..	..	22
Procedures to start a business (number)	..	..	7
Firing cost (weeks of wages)	..	..	34.9
Closing a business (years to resolve insolvency)	..	..	2.0
Total tax rate (% of profit)	..	..	41.5
Highest marginal tax rate, corporate (%)	35	35	
Business entry rate (new registrations as % of total)	..	..	10.1
Enterprise surveys			
Time dealing with gov't officials (% of management time)	..	..	
Firms expected to give gifts in meetings w/tax officials (%)	..	..	
Firms using banks to finance investments (% of firms)	..	..	
Delay in obtaining an electrical connection (days)	..	..	
ISO certification ownership (% of firms)	..	..	
Private sector investment			
Invest. in infrastructure w/private participation ($ millions)	..	..	849
Private foreign direct investment, net (% of GDP)	..	..	2.7
Gross fixed capital formation (% of GDP)	..	..	20.4
Gross fixed private capital formation (% of GDP)	..	..	..
Finance and banking			
Government cash surplus or deficit (% of GDP)	..	..	-1.3
Government debt (% of GDP)	..	..	47.6
Deposit money banks' assets (% of GDP)	..	..	99.7
Total financial system deposits (% of GDP)	..	..	..
Bank capital to asset ratio (%)	..	..	6.2
Bank nonperforming loans to total gross loans ratio (%)	..	..	1.1
Domestic credit to the private sector (% of GDP)	..	..	162.0
Real interest rate (%)	..	..	
Interest rate spread (percentage points)	6.2	6.5	4.4
Infrastructure			
Paved roads (% of total roads)	..	..	90.9
Electric power consumption (kWh per capita)	5,402	5,172	9,760
Power outages in a typical month (number)	..	..	
Fixed line and mobile subscribers (per 100 people)	60	..	143
Internet users (per 100 people)	1.1	..	59.3
Cost of telephone call to U.S. ($ per 3 minutes)	..	..	0.77

New Caledonia

	Country data		High-income group
	2000	**2006**	**2006**
Economic and social context			
Population (millions)	0.21	0.24	1,031
Labor force (millions)	0.09	0.10	504
Unemployment rate (% of labor force)	..	..	6.2
GNI per capita, *World Bank Atlas* method ($)	14,020	..	36,608
GDP growth, 1995–2000 and 2000–06 (average annual %)	0.2	..	2.3
Agriculture value added (% of GDP)	3.7	..	1.5
Industry value added (% of GDP)	19.6	..	26.2
Manufacturing value added (% of GDP)	4.0	..	16.8
Services value added (% of GDP)	76.7	..	72.3
Inflation (annual % change in consumer price index)	..	..	
Exchange rate (local currency units per $)	129.5	95.1	
Exports of goods and services (% of GDP)	13.1	..	25.6
Imports of goods and services (% of GDP)	33.0	..	26.3
Business environment			
Ease of doing business (ranking 1-178; 1=best)	..	..	
Time to start a business (days)	..	..	22
Procedures to start a business (number)	..	..	7
Firing cost (weeks of wages)	..	..	34.9
Closing a business (years to resolve insolvency)	..	..	2.0
Total tax rate (% of profit)	..	..	41.5
Highest marginal tax rate, corporate (%)	30	30	
Business entry rate (new registrations as % of total)	..	..	10.1
Enterprise surveys			
Time dealing with gov't officials (% of management time)	..	..	
Firms expected to give gifts in meetings w/tax officials (%)	..	..	
Firms using banks to finance investments (% of firms)	..	..	
Delay in obtaining an electrical connection (days)	..	..	
ISO certification ownership (% of firms)	..	..	
Private sector investment			
Invest. in infrastructure w/private participation ($ millions)	..	..	849
Private foreign direct investment, net (% of GDP)	..	..	2.7
Gross fixed capital formation (% of GDP)	..	..	20.4
Gross fixed private capital formation (% of GDP)	..	..	..
Finance and banking			
Government cash surplus or deficit (% of GDP)	..	..	-1.3
Government debt (% of GDP)	..	..	47.6
Deposit money banks' assets (% of GDP)	..	..	99.7
Total financial system deposits (% of GDP)	..	..	..
Bank capital to asset ratio (%)	..	..	6.2
Bank nonperforming loans to total gross loans ratio (%)	..	..	1.1
Domestic credit to the private sector (% of GDP)	..	..	162.0
Real interest rate (%)	..	..	
Interest rate spread (percentage points)	..	..	4.4
Infrastructure			
Paved roads (% of total roads)	..	..	90.9
Electric power consumption (kWh per capita)	..	..	9,760
Power outages in a typical month (number)	..	..	
Fixed line and mobile subscribers (per 100 people)	47	81	143
Internet users (per 100 people)	14.1	33.6	59.3
Cost of telephone call to U.S. ($ per 3 minutes)	3.43	3.13	0.77

New Zealand

	Country data		High-income group
	2000	2006	2006
Economic and social context			
Population (millions)	3.9	4.2	1,031
Labor force (millions)	1.9	2.2	504
Unemployment rate (% of labor force)	5.9	3.7	6.2
GNI per capita, *World Bank Atlas* method ($)	13,760	26,750	36,608
GDP growth, 1995–2000 and 2000–06 (average annual %)	2.5	3.3	2.3
Agriculture value added (% of GDP)	8.9	..	1.5
Industry value added (% of GDP)	25.3	..	26.2
Manufacturing value added (% of GDP)	16.9	..	16.8
Services value added (% of GDP)	65.8	..	72.3
Inflation (annual % change in consumer price index)	2.6	3.4	
Exchange rate (local currency units per $)	2.2	1.5	
Exports of goods and services (% of GDP)	35.5	27.8	25.6
Imports of goods and services (% of GDP)	33.8	30.5	26.3
Business environment			
Ease of doing business (ranking 1-178; 1=best)	..	2	
Time to start a business (days)	..	12	22
Procedures to start a business (number)	..	2	7
Firing cost (weeks of wages)	..	..	34.9
Closing a business (years to resolve insolvency)	..	1.3	2.0
Total tax rate (% of profit)	..	35.1	41.5
Highest marginal tax rate, corporate (%)	33	33	
Business entry rate (new registrations as % of total)	15.6	16.1	10.1
Enterprise surveys			
Time dealing with gov't officials (% of management time)	..	..	
Firms expected to give gifts in meetings w/tax officials (%)	..	..	
Firms using banks to finance investments (% of firms)	..	..	
Delay in obtaining an electrical connection (days)	..	..	
ISO certification ownership (% of firms)	..	..	
Private sector investment			
Invest. in infrastructure w/private participation ($ millions)	..	..	849
Private foreign direct investment, net (% of GDP)	7.4	7.6	2.7
Gross fixed capital formation (% of GDP)	20.4	23.9	20.4
Gross fixed private capital formation (% of GDP)	..	..	..
Finance and banking			
Government cash surplus or deficit (% of GDP)	1.7	4.7	–1.3
Government debt (% of GDP)	33.9	45.9	47.6
Deposit money banks' assets (% of GDP)	..	..	99.7
Total financial system deposits (% of GDP)	..	..	..
Bank capital to asset ratio (%)	..	..	6.2
Bank nonperforming loans to total gross loans ratio (%)	..	..	1.1
Domestic credit to the private sector (% of GDP)	111.5	144.2	162.0
Real interest rate (%)	6.5	10.8	
Interest rate spread (percentage points)	3.9	5.3	4.4
Infrastructure			
Paved roads (% of total roads)	62.8	64.9	90.9
Electric power consumption (kWh per capita)	9,076	9,656	9,760
Power outages in a typical month (number)	..		
Fixed line and mobile subscribers (per 100 people)	87	127	143
Internet users (per 100 people)	39.3	76.5	59.3
Cost of telephone call to U.S. ($ per 3 minutes)	0.80	1.30	0.77

Nicaragua

Lower middle income

	Country data		Lower middle-income group
	2000	2006	2006
Economic and social context			
Population (millions)	5.1	5.5	2,276
Labor force (millions)	1.8	2.1	1,209
Unemployment rate (% of labor force)	6.2	8.0	5.7
GNI per capita, World Bank Atlas method ($)	730	930	2,038
GDP growth, 1995–2000 and 2000–06 (average annual %)	5.0	3.3	7.6
Agriculture value added (% of GDP)	20.9	19.7	11.9
Industry value added (% of GDP)	28.2	29.5	43.5
Manufacturing value added (% of GDP)	17.0	18.5	26.7
Services value added (% of GDP)	50.9	50.8	44.6
Inflation (annual % change in consumer price index)	3.8	9.1	
Exchange rate (local currency units per $)	12.7	17.6	
Exports of goods and services (% of GDP)	23.9	31.1	40.4
Imports of goods and services (% of GDP)	51.1	61.0	36.4
Business environment			
Ease of doing business (ranking 1-178; 1=best)	..	93	
Time to start a business (days)	..	39	53
Procedures to start a business (number)	..	6	10
Firing cost (weeks of wages)	..	24.0	50.2
Closing a business (years to resolve insolvency)	..	2.2	3.3
Total tax rate (% of profit)	..	63.2	45.8
Highest marginal tax rate, corporate (%)	25	30	
Business entry rate (new registrations as % of total)	..	..	7.6
Enterprise surveys			
Time dealing with gov't officials (% of management time)	..	9.3	
Firms expected to give gifts in meetings w/tax officials (%)	..	2.6	
Firms using banks to finance investments (% of firms)	..	13.0	
Delay in obtaining an electrical connection (days)	..	62.7	
ISO certification ownership (% of firms)	..	18.7	
Private sector investment			
Invest. in infrastructure w/private participation ($ millions)	219	76	38,154
Private foreign direct investment, net (% of GDP)	6.8	5.3	3.0
Gross fixed capital formation (% of GDP)	26.5	27.9	33.5
Gross fixed private capital formation (% of GDP)	19.8	22.1	10.9
Finance and banking			
Government cash surplus or deficit (% of GDP)	-3.6	0.1	-0.9
Government debt (% of GDP)	..	..	..
Deposit money banks' assets (% of GDP)	..	36.1	87.8
Total financial system deposits (% of GDP)	..	33.3	43.1
Bank capital to asset ratio (%)	6.3	8.8	10.7
Bank nonperforming loans to total gross loans ratio (%)	5.2	8.0	4.0
Domestic credit to the private sector (% of GDP)	33.2	33.8	81.3
Real interest rate (%)	8.8	0.9	
Interest rate spread (percentage points)	7.3	6.7	7.2
Infrastructure			
Paved roads (% of total roads)	11.1	..	65.8
Electric power consumption (kWh per capita)	337	414	1,502
Power outages in a typical month (number)	..	13.2	
Fixed line and mobile subscribers (per 100 people)	5	38	60
Internet users (per 100 people)	1.0	2.8	11.4
Cost of telephone call to U.S. ($ per 3 minutes)	3.20	3.15	2.08

Niger

Sub-Saharan Africa   **Low income**

	Country data		Low-income group
	2000	2006	2006
Economic and social context			
Population (millions)	11.1	13.7	2,420
Labor force (millions)	4.8	5.9	995
Unemployment rate (% of labor force)	..	..	..
GNI per capita, *World Bank Atlas* method ($)	170	270	649
GDP growth, 1995–2000 and 2000–06 (average annual %)	3.4	3.9	6.5
Agriculture value added (% of GDP)	37.8	39.9	20.4
Industry value added (% of GDP)	17.8	16.8	27.7
Manufacturing value added (% of GDP)	6.8	6.6	15.8
Services value added (% of GDP)	44.4	43.4	51.9
Inflation (annual % change in consumer price index)	2.9	0.0	
Exchange rate (local currency units per $)	712.0	522.9	
Exports of goods and services (% of GDP)	17.8	14.9	26.7
Imports of goods and services (% of GDP)	25.7	24.0	30.1
Business environment			
Ease of doing business (ranking 1-178; 1=best)	..	169	
Time to start a business (days)	..	23	54
Procedures to start a business (number)	..	11	10
Firing cost (weeks of wages)	..	31.0	62.6
Closing a business (years to resolve insolvency)	..	5.0	3.8
Total tax rate (% of profit)	..	42.4	67.4
Highest marginal tax rate, corporate (%)	..	..	
Business entry rate (new registrations as % of total)	..	..	6.4
Enterprise surveys			
Time dealing with gov't officials (% of management time)	..	11.5	
Firms expected to give gifts in meetings w/tax officials (%)	..	17.1	
Firms using banks to finance investments (% of firms)	..	14.6	
Delay in obtaining an electrical connection (days)	..	20.6	
ISO certification ownership (% of firms)	..	4.8	
Private sector investment			
Invest. in infrastructure w/private participation ($ millions)	13	47	29,785
Private foreign direct investment, net (% of GDP)	0.5	0.6	2.6
Gross fixed capital formation (% of GDP)	11.2	18.4	26.7
Gross fixed private capital formation (% of GDP)	4.6	8.7	19.6
Finance and banking			
Government cash surplus or deficit (% of GDP)	..	..	-2.6
Government debt (% of GDP)	..	..	..
Deposit money banks' assets (% of GDP)	5.8	8.5	50.5
Total financial system deposits (% of GDP)	5.5	7.9	44.6
Bank capital to asset ratio (%)	..	..	..
Bank nonperforming loans to total gross loans ratio (%)	..	..	..
Domestic credit to the private sector (% of GDP)	4.8	8.3	38.3
Real interest rate (%)	..	..	
Interest rate spread (percentage points)	..	..	11.3
Infrastructure			
Paved roads (% of total roads)	25.7	20.6	..
Electric power consumption (kWh per capita)	..	..	391
Power outages in a typical month (number)	..	20.7	
Fixed line and mobile subscribers (per 100 people)	0	3	17
Internet users (per 100 people)	0.0	0.3	4.2
Cost of telephone call to U.S. ($ per 3 minutes)	9.03	..	1.99

Nigeria

Low income

	Country data		Low-income group
	2000	**2006**	**2006**
Economic and social context			
Population (millions)	124.8	144.7	2,420
Labor force (millions)	45.0	52.7	995
Unemployment rate (% of labor force)	..	..	..
GNI per capita, *World Bank Atlas* method ($)	270	620	649
GDP growth, 1995–2000 and 2000–06 (average annual %)	2.7	6.0	6.5
Agriculture value added (% of GDP)	26.3	23.3	20.4
Industry value added (% of GDP)	52.7	56.8	27.7
Manufacturing value added (% of GDP)	3.7	4.0	15.8
Services value added (% of GDP)	21.0	19.9	51.9
Inflation (annual % change in consumer price index)	6.9	8.2	
Exchange rate (local currency units per $)	101.7	128.7	
Exports of goods and services (% of GDP)	54.3	56.3	26.7
Imports of goods and services (% of GDP)	32.2	34.7	30.1
Business environment			
Ease of doing business (ranking 1-178; 1=best)	..	108	
Time to start a business (days)	..	34	54
Procedures to start a business (number)	..	9	10
Firing cost (weeks of wages)	..	50.0	62.6
Closing a business (years to resolve insolvency)	..	2.0	3.8
Total tax rate (% of profit)	..	29.9	67.4
Highest marginal tax rate, corporate (%)	30	..	
Business entry rate (new registrations as % of total)	..	..	6.4
Enterprise surveys			
Time dealing with gov't officials (% of management time)	..	..	
Firms expected to give gifts in meetings w/tax officials (%)	..	..	
Firms using banks to finance investments (% of firms)	..	..	
Delay in obtaining an electrical connection (days)	..	..	
ISO certification ownership (% of firms)	..	..	
Private sector investment			
Invest. in infrastructure w/private participation ($ millions)	76	2,797	29,785
Private foreign direct investment, net (% of GDP)	2.5	4.7	2.6
Gross fixed capital formation (% of GDP)	20.3	22.0	26.7
Gross fixed private capital formation (% of GDP)	10.7	11.7	19.6
Finance and banking			
Government cash surplus or deficit (% of GDP)	..	..	-2.6
Government debt (% of GDP)	..	..	..
Deposit money banks' assets (% of GDP)	15.5	17.0	50.5
Total financial system deposits (% of GDP)	12.6	13.2	44.6
Bank capital to asset ratio (%)	7.4	14.7	..
Bank nonperforming loans to total gross loans ratio (%)	22.6	21.9	..
Domestic credit to the private sector (% of GDP)	12.5	15.0	38.3
Real interest rate (%)	-12.2	8.3	
Interest rate spread (percentage points)	9.6	7.2	11.3
Infrastructure			
Paved roads (% of total roads)	30.9	15.0	..
Electric power consumption (kWh per capita)	73	127	391
Power outages in a typical month (number)	..	..	
Fixed line and mobile subscribers (per 100 people)	0	24	17
Internet users (per 100 people)	0.1	5.5	4.2
Cost of telephone call to U.S. ($ per 3 minutes)	7.15	1.49	1.99

Northern Mariana Islands

East Asia & Pacific   **Upper middle income**

	Country data		Upper middle-income group
	2000	**2006**	**2006**
Economic and social context			
Population (millions)	..	0.08	811
Labor force (millions)	..	..	374
Unemployment rate (% of labor force)	..	..	9.8
GNI per capita, *World Bank Atlas* method ($)	..	..	5,913
GDP growth, 1995–2000 and 2000–06 (average annual %)	..	..	3.9
Agriculture value added (% of GDP)	..	..	5.7
Industry value added (% of GDP)	..	..	32.4
Manufacturing value added (% of GDP)	..	..	19.4
Services value added (% of GDP)	..	..	62.0
Inflation (annual % change in consumer price index)	..	..	
Exchange rate (local currency units per $)	..	..	
Exports of goods and services (% of GDP)	..	..	32.7
Imports of goods and services (% of GDP)	..	..	30.3
Business environment			
Ease of doing business (ranking 1-178; 1=best)	..	..	
Time to start a business (days)	..	..	41
Procedures to start a business (number)	..	..	9
Firing cost (weeks of wages)	..	..	39.7
Closing a business (years to resolve insolvency)	..	..	2.9
Total tax rate (% of profit)	..	..	44.5
Highest marginal tax rate, corporate (%)	..	..	
Business entry rate (new registrations as % of total)	..	..	9.1
Enterprise surveys			
Time dealing with gov't officials (% of management time)	..	..	
Firms expected to give gifts in meetings w/tax officials (%)	..	..	
Firms using banks to finance investments (% of firms)	..	..	
Delay in obtaining an electrical connection (days)	..	..	
ISO certification ownership (% of firms)	..	..	
Private sector investment			
Invest. in infrastructure w/private participation ($ millions)	..	..	45,869
Private foreign direct investment, net (% of GDP)	..	..	3.5
Gross fixed capital formation (% of GDP)	..	..	19.9
Gross fixed private capital formation (% of GDP)	..	..	..
Finance and banking			
Government cash surplus or deficit (% of GDP)	..	..	..
Government debt (% of GDP)	..	..	
Deposit money banks' assets (% of GDP)	..	..	52.9
Total financial system deposits (% of GDP)	..	..	41.4
Bank capital to asset ratio (%)	..	..	9.8
Bank nonperforming loans to total gross loans ratio (%)	..	..	3.2
Domestic credit to the private sector (% of GDP)	..	..	41.4
Real interest rate (%)	..	..	
Interest rate spread (percentage points)	..	..	5.9
Infrastructure			
Paved roads (% of total roads)	..	..	..
Electric power consumption (kWh per capita)	..	..	3,131
Power outages in a typical month (number)	..	..	
Fixed line and mobile subscribers (per 100 people)	..	..	88
Internet users (per 100 people)	..	..	22.2
Cost of telephone call to U.S. ($ per 3 minutes)	..	..	1.06

Norway

	Country data		High-income group
	2000	2006	2006
Economic and social context			
Population (millions)	4.5	4.7	1,031
Labor force (millions)	2.4	2.6	504
Unemployment rate (% of labor force)	3.4	4.6	6.2
GNI per capita, *World Bank Atlas* method ($)	35,870	68,440	36,608
GDP growth, 1995–2000 and 2000–06 (average annual %)	3.6	2.3	2.3
Agriculture value added (% of GDP)	2.1	1.6	1.5
Industry value added (% of GDP)	42.0	44.9	26.2
Manufacturing value added (% of GDP)	10.6	9.4	16.8
Services value added (% of GDP)	56.0	53.6	72.3
Inflation (annual % change in consumer price index)	3.1	2.3	
Exchange rate (local currency units per $)	8.8	6.4	
Exports of goods and services (% of GDP)	46.5	46.4	25.6
Imports of goods and services (% of GDP)	29.4	28.6	26.3
Business environment			
Ease of doing business (ranking 1-178; 1=best)	..	11	
Time to start a business (days)	..	10	22
Procedures to start a business (number)	..	6	7
Firing cost (weeks of wages)	..	13.0	34.9
Closing a business (years to resolve insolvency)	..	0.9	2.0
Total tax rate (% of profit)	..	42.0	41.5
Highest marginal tax rate, corporate (%)	28	28	
Business entry rate (new registrations as % of total)	*14.5*	15.9	*10.1*
Enterprise surveys			
Time dealing with gov't officials (% of management time)	..	..	
Firms expected to give gifts in meetings w/tax officials (%)	..	..	
Firms using banks to finance investments (% of firms)	..	..	
Delay in obtaining an electrical connection (days)	..	..	
ISO certification ownership (% of firms)	..	..	
Private sector investment			
Invest. in infrastructure w/private participation ($ millions)	..	..	849
Private foreign direct investment, net (% of GDP)	4.1	1.4	2.7
Gross fixed capital formation (% of GDP)	18.4	18.8	*20.4*
Gross fixed private capital formation (% of GDP)	..	..	..
Finance and banking			
Government cash surplus or deficit (% of GDP)	15.7	17.9	-1.3
Government debt (% of GDP)	23.5	48.4	47.6
Deposit money banks' assets (% of GDP)	66.3	83.1	99.7
Total financial system deposits (% of GDP)	44.0	50.5	
Bank capital to asset ratio (%)	7.0	5.0	6.2
Bank nonperforming loans to total gross loans ratio (%)	1.2	0.6	1.1
Domestic credit to the private sector (% of GDP)	75.8	87.9	162.0
Real interest rate (%)	-5.8	-4.2	
Interest rate spread (percentage points)	2.2	2.2	*4.4*
Infrastructure			
Paved roads (% of total roads)	76.0	..	*90.9*
Electric power consumption (kWh per capita)	24,994	25,137	*9,760*
Power outages in a typical month (number)	..	..	
Fixed line and mobile subscribers (per 100 people)	125	152	143
Internet users (per 100 people)	26.7	87.4	59.3
Cost of telephone call to U.S. ($ per 3 minutes)	0.40	..	*0.77*

Oman

	Middle East & North Africa		Upper middle income

	Country data		Upper middle-income group
	2000	2006	2006
Economic and social context			
Population (millions)	2.4	2.5	811
Labor force (millions)	0.88	0.97	374
Unemployment rate (% of labor force)	..	..	9.8
GNI per capita, World Bank Atlas method ($)	6,720	11,120	5,913
GDP growth, 1995–2000 and 2000–06 (average annual %)	3.2	4.2	3.9
Agriculture value added (% of GDP)	2.0	1.9	5.7
Industry value added (% of GDP)	57.2	54.9	32.4
Manufacturing value added (% of GDP)	5.4	8.3	19.4
Services value added (% of GDP)	40.8	43.2	62.0
Inflation (annual % change in consumer price index)	-0.8	3.2	
Exchange rate (local currency units per $)	0.4	0.4	
Exports of goods and services (% of GDP)	59.2	63.3	32.7
Imports of goods and services (% of GDP)	31.4	35.9	30.3
Business environment			
Ease of doing business (ranking 1-178; 1=best)	..	49	
Time to start a business (days)	..	34	41
Procedures to start a business (number)	..	9	9
Firing cost (weeks of wages)	..	4.0	39.7
Closing a business (years to resolve insolvency)	..	4.0	2.9
Total tax rate (% of profit)	..	21.6	44.5
Highest marginal tax rate, corporate (%)	12	12	
Business entry rate (new registrations as % of total)	..	..	9.1
Enterprise surveys			
Time dealing with gov't officials (% of management time)	..	..	
Firms expected to give gifts in meetings w/tax officials (%)	..	..	
Firms using banks to finance investments (% of firms)	..	6.5	
Delay in obtaining an electrical connection (days)	..	14.7	
ISO certification ownership (% of firms)	..	10.8	
Private sector investment			
Invest. in infrastructure w/private participation ($ millions)	29	1,047	45,869
Private foreign direct investment, net (% of GDP)	0.4	2.9	3.5
Gross fixed capital formation (% of GDP)	11.9	18.1	19.9
Gross fixed private capital formation (% of GDP)	4.4	..	..
Finance and banking			
Government cash surplus or deficit (% of GDP)	-4.4	..	..
Government debt (% of GDP)	19.1	..	..
Deposit money banks' assets (% of GDP)	43.8	32.8	52.9
Total financial system deposits (% of GDP)	30.7	24.4	41.4
Bank capital to asset ratio (%)	12.8	13.2	9.8
Bank nonperforming loans to total gross loans ratio (%)	11.3	7.8	3.2
Domestic credit to the private sector (% of GDP)	36.8	30.9	41.4
Real interest rate (%)	-8.3	-9.2	
Interest rate spread (percentage points)	2.4	3.4	5.9
Infrastructure			
Paved roads (% of total roads)	30.0	..	..
Electric power consumption (kWh per capita)	3,140	3,757	3,131
Power outages in a typical month (number)	..	..	
Fixed line and mobile subscribers (per 100 people)	16	82	88
Internet users (per 100 people)	3.7	12.5	22.2
Cost of telephone call to U.S. ($ per 3 minutes)	7.89	1.87	1.06

Pakistan

	Country data		Low-income group
	2000	2006	2006
Economic and social context			
Population (millions)	138.1	159.0	2,420
Labor force (millions)	46.3	59.6	995
Unemployment rate (% of labor force)	7.2	7.7	..
GNI per capita, *World Bank Atlas* method ($)	490	800	649
GDP growth, 1995–2000 and 2000–06 (average annual %)	3.0	5.5	6.5
Agriculture value added (% of GDP)	25.9	19.4	20.4
Industry value added (% of GDP)	23.3	27.2	27.7
Manufacturing value added (% of GDP)	14.7	19.5	15.8
Services value added (% of GDP)	50.7	53.4	51.9
Inflation (annual % change in consumer price index)	4.4	7.9	
Exchange rate (local currency units per $)	53.6	60.3	
Exports of goods and services (% of GDP)	13.4	15.3	26.7
Imports of goods and services (% of GDP)	14.7	23.3	30.1
Business environment			
Ease of doing business (ranking 1-178; 1=best)	..	76	
Time to start a business (days)	..	24	54
Procedures to start a business (number)	..	11	10
Firing cost (weeks of wages)	..	90.0	62.6
Closing a business (years to resolve insolvency)	..	2.8	3.8
Total tax rate (% of profit)	..	40.7	67.4
Highest marginal tax rate, corporate (%)	..	37	
Business entry rate (new registrations as % of total)	3.5	9.4	6.4
Enterprise surveys			
Time dealing with gov't officials (% of management time)	8.7	..	
Firms expected to give gifts in meetings w/tax officials (%)	..	..	
Firms using banks to finance investments (% of firms)	3.6	..	
Delay in obtaining an electrical connection (days)	32.9	..	
ISO certification ownership (% of firms)	17.0	..	
Private sector investment			
Invest. in infrastructure w/private participation ($ millions)	77	2,926	29,785
Private foreign direct investment, net (% of GDP)	0.4	3.4	2.6
Gross fixed capital formation (% of GDP)	15.9	20.1	26.7
Gross fixed private capital formation (% of GDP)	10.3	15.4	19.6
Finance and banking			
Government cash surplus or deficit (% of GDP)	–4.1	–4.2	–2.6
Government debt (% of GDP)	74.0	..	
Deposit money banks' assets (% of GDP)	30.2	37.0	50.5
Total financial system deposits (% of GDP)	26.5	34.5	44.6
Bank capital to asset ratio (%)	4.9	8.8	..
Bank nonperforming loans to total gross loans ratio (%)	19.5	7.7	..
Domestic credit to the private sector (% of GDP)	22.3	29.0	38.3
Real interest rate (%)	..	1.6	
Interest rate spread (percentage points)	..	6.8	11.3
Infrastructure			
Paved roads (% of total roads)	56.0	64.7	..
Electric power consumption (kWh per capita)	374	456	391
Power outages in a typical month (number)	..	..	
Fixed line and mobile subscribers (per 100 people)	2	25	17
Internet users (per 100 people)	0.2	7.5	4.2
Cost of telephone call to U.S. ($ per 3 minutes)	3.60	1.03	1.99

Palau

East Asia & Pacific   **Upper middle income**

	Country data		Upper middle-income group
	2000	2006	2006
Economic and social context			
Population (millions)	..	0.02	811
Labor force (millions)	..	..	374
Unemployment rate (% of labor force)	..	..	9.8
GNI per capita, *World Bank Atlas* method ($)	..	7,990	5,913
GDP growth, 1995–2000 and 2000–06 (average annual %)	1.2	1.8	3.9
Agriculture value added (% of GDP)	3.9	3.1	5.7
Industry value added (% of GDP)	15.1	19.0	32.4
Manufacturing value added (% of GDP)	1.4	0.4	19.4
Services value added (% of GDP)	80.0	76.9	62.0
Inflation (annual % change in consumer price index)	..	..	
Exchange rate (local currency units per $)	..	..	
Exports of goods and services (% of GDP)	9.6	71.7	32.7
Imports of goods and services (% of GDP)	106.1	81.9	30.3
Business environment			
Ease of doing business (ranking 1-178; 1=best)	..	82	
Time to start a business (days)	..	28	41
Procedures to start a business (number)	..	8	9
Firing cost (weeks of wages)	..	..	39.7
Closing a business (years to resolve insolvency)	..	1.0	2.9
Total tax rate (% of profit)	..	73.0	44.5
Highest marginal tax rate, corporate (%)	..	..	
Business entry rate (new registrations as % of total)	..	..	9.1
Enterprise surveys			
Time dealing with gov't officials (% of management time)	..	..	
Firms expected to give gifts in meetings w/tax officials (%)	..	..	
Firms using banks to finance investments (% of firms)	..	..	
Delay in obtaining an electrical connection (days)	..	..	
ISO certification ownership (% of firms)	..	..	
Private sector investment			
Invest. in infrastructure w/private participation ($ millions)	..	..	45,869
Private foreign direct investment, net (% of GDP)	..	..	3.5
Gross fixed capital formation (% of GDP)	..	..	19.9
Gross fixed private capital formation (% of GDP)	..	..	..
Finance and banking			
Government cash surplus or deficit (% of GDP)	..	..	..
Government debt (% of GDP)	..	..	..
Deposit money banks' assets (% of GDP)	..	..	52.9
Total financial system deposits (% of GDP)	..	..	41.4
Bank capital to asset ratio (%)	..	..	9.8
Bank nonperforming loans to total gross loans ratio (%)	..	..	3.2
Domestic credit to the private sector (% of GDP)	..	..	41.4
Real interest rate (%)	..	..	
Interest rate spread (percentage points)	..	..	5.9
Infrastructure			
Paved roads (% of total roads)	..	..	..
Electric power consumption (kWh per capita)	..	..	3,131
Power outages in a typical month (number)	..	..	
Fixed line and mobile subscribers (per 100 people)	..	78	88
Internet users (per 100 people)	..	27.0	22.2
Cost of telephone call to U.S. ($ per 3 minutes)	..	..	1.06

Panama

	Latin America & Caribbean		Upper middle income

	Country data		Upper middle-income group
	2000	2006	2006

Economic and social context

Population (millions)	2.9	3.3	811
Labor force (millions)	1.3	1.5	374
Unemployment rate (% of labor force)	13.5	10.3	9.8
GNI per capita, *World Bank Atlas* method ($)	3,740	5,000	5,913
GDP growth, 1995-2000 and 2000-06 (average annual %)	5.0	5.0	3.9
Agriculture value added (% of GDP)	7.2	8.2	5.7
Industry value added (% of GDP)	19.1	18.6	32.4
Manufacturing value added (% of GDP)	10.1	8.5	19.4
Services value added (% of GDP)	73.6	73.2	62.0
Inflation (annual % change in consumer price index)	1.5	2.1	
Exchange rate (local currency units per $)	1.0	1.0	
Exports of goods and services (% of GDP)	72.6	73.4	32.7
Imports of goods and services (% of GDP)	69.8	71.1	30.3

Business environment

Ease of doing business (ranking 1-178; 1=best)	..	65	
Time to start a business (days)	..	19	41
Procedures to start a business (number)	..	7	9
Firing cost (weeks of wages)	..	44.0	39.7
Closing a business (years to resolve insolvency)	..	2.5	2.9
Total tax rate (% of profit)	..	50.8	44.5
Highest marginal tax rate, corporate (%)	30	30	
Business entry rate (new registrations as % of total)	..	..	9.1
Enterprise surveys			
Time dealing with gov't officials (% of management time)	..	10.3	
Firms expected to give gifts in meetings w/tax officials (%)	..	7.7	
Firms using banks to finance investments (% of firms)	..	19.2	
Delay in obtaining an electrical connection (days)	..	11.8	
ISO certification ownership (% of firms)	..	14.7	

Private sector investment

Invest. in infrastructure w/private participation ($ millions)	111	122	45,869
Private foreign direct investment, net (% of GDP)	5.4	15.1	3.5
Gross fixed capital formation (% of GDP)	21.2	18.4	19.9
Gross fixed private capital formation (% of GDP)	17.9	12.9	..

Finance and banking

Government cash surplus or deficit (% of GDP)	-0.8	..	..
Government debt (% of GDP)	..	..	..
Deposit money banks' assets (% of GDP)	94.5	79.9	52.9
Total financial system deposits (% of GDP)	73.8	74.3	41.4
Bank capital to asset ratio (%)	9.6	11.3	9.8
Bank nonperforming loans to total gross loans ratio (%)	1.4	1.5	3.2
Domestic credit to the private sector (% of GDP)	101.9	88.6	41.4
Real interest rate (%)	11.9	6.1	
Interest rate spread (percentage points)	3.4	4.6	5.9

Infrastructure

Paved roads (% of total roads)	34.6	..	..
Electric power consumption (kWh per capita)	1,301	1,500	3,131
Power outages in a typical month (number)	..	4.2	
Fixed line and mobile subscribers (per 100 people)	28	67	88
Internet users (per 100 people)	3.6	6.7	22.2
Cost of telephone call to U.S. ($ per 3 minutes)	4.36	..	1.06

Papua New Guinea

East Asia & Pacific   **Low income**

	Country data		Low-income group
	2000	**2006**	**2006**
Economic and social context			
Population (millions)	5.4	6.2	2,420
Labor force (millions)	2.3	2.7	995
Unemployment rate (% of labor force)	2.8	..	..
GNI per capita, World Bank Atlas method ($)	640	740	649
GDP growth, 1995–2000 and 2000–06 (average annual %)	0.7	1.9	6.5
Agriculture value added (% of GDP)	28.4	41.8	20.4
Industry value added (% of GDP)	44.0	39.1	27.7
Manufacturing value added (% of GDP)	8.9	6.3	15.8
Services value added (% of GDP)	27.7	19.0	51.9
Inflation (annual % change in consumer price index)	15.6	2.3	
Exchange rate (local currency units per $)	2.8	3.1	
Exports of goods and services (% of GDP)	72.0	..	26.7
Imports of goods and services (% of GDP)	62.8	..	30.1
Business environment			
Ease of doing business (ranking 1-178; 1=best)	..	84	
Time to start a business (days)	..	56	54
Procedures to start a business (number)	..	8	10
Firing cost (weeks of wages)	..	39.0	62.6
Closing a business (years to resolve insolvency)	..	3.0	3.8
Total tax rate (% of profit)	..	41.7	67.4
Highest marginal tax rate, corporate (%)	25	25	
Business entry rate (new registrations as % of total)	..	..	6.4
Enterprise surveys			
Time dealing with gov't officials (% of management time)	..	..	
Firms expected to give gifts in meetings w/tax officials (%)	..	..	
Firms using banks to finance investments (% of firms)	..	..	
Delay in obtaining an electrical connection (days)	..	..	
ISO certification ownership (% of firms)	..	..	
Private sector investment			
Invest. in infrastructure w/private participation ($ millions)	71	..	29,785
Private foreign direct investment, net (% of GDP)	2.8	0.6	2.6
Gross fixed capital formation (% of GDP)	12.1	..	26.7
Gross fixed private capital formation (% of GDP)	..	..	19.6
Finance and banking			
Government cash surplus or deficit (% of GDP)	–1.9	..	–2.6
Government debt (% of GDP)	59.1	..	..
Deposit money banks' assets (% of GDP)	..	..	50.5
Total financial system deposits (% of GDP)	..	..	44.6
Bank capital to asset ratio (%)	..	..	..
Bank nonperforming loans to total gross loans ratio (%)	..	..	..
Domestic credit to the private sector (% of GDP)	17.6	17.1	38.3
Real interest rate (%)	7.2	0.8	
Interest rate spread (percentage points)	9.1	9.6	11.3
Infrastructure			
Paved roads (% of total roads)	3.5	..	
Electric power consumption (kWh per capita)	..	..	391
Power outages in a typical month (number)	..	..	
Fixed line and mobile subscribers (per 100 people)	1	2	17
Internet users (per 100 people)	0.8	1.8	4.2
Cost of telephone call to U.S. ($ per 3 minutes)	4.32	..	1.99

Paraguay

Lower middle income

	Country data		Lower middle-income group
	2000	**2006**	**2006**
Economic and social context			
Population (millions)	5.3	6.0	2,276
Labor force (millions)	2.4	2.9	1,209
Unemployment rate (% of labor force)	7.6	7.9	5.7
GNI per capita, *World Bank Atlas* method ($)	1,350	1,410	2,038
GDP growth, 1995–2000 and 2000–06 (average annual %)	0.1	2.9	7.6
Agriculture value added (% of GDP)	17.0	21.0	11.9
Industry value added (% of GDP)	22.5	18.3	43.5
Manufacturing value added (% of GDP)	15.5	11.8	26.7
Services value added (% of GDP)	60.5	60.7	44.6
Inflation (annual % change in consumer price index)	9.0	9.6	
Exchange rate (local currency units per $)	3,486.4	5,635.5	
Exports of goods and services (% of GDP)	38.2	49.2	40.4
Imports of goods and services (% of GDP)	49.0	66.0	36.4
Business environment			
Ease of doing business (ranking 1-178; 1=best)	..	103	
Time to start a business (days)	..	35	53
Procedures to start a business (number)	..	7	10
Firing cost (weeks of wages)	..	113.0	50.2
Closing a business (years to resolve insolvency)	..	3.9	3.3
Total tax rate (% of profit)	..	35.3	45.8
Highest marginal tax rate, corporate (%)	30	30	
Business entry rate (new registrations as % of total)	..	..	7.6
Enterprise surveys			
Time dealing with gov't officials (% of management time)	..	7.9	
Firms expected to give gifts in meetings w/tax officials (%)	..	24.5	
Firms using banks to finance investments (% of firms)	..	8.2	
Delay in obtaining an electrical connection (days)	..	27.2	
ISO certification ownership (% of firms)	..	7.1	
Private sector investment			
Invest. in infrastructure w/private participation ($ millions)	30	167	38,154
Private foreign direct investment, net (% of GDP)	1.5	2.0	3.0
Gross fixed capital formation (% of GDP)	17.5	19.2	33.5
Gross fixed private capital formation (% of GDP)	..	..	10.9
Finance and banking			
Government cash surplus or deficit (% of GDP)	..	1.2	–0.9
Government debt (% of GDP)	..	..	..
Deposit money banks' assets (% of GDP)	28.4	17.2	87.8
Total financial system deposits (% of GDP)	22.0	17.1	43.1
Bank capital to asset ratio (%)	12.4	12.5	10.7
Bank nonperforming loans to total gross loans ratio (%)	12.3	3.3	4.0
Domestic credit to the private sector (% of GDP)	29.8	16.9	81.3
Real interest rate (%)	13.1	17.5	
Interest rate spread (percentage points)	11.1	23.4	7.2
Infrastructure			
Paved roads (% of total roads)	50.8	..	65.8
Electric power consumption (kWh per capita)	880	849	1,502
Power outages in a typical month (number)	..	2.5	
Fixed line and mobile subscribers (per 100 people)	21	59	60
Internet users (per 100 people)	0.7	4.3	11.4
Cost of telephone call to U.S. ($ per 3 minutes)	0.97	0.90	2.08

Peru

Latin America & Caribbean			Lower middle income

	Country data		Lower middle-income group
	2000	2006	2006

Economic and social context

Population (millions)	25.7	27.6	2,276
Labor force (millions)	11.4	13.4	1,209
Unemployment rate (% of labor force)	7.3	11.4	5.7
GNI per capita, *World Bank Atlas* method ($)	2,080	2,980	2,038
GDP growth, 1995–2000 and 2000–06 (average annual %)	2.4	4.9	7.6
Agriculture value added (% of GDP)	8.5	6.9	11.9
Industry value added (% of GDP)	29.9	37.9	43.5
Manufacturing value added (% of GDP)	15.8	16.5	26.7
Services value added (% of GDP)	61.6	55.3	44.6
Inflation (annual % change in consumer price index)	3.8	2.0	
Exchange rate (local currency units per $)	3.5	3.3	
Exports of goods and services (% of GDP)	16.0	28.7	40.4
Imports of goods and services (% of GDP)	18.2	19.7	36.4

Business environment

Ease of doing business (ranking 1-178; 1=best)	..	58	
Time to start a business (days)	..	72	53
Procedures to start a business (number)	..	10	10
Firing cost (weeks of wages)	..	52.0	50.2
Closing a business (years to resolve insolvency)	..	3.1	3.3
Total tax rate (% of profit)	..	41.5	45.8
Highest marginal tax rate, corporate (%)	30	30	
Business entry rate (new registrations as % of total)	4.9	6.0	7.6
Enterprise surveys			
Time dealing with gov't officials (% of management time)	..	13.5	
Firms expected to give gifts in meetings w/tax officials (%)	..	1.6	
Firms using banks to finance investments (% of firms)	3.1	30.9	
Delay in obtaining an electrical connection (days)	22.5	81.6	
ISO certification ownership (% of firms)	..	14.6	

Private sector investment

Invest. in infrastructure w/private participation ($ millions)	952	1,458	38,154
Private foreign direct investment, net (% of GDP)	1.5	3.8	3.0
Gross fixed capital formation (% of GDP)	20.2	19.3	33.5
Gross fixed private capital formation (% of GDP)	16.3	16.5	10.9

Finance and banking

Government cash surplus or deficit (% of GDP)	-2.1	-0.8	-0.9
Government debt (% of GDP)	..	..	..
Deposit money banks' assets (% of GDP)	29.0	18.9	87.8
Total financial system deposits (% of GDP)	26.1	21.3	43.1
Bank capital to asset ratio (%)	9.1	9.5	10.7
Bank nonperforming loans to total gross loans ratio (%)	9.0	1.6	4.0
Domestic credit to the private sector (% of GDP)	26.0	17.8	81.3
Real interest rate (%)	25.4	15.5	
Interest rate spread (percentage points)	20.2	20.7	7.2

Infrastructure

Paved roads (% of total roads)	13.4	14.4	65.8
Electric power consumption (kWh per capita)	687	848	1,502
Power outages in a typical month (number)	..	1.1	
Fixed line and mobile subscribers (per 100 people)	12	39	60
Internet users (per 100 people)	3.1	22.1	11.4
Cost of telephone call to U.S. ($ per 3 minutes)	2.08	1.80	2.08

Philippines

Lower middle income

	Country data		Lower middle-income group
	2000	2006	2006
Economic and social context			
Population (millions)	76.2	86.3	2,276
Labor force (millions)	30.8	38.4	1,209
Unemployment rate (% of labor force)	10.1	7.4	5.7
GNI per capita, *World Bank Atlas* method ($)	1,050	1,390	2,038
GDP growth, 1995-2000 and 2000-06 (average annual %)	3.5	4.9	7.6
Agriculture value added (% of GDP)	15.8	14.2	11.9
Industry value added (% of GDP)	32.3	31.6	43.5
Manufacturing value added (% of GDP)	22.2	22.9	26.7
Services value added (% of GDP)	52.0	54.2	44.6
Inflation (annual % change in consumer price index)	4.0	6.2	
Exchange rate (local currency units per $)	44.2	51.3	
Exports of goods and services (% of GDP)	55.4	46.4	40.4
Imports of goods and services (% of GDP)	53.5	47.6	36.4
Business environment			
Ease of doing business (ranking 1-178; 1=best)	..	133	
Time to start a business (days)	..	58	53
Procedures to start a business (number)	..	15	10
Firing cost (weeks of wages)	..	91.0	50.2
Closing a business (years to resolve insolvency)	..	5.7	3.3
Total tax rate (% of profit)	..	52.8	45.8
Highest marginal tax rate, corporate (%)	32	35	
Business entry rate (new registrations as % of total)	..	..	7.6
Enterprise surveys			
Time dealing with gov't officials (% of management time)	..	6.9	
Firms expected to give gifts in meetings w/tax officials (%)	..	27.6	
Firms using banks to finance investments (% of firms)	..	5.5	
Delay in obtaining an electrical connection (days)	..	13.5	
ISO certification ownership (% of firms)	..	15.8	
Private sector investment			
Invest. in infrastructure w/private participation ($ millions)	2,153	1,815	38,154
Private foreign direct investment, net (% of GDP)	3.0	2.0	3.0
Gross fixed capital formation (% of GDP)	21.2	13.8	33.5
Gross fixed private capital formation (% of GDP)	17.8	11.6	10.9
Finance and banking			
Government cash surplus or deficit (% of GDP)	-3.9	-1.3	-0.9
Government debt (% of GDP)	52.9	77.7	..
Deposit money banks' assets (% of GDP)	50.3	40.1	87.8
Total financial system deposits (% of GDP)	54.0	51.3	43.1
Bank capital to asset ratio (%)	13.6	11.7	10.7
Bank nonperforming loans to total gross loans ratio (%)	24.0	18.6	4.0
Domestic credit to the private sector (% of GDP)	43.8	30.0	81.3
Real interest rate (%)	4.3	4.3	
Interest rate spread (percentage points)	2.6	4.5	7.2
Infrastructure			
Paved roads (% of total roads)	20.0	9.9	65.8
Electric power consumption (kWh per capita)	511	588	1,502
Power outages in a typical month (number)	..	..	
Fixed line and mobile subscribers (per 100 people)	12	54	60
Internet users (per 100 people)	2.0	5.5	11.4
Cost of telephone call to U.S. ($ per 3 minutes)	2.07	1.20	2.08

Poland

Europe & Central Asia **Upper middle income**

	Country data		Upper middle-income group
	2000	2006	2006
Economic and social context			
Population (millions)	38.5	38.1	811
Labor force (millions)	17.4	17.2	374
Unemployment rate (% of labor force)	16.1	17.7	9.8
GNI per capita, *World Bank Atlas* method ($)	4,570	8,210	5,913
GDP growth, 1995–2000 and 2000–06 (average annual %)	5.4	3.7	3.9
Agriculture value added (% of GDP)	5.0	4.5	5.7
Industry value added (% of GDP)	31.7	31.5	32.4
Manufacturing value added (% of GDP)	18.5	18.8	19.4
Services value added (% of GDP)	63.3	63.9	62.0
Inflation (annual % change in consumer price index)	10.1	1.1	
Exchange rate (local currency units per $)	4.3	3.1	
Exports of goods and services (% of GDP)	27.1	40.6	32.7
Imports of goods and services (% of GDP)	33.5	41.3	30.3
Business environment			
Ease of doing business (ranking 1-178; 1=best)	..	74	
Time to start a business (days)	..	31	41
Procedures to start a business (number)	..	10	9
Firing cost (weeks of wages)	..	13.0	39.7
Closing a business (years to resolve insolvency)	..	3.0	2.9
Total tax rate (% of profit)	..	38.4	44.5
Highest marginal tax rate, corporate (%)	28	19	
Business entry rate (new registrations as % of total)	4.9	4.7	9.1
Enterprise surveys			
Time dealing with gov't officials (% of management time)	..	3.0	
Firms expected to give gifts in meetings w/tax officials (%)	27.4	30.0	
Firms using banks to finance investments (% of firms)	17.2	20.7	
Delay in obtaining an electrical connection (days)	..	13.4	
ISO certification ownership (% of firms)	..	13.9	
Private sector investment			
Invest. in infrastructure w/private participation ($ millions)	7,807	1,390	45,869
Private foreign direct investment, net (% of GDP)	5.5	5.7	3.5
Gross fixed capital formation (% of GDP)	23.7	20.0	19.9
Gross fixed private capital formation (% of GDP)	20.9	16.3	..
Finance and banking			
Government cash surplus or deficit (% of GDP)	-2.8	-3.6	..
Government debt (% of GDP)	33.0	47.9	..
Deposit money banks' assets (% of GDP)	33.6	41.4	52.9
Total financial system deposits (% of GDP)	34.0	38.1	41.4
Bank capital to asset ratio (%)	7.1	7.9	9.8
Bank nonperforming loans to total gross loans ratio (%)	15.5	9.4	3.2
Domestic credit to the private sector (% of GDP)	26.6	33.6	41.4
Real interest rate (%)	12.0	4.5	
Interest rate spread (percentage points)	5.8	4.0	5.9
Infrastructure			
Paved roads (% of total roads)	68.3	69.7	..
Electric power consumption (kWh per capita)	3,240	3,437	3,131
Power outages in a typical month (number)	..	..	
Fixed line and mobile subscribers (per 100 people)	46	126	88
Internet users (per 100 people)	7.3	28.8	22.2
Cost of telephone call to U.S. ($ per 3 minutes)	2.92	1.35	1.06

Portugal

	Country data		High-income group
	2000	2006	2006
Economic and social context			
Population (millions)	10.2	10.6	1,031
Labor force (millions)	5.2	5.6	504
Unemployment rate (% of labor force)	3.9	7.6	6.2
GNI per capita, World Bank Atlas method ($)	11,600	17,850	36,608
GDP growth, 1995–2000 and 2000–06 (average annual %)	4.2	0.7	2.3
Agriculture value added (% of GDP)	3.8	2.8	1.5
Industry value added (% of GDP)	27.6	25.0	26.2
Manufacturing value added (% of GDP)	17.1	15.7	16.8
Services value added (% of GDP)	68.6	72.2	72.3
Inflation (annual % change in consumer price index)	2.8	2.7	
Exchange rate (local currency units per $)	1.1	0.8	
Exports of goods and services (% of GDP)	29.8	31.1	25.6
Imports of goods and services (% of GDP)	40.6	38.9	26.3
Business environment			
Ease of doing business (ranking 1-178; 1=best)	..	37	
Time to start a business (days)	..	7	22
Procedures to start a business (number)	..	7	7
Firing cost (weeks of wages)	..	95.0	34.9
Closing a business (years to resolve insolvency)	..	2.0	2.0
Total tax rate (% of profit)	..	44.8	41.5
Highest marginal tax rate, corporate (%)	34	25	
Business entry rate (new registrations as % of total)	6.0	6.4	10.1
Enterprise surveys			
Time dealing with gov't officials (% of management time)	..	..	
Firms expected to give gifts in meetings w/tax officials (%)	..	..	
Firms using banks to finance investments (% of firms)	..	..	
Delay in obtaining an electrical connection (days)	..	..	
ISO certification ownership (% of firms)	..	..	
Private sector investment			
Invest. in infrastructure w/private participation ($ millions)	..	..	849
Private foreign direct investment, net (% of GDP)	5.9	3.8	2.7
Gross fixed capital formation (% of GDP)	27.1	21.2	20.4
Gross fixed private capital formation (% of GDP)	..	..	..
Finance and banking			
Government cash surplus or deficit (% of GDP)	-2.4	-3.9	-1.3
Government debt (% of GDP)	..	72.2	47.6
Deposit money banks' assets (% of GDP)	106.4	..	99.7
Total financial system deposits (% of GDP)	88.5	..	..
Bank capital to asset ratio (%)	5.8	6.4	6.2
Bank nonperforming loans to total gross loans ratio (%)	2.2	1.3	1.1
Domestic credit to the private sector (% of GDP)	131.5	157.4	162.0
Real interest rate (%)	1.9	..	
Interest rate spread (percentage points)	2.8	..	4.4
Infrastructure			
Paved roads (% of total roads)	86.0	86.0	90.9
Electric power consumption (kWh per capita)	4,014	4,663	9,760
Power outages in a typical month (number)	..	..	
Fixed line and mobile subscribers (per 100 people)	107	155	143
Internet users (per 100 people)	16.4	30.3	59.3
Cost of telephone call to U.S. ($ per 3 minutes)	0.83	1.04	0.77

Puerto Rico

High income

	Country data		High-income group
	2000	2006	2006
Economic and social context			
Population (millions)	3.8	3.9	1,031
Labor force (millions)	1.4	1.5	504
Unemployment rate (% of labor force)	10.2	11.3	6.2
GNI per capita, World Bank Atlas method ($)	10,560	..	36,608
GDP growth, 1995–2000 and 2000–06 (average annual %)	4.4	..	2.3
Agriculture value added (% of GDP)	0.9	..	1.5
Industry value added (% of GDP)	41.3	..	26.2
Manufacturing value added (% of GDP)	38.3	..	16.8
Services value added (% of GDP)	57.8	..	72.3
Inflation (annual % change in consumer price index)	..	..	
Exchange rate (local currency units per $)	..	..	
Exports of goods and services (% of GDP)	75.2	..	25.6
Imports of goods and services (% of GDP)	98.0	..	26.3
Business environment			
Ease of doing business (ranking 1-178; 1=best)	..	28	
Time to start a business (days)	..	7	22
Procedures to start a business (number)	..	7	7
Firing cost (weeks of wages)	..	..	34.9
Closing a business (years to resolve insolvency)	..	3.8	2.0
Total tax rate (% of profit)	..	44.3	41.5
Highest marginal tax rate, corporate (%)	20	20	
Business entry rate (new registrations as % of total)	..	..	10.1
Enterprise surveys			
Time dealing with gov't officials (% of management time)	..	..	
Firms expected to give gifts in meetings w/tax officials (%)	..	..	
Firms using banks to finance investments (% of firms)	..	..	
Delay in obtaining an electrical connection (days)	..	..	
ISO certification ownership (% of firms)	..	..	
Private sector investment			
Invest. in infrastructure w/private participation ($ millions)	..	..	849
Private foreign direct investment, net (% of GDP)	..	..	2.7
Gross fixed capital formation (% of GDP)	..	..	20.4
Gross fixed private capital formation (% of GDP)	..	..	..
Finance and banking			
Government cash surplus or deficit (% of GDP)	..	..	-1.3
Government debt (% of GDP)	..	..	47.6
Deposit money banks' assets (% of GDP)	..	..	99.7
Total financial system deposits (% of GDP)	..	..	..
Bank capital to asset ratio (%)	..	..	6.2
Bank nonperforming loans to total gross loans ratio (%)	..	..	1.1
Domestic credit to the private sector (% of GDP)	..	..	162.0
Real interest rate (%)	..	..	
Interest rate spread (percentage points)	..	..	4.4
Infrastructure			
Paved roads (% of total roads)	94.0	95.0	90.9
Electric power consumption (kWh per capita)	..	..	9,760
Power outages in a typical month (number)	..	..	
Fixed line and mobile subscribers (per 100 people)	58	112	143
Internet users (per 100 people)	10.5	23.4	59.3
Cost of telephone call to U.S. ($ per 3 minutes)	0.87	..	0.77

Qatar

	Country data		High-income group
	2000	**2006**	**2006**
Economic and social context			
Population (millions)	0.62	0.82	1,031
Labor force (millions)	0.33	0.48	504
Unemployment rate (% of labor force)	3.9	..	6.2
GNI per capita, *World Bank Atlas* method ($)	..	..	36,608
GDP growth, 1995–2000 and 2000–06 (average annual %)	..	9.7	2.3
Agriculture value added (% of GDP)	..	..	1.5
Industry value added (% of GDP)	..	..	26.2
Manufacturing value added (% of GDP)	..	..	16.8
Services value added (% of GDP)	..	..	72.3
Inflation (annual % change in consumer price index)	1.7	11.8	
Exchange rate (local currency units per $)	3.6	3.6	
Exports of goods and services (% of GDP)	67.3	68.3	25.6
Imports of goods and services (% of GDP)	22.3	33.5	26.3
Business environment			
Ease of doing business (ranking 1-178; 1=best)	..	..	
Time to start a business (days)	..	..	22
Procedures to start a business (number)	..	..	7
Firing cost (weeks of wages)	..	..	34.9
Closing a business (years to resolve insolvency)	..	..	2.0
Total tax rate (% of profit)	..	..	41.5
Highest marginal tax rate, corporate (%)	35	..	
Business entry rate (new registrations as % of total)	..	..	10.1
Enterprise surveys			
Time dealing with gov't officials (% of management time)	..	..	
Firms expected to give gifts in meetings w/tax officials (%)	..	..	
Firms using banks to finance investments (% of firms)	..	..	
Delay in obtaining an electrical connection (days)	..	..	
ISO certification ownership (% of firms)	..	..	
Private sector investment			
Invest. in infrastructure w/private participation ($ millions)	..	..	849
Private foreign direct investment, net (% of GDP)	..	..	2.7
Gross fixed capital formation (% of GDP)	19.5	33.6	20.4
Gross fixed private capital formation (% of GDP)	..	..	..
Finance and banking			
Government cash surplus or deficit (% of GDP)	..	9.7	-1.3
Government debt (% of GDP)	..	..	47.6
Deposit money banks' assets (% of GDP)	..	55.5	99.7
Total financial system deposits (% of GDP)	..	38.3	..
Bank capital to asset ratio (%)	..	..	6.2
Bank nonperforming loans to total gross loans ratio (%)	..	..	1.1
Domestic credit to the private sector (% of GDP)	26.8	35.4	162.0
Real interest rate (%)	..	-15.5	
Interest rate spread (percentage points)	..	..	4.4
Infrastructure			
Paved roads (% of total roads)	90.0	..	90.9
Electric power consumption (kWh per capita)	13,784	16,801	9,760
Power outages in a typical month (number)	..	..	
Fixed line and mobile subscribers (per 100 people)	46	140	143
Internet users (per 100 people)	4.9	35.3	59.3
Cost of telephone call to U.S. ($ per 3 minutes)	4.45	1.95	0.77

Romania

Europe & Central Asia   **Upper middle income**

	Country data		Upper middle-income group
	2000	2006	2006
Economic and social context			
Population (millions)	22.4	21.6	811
Labor force (millions)	11.6	10.1	374
Unemployment rate (% of labor force)	7.1	7.2	9.8
GNI per capita, World Bank Atlas method ($)	1,690	4,830	5,913
GDP growth, 1995–2000 and 2000–06 (average annual %)	-2.1	6.0	3.9
Agriculture value added (% of GDP)	12.5	10.5	5.7
Industry value added (% of GDP)	36.4	37.9	32.4
Manufacturing value added (% of GDP)	14.5	25.5	19.4
Services value added (% of GDP)	51.1	51.5	62.0
Inflation (annual % change in consumer price index)	45.7	6.6	
Exchange rate (local currency units per $)	2.2	2.8	
Exports of goods and services (% of GDP)	32.9	34.0	32.7
Imports of goods and services (% of GDP)	38.5	44.5	30.3
Business environment			
Ease of doing business (ranking 1-178; 1=best)	..	48	
Time to start a business (days)	..	14	41
Procedures to start a business (number)	..	6	9
Firing cost (weeks of wages)	..	8.0	39.7
Closing a business (years to resolve insolvency)	..	3.3	2.9
Total tax rate (% of profit)	..	46.9	44.5
Highest marginal tax rate, corporate (%)	25	16	
Business entry rate (new registrations as % of total)	8.0	10.7	9.1
Enterprise surveys			
Time dealing with gov't officials (% of management time)	..	1.1	
Firms expected to give gifts in meetings w/tax officials (%)	37.7	27.1	
Firms using banks to finance investments (% of firms)	13.3	23.2	
Delay in obtaining an electrical connection (days)	27.8	23.0	
ISO certification ownership (% of firms)	..	16.8	
Private sector investment			
Invest. in infrastructure w/private participation ($ millions)	1,901	531	45,869
Private foreign direct investment, net (% of GDP)	2.8	9.4	3.5
Gross fixed capital formation (% of GDP)	18.9	23.7	19.9
Gross fixed private capital formation (% of GDP)	..	18.7	..
Finance and banking			
Government cash surplus or deficit (% of GDP)	-2.0	-1.0	..
Government debt (% of GDP)	..	..	..
Deposit money banks' assets (% of GDP)	11.7	23.2	52.9
Total financial system deposits (% of GDP)	17.4	24.1	41.4
Bank capital to asset ratio (%)	8.6	8.9	9.8
Bank nonperforming loans to total gross loans ratio (%)	3.3	8.4	3.2
Domestic credit to the private sector (% of GDP)	7.2	26.3	41.4
Real interest rate (%)	..	..	
Interest rate spread (percentage points)	..	..	5.9
Infrastructure			
Paved roads (% of total roads)	49.5	30.2	..
Electric power consumption (kWh per capita)	1,988	2,342	3,131
Power outages in a typical month (number)	..	..	
Fixed line and mobile subscribers (per 100 people)	29	100	88
Internet users (per 100 people)	3.6	32.4	22.2
Cost of telephone call to U.S. ($ per 3 minutes)	2.49	0.82	1.06

Russian Federation

	Country data		Upper middle-income group
	2000	2006	2006
Economic and social context			
Population (millions)	146.3	142.5	811
Labor force (millions)	71.4	73.5	374
Unemployment rate (% of labor force)	9.8	7.9	9.8
GNI per capita, World Bank Atlas method ($)	1,710	5,770	5,913
GDP growth, 1995-2000 and 2000-06 (average annual %)	1.2	6.4	3.9
Agriculture value added (% of GDP)	6.4	4.9	5.7
Industry value added (% of GDP)	37.9	39.4	32.4
Manufacturing value added (% of GDP)	17.6	19.4	19.4
Services value added (% of GDP)	55.6	55.8	62.0
Inflation (annual % change in consumer price index)	20.8	9.7	
Exchange rate (local currency units per $)	28.1	27.2	
Exports of goods and services (% of GDP)	44.1	33.9	32.7
Imports of goods and services (% of GDP)	24.0	21.2	30.3
Business environment			
Ease of doing business (ranking 1-178; 1=best)	..	106	
Time to start a business (days)	..	29	41
Procedures to start a business (number)	..	8	9
Firing cost (weeks of wages)	..	17.0	39.7
Closing a business (years to resolve insolvency)	..	3.8	2.9
Total tax rate (% of profit)	..	51.4	44.5
Highest marginal tax rate, corporate (%)	35	24	
Business entry rate (new registrations as % of total)	8.1	9.4	9.1
Enterprise surveys			
Time dealing with gov't officials (% of management time)	..	6.3	
Firms expected to give gifts in meetings w/tax officials (%)	53.5	58.0	
Firms using banks to finance investments (% of firms)	5.7	10.2	
Delay in obtaining an electrical connection (days)	19.9	16.1	
ISO certification ownership (% of firms)	..	9.3	
Private sector investment			
Invest. in infrastructure w/private participation ($ millions)	1,939	6,073	45,869
Private foreign direct investment, net (% of GDP)	1.0	3.1	3.5
Gross fixed capital formation (% of GDP)	16.9	17.9	19.9
Gross fixed private capital formation (% of GDP)	15.1	15.2	..
Finance and banking			
Government cash surplus or deficit (% of GDP)	2.5	8.1	..
Government debt (% of GDP)	62.1	..	..
Deposit money banks' assets (% of GDP)	..	..	52.9
Total financial system deposits (% of GDP)	..	..	41.4
Bank capital to asset ratio (%)	12.1	12.5	9.8
Bank nonperforming loans to total gross loans ratio (%)	7.7	2.6	3.2
Domestic credit to the private sector (% of GDP)	13.3	30.8	41.4
Real interest rate (%)	-9.6	-4.9	
Interest rate spread (percentage points)	17.9	6.4	5.9
Infrastructure			
Paved roads (% of total roads)	67.4	..	..
Electric power consumption (kWh per capita)	5,209	5,785	3,131
Power outages in a typical month (number)	..	..	
Fixed line and mobile subscribers (per 100 people)	24	112	88
Internet users (per 100 people)	2.0	18.0	22.2
Cost of telephone call to U.S. ($ per 3 minutes)	2.56	2.03	1.06

Rwanda

	Country data		Low-income group
	2000	2006	2006
Economic and social context			
Population (millions)	8.2	9.5	2,420
Labor force (millions)	3.6	4.4	995
Unemployment rate (% of labor force)	..	..	..
GNI per capita, *World Bank Atlas* method ($)	240	250	649
GDP growth, 1995-2000 and 2000-06 (average annual %)	9.8	5.0	6.5
Agriculture value added (% of GDP)	41.4	41.0	20.4
Industry value added (% of GDP)	20.5	21.2	27.7
Manufacturing value added (% of GDP)	11.3	8.5	15.8
Services value added (% of GDP)	38.1	37.8	51.9
Inflation (annual % change in consumer price index)	4.3	8.9	
Exchange rate (local currency units per $)	389.7	551.7	
Exports of goods and services (% of GDP)	8.3	11.7	26.7
Imports of goods and services (% of GDP)	24.6	31.5	30.1
Business environment			
Ease of doing business (ranking 1-178; 1=best)	..	150	
Time to start a business (days)	..	16	54
Procedures to start a business (number)	..	9	10
Firing cost (weeks of wages)	..	26.0	62.6
Closing a business (years to resolve insolvency)	..	..	3.8
Total tax rate (% of profit)	..	33.8	67.4
Highest marginal tax rate, corporate (%)	..	..	
Business entry rate (new registrations as % of total)	..	..	*6.4*
Enterprise surveys			
Time dealing with gov't officials (% of management time)	..	5.9	
Firms expected to give gifts in meetings w/tax officials (%)	..	4.9	
Firms using banks to finance investments (% of firms)	..	15.9	
Delay in obtaining an electrical connection (days)	..	18.2	
ISO certification ownership (% of firms)	..	10.8	
Private sector investment			
Invest. in infrastructure w/private participation ($ millions)	8	10	29,785
Private foreign direct investment, net (% of GDP)	0.5	0.5	2.6
Gross fixed capital formation (% of GDP)	17.5	21.4	26.7
Gross fixed private capital formation (% of GDP)	11.6	12.8	19.6
Finance and banking			
Government cash surplus or deficit (% of GDP)	..	..	-2.6
Government debt (% of GDP)	..	..	..
Deposit money banks' assets (% of GDP)	10.2	12.7	50.5
Total financial system deposits (% of GDP)	11.6	14.6	44.6
Bank capital to asset ratio (%)	*8.1*	9.2	..
Bank nonperforming loans to total gross loans ratio (%)	*57.0*	27.2	..
Domestic credit to the private sector (% of GDP)	10.0	*13.5*	38.3
Real interest rate (%)	13.3	6.4	
Interest rate spread (percentage points)	8.1	*8.1*	*11.3*
Infrastructure			
Paved roads (% of total roads)	8.3	*19.0*	..
Electric power consumption (kWh per capita)	..	..	391
Power outages in a typical month (number)	..	13.7	
Fixed line and mobile subscribers (per 100 people)	1	3	17
Internet users (per 100 people)	0.1	0.7	*4.2*
Cost of telephone call to U.S. ($ per 3 minutes)	*11.23*	2.43	*1.99*

Samoa

	Country data		Lower middle-income group
	2000	2006	2006
Economic and social context			
Population (millions)	0.18	0.19	2,276
Labor force (millions)	0.06	0.07	1,209
Unemployment rate (% of labor force)	..	..	5.7
GNI per capita, World Bank Atlas method ($)	1,350	2,270	2,038
GDP growth, 1995–2000 and 2000–06 (average annual %)	3.3	3.8	7.6
Agriculture value added (% of GDP)	16.8	12.2	11.9
Industry value added (% of GDP)	26.0	27.4	43.5
Manufacturing value added (% of GDP)	14.8	13.9	26.7
Services value added (% of GDP)	57.2	60.5	44.6
Inflation (annual % change in consumer price index)	1.0	3.8	
Exchange rate (local currency units per $)	3.3	2.8	
Exports of goods and services (% of GDP)	33.8	28.0	40.4
Imports of goods and services (% of GDP)	57.2	50.1	36.4
Business environment			
Ease of doing business (ranking 1-178; 1=best)	..	61	
Time to start a business (days)	..	35	53
Procedures to start a business (number)	..	9	10
Firing cost (weeks of wages)	..	9.0	50.2
Closing a business (years to resolve insolvency)	..	2.5	3.3
Total tax rate (% of profit)	..	19.8	45.8
Highest marginal tax rate, corporate (%)	..	..	
Business entry rate (new registrations as % of total)	..	..	7.6
Enterprise surveys			
Time dealing with gov't officials (% of management time)	..	..	
Firms expected to give gifts in meetings w/tax officials (%)	..	..	
Firms using banks to finance investments (% of firms)	..	..	
Delay in obtaining an electrical connection (days)	..	..	
ISO certification ownership (% of firms)	..	..	
Private sector investment			
Invest. in infrastructure w/private participation ($ millions)	10	..	38,154
Private foreign direct investment, net (% of GDP)	-0.7	4.9	3.0
Gross fixed capital formation (% of GDP)	..	..	33.5
Gross fixed private capital formation (% of GDP)	..	..	10.9
Finance and banking			
Government cash surplus or deficit (% of GDP)	..	..	-0.9
Government debt (% of GDP)	..	..	..
Deposit money banks' assets (% of GDP)	31.7	38.2	87.8
Total financial system deposits (% of GDP)	32.6	39.3	43.1
Bank capital to asset ratio (%)	..	..	10.7
Bank nonperforming loans to total gross loans ratio (%)	..	..	4.0
Domestic credit to the private sector (% of GDP)	30.6	45.7	81.3
Real interest rate (%)	8.0	6.2	
Interest rate spread (percentage points)	4.5	7.1	7.2
Infrastructure			
Paved roads (% of total roads)	14.2	..	65.8
Electric power consumption (kWh per capita)	..	..	1,502
Power outages in a typical month (number)	..	..	
Fixed line and mobile subscribers (per 100 people)	6	24	60
Internet users (per 100 people)	0.6	4.3	11.4
Cost of telephone call to U.S. ($ per 3 minutes)	1.36	..	2.08

San Marino

	Country data		High-income group
	2000	2006	2006
Economic and social context			
Population (millions)	..	0.03	1,031
Labor force (millions)	..	..	504
Unemployment rate (% of labor force)	..	..	6.2
GNI per capita, *World Bank Atlas* method ($)	..	45,130	36,608
GDP growth, 1995–2000 and 2000–06 (average annual %)	..	3.7	2.3
Agriculture value added (% of GDP)	..	..	1.5
Industry value added (% of GDP)	..	..	26.2
Manufacturing value added (% of GDP)	..	..	16.8
Services value added (% of GDP)	..	..	72.3
Inflation (annual % change in consumer price index)	..	..	
Exchange rate (local currency units per $)	1.1	0.8	
Exports of goods and services (% of GDP)	..	..	25.6
Imports of goods and services (% of GDP)	..	..	26.3
Business environment			
Ease of doing business (ranking 1-178; 1=best)	..	..	
Time to start a business (days)	..	..	22
Procedures to start a business (number)	..	..	7
Firing cost (weeks of wages)	..	..	34.9
Closing a business (years to resolve insolvency)	..	..	2.0
Total tax rate (% of profit)	..	..	41.5
Highest marginal tax rate, corporate (%)	..	..	
Business entry rate (new registrations as % of total)	..	..	10.1
Enterprise surveys			
Time dealing with gov't officials (% of management time)	..	..	
Firms expected to give gifts in meetings w/tax officials (%)	..	..	
Firms using banks to finance investments (% of firms)	..	..	
Delay in obtaining an electrical connection (days)	..	..	
ISO certification ownership (% of firms)	..	..	
Private sector investment			
Invest. in infrastructure w/private participation ($ millions)	..	..	849
Private foreign direct investment, net (% of GDP)	..	..	2.7
Gross fixed capital formation (% of GDP)	..	..	20.4
Gross fixed private capital formation (% of GDP)	..	..	..
Finance and banking			
Government cash surplus or deficit (% of GDP)	1.3	5.2	–1.3
Government debt (% of GDP)	16.5	49.8	47.6
Deposit money banks' assets (% of GDP)	..	..	99.7
Total financial system deposits (% of GDP)	..	..	..
Bank capital to asset ratio (%)	..	..	6.2
Bank nonperforming loans to total gross loans ratio (%)	..	..	1.1
Domestic credit to the private sector (% of GDP)	257,795.3	..	162.0
Real interest rate (%)	6.5	..	
Interest rate spread (percentage points)	6.6	5.7	4.4
Infrastructure			
Paved roads (% of total roads)	..	..	90.9
Electric power consumption (kWh per capita)	..	..	9,760
Power outages in a typical month (number)	..	..	
Fixed line and mobile subscribers (per 100 people)	..	134	143
Internet users (per 100 people)	..	53.8	59.3
Cost of telephone call to U.S. ($ per 3 minutes)	..	..	0.77

São Tomé and Principe

Sub-Saharan Africa   **Low income**

	Country data		Low-income group
	2000	2006	2006
Economic and social context			
Population (millions)	0.14	0.16	2,420
Labor force (millions)	0.04	0.05	995
Unemployment rate (% of labor force)	14.4	..	..
GNI per capita, *World Bank Atlas* method ($)	..	800	649
GDP growth, 1995–2000 and 2000–06 (average annual %)	..	6.7	6.5
Agriculture value added (% of GDP)	19.7	17.0	20.4
Industry value added (% of GDP)	16.9	20.8	27.7
Manufacturing value added (% of GDP)	5.7	6.4	15.8
Services value added (% of GDP)	63.5	62.3	51.9
Inflation (annual % change in consumer price index)	..	..	
Exchange rate (local currency units per $)	7,978.2	12,445.4	
Exports of goods and services (% of GDP)	..	..	26.7
Imports of goods and services (% of GDP)	..	..	30.1
Business environment			
Ease of doing business (ranking 1-178; 1=best)	..	163	
Time to start a business (days)	..	144	54
Procedures to start a business (number)	..	10	10
Firing cost (weeks of wages)	..	91.0	62.6
Closing a business (years to resolve insolvency)	..	..	3.8
Total tax rate (% of profit)	..	51.0	67.4
Highest marginal tax rate, corporate (%)	..	..	
Business entry rate (new registrations as % of total)	..	..	6.4
Enterprise surveys			
Time dealing with gov't officials (% of management time)	..	..	
Firms expected to give gifts in meetings w/tax officials (%)	..	..	
Firms using banks to finance investments (% of firms)	..	..	
Delay in obtaining an electrical connection (days)	..	..	
ISO certification ownership (% of firms)	..	..	
Private sector investment			
Invest. in infrastructure w/private participation ($ millions)	..	50	29,785
Private foreign direct investment, net (% of GDP)	3.9	−0.4	2.6
Gross fixed capital formation (% of GDP)	..	..	26.7
Gross fixed private capital formation (% of GDP)	..	..	19.6
Finance and banking			
Government cash surplus or deficit (% of GDP)	..	..	−2.6
Government debt (% of GDP)	..	..	..
Deposit money banks' assets (% of GDP)	..	..	50.5
Total financial system deposits (% of GDP)	..	..	44.6
Bank capital to asset ratio (%)	..	..	..
Bank nonperforming loans to total gross loans ratio (%)	..	..	..
Domestic credit to the private sector (% of GDP)	4.3	33.3	38.3
Real interest rate (%)	23.8	19.2	
Interest rate spread (percentage points)	18.7	18.3	11.3
Infrastructure			
Paved roads (% of total roads)	68.1	..	..
Electric power consumption (kWh per capita)	..	..	391
Power outages in a typical month (number)	..	..	
Fixed line and mobile subscribers (per 100 people)	3	17	17
Internet users (per 100 people)	4.6	18.7	4.2
Cost of telephone call to U.S. ($ per 3 minutes)	5.56	5.11	1.99

Saudi Arabia

High income

	Country data		High-income group
	2000	2006	2006
Economic and social context			
Population (millions)	20.7	23.7	1,031
Labor force (millions)	6.8	8.4	504
Unemployment rate (% of labor force)	4.6	6.2	6.2
GNI per capita, *World Bank Atlas* method ($)	8,140	13,980	36,608
GDP growth, 1995–2000 and 2000–06 (average annual %)	2.3	4.4	2.3
Agriculture value added (% of GDP)	4.9	3.0	1.5
Industry value added (% of GDP)	53.9	65.0	26.2
Manufacturing value added (% of GDP)	9.7	9.5	16.8
Services value added (% of GDP)	41.1	32.0	72.3
Inflation (annual % change in consumer price index)	–1.1	2.2	
Exchange rate (local currency units per $)	3.8	3.7	
Exports of goods and services (% of GDP)	43.7	62.2	25.6
Imports of goods and services (% of GDP)	24.9	30.7	26.3
Business environment			
Ease of doing business (ranking 1-178; 1=best)	..	23	
Time to start a business (days)	..	15	22
Procedures to start a business (number)	..	7	7
Firing cost (weeks of wages)	..	80.0	34.9
Closing a business (years to resolve insolvency)	..	2.8	2.0
Total tax rate (% of profit)	..	14.5	41.5
Highest marginal tax rate, corporate (%)	45	..	
Business entry rate (new registrations as % of total)	..	..	10.1
Enterprise surveys			
Time dealing with gov't officials (% of management time)	..	..	
Firms expected to give gifts in meetings w/tax officials (%)	..	..	
Firms using banks to finance investments (% of firms)	..	..	
Delay in obtaining an electrical connection (days)	..	..	
ISO certification ownership (% of firms)	..	..	
Private sector investment			
Invest. in infrastructure w/private participation ($ millions)	..	..	849
Private foreign direct investment, net (% of GDP)	–1.0	0.2	2.7
Gross fixed capital formation (% of GDP)	17.5	17.0	20.4
Gross fixed private capital formation (% of GDP)	..	..	..
Finance and banking			
Government cash surplus or deficit (% of GDP)	..	..	–1.3
Government debt (% of GDP)	..	..	47.6
Deposit money banks' assets (% of GDP)	40.6	46.9	99.7
Total financial system deposits (% of GDP)	15.3	17.7	..
Bank capital to asset ratio (%)	9.6	9.3	6.2
Bank nonperforming loans to total gross loans ratio (%)	10.4	2.0	1.1
Domestic credit to the private sector (% of GDP)	52.5	50.7	162.0
Real interest rate (%)	..	..	
Interest rate spread (percentage points)	..	..	4.4
Infrastructure			
Paved roads (% of total roads)	29.9	..	90.9
Electric power consumption (kWh per capita)	5,666	6,813	9,760
Power outages in a typical month (number)	..	..	
Fixed line and mobile subscribers (per 100 people)	21	100	143
Internet users (per 100 people)	2.2	19.8	59.3
Cost of telephone call to U.S. ($ per 3 minutes)	5.20	..	0.77

Senegal

	Country data		Low-income group
	2000	2006	2006
Economic and social context			
Population (millions)	10.3	12.1	2,420
Labor force (millions)	4.1	4.8	995
Unemployment rate (% of labor force)	..	..	
GNI per capita, *World Bank Atlas* method ($)	490	760	649
GDP growth, 1995–2000 and 2000–06 (average annual %)	4.4	4.5	6.5
Agriculture value added (% of GDP)	19.1	15.9	20.4
Industry value added (% of GDP)	23.2	23.0	27.7
Manufacturing value added (% of GDP)	14.7	13.9	15.8
Services value added (% of GDP)	57.6	61.1	51.9
Inflation (annual % change in consumer price index)	0.7	2.1	
Exchange rate (local currency units per $)	712.0	522.9	
Exports of goods and services (% of GDP)	27.9	25.6	26.7
Imports of goods and services (% of GDP)	37.2	44.2	30.1
Business environment			
Ease of doing business (ranking 1-178; 1=best)	..	162	
Time to start a business (days)	..	58	54
Procedures to start a business (number)	..	10	10
Firing cost (weeks of wages)	..	38.0	62.6
Closing a business (years to resolve insolvency)	..	3.0	3.8
Total tax rate (% of profit)	..	46.0	67.4
Highest marginal tax rate, corporate (%)	35	..	
Business entry rate (new registrations as % of total)	*3.1*	*2.3*	*6.4*
Enterprise surveys			
Time dealing with gov't officials (% of management time)	..	..	
Firms expected to give gifts in meetings w/tax officials (%)	..	10.2	
Firms using banks to finance investments (% of firms)	..	26.3	
Delay in obtaining an electrical connection (days)	..	13.2	
ISO certification ownership (% of firms)	..	6.1	
Private sector investment			
Invest. in infrastructure w/private participation ($ millions)	79	212	29,785
Private foreign direct investment, net (% of GDP)	1.3	0.6	2.6
Gross fixed capital formation (% of GDP)	22.4	29.2	26.7
Gross fixed private capital formation (% of GDP)	17.9	19.3	19.6
Finance and banking			
Government cash surplus or deficit (% of GDP)	–0.9	..	–2.6
Government debt (% of GDP)	73.7	..	..
Deposit money banks' assets (% of GDP)	19.6	24.4	50.5
Total financial system deposits (% of GDP)	17.1	25.3	44.6
Bank capital to asset ratio (%)	9.9	8.1	..
Bank nonperforming loans to total gross loans ratio (%)	18.1	16.0	..
Domestic credit to the private sector (% of GDP)	18.7	23.1	38.3
Real interest rate (%)	..	..	
Interest rate spread (percentage points)	..	..	11.3
Infrastructure			
Paved roads (% of total roads)	29.3	*29.3*	..
Electric power consumption (kWh per capita)	97	*151*	391
Power outages in a typical month (number)	..	..	
Fixed line and mobile subscribers (per 100 people)	4	27	17
Internet users (per 100 people)	0.4	5.4	*4.2*
Cost of telephone call to U.S. ($ per 3 minutes)	2.23	*1.02*	*1.99*

Serbia

| Europe & Central Asia | | | Upper middle income |

	Country data		Upper middle-income group
	2000	2006	2006
Economic and social context			
Population (millions)	7.5	7.4	811
Labor force (millions)	3.5	3.6	374
Unemployment rate (% of labor force)	..	..	9.8
GNI per capita, *World Bank Atlas* method ($)	1,460	4,030	5,913
GDP growth, 1995–2000 and 2000–06 (average annual %)	..	5.3	3.9
Agriculture value added (% of GDP)	19.4	12.7	5.7
Industry value added (% of GDP)	29.6	25.5	32.4
Manufacturing value added (% of GDP)	..	..	19.4
Services value added (% of GDP)	51.0	61.8	62.0
Inflation (annual % change in consumer price index)	71.1	11.7	
Exchange rate (local currency units per $)	63.2	67.1	
Exports of goods and services (% of GDP)	23.0	26.9	32.7
Imports of goods and services (% of GDP)	39.1	46.5	30.3
Business environment			
Ease of doing business (ranking 1-178; 1=best)	..	86	
Time to start a business (days)	..	23	41
Procedures to start a business (number)	..	11	9
Firing cost (weeks of wages)	..	25.0	39.7
Closing a business (years to resolve insolvency)	..	2.7	2.9
Total tax rate (% of profit)	..	35.8	44.5
Highest marginal tax rate, corporate (%)	..	..	
Business entry rate (new registrations as % of total)	3.8	5.4	9.1
Enterprise surveys			
Time dealing with gov't officials (% of management time)	..	8.1	
Firms expected to give gifts in meetings w/tax officials (%)	42.5	61.1	
Firms using banks to finance investments (% of firms)	8.4	16.7	
Delay in obtaining an electrical connection (days)	..	16.8	
ISO certification ownership (% of firms)	..	11.7	
Private sector investment			
Invest. in infrastructure w/private participation ($ millions)	355	2,385	45,869
Private foreign direct investment, net (% of GDP)	0.3	16.0	3.5
Gross fixed capital formation (% of GDP)	12.3	17.9	19.9
Gross fixed private capital formation (% of GDP)	9.5	14.2	..
Finance and banking			
Government cash surplus or deficit (% of GDP)	..	..	..
Government debt (% of GDP)	..	..	..
Deposit money banks' assets (% of GDP)	..	..	52.9
Total financial system deposits (% of GDP)	..	..	41.4
Bank capital to asset ratio (%)	18.3	15.6	9.8
Bank nonperforming loans to total gross loans ratio (%)	21.6	21.4	3.2
Domestic credit to the private sector (% of GDP)	47.5	26.8	41.4
Real interest rate (%)	-41.3	0.8	
Interest rate spread (percentage points)	0.0	11.5	5.9
Infrastructure			
Paved roads (% of total roads)	62.7	..	..
Electric power consumption (kWh per capita)	..	..	3,131
Power outages in a typical month (number)	..	..	
Fixed line and mobile subscribers (per 100 people)	49	99	88
Internet users (per 100 people)	5.3	20.3	22.2
Cost of telephone call to U.S. ($ per 3 minutes)	..	..	1.06

Seychelles

<table>
<tr><td>Sub-Saharan Africa</td><td colspan="2"></td><td>Upper middle income</td></tr>
<tr><td></td><td colspan="2">Country data</td><td>Upper middle-income group</td></tr>
<tr><td></td><td>2000</td><td>2006</td><td>2006</td></tr>
</table>

	2000	2006	2006
Economic and social context			
Population (millions)	0.08	0.08	811
Labor force (millions)	..	..	374
Unemployment rate (% of labor force)	..	..	9.8
GNI per capita, *World Bank Atlas* method ($)	7,420	8,870	5,913
GDP growth, 1995-2000 and 2000-06 (average annual %)	6.6	-1.2	3.9
Agriculture value added (% of GDP)	3.0	3.0	5.7
Industry value added (% of GDP)	29.0	25.5	32.4
Manufacturing value added (% of GDP)	19.2	15.2	19.4
Services value added (% of GDP)	68.0	71.5	62.0
Inflation (annual % change in consumer price index)	6.3	-0.3	
Exchange rate (local currency units per $)	5.7	5.5	
Exports of goods and services (% of GDP)	78.2	111.0	32.7
Imports of goods and services (% of GDP)	81.4	133.5	30.3
Business environment			
Ease of doing business (ranking 1-178; 1=best)	..	90	
Time to start a business (days)	..	38	41
Procedures to start a business (number)	..	9	9
Firing cost (weeks of wages)	..	39.0	39.7
Closing a business (years to resolve insolvency)	..	..	2.9
Total tax rate (% of profit)	..	48.4	44.5
Highest marginal tax rate, corporate (%)	..	..	
Business entry rate (new registrations as % of total)	..	..	9.1
Enterprise surveys			
Time dealing with gov't officials (% of management time)	..	..	
Firms expected to give gifts in meetings w/tax officials (%)	..	..	
Firms using banks to finance investments (% of firms)	..	..	
Delay in obtaining an electrical connection (days)	..	..	
ISO certification ownership (% of firms)	..	..	
Private sector investment			
Invest. in infrastructure w/private participation ($ millions)	7	15	45,869
Private foreign direct investment, net (% of GDP)	4.0	18.8	3.5
Gross fixed capital formation (% of GDP)	25.2	32.7	19.9
Gross fixed private capital formation (% of GDP)	13.8	22.6	..
Finance and banking			
Government cash surplus or deficit (% of GDP)	-13.9	-2.6	..
Government debt (% of GDP)	..	..	..
Deposit money banks' assets (% of GDP)	90.2	104.5	52.9
Total financial system deposits (% of GDP)	80.7	105.4	41.4
Bank capital to asset ratio (%)	..	..	9.8
Bank nonperforming loans to total gross loans ratio (%)	..	..	3.2
Domestic credit to the private sector (% of GDP)	22.3	36.9	41.4
Real interest rate (%)	9.4	7.7	
Interest rate spread (percentage points)	6.0	7.4	5.9
Infrastructure			
Paved roads (% of total roads)	84.5	96.0	..
Electric power consumption (kWh per capita)	..	..	3,131
Power outages in a typical month (number)	..	..	
Fixed line and mobile subscribers (per 100 people)	57	108	88
Internet users (per 100 people)	7.4	34.3	22.2
Cost of telephone call to U.S. ($ per 3 minutes)	5.59	3.78	1.06

Sierra Leone

	Country data		Low-income group
	2000	2006	2006
Economic and social context			
Population (millions)	4.5	5.7	2,420
Labor force (millions)	1.9	2.5	995
Unemployment rate (% of labor force)	..	..	..
GNI per capita, *World Bank Atlas* method ($)	140	240	649
GDP growth, 1995–2000 and 2000–06 (average annual %)	-5.2	12.3	6.5
Agriculture value added (% of GDP)	58.4	46.4	20.4
Industry value added (% of GDP)	28.4	25.0	27.7
Manufacturing value added (% of GDP)	3.5	3.7	15.8
Services value added (% of GDP)	13.3	28.6	51.9
Inflation (annual % change in consumer price index)	-0.8	9.5	
Exchange rate (local currency units per $)	2,092.1	2,961.9	
Exports of goods and services (% of GDP)	18.1	23.0	26.7
Imports of goods and services (% of GDP)	39.4	36.5	30.1
Business environment			
Ease of doing business (ranking 1-178; 1=best)	..	160	
Time to start a business (days)	..	26	54
Procedures to start a business (number)	..	9	10
Firing cost (weeks of wages)	..	189.0	62.6
Closing a business (years to resolve insolvency)	..	2.6	3.8
Total tax rate (% of profit)	..	233.5	67.4
Highest marginal tax rate, corporate (%)	..	..	
Business entry rate (new registrations as % of total)	..	..	6.4
Enterprise surveys			
Time dealing with gov't officials (% of management time)	..	..	
Firms expected to give gifts in meetings w/tax officials (%)	..	..	
Firms using banks to finance investments (% of firms)	..	..	
Delay in obtaining an electrical connection (days)	..	..	
ISO certification ownership (% of firms)	..	..	
Private sector investment			
Invest. in infrastructure w/private participation ($ millions)	3	40	29,785
Private foreign direct investment, net (% of GDP)	6.2	4.1	2.6
Gross fixed capital formation (% of GDP)	8.0	15.3	26.7
Gross fixed private capital formation (% of GDP)	1.7	10.2	19.6
Finance and banking			
Government cash surplus or deficit (% of GDP)	-9.3	-2.5	-2.6
Government debt (% of GDP)	247.4	..	..
Deposit money banks' assets (% of GDP)	7.3	9.7	50.5
Total financial system deposits (% of GDP)	8.5	11.9	44.6
Bank capital to asset ratio (%)	18.5	19.0	..
Bank nonperforming loans to total gross loans ratio (%)	37.9	20.9	..
Domestic credit to the private sector (% of GDP)	2.1	4.4	38.3
Real interest rate (%)	19.0	8.6	
Interest rate spread (percentage points)	17.0	13.6	11.3
Infrastructure			
Paved roads (% of total roads)	7.9	..	..
Electric power consumption (kWh per capita)	..	..	391
Power outages in a typical month (number)	..	..	
Fixed line and mobile subscribers (per 100 people)	1	..	17
Internet users (per 100 people)	0.1	0.2	4.2
Cost of telephone call to U.S. ($ per 3 minutes)	2.74	..	1.99

Singapore

	Country data		High-income group
	2000	2006	2006
Economic and social context			
Population (millions)	4.0	4.5	1,031
Labor force (millions)	2.1	2.3	504
Unemployment rate (% of labor force)	3.4	4.2	6.2
GNI per capita, *World Bank Atlas* method ($)	22,970	28,730	36,608
GDP growth, 1995–2000 and 2000–06 (average annual %)	5.7	5.0	2.3
Agriculture value added (% of GDP)	0.1	0.1	1.5
Industry value added (% of GDP)	35.6	34.7	26.2
Manufacturing value added (% of GDP)	27.7	29.2	16.8
Services value added (% of GDP)	64.3	65.2	72.3
Inflation (annual % change in consumer price index)	1.4	1.0	
Exchange rate (local currency units per $)	1.7	1.6	
Exports of goods and services (% of GDP)	191.8	252.6	25.6
Imports of goods and services (% of GDP)	176.7	220.9	26.3
Business environment			
Ease of doing business (ranking 1-178; 1=best)	..	1	
Time to start a business (days)	..	5	22
Procedures to start a business (number)	..	5	7
Firing cost (weeks of wages)	..	4.0	34.9
Closing a business (years to resolve insolvency)	..	0.8	2.0
Total tax rate (% of profit)	..	23.2	41.5
Highest marginal tax rate, corporate (%)	26	20	
Business entry rate (new registrations as % of total)	12.9	19.0	10.1
Enterprise surveys			
Time dealing with gov't officials (% of management time)	..	..	
Firms expected to give gifts in meetings w/tax officials (%)	..	..	
Firms using banks to finance investments (% of firms)	..	..	
Delay in obtaining an electrical connection (days)	..	..	
ISO certification ownership (% of firms)	..	..	
Private sector investment			
Invest. in infrastructure w/private participation ($ millions)	..	..	849
Private foreign direct investment, net (% of GDP)	17.8	18.3	2.7
Gross fixed capital formation (% of GDP)	30.6	23.1	20.4
Gross fixed private capital formation (% of GDP)	22.6	17.3	..
Finance and banking			
Government cash surplus or deficit (% of GDP)	11.4	7.0	–1.3
Government debt (% of GDP)	86.9	104.0	47.6
Deposit money banks' assets (% of GDP)	117.0	114.8	99.7
Total financial system deposits (% of GDP)	109.8	110.6	..
Bank capital to asset ratio (%)	10.0	9.6	6.2
Bank nonperforming loans to total gross loans ratio (%)	3.4	2.8	1.1
Domestic credit to the private sector (% of GDP)	109.5	98.6	162.0
Real interest rate (%)	2.0	5.1	
Interest rate spread (percentage points)	4.1	4.7	4.4
Infrastructure			
Paved roads (% of total roads)	100.0	100.0	90.9
Electric power consumption (kWh per capita)	7,575	8,358	9,760
Power outages in a typical month (number)	..	..	
Fixed line and mobile subscribers (per 100 people)	117	148	143
Internet users (per 100 people)	32.3	38.3	59.3
Cost of telephone call to U.S. ($ per 3 minutes)	0.68	0.69	0.77

Slovak Republic

Europe & Central Asia **Upper middle income**

	Country data		Upper middle-income group
	2000	2006	2006
Economic and social context			
Population (millions)	5.4	5.4	811
Labor force (millions)	2.6	2.7	374
Unemployment rate (% of labor force)	18.8	16.2	9.8
GNI per capita, *World Bank Atlas* method ($)	3,860	9,610	5,913
GDP growth, 1995–2000 and 2000–06 (average annual %)	3.5	5.1	3.9
Agriculture value added (% of GDP)	4.0	3.6	5.7
Industry value added (% of GDP)	32.2	31.6	32.4
Manufacturing value added (% of GDP)	22.0	19.8	19.4
Services value added (% of GDP)	63.8	64.8	62.0
Inflation (annual % change in consumer price index)	12.0	4.5	
Exchange rate (local currency units per $)	46.0	29.7	
Exports of goods and services (% of GDP)	70.3	85.7	32.7
Imports of goods and services (% of GDP)	72.8	90.3	30.3
Business environment			
Ease of doing business (ranking 1-178; 1=best)	..	32	
Time to start a business (days)	..	25	41
Procedures to start a business (number)	..	9	9
Firing cost (weeks of wages)	..	13.0	39.7
Closing a business (years to resolve insolvency)	..	4.0	2.9
Total tax rate (% of profit)	..	50.5	44.5
Highest marginal tax rate, corporate (%)	29	19	
Business entry rate (new registrations as % of total)	4.1	9.2	9.1
Enterprise surveys			
Time dealing with gov't officials (% of management time)	..	3.0	
Firms expected to give gifts in meetings w/tax officials (%)	38.6	29.1	
Firms using banks to finance investments (% of firms)	9.4	13.2	
Delay in obtaining an electrical connection (days)	13.1	6.0	
ISO certification ownership (% of firms)	..	10.0	
Private sector investment			
Invest. in infrastructure w/private participation ($ millions)	963	1,415	45,869
Private foreign direct investment, net (% of GDP)	9.4	7.6	3.5
Gross fixed capital formation (% of GDP)	25.7	26.4	19.9
Gross fixed private capital formation (% of GDP)	23.8	22.5	..
Finance and banking			
Government cash surplus or deficit (% of GDP)	..	-3.4	..
Government debt (% of GDP)	..	42.4	..
Deposit money banks' assets (% of GDP)	81.2	51.5	52.9
Total financial system deposits (% of GDP)	54.4	47.8	41.4
Bank capital to asset ratio (%)	4.6	8.0	9.8
Bank nonperforming loans to total gross loans ratio (%)	13.7	3.7	3.2
Domestic credit to the private sector (% of GDP)	50.9	39.2	41.4
Real interest rate (%)	4.8	4.8	
Interest rate spread (percentage points)	6.4	4.1	5.9
Infrastructure			
Paved roads (% of total roads)	87.0	87.3	..
Electric power consumption (kWh per capita)	4,956	4,920	3,131
Power outages in a typical month (number)	..	..	
Fixed line and mobile subscribers (per 100 people)	55	112	88
Internet users (per 100 people)	9.4	41.8	22.2
Cost of telephone call to U.S. ($ per 3 minutes)	1.13	1.06	1.06

Slovenia

High income

	Country data		High-income group
	2000	2006	2006
Economic and social context			
Population (millions)	2.0	2.0	1,031
Labor force (millions)	0.97	1.0	504
Unemployment rate (% of labor force)	7.2	5.8	6.2
GNI per capita, *World Bank Atlas* method ($)	10,780	18,660	36,608
GDP growth, 1995–2000 and 2000–06 (average annual %)	4.5	3.7	2.3
Agriculture value added (% of GDP)	3.2	2.3	1.5
Industry value added (% of GDP)	36.2	34.6	26.2
Manufacturing value added (% of GDP)	26.5	24.6	16.8
Services value added (% of GDP)	60.6	63.1	72.3
Inflation (annual % change in consumer price index)	8.9	2.5	
Exchange rate (local currency units per $)	222.7	191.0	
Exports of goods and services (% of GDP)	55.6	69.2	25.6
Imports of goods and services (% of GDP)	59.1	69.9	26.3
Business environment			
Ease of doing business (ranking 1-178; 1=best)	..	55	
Time to start a business (days)	..	60	22
Procedures to start a business (number)	..	9	7
Firing cost (weeks of wages)	..	40.0	34.9
Closing a business (years to resolve insolvency)	..	2.0	2.0
Total tax rate (% of profit)	..	39.2	41.5
Highest marginal tax rate, corporate (%)	25	25	
Business entry rate (new registrations as % of total)	6.4	8.0	10.1
Enterprise surveys			
Time dealing with gov't officials (% of management time)	..	3.7	
Firms expected to give gifts in meetings w/tax officials (%)	15.6	14.5	
Firms using banks to finance investments (% of firms)	10.6	29.6	
Delay in obtaining an electrical connection (days)	14.2	13.8	
ISO certification ownership (% of firms)	..	20.2	
Private sector investment			
Invest. in infrastructure w/private participation ($ millions)	..	..	849
Private foreign direct investment, net (% of GDP)	0.7	1.7	2.7
Gross fixed capital formation (% of GDP)	25.6	25.8	20.4
Gross fixed private capital formation (% of GDP)	59.1	61.2	..
Finance and banking			
Government cash surplus or deficit (% of GDP)	–1.1	–0.8	–1.3
Government debt (% of GDP)	22.8	..	47.6
Deposit money banks' assets (% of GDP)	44.9	71.3	99.7
Total financial system deposits (% of GDP)	42.4	52.9	..
Bank capital to asset ratio (%)	10.1	7.4	6.2
Bank nonperforming loans to total gross loans ratio (%)	6.5	4.9	1.1
Domestic credit to the private sector (% of GDP)	37.0	68.8	162.0
Real interest rate (%)	9.8	5.0	
Interest rate spread (percentage points)	5.7	4.6	4.4
Infrastructure			
Paved roads (% of total roads)	100.0	100.0	90.9
Electric power consumption (kWh per capita)	5,778	6,918	9,760
Power outages in a typical month (number)	..	..	
Fixed line and mobile subscribers (per 100 people)	101	132	143
Internet users (per 100 people)	15.1	62.3	59.3
Cost of telephone call to U.S. ($ per 3 minutes)	0.81	0.65	0.77

Solomon Islands

East Asia & Pacific **Low income**

	Country data		Low-income group
	2000	2006	2006
Economic and social context			
Population (millions)	0.42	0.48	2,420
Labor force (millions)	0.17	0.20	995
Unemployment rate (% of labor force)	..	..	..
GNI per capita, *World Bank Atlas* method ($)	690	690	649
GDP growth, 1995–2000 and 2000–06 (average annual %)	-1.7	3.2	6.5
Agriculture value added (% of GDP)	..	..	20.4
Industry value added (% of GDP)	..	..	27.7
Manufacturing value added (% of GDP)	..	..	15.8
Services value added (% of GDP)	..	..	51.9
Inflation (annual % change in consumer price index)	7.9	7.5	
Exchange rate (local currency units per $)	5.1	7.6	
Exports of goods and services (% of GDP)	39.6	47.9	26.7
Imports of goods and services (% of GDP)	59.0	54.3	30.1
Business environment			
Ease of doing business (ranking 1-178; 1=best)	..	79	
Time to start a business (days)	..	57	54
Procedures to start a business (number)	..	7	10
Firing cost (weeks of wages)	..	44.0	62.6
Closing a business (years to resolve insolvency)	..	1.0	3.8
Total tax rate (% of profit)	..	32.6	67.4
Highest marginal tax rate, corporate (%)	30	30	
Business entry rate (new registrations as % of total)	..	..	6.4
Enterprise surveys			
Time dealing with gov't officials (% of management time)	..	..	
Firms expected to give gifts in meetings w/tax officials (%)	..	..	
Firms using banks to finance investments (% of firms)	..	..	
Delay in obtaining an electrical connection (days)	..	..	
ISO certification ownership (% of firms)	..	..	
Private sector investment			
Invest. in infrastructure w/private participation ($ millions)	..	..	29,785
Private foreign direct investment, net (% of GDP)	4.4	5.5	2.6
Gross fixed capital formation (% of GDP)	21.7	35.3	26.7
Gross fixed private capital formation (% of GDP)	17.1	17.2	19.6
Finance and banking			
Government cash surplus or deficit (% of GDP)	..	..	-2.6
Government debt (% of GDP)	..	..	
Deposit money banks' assets (% of GDP)	22.5	..	50.5
Total financial system deposits (% of GDP)	22.9	..	44.6
Bank capital to asset ratio (%)	..	..	..
Bank nonperforming loans to total gross loans ratio (%)	..	..	..
Domestic credit to the private sector (% of GDP)	22.2	28.8	38.3
Real interest rate (%)	3.5	6.6	
Interest rate spread (percentage points)	12.0	13.1	11.3
Infrastructure			
Paved roads (% of total roads)	2.4	..	..
Electric power consumption (kWh per capita)	..	..	391
Power outages in a typical month (number)	..	..	
Fixed line and mobile subscribers (per 100 people)	2	3	17
Internet users (per 100 people)	0.5	1.7	4.2
Cost of telephone call to U.S. ($ per 3 minutes)	..	..	1.99

Somalia

	Country data		Low-income group
	2000	2006	2006
Economic and social context			
Population (millions)	7.1	8.4	2,420
Labor force (millions)	3.0	3.6	995
Unemployment rate (% of labor force)	..	..	..
GNI per capita, *World Bank Atlas* method ($)	..	..	649
GDP growth, 1995–2000 and 2000–06 (average annual %)	..	..	6.5
Agriculture value added (% of GDP)	..	..	20.4
Industry value added (% of GDP)	..	..	27.7
Manufacturing value added (% of GDP)	..	..	15.8
Services value added (% of GDP)	..	..	51.9
Inflation (annual % change in consumer price index)	..	..	
Exchange rate (local currency units per $)	..	..	
Exports of goods and services (% of GDP)	..	..	26.7
Imports of goods and services (% of GDP)	..	..	30.1
Business environment			
Ease of doing business (ranking 1-178; 1=best)	..	..	
Time to start a business (days)	..	..	54
Procedures to start a business (number)	..	..	10
Firing cost (weeks of wages)	..	..	62.6
Closing a business (years to resolve insolvency)	..	..	3.8
Total tax rate (% of profit)	..	..	67.4
Highest marginal tax rate, corporate (%)	..	..	
Business entry rate (new registrations as % of total)	..	..	6.4
Enterprise surveys			
Time dealing with gov't officials (% of management time)	..	..	
Firms expected to give gifts in meetings w/tax officials (%)	..	..	
Firms using banks to finance investments (% of firms)	..	..	
Delay in obtaining an electrical connection (days)	..	..	
ISO certification ownership (% of firms)	..	..	
Private sector investment			
Invest. in infrastructure w/private participation ($ millions)	1	1	29,785
Private foreign direct investment, net (% of GDP)	..	..	2.6
Gross fixed capital formation (% of GDP)	..	..	26.7
Gross fixed private capital formation (% of GDP)	..	..	19.6
Finance and banking			
Government cash surplus or deficit (% of GDP)	..	..	-2.6
Government debt (% of GDP)	..	..	..
Deposit money banks' assets (% of GDP)	..	..	50.5
Total financial system deposits (% of GDP)	..	..	44.6
Bank capital to asset ratio (%)	..	..	..
Bank nonperforming loans to total gross loans ratio (%)	..	..	..
Domestic credit to the private sector (% of GDP)	..	..	38.3
Real interest rate (%)	..	..	
Interest rate spread (percentage points)	..	..	11.3
Infrastructure			
Paved roads (% of total roads)	11.8	..	..
Electric power consumption (kWh per capita)	..	..	391
Power outages in a typical month (number)	..	..	
Fixed line and mobile subscribers (per 100 people)	1	7	17
Internet users (per 100 people)	0.2	1.1	4.2
Cost of telephone call to U.S. ($ per 3 minutes)	..	..	1.99

South Africa

Sub-Saharan Africa   **Upper middle income**

	Country data		Upper middle-income group
	2000	2006	2006
Economic and social context			
Population (millions)	44.0	47.4	811
Labor force (millions)	18.7	20.0	374
Unemployment rate (% of labor force)	26.7	26.7	9.8
GNI per capita, *World Bank Atlas* method ($)	3,050	5,390	5,913
GDP growth, 1995–2000 and 2000–06 (average annual %)	2.5	4.1	3.9
Agriculture value added (% of GDP)	3.3	2.7	5.7
Industry value added (% of GDP)	31.8	30.9	32.4
Manufacturing value added (% of GDP)	19.0	18.2	19.4
Services value added (% of GDP)	64.9	66.4	62.0
Inflation (annual % change in consumer price index)	5.3	4.6	
Exchange rate (local currency units per $)	6.9	6.8	
Exports of goods and services (% of GDP)	27.9	29.8	32.7
Imports of goods and services (% of GDP)	24.9	33.2	30.3
Business environment			
Ease of doing business (ranking 1-178; 1=best)	..	35	
Time to start a business (days)	..	31	41
Procedures to start a business (number)	..	8	9
Firing cost (weeks of wages)	..	24.0	39.7
Closing a business (years to resolve insolvency)	..	2.0	2.9
Total tax rate (% of profit)	..	37.1	44.5
Highest marginal tax rate, corporate (%)	30	29	
Business entry rate (new registrations as % of total)	5.8	7.5	9.1
Enterprise surveys			
Time dealing with gov't officials (% of management time)	..	9.2	
Firms expected to give gifts in meetings w/tax officials (%)	..	0.6	
Firms using banks to finance investments (% of firms)	..	24.2	
Delay in obtaining an electrical connection (days)	..	7.3	
ISO certification ownership (% of firms)	..	42.4	
Private sector investment			
Invest. in infrastructure w/private participation ($ millions)	584	4,850	45,869
Private foreign direct investment, net (% of GDP)	0.7	0.0	3.5
Gross fixed capital formation (% of GDP)	15.1	18.7	19.9
Gross fixed private capital formation (% of GDP)	12.4	15.8	..
Finance and banking			
Government cash surplus or deficit (% of GDP)	–2.0	1.2	..
Government debt (% of GDP)	45.3	..	..
Deposit money banks' assets (% of GDP)	70.7	76.7	52.9
Total financial system deposits (% of GDP)	50.1	56.9	41.4
Bank capital to asset ratio (%)	8.7	7.8	9.8
Bank nonperforming loans to total gross loans ratio (%)	3.1	1.2	3.2
Domestic credit to the private sector (% of GDP)	133.7	160.8	41.4
Real interest rate (%)	5.2	4.0	
Interest rate spread (percentage points)	5.3	4.0	5.9
Infrastructure			
Paved roads (% of total roads)	20.3	..	..
Electric power consumption (kWh per capita)	4,417	4,847	3,131
Power outages in a typical month (number)	..	..	
Fixed line and mobile subscribers (per 100 people)	30	83	88
Internet users (per 100 people)	5.5	10.9	22.2
Cost of telephone call to U.S. ($ per 3 minutes)	1.98	0.79	1.06

Spain

	Country data		High-income group
	2000	2006	2006
Economic and social context			
Population (millions)	40.3	44.1	1,031
Labor force (millions)	18.3	21.1	504
Unemployment rate (% of labor force)	13.9	9.2	6.2
GNI per capita, *World Bank Atlas* method ($)	15,420	27,340	36,608
GDP growth, 1995–2000 and 2000–06 (average annual %)	4.2	3.3	2.3
Agriculture value added (% of GDP)	4.4	3.1	1.5
Industry value added (% of GDP)	29.2	29.7	26.2
Manufacturing value added (% of GDP)	18.6	15.5	16.8
Services value added (% of GDP)	66.4	67.2	72.3
Inflation (annual % change in consumer price index)	3.4	3.5	
Exchange rate (local currency units per $)	1.1	0.8	
Exports of goods and services (% of GDP)	29.0	26.1	25.6
Imports of goods and services (% of GDP)	32.2	32.3	26.3
Business environment			
Ease of doing business (ranking 1-178; 1=best)	..	38	
Time to start a business (days)	..	47	22
Procedures to start a business (number)	..	10	7
Firing cost (weeks of wages)	..	56.0	34.9
Closing a business (years to resolve insolvency)	..	1.0	2.0
Total tax rate (% of profit)	..	62.0	41.5
Highest marginal tax rate, corporate (%)	35	35	
Business entry rate (new registrations as % of total)	6.4	6.3	10.1
Enterprise surveys			
Time dealing with gov't officials (% of management time)	..	..	
Firms expected to give gifts in meetings w/tax officials (%)	..	..	
Firms using banks to finance investments (% of firms)	..	..	
Delay in obtaining an electrical connection (days)	..	..	
ISO certification ownership (% of firms)	..	..	
Private sector investment			
Invest. in infrastructure w/private participation ($ millions)	..	..	849
Private foreign direct investment, net (% of GDP)	6.7	1.6	2.7
Gross fixed capital formation (% of GDP)	25.8	30.3	20.4
Gross fixed private capital formation (% of GDP)	..	..	..
Finance and banking			
Government cash surplus or deficit (% of GDP)	−0.5	1.9	−1.3
Government debt (% of GDP)	58.9	39.8	47.6
Deposit money banks' assets (% of GDP)	105.6	..	99.7
Total financial system deposits (% of GDP)	58.1	..	..
Bank capital to asset ratio (%)	8.5	7.2	6.2
Bank nonperforming loans to total gross loans ratio (%)	1.2	0.6	1.1
Domestic credit to the private sector (% of GDP)	97.7	167.4	162.0
Real interest rate (%)	1.7	..	
Interest rate spread (percentage points)	2.2	..	4.4
Infrastructure			
Paved roads (% of total roads)	99.0	99.0	90.9
Electric power consumption (kWh per capita)	5,207	6,147	9,760
Power outages in a typical month (number)	..	..	
Fixed line and mobile subscribers (per 100 people)	103	146	143
Internet users (per 100 people)	13.6	42.1	59.3
Cost of telephone call to U.S. ($ per 3 minutes)	1.08	0.60	0.77

Sri Lanka

South Asia   **Lower middle income**

	Country data		Lower middle-income group
	2000	2006	2006
Economic and social context			
Population (millions)	19.4	19.9	2,276
Labor force (millions)	8.0	8.4	1,209
Unemployment rate (% of labor force)	7.4	7.6	5.7
GNI per capita, *World Bank Atlas* method ($)	850	1,310	2,038
GDP growth, 1995–2000 and 2000–06 (average annual %)	5.0	4.8	7.6
Agriculture value added (% of GDP)	19.9	16.5	11.9
Industry value added (% of GDP)	27.3	27.1	43.5
Manufacturing value added (% of GDP)	16.8	13.9	26.7
Services value added (% of GDP)	52.8	56.5	44.6
Inflation (annual % change in consumer price index)	6.2	13.7	
Exchange rate (local currency units per $)	77.0	103.9	
Exports of goods and services (% of GDP)	39.0	31.6	40.4
Imports of goods and services (% of GDP)	49.6	43.2	36.4
Business environment			
Ease of doing business (ranking 1-178; 1=best)	..	101	
Time to start a business (days)	..	39	53
Procedures to start a business (number)	..	5	10
Firing cost (weeks of wages)	..	169.0	50.2
Closing a business (years to resolve insolvency)	..	1.7	3.3
Total tax rate (% of profit)	..	63.7	45.8
Highest marginal tax rate, corporate (%)	35	35	
Business entry rate (new registrations as % of total)	6.8	8.1	7.6
Enterprise surveys			
Time dealing with gov't officials (% of management time)	..	3.5	
Firms expected to give gifts in meetings w/tax officials (%)	..	2.7	
Firms using banks to finance investments (% of firms)	..	16.2	
Delay in obtaining an electrical connection (days)	..	83.4	
ISO certification ownership (% of firms)	..	..	
Private sector investment			
Invest. in infrastructure w/private participation ($ millions)	159	310	38,154
Private foreign direct investment, net (% of GDP)	1.1	1.8	3.0
Gross fixed capital formation (% of GDP)	28.0	28.7	33.5
Gross fixed private capital formation (% of GDP)	24.8	24.8	10.9
Finance and banking			
Government cash surplus or deficit (% of GDP)	-8.4	-7.2	-0.9
Government debt (% of GDP)	96.9	93.0	..
Deposit money banks' assets (% of GDP)	32.1	35.8	87.8
Total financial system deposits (% of GDP)	31.1	34.6	43.1
Bank capital to asset ratio (%)	4.4	6.7	10.7
Bank nonperforming loans to total gross loans ratio (%)	15.3	9.6	4.0
Domestic credit to the private sector (% of GDP)	28.8	32.8	81.3
Real interest rate (%)	8.3	-2.7	
Interest rate spread (percentage points)	7.0	-3.2	7.2
Infrastructure			
Paved roads (% of total roads)	85.8	81.0	65.8
Electric power consumption (kWh per capita)	288	378	1,502
Power outages in a typical month (number)	..	..	
Fixed line and mobile subscribers (per 100 people)	6	37	60
Internet users (per 100 people)	0.6	2.2	11.4
Cost of telephone call to U.S. ($ per 3 minutes)	3.29	2.11	2.08

St. Kitts and Nevis

Latin America & Caribbean　　　　　　**Upper middle income**

	Country data		Upper middle-income group
	2000	2006	2006
Economic and social context			
Population (millions)	0.04	0.05	811
Labor force (millions)	..	..	374
Unemployment rate (% of labor force)	..	..	9.8
GNI per capita, *World Bank Atlas* method ($)	6,490	8,460	5,913
GDP growth, 1995–2000 and 2000–06 (average annual %)	4.3	3.9	3.9
Agriculture value added (% of GDP)	2.7	3.0	5.7
Industry value added (% of GDP)	28.8	27.6	32.4
Manufacturing value added (% of GDP)	10.4	9.7	19.4
Services value added (% of GDP)	68.5	69.4	62.0
Inflation (annual % change in consumer price index)	2.0	1.8	
Exchange rate (local currency units per $)	2.7	2.7	
Exports of goods and services (% of GDP)	45.6	46.9	32.7
Imports of goods and services (% of GDP)	75.6	66.6	30.3
Business environment			
Ease of doing business (ranking 1-178; 1=best)	..	64	
Time to start a business (days)	..	46	41
Procedures to start a business (number)	..	9	9
Firing cost (weeks of wages)	..	8.0	39.7
Closing a business (years to resolve insolvency)	..	..	2.9
Total tax rate (% of profit)	..	52.6	44.5
Highest marginal tax rate, corporate (%)	..	..	
Business entry rate (new registrations as % of total)	..	..	9.1
Enterprise surveys			
Time dealing with gov't officials (% of management time)	..	..	
Firms expected to give gifts in meetings w/tax officials (%)	..	..	
Firms using banks to finance investments (% of firms)	..	..	
Delay in obtaining an electrical connection (days)	..	..	
ISO certification ownership (% of firms)	..	..	
Private sector investment			
Invest. in infrastructure w/private participation ($ millions)	..	..	45,869
Private foreign direct investment, net (% of GDP)	29.2	42.4	3.5
Gross fixed capital formation (% of GDP)	49.6	45.5	19.9
Gross fixed private capital formation (% of GDP)	39.3	41.9	..
Finance and banking			
Government cash surplus or deficit (% of GDP)	..	1.3	..
Government debt (% of GDP)	..	..	
Deposit money banks' assets (% of GDP)	117.3	119.6	52.9
Total financial system deposits (% of GDP)	108.6	128.5	41.4
Bank capital to asset ratio (%)	..	..	9.8
Bank nonperforming loans to total gross loans ratio (%)	..	..	3.2
Domestic credit to the private sector (% of GDP)	76.6	69.8	41.4
Real interest rate (%)	5.7	3.9	
Interest rate spread (percentage points)	6.8	4.7	5.9
Infrastructure			
Paved roads (% of total roads)	42.5	..	..
Electric power consumption (kWh per capita)	..	..	3,131
Power outages in a typical month (number)	..	..	
Fixed line and mobile subscribers (per 100 people)	52	74	88
Internet users (per 100 people)	6.1	..	22.2
Cost of telephone call to U.S. ($ per 3 minutes)	..	..	1.06

St. Lucia

Latin America & Caribbean　　　　**Upper middle income**

	Country data		Upper middle-income group
	2000	2006	2006
Economic and social context			
Population (millions)	0.16	0.17	811
Labor force (millions)	0.07	0.08	374
Unemployment rate (% of labor force)	16.5	24.8	9.8
GNI per capita, *World Bank Atlas* method ($)	3,910	5,060	5,913
GDP growth, 1995–2000 and 2000–06 (average annual %)	3.0	3.8	3.9
Agriculture value added (% of GDP)	6.5	3.9	5.7
Industry value added (% of GDP)	18.2	18.8	32.4
Manufacturing value added (% of GDP)	5.0	5.5	19.4
Services value added (% of GDP)	75.3	77.3	62.0
Inflation (annual % change in consumer price index)	3.6	2.3	
Exchange rate (local currency units per $)	2.7	2.7	
Exports of goods and services (% of GDP)	57.2	52.0	32.7
Imports of goods and services (% of GDP)	67.7	65.5	30.3
Business environment			
Ease of doing business (ranking 1-178; 1=best)	..	34	
Time to start a business (days)	..	40	41
Procedures to start a business (number)	..	6	9
Firing cost (weeks of wages)	..	56.0	39.7
Closing a business (years to resolve insolvency)	..	2.0	2.9
Total tax rate (% of profit)	..	36.9	44.5
Highest marginal tax rate, corporate (%)	33	30	
Business entry rate (new registrations as % of total)	..	..	9.1
Enterprise surveys			
Time dealing with gov't officials (% of management time)	..	..	
Firms expected to give gifts in meetings w/tax officials (%)	..	..	
Firms using banks to finance investments (% of firms)	..	..	
Delay in obtaining an electrical connection (days)	..	..	
ISO certification ownership (% of firms)	..	..	
Private sector investment			
Invest. in infrastructure w/private participation ($ millions)	15	10	45,869
Private foreign direct investment, net (% of GDP)	8.2	13.2	3.5
Gross fixed capital formation (% of GDP)	27.6	23.1	19.9
Gross fixed private capital formation (% of GDP)	17.7	18.4	..
Finance and banking			
Government cash surplus or deficit (% of GDP)	..	..	..
Government debt (% of GDP)	..	..	..
Deposit money banks' assets (% of GDP)	84.4	89.2	52.9
Total financial system deposits (% of GDP)	70.8	80.1	41.4
Bank capital to asset ratio (%)	..	..	9.8
Bank nonperforming loans to total gross loans ratio (%)	..	..	3.2
Domestic credit to the private sector (% of GDP)	83.3	37.1	41.4
Real interest rate (%)	5.5	13.6	
Interest rate spread (percentage points)	8.3	7.8	5.9
Infrastructure			
Paved roads (% of total roads)	..	..	..
Electric power consumption (kWh per capita)	..	..	3,131
Power outages in a typical month (number)	..	..	
Fixed line and mobile subscribers (per 100 people)	33	..	88
Internet users (per 100 people)	5.1	33.9	22.2
Cost of telephone call to U.S. ($ per 3 minutes)	..	..	1.06

St. Vincent & Grenadines

Latin America & Caribbean			Upper middle income

	Country data		Upper middle-income group
	2000	2006	2006

Economic and social context

Population (millions)	0.12	0.12	811
Labor force (millions)	0.05	0.06	374
Unemployment rate (% of labor force)	..	..	9.8
GNI per capita, *World Bank Atlas* method ($)	2,740	3,320	5,913
GDP growth, 1995–2000 and 2000–06 (average annual %)	5.7	3.5	3.9
Agriculture value added (% of GDP)	10.8	8.1	5.7
Industry value added (% of GDP)	24.0	24.7	32.4
Manufacturing value added (% of GDP)	6.0	5.7	19.4
Services value added (% of GDP)	65.2	67.2	62.0
Inflation (annual % change in consumer price index)	0.2	3.0	
Exchange rate (local currency units per $)	2.7	2.7	
Exports of goods and services (% of GDP)	53.6	48.4	32.7
Imports of goods and services (% of GDP)	59.9	76.5	30.3

Business environment

Ease of doing business (ranking 1-178; 1=best)	..	54	
Time to start a business (days)	..	12	41
Procedures to start a business (number)	..	8	9
Firing cost (weeks of wages)	..	54.0	39.7
Closing a business (years to resolve insolvency)	..	..	2.9
Total tax rate (% of profit)	..	45.0	44.5
Highest marginal tax rate, corporate (%)	..	..	
Business entry rate (new registrations as % of total)	..	..	9.1
Enterprise surveys			
Time dealing with gov't officials (% of management time)	..	..	
Firms expected to give gifts in meetings w/tax officials (%)	..	..	
Firms using banks to finance investments (% of firms)	..	..	
Delay in obtaining an electrical connection (days)	..	..	
ISO certification ownership (% of firms)	..	..	

Private sector investment

Invest. in infrastructure w/private participation ($ millions)	..	35	45,869
Private foreign direct investment, net (% of GDP)	11.3	20.1	3.5
Gross fixed capital formation (% of GDP)	27.4	36.5	19.9
Gross fixed private capital formation (% of GDP)	20.3	27.8	..

Finance and banking

Government cash surplus or deficit (% of GDP)	..	..	..
Government debt (% of GDP)	..	..	
Deposit money banks' assets (% of GDP)	76.6	76.8	52.9
Total financial system deposits (% of GDP)	85.6	82.5	41.4
Bank capital to asset ratio (%)	..	..	9.8
Bank nonperforming loans to total gross loans ratio (%)	..	..	3.2
Domestic credit to the private sector (% of GDP)	65.5	67.9	41.4
Real interest rate (%)	12.5	19.6	
Interest rate spread (percentage points)	6.9	6.8	5.9

Infrastructure

Paved roads (% of total roads)	68.0	70.0	..
Electric power consumption (kWh per capita)	..	..	3,131
Power outages in a typical month (number)	..	..	
Fixed line and mobile subscribers (per 100 people)	24	92	88
Internet users (per 100 people)	3.0	8.4	22.2
Cost of telephone call to U.S. ($ per 3 minutes)	3.97	..	1.06

Sudan

Sub-Saharan Africa   **Low income**

	Country data		Low-income group
	2000	**2006**	**2006**
Economic and social context			
Population (millions)	33.3	37.7	2,420
Labor force (millions)	9.1	10.7	995
Unemployment rate (% of labor force)	..	..	..
GNI per capita, *World Bank Atlas* method ($)	310	800	649
GDP growth, 1995–2000 and 2000–06 (average annual %)	6.2	7.0	6.5
Agriculture value added (% of GDP)	41.7	32.3	20.4
Industry value added (% of GDP)	21.5	28.5	27.7
Manufacturing value added (% of GDP)	8.6	6.2	15.8
Services value added (% of GDP)	36.8	39.2	51.9
Inflation (annual % change in consumer price index)	6.9	7.2	
Exchange rate (local currency units per $)	2.6	2.2	
Exports of goods and services (% of GDP)	15.3	16.1	26.7
Imports of goods and services (% of GDP)	17.7	26.7	30.1
Business environment			
Ease of doing business (ranking 1-178; 1=best)	..	143	
Time to start a business (days)	..	39	54
Procedures to start a business (number)	..	10	10
Firing cost (weeks of wages)	..	118.0	62.6
Closing a business (years to resolve insolvency)	..		3.8
Total tax rate (% of profit)	..	31.6	67.4
Highest marginal tax rate, corporate (%)	..	..	
Business entry rate (new registrations as % of total)	..	..	*6.4*
Enterprise surveys			
Time dealing with gov't officials (% of management time)	..	..	
Firms expected to give gifts in meetings w/tax officials (%)	..	..	
Firms using banks to finance investments (% of firms)	..	..	
Delay in obtaining an electrical connection (days)	..	..	
ISO certification ownership (% of firms)	..	..	
Private sector investment			
Invest. in infrastructure w/private participation ($ millions)	*12*	736	29,785
Private foreign direct investment, net (% of GDP)	3.2	9.4	2.6
Gross fixed capital formation (% of GDP)	12.1	20.4	26.7
Gross fixed private capital formation (% of GDP)	9.7	14.1	19.6
Finance and banking			
Government cash surplus or deficit (% of GDP)	–0.4	..	–2.6
Government debt (% of GDP)	8.7	..	..
Deposit money banks' assets (% of GDP)	2.1	13.3	50.5
Total financial system deposits (% of GDP)	5.3	14.3	44.6
Bank capital to asset ratio (%)	..	..	..
Bank nonperforming loans to total gross loans ratio (%)	..	..	..
Domestic credit to the private sector (% of GDP)	2.2	12.7	38.3
Real interest rate (%)	..	..	
Interest rate spread (percentage points)	..	..	*11.3*
Infrastructure			
Paved roads (% of total roads)	36.3	..	..
Electric power consumption (kWh per capita)	62	94	*391*
Power outages in a typical month (number)	..	..	
Fixed line and mobile subscribers (per 100 people)	1	14	17
Internet users (per 100 people)	0.1	9.3	*4.2*
Cost of telephone call to U.S. ($ per 3 minutes)	42.02	..	*1.99*

Suriname

Latin America & Caribbean **Lower middle income**

	Country data		Lower middle-income group
	2000	**2006**	**2006**
Economic and social context			
Population (millions)	0.44	0.46	2,276
Labor force (millions)	0.14	0.16	1,209
Unemployment rate (% of labor force)	13.8	..	5.7
GNI per capita, *World Bank Atlas* method ($)	2,060	4,210	2,038
GDP growth, 1995–2000 and 2000–06 (average annual %)	1.7	6.0	7.6
Agriculture value added (% of GDP)	11.2	5.2	11.9
Industry value added (% of GDP)	25.2	35.7	43.5
Manufacturing value added (% of GDP)	9.0	14.2	26.7
Services value added (% of GDP)	63.7	59.1	44.6
Inflation (annual % change in consumer price index)	59.4	11.3	
Exchange rate (local currency units per $)	1.3	2.7	
Exports of goods and services (% of GDP)	19.7	30.7	40.4
Imports of goods and services (% of GDP)	33.2	45.6	36.4
Business environment			
Ease of doing business (ranking 1-178; 1=best)	..	142	
Time to start a business (days)	..	694	53
Procedures to start a business (number)	..	13	10
Firing cost (weeks of wages)	..	26.0	50.2
Closing a business (years to resolve insolvency)	..	5.0	3.3
Total tax rate (% of profit)	..	27.9	45.8
Highest marginal tax rate, corporate (%)	..	..	
Business entry rate (new registrations as % of total)	..	..	7.6
Enterprise surveys			
Time dealing with gov't officials (% of management time)	..	..	
Firms expected to give gifts in meetings w/tax officials (%)	..	..	
Firms using banks to finance investments (% of firms)	..	..	
Delay in obtaining an electrical connection (days)	..	..	
ISO certification ownership (% of firms)	..	..	
Private sector investment			
Invest. in infrastructure w/private participation ($ millions)	..	..	38,154
Private foreign direct investment, net (% of GDP)	..	..	3.0
Gross fixed capital formation (% of GDP)	12.4	25.1	33.5
Gross fixed private capital formation (% of GDP)	9.8	19.8	10.9
Finance and banking			
Government cash surplus or deficit (% of GDP)	..	..	-0.9
Government debt (% of GDP)	..	..	..
Deposit money banks' assets (% of GDP)	12.3	26.5	87.8
Total financial system deposits (% of GDP)	17.6	48.2	43.1
Bank capital to asset ratio (%)	..	..	10.7
Bank nonperforming loans to total gross loans ratio (%)	..	..	4.0
Domestic credit to the private sector (% of GDP)	8.4	20.8	81.3
Real interest rate (%)	-16.7	2.3	
Interest rate spread (percentage points)	13.5	9.0	7.2
Infrastructure			
Paved roads (% of total roads)	26.0	26.3	65.8
Electric power consumption (kWh per capita)	..	..	1,502
Power outages in a typical month (number)	..	..	
Fixed line and mobile subscribers (per 100 people)	27	88	60
Internet users (per 100 people)	2.7	7.1	11.4
Cost of telephone call to U.S. ($ per 3 minutes)	2.29	1.33	2.08

Swaziland

Sub-Saharan Africa   **Lower middle income**

	Country data		Lower middle-income group
	2000	2006	2006
Economic and social context			
Population (millions)	1.0	1.1	2,276
Labor force (millions)	0.32	0.36	1,209
Unemployment rate (% of labor force)	25.2	..	5.7
GNI per capita, World Bank Atlas method ($)	1,370	2,400	2,038
GDP growth, 1995–2000 and 2000–06 (average annual %)	3.4	2.4	7.6
Agriculture value added (% of GDP)	15.5	10.9	11.9
Industry value added (% of GDP)	44.8	45.6	43.5
Manufacturing value added (% of GDP)	35.8	36.8	26.7
Services value added (% of GDP)	39.7	43.5	44.6
Inflation (annual % change in consumer price index)	12.2	5.3	
Exchange rate (local currency units per $)	6.9	6.8	
Exports of goods and services (% of GDP)	81.6	81.2	40.4
Imports of goods and services (% of GDP)	97.2	86.3	36.4
Business environment			
Ease of doing business (ranking 1–178; 1=best)	..	95	
Time to start a business (days)	..	61	53
Procedures to start a business (number)	..	13	10
Firing cost (weeks of wages)	..	53.0	50.2
Closing a business (years to resolve insolvency)	..	2.0	3.3
Total tax rate (% of profit)	..	36.6	45.8
Highest marginal tax rate, corporate (%)	30	30	
Business entry rate (new registrations as % of total)	..	..	7.6
Enterprise surveys			
Time dealing with gov't officials (% of management time)	..	4.4	
Firms expected to give gifts in meetings w/tax officials (%)	..	3.3	
Firms using banks to finance investments (% of firms)	..	7.7	
Delay in obtaining an electrical connection (days)	..	16.9	
ISO certification ownership (% of firms)	..	22.1	
Private sector investment			
Invest. in infrastructure w/private participation ($ millions)	5	3	38,154
Private foreign direct investment, net (% of GDP)	6.6	1.4	3.0
Gross fixed capital formation (% of GDP)	18.6	17.2	33.5
Gross fixed private capital formation (% of GDP)	12.3	9.4	10.9
Finance and banking			
Government cash surplus or deficit (% of GDP)	..	-2.6	-0.9
Government debt (% of GDP)	..	..	..
Deposit money banks' assets (% of GDP)	13.2	22.6	87.8
Total financial system deposits (% of GDP)	19.6	19.5	43.1
Bank capital to asset ratio (%)	..	..	10.7
Bank nonperforming loans to total gross loans ratio (%)	..	2.0	4.0
Domestic credit to the private sector (% of GDP)	13.7	23.7	81.3
Real interest rate (%)	1.5	5.2	
Interest rate spread (percentage points)	7.5	6.2	7.2
Infrastructure			
Paved roads (% of total roads)	30.0	..	65.8
Electric power consumption (kWh per capita)	..	..	1,502
Power outages in a typical month (number)	..	2.5	
Fixed line and mobile subscribers (per 100 people)	6	26	60
Internet users (per 100 people)	1.0	3.7	11.4
Cost of telephone call to U.S. ($ per 3 minutes)	3.68	2.97	2.08

Sweden

	Country data		High-income group
	2000	2006	2006
Economic and social context			
Population (millions)	8.9	9.1	1,031
Labor force (millions)	4.6	4.7	504
Unemployment rate (% of labor force)	5.8	7.7	6.2
GNI per capita, *World Bank Atlas* method ($)	28,870	43,530	36,608
GDP growth, 1995–2000 and 2000–06 (average annual %)	3.3	2.7	2.3
Agriculture value added (% of GDP)	1.9	1.4	1.5
Industry value added (% of GDP)	28.6	29.0	26.2
Manufacturing value added (% of GDP)	22.0	19.7	16.8
Services value added (% of GDP)	69.5	69.6	72.3
Inflation (annual % change in consumer price index)	0.9	1.4	
Exchange rate (local currency units per $)	9.2	7.4	
Exports of goods and services (% of GDP)	45.9	51.3	25.6
Imports of goods and services (% of GDP)	40.0	43.2	26.3
Business environment			
Ease of doing business (ranking 1-178; 1=best)	..	14	
Time to start a business (days)	..	15	22
Procedures to start a business (number)	..	3	7
Firing cost (weeks of wages)	..	26.0	34.9
Closing a business (years to resolve insolvency)	..	2.0	2.0
Total tax rate (% of profit)	..	54.5	41.5
Highest marginal tax rate, corporate (%)	28	28	
Business entry rate (new registrations as % of total)	5.8	7.2	10.1
Enterprise surveys			
Time dealing with gov't officials (% of management time)	..	..	
Firms expected to give gifts in meetings w/tax officials (%)	..	..	
Firms using banks to finance investments (% of firms)	..	..	
Delay in obtaining an electrical connection (days)	..	..	
ISO certification ownership (% of firms)	..	..	
Private sector investment			
Invest. in infrastructure w/private participation ($ millions)	..	..	849
Private foreign direct investment, net (% of GDP)	9.1	7.1	2.7
Gross fixed capital formation (% of GDP)	17.5	17.9	20.4
Gross fixed private capital formation (% of GDP)	..	..	..
Finance and banking			
Government cash surplus or deficit (% of GDP)	3.2	1.9	-1.3
Government debt (% of GDP)	61.9	48.5	47.6
Deposit money banks' assets (% of GDP)	46.4	117.9	99.7
Total financial system deposits (% of GDP)	0.1	46.4	..
Bank capital to asset ratio (%)	6.5	4.9	6.2
Bank nonperforming loans to total gross loans ratio (%)	1.6	0.5	1.1
Domestic credit to the private sector (% of GDP)	43.2	117.3	162.0
Real interest rate (%)	4.4	2.1	
Interest rate spread (percentage points)	3.7	2.5	4.4
Infrastructure			
Paved roads (% of total roads)	77.5	31.5	90.9
Electric power consumption (kWh per capita)	15,687	15,440	9,760
Power outages in a typical month (number)	..	..	
Fixed line and mobile subscribers (per 100 people)	137	165	143
Internet users (per 100 people)	45.6	76.9	59.3
Cost of telephone call to U.S. ($ per 3 minutes)	0.36	0.41	0.77

Switzerland

	Country data		High-income group
	2000	2006	2006
Economic and social context			
Population (millions)	7.2	7.5	1,031
Labor force (millions)	4.0	4.2	504
Unemployment rate (% of labor force)	2.7	4.4	6.2
GNI per capita, *World Bank Atlas* method ($)	40,110	58,050	36,608
GDP growth, 1995–2000 and 2000–06 (average annual %)	2.0	1.3	2.3
Agriculture value added (% of GDP)	1.7	1.3	1.5
Industry value added (% of GDP)	28.7	28.4	26.2
Manufacturing value added (% of GDP)	20.2	19.8	16.8
Services value added (% of GDP)	69.6	70.3	72.3
Inflation (annual % change in consumer price index)	1.5	1.1	
Exchange rate (local currency units per $)	1.7	1.3	
Exports of goods and services (% of GDP)	45.7	47.9	25.6
Imports of goods and services (% of GDP)	40.0	41.1	26.3
Business environment			
Ease of doing business (ranking 1-178; 1=best)	..	16	
Time to start a business (days)	..	20	22
Procedures to start a business (number)	..	6	7
Firing cost (weeks of wages)	..	13.0	34.9
Closing a business (years to resolve insolvency)	..	3.0	2.0
Total tax rate (% of profit)	..	29.1	41.5
Highest marginal tax rate, corporate (%)	45	9	
Business entry rate (new registrations as % of total)	13.1	6.4	10.1
Enterprise surveys			
Time dealing with gov't officials (% of management time)	..	..	
Firms expected to give gifts in meetings w/tax officials (%)	..	..	
Firms using banks to finance investments (% of firms)	..	..	
Delay in obtaining an electrical connection (days)	..	..	
ISO certification ownership (% of firms)	..	..	
Private sector investment			
Invest. in infrastructure w/private participation ($ millions)	..	..	849
Private foreign direct investment, net (% of GDP)	8.0	7.1	2.7
Gross fixed capital formation (% of GDP)	22.8	21.4	20.4
Gross fixed private capital formation (% of GDP)	..	..	..
Finance and banking			
Government cash surplus or deficit (% of GDP)	2.2	-0.4	-1.3
Government debt (% of GDP)	26.0	28.6	47.6
Deposit money banks' assets (% of GDP)	172.9	175.7	99.7
Total financial system deposits (% of GDP)	129.4	137.0	..
Bank capital to asset ratio (%)	6.0	4.9	6.2
Bank nonperforming loans to total gross loans ratio (%)	4.1	0.3	1.1
Domestic credit to the private sector (% of GDP)	161.0	174.3	162.0
Real interest rate (%)	3.5	1.6	
Interest rate spread (percentage points)	1.3	1.6	4.4
Infrastructure			
Paved roads (% of total roads)	..	100.0	90.9
Electric power consumption (kWh per capita)	7,847	8,305	9,760
Power outages in a typical month (number)	..	..	
Fixed line and mobile subscribers (per 100 people)	137	166	143
Internet users (per 100 people)	29.2	58.2	59.3
Cost of telephone call to U.S. ($ per 3 minutes)	0.21	0.32	0.77

Syrian Arab Republic

Middle East & North Africa **Lower middle income**

	Country data		Lower middle-income group
	2000	2006	2006
Economic and social context			
Population (millions)	16.5	19.4	2,276
Labor force (millions)	5.9	7.9	1,209
Unemployment rate (% of labor force)	11.6	12.3	5.7
GNI per capita, *World Bank Atlas* method ($)	960	1,560	2,038
GDP growth, 1995–2000 and 2000–06 (average annual %)	2.2	4.2	7.6
Agriculture value added (% of GDP)	23.8	18.3	11.9
Industry value added (% of GDP)	37.9	32.2	43.5
Manufacturing value added (% of GDP)	6.5	7.1	26.7
Services value added (% of GDP)	38.3	49.5	44.6
Inflation (annual % change in consumer price index)	-3.8	10.0	
Exchange rate (local currency units per $)	11.2	11.2	
Exports of goods and services (% of GDP)	35.4	39.4	40.4
Imports of goods and services (% of GDP)	28.6	35.6	36.4
Business environment			
Ease of doing business (ranking 1-178; 1=best)	..	137	
Time to start a business (days)	..	43	53
Procedures to start a business (number)	..	13	10
Firing cost (weeks of wages)	..	80.0	50.2
Closing a business (years to resolve insolvency)	..	4.1	3.3
Total tax rate (% of profit)	..	46.7	45.8
Highest marginal tax rate, corporate (%)	..	..	
Business entry rate (new registrations as % of total)	9.2	9.5	7.6
Enterprise surveys			
Time dealing with gov't officials (% of management time)	..	10.3	
Firms expected to give gifts in meetings w/tax officials (%)	..	68.8	
Firms using banks to finance investments (% of firms)	..	2.9	
Delay in obtaining an electrical connection (days)	..	61.8	
ISO certification ownership (% of firms)	..	7.4	
Private sector investment			
Invest. in infrastructure w/private participation ($ millions)	161	82	38,154
Private foreign direct investment, net (% of GDP)	1.4	1.8	3.0
Gross fixed capital formation (% of GDP)	17.3	21.4	33.5
Gross fixed private capital formation (% of GDP)	6.3	11.4	10.9
Finance and banking			
Government cash surplus or deficit (% of GDP)	..	..	-0.9
Government debt (% of GDP)	..	..	..
Deposit money banks' assets (% of GDP)	33.6	32.5	87.8
Total financial system deposits (% of GDP)	32.6	42.3	43.1
Bank capital to asset ratio (%)	..	..	10.7
Bank nonperforming loans to total gross loans ratio (%)	..	..	4.0
Domestic credit to the private sector (% of GDP)	8.3	14.9	81.3
Real interest rate (%)	-0.6	-4.4	
Interest rate spread (percentage points)	5.0	7.0	7.2
Infrastructure			
Paved roads (% of total roads)	20.1	20.1	65.8
Electric power consumption (kWh per capita)	1,058	1,411	1,502
Power outages in a typical month (number)	..	..	
Fixed line and mobile subscribers (per 100 people)	10	41	60
Internet users (per 100 people)	0.2	7.7	11.4
Cost of telephone call to U.S. ($ per 3 minutes)	4.81	..	2.08

Tajikistan

Europe & Central Asia			**Low income**

	Country data		Low-income group
	2000	**2006**	**2006**
Economic and social context			
Population (millions)	6.2	6.6	2,420
Labor force (millions)	2.0	2.2	995
Unemployment rate (% of labor force)	..	..	..
GNI per capita, *World Bank Atlas* method ($)	180	390	649
GDP growth, 1995–2000 and 2000–06 (average annual %)	1.1	9.1	6.5
Agriculture value added (% of GDP)	27.4	24.8	20.4
Industry value added (% of GDP)	38.9	27.4	27.7
Manufacturing value added (% of GDP)	33.7	19.3	15.8
Services value added (% of GDP)	33.7	47.8	51.9
Inflation (annual % change in consumer price index)	..	..	
Exchange rate (local currency units per $)	2.1	3.3	
Exports of goods and services (% of GDP)	86.7	23.2	26.7
Imports of goods and services (% of GDP)	88.6	57.5	30.1
Business environment			
Ease of doing business (ranking 1-178; 1=best)	..	153	
Time to start a business (days)	..	49	54
Procedures to start a business (number)	..	13	10
Firing cost (weeks of wages)	..	22.0	62.6
Closing a business (years to resolve insolvency)	..	3.0	3.8
Total tax rate (% of profit)	..	82.2	67.4
Highest marginal tax rate, corporate (%)	..	..	
Business entry rate (new registrations as % of total)	..	..	6.4
Enterprise surveys			
Time dealing with gov't officials (% of management time)	..	3.3	
Firms expected to give gifts in meetings w/tax officials (%)	82.4	67.5	
Firms using banks to finance investments (% of firms)	2.3	1.0	
Delay in obtaining an electrical connection (days)	12.7	5.4	
ISO certification ownership (% of firms)	..	6.5	
Private sector investment			
Invest. in infrastructure w/private participation ($ millions)	9	..	29,785
Private foreign direct investment, net (% of GDP)	2.4	12.0	2.6
Gross fixed capital formation (% of GDP)	9.5	13.1	26.7
Gross fixed private capital formation (% of GDP)	2.8	6.1	19.6
Finance and banking			
Government cash surplus or deficit (% of GDP)	-0.8	-6.6	-2.6
Government debt (% of GDP)	114.1	..	
Deposit money banks' assets (% of GDP)	..	..	50.5
Total financial system deposits (% of GDP)	..	..	44.6
Bank capital to asset ratio (%)	..	..	..
Bank nonperforming loans to total gross loans ratio (%)	..	..	..
Domestic credit to the private sector (% of GDP)	13.8	16.0	38.3
Real interest rate (%)	2.4	3.4	
Interest rate spread (percentage points)	24.3	15.3	11.3
Infrastructure			
Paved roads (% of total roads)	..	..	..
Electric power consumption (kWh per capita)	2,177	2,267	391
Power outages in a typical month (number)	..	..	
Fixed line and mobile subscribers (per 100 people)	4	8	17
Internet users (per 100 people)	0.0	0.3	4.2
Cost of telephone call to U.S. ($ per 3 minutes)	8.10	7.84	1.99

Tanzania

	Country data		Low-income group
	2000	2006	2006
Economic and social context			
Population (millions)	33.8	39.5	2,420
Labor force (millions)	16.7	19.3	995
Unemployment rate (% of labor force)	5.1	..	..
GNI per capita, *World Bank Atlas* method ($)	270	350	649
GDP growth, 1995–2000 and 2000–06 (average annual %)	3.9	6.5	6.5
Agriculture value added (% of GDP)	45.0	45.3	20.4
Industry value added (% of GDP)	15.7	17.4	27.7
Manufacturing value added (% of GDP)	7.5	6.9	15.8
Services value added (% of GDP)	39.2	37.3	51.9
Inflation (annual % change in consumer price index)	5.9	6.4	
Exchange rate (local currency units per $)	800.4	1,251.9	
Exports of goods and services (% of GDP)	16.8	24.3	26.7
Imports of goods and services (% of GDP)	24.2	30.8	30.1
Business environment			
Ease of doing business (ranking 1-178; 1=best)	..	130	
Time to start a business (days)	..	29	54
Procedures to start a business (number)	..	12	10
Firing cost (weeks of wages)	..	32.0	62.6
Closing a business (years to resolve insolvency)	..	3.0	3.8
Total tax rate (% of profit)	..	44.3	67.4
Highest marginal tax rate, corporate (%)	30	30	
Business entry rate (new registrations as % of total)		6.6	6.4
Enterprise surveys			
Time dealing with gov't officials (% of management time)	..	4.0	
Firms expected to give gifts in meetings w/tax officials (%)	..	14.7	
Firms using banks to finance investments (% of firms)	..	6.8	
Delay in obtaining an electrical connection (days)	..	44.3	
ISO certification ownership (% of firms)	..	14.7	
Private sector investment			
Invest. in infrastructure w/private participation ($ millions)	61	98	29,785
Private foreign direct investment, net (% of GDP)	5.1	3.7	2.6
Gross fixed capital formation (% of GDP)	17.4	18.4	26.7
Gross fixed private capital formation (% of GDP)	11.4	11.0	19.6
Finance and banking			
Government cash surplus or deficit (% of GDP)	..	..	-2.6
Government debt (% of GDP)	..	..	
Deposit money banks' assets (% of GDP)	..	..	50.5
Total financial system deposits (% of GDP)	..	..	44.6
Bank capital to asset ratio (%)	..	..	
Bank nonperforming loans to total gross loans ratio (%)	..	..	
Domestic credit to the private sector (% of GDP)	4.6	12.2	38.3
Real interest rate (%)	13.1	8.6	
Interest rate spread (percentage points)	14.2	8.8	11.3
Infrastructure			
Paved roads (% of total roads)	4.2	8.6	..
Electric power consumption (kWh per capita)	58	61	391
Power outages in a typical month (number)	..	12.0	
Fixed line and mobile subscribers (per 100 people)	1	15	17
Internet users (per 100 people)	0.1	1.0	4.2
Cost of telephone call to U.S. ($ per 3 minutes)	10.70	3.17	1.99

Thailand

East Asia & Pacific

Lower middle income

	Country data		Lower middle-income group
	2000	2006	2006
Economic and social context			
Population (millions)	60.7	63.4	2,276
Labor force (millions)	34.1	36.5	1,209
Unemployment rate (% of labor force)	2.4	1.3	5.7
GNI per capita, World Bank Atlas method ($)	2,010	3,050	2,038
GDP growth, 1995-2000 and 2000-06 (average annual %)	-0.7	5.4	7.6
Agriculture value added (% of GDP)	9.0	10.7	11.9
Industry value added (% of GDP)	42.0	44.6	43.5
Manufacturing value added (% of GDP)	33.6	35.0	26.7
Services value added (% of GDP)	49.0	44.7	44.6
Inflation (annual % change in consumer price index)	1.6	4.6	
Exchange rate (local currency units per $)	40.1	37.9	
Exports of goods and services (% of GDP)	66.8	73.7	40.4
Imports of goods and services (% of GDP)	58.1	69.8	36.4
Business environment			
Ease of doing business (ranking 1-178; 1=best)	..	15	
Time to start a business (days)	..	33	53
Procedures to start a business (number)	..	8	10
Firing cost (weeks of wages)	..	54.0	50.2
Closing a business (years to resolve insolvency)	..	2.7	3.3
Total tax rate (% of profit)	..	37.7	45.8
Highest marginal tax rate, corporate (%)	30	30	
Business entry rate (new registrations as % of total)	..	..	7.6
Enterprise surveys			
Time dealing with gov't officials (% of management time)	..	1.3	
Firms expected to give gifts in meetings w/tax officials (%)	..	..	
Firms using banks to finance investments (% of firms)	..	74.7	
Delay in obtaining an electrical connection (days)	..	24.2	
ISO certification ownership (% of firms)	..	44.6	
Private sector investment			
Invest. in infrastructure w/private participation ($ millions)	1,377	1,149	38,154
Private foreign direct investment, net (% of GDP)	2.7	4.4	3.0
Gross fixed capital formation (% of GDP)	22.0	28.6	33.5
Gross fixed private capital formation (% of GDP)	13.8	21.4	10.9
Finance and banking			
Government cash surplus or deficit (% of GDP)	..	1.9	-0.9
Government debt (% of GDP)	..	26.2	..
Deposit money banks' assets (% of GDP)	131.6	99.2	87.8
Total financial system deposits (% of GDP)	103.3	94.1	43.1
Bank capital to asset ratio (%)	7.5	9.2	10.7
Bank nonperforming loans to total gross loans ratio (%)	17.7	7.5	4.0
Domestic credit to the private sector (% of GDP)	108.3	88.0	81.3
Real interest rate (%)	6.4	2.2	
Interest rate spread (percentage points)	4.5	2.9	7.2
Infrastructure			
Paved roads (% of total roads)	98.5	..	65.8
Electric power consumption (kWh per capita)	1,503	1,988	1,502
Power outages in a typical month (number)	..	..	
Fixed line and mobile subscribers (per 100 people)	14	75	60
Internet users (per 100 people)	3.8	13.3	11.4
Cost of telephone call to U.S. ($ per 3 minutes)	2.19	0.67	2.08

Timor-Leste

Low income

	Country data		Low-income group
	2000	2006	2006
Economic and social context			
Population (millions)	0.78	1.0	2,420
Labor force (millions)	0.26	0.40	995
Unemployment rate (% of labor force)	..	..	..
GNI per capita, *World Bank Atlas* method ($)	420	840	649
GDP growth, 1995–2000 and 2000–06 (average annual %)	..	-0.7	6.5
Agriculture value added (% of GDP)	25.8	32.2	20.4
Industry value added (% of GDP)	18.5	12.8	27.7
Manufacturing value added (% of GDP)	2.8	2.6	15.8
Services value added (% of GDP)	55.7	55.0	51.9
Inflation (annual % change in consumer price index)	..	..	
Exchange rate (local currency units per $)	180.1	..	
Exports of goods and services (% of GDP)	..	..	26.7
Imports of goods and services (% of GDP)	..	..	30.1
Business environment			
Ease of doing business (ranking 1-178; 1=best)	..	168	
Time to start a business (days)	..	82	54
Procedures to start a business (number)	..	9	10
Firing cost (weeks of wages)	..	17.0	62.6
Closing a business (years to resolve insolvency)	..	..	3.8
Total tax rate (% of profit)	..	28.3	67.4
Highest marginal tax rate, corporate (%)	..	..	
Business entry rate (new registrations as % of total)	..	..	6.4
Enterprise surveys			
Time dealing with gov't officials (% of management time)	..	..	
Firms expected to give gifts in meetings w/tax officials (%)	..	..	
Firms using banks to finance investments (% of firms)	..	..	
Delay in obtaining an electrical connection (days)	..	..	
ISO certification ownership (% of firms)	..	..	
Private sector investment			
Invest. in infrastructure w/private participation ($ millions)	..	..	29,785
Private foreign direct investment, net (% of GDP)	..	..	2.6
Gross fixed capital formation (% of GDP)	21.8	17.1	26.7
Gross fixed private capital formation (% of GDP)	7.7	2.1	19.6
Finance and banking			
Government cash surplus or deficit (% of GDP)	..	..	-2.6
Government debt (% of GDP)	..	..	
Deposit money banks' assets (% of GDP)	..	..	50.5
Total financial system deposits (% of GDP)	..	..	44.6
Bank capital to asset ratio (%)	..	..	
Bank nonperforming loans to total gross loans ratio (%)	..	..	..
Domestic credit to the private sector (% of GDP)	..	..	38.3
Real interest rate (%)	..	..	
Interest rate spread (percentage points)	..	..	11.3
Infrastructure			
Paved roads (% of total roads)	..	..	..
Electric power consumption (kWh per capita)	..	..	391
Power outages in a typical month (number)	..	..	
Fixed line and mobile subscribers (per 100 people)	..	..	17
Internet users (per 100 people)	..	..	4.2
Cost of telephone call to U.S. ($ per 3 minutes)	..	..	1.99

Togo

	Country data		Low-income group
	2000	2006	2006
Economic and social context			
Population (millions)	5.4	6.4	2,420
Labor force (millions)	2.1	2.5	995
Unemployment rate (% of labor force)	..	..	..
GNI per capita, *World Bank Atlas* method ($)	270	350	649
GDP growth, 1995–2000 and 2000–06 (average annual %)	4.2	2.6	6.5
Agriculture value added (% of GDP)	34.2	43.6	20.4
Industry value added (% of GDP)	17.8	24.0	27.7
Manufacturing value added (% of GDP)	8.4	10.1	15.8
Services value added (% of GDP)	47.9	32.4	51.9
Inflation (annual % change in consumer price index)	1.9	2.2	
Exchange rate (local currency units per $)	712.0	522.9	
Exports of goods and services (% of GDP)	30.7	35.2	26.7
Imports of goods and services (% of GDP)	50.7	48.6	30.1
Business environment			
Ease of doing business (ranking 1-178; 1=best)	..	156	
Time to start a business (days)	..	53	54
Procedures to start a business (number)	..	13	10
Firing cost (weeks of wages)	..	36.0	62.6
Closing a business (years to resolve insolvency)	..	3.0	3.8
Total tax rate (% of profit)	..	48.2	67.4
Highest marginal tax rate, corporate (%)	..	..	
Business entry rate (new registrations as % of total)	..	..	6.4
Enterprise surveys			
Time dealing with gov't officials (% of management time)	..	..	
Firms expected to give gifts in meetings w/tax officials (%)	..	..	
Firms using banks to finance investments (% of firms)	..	..	
Delay in obtaining an electrical connection (days)	..	..	
ISO certification ownership (% of firms)	..	..	
Private sector investment			
Invest. in infrastructure w/private participation ($ millions)	68	590	29,785
Private foreign direct investment, net (% of GDP)	3.2	2.6	2.6
Gross fixed capital formation (% of GDP)	17.8	22.2	26.7
Gross fixed private capital formation (% of GDP)	14.8	18.1	19.6
Finance and banking			
Government cash surplus or deficit (% of GDP)	..	-0.1	-2.6
Government debt (% of GDP)	..	..	
Deposit money banks' assets (% of GDP)	17.0	19.8	50.5
Total financial system deposits (% of GDP)	14.8	23.4	44.6
Bank capital to asset ratio (%)	..	..	..
Bank nonperforming loans to total gross loans ratio (%)	..	..	
Domestic credit to the private sector (% of GDP)	15.6	16.9	38.3
Real interest rate (%)	..	..	
Interest rate spread (percentage points)	..	..	11.3
Infrastructure			
Paved roads (% of total roads)	31.6	..	..
Electric power consumption (kWh per capita)	86	94	391
Power outages in a typical month (number)	..	..	
Fixed line and mobile subscribers (per 100 people)	2	12	17
Internet users (per 100 people)	1.9	5.0	4.2
Cost of telephone call to U.S. ($ per 3 minutes)	7.90	3.98	1.99

Tonga

Lower middle income

	Country data		Lower middle-income group
	2000	2006	2006
Economic and social context			
Population (millions)	0.10	0.10	2,276
Labor force (millions)	0.04	0.04	1,209
Unemployment rate (% of labor force)	..	..	5.7
GNI per capita, *World Bank Atlas* method ($)	1,600	2,250	2,038
GDP growth, 1995–2000 and 2000–06 (average annual %)	1.4	2.4	7.6
Agriculture value added (% of GDP)	29.7	28.5	11.9
Industry value added (% of GDP)	17.2	15.3	43.5
Manufacturing value added (% of GDP)	5.4	4.8	26.7
Services value added (% of GDP)	53.1	56.2	44.6
Inflation (annual % change in consumer price index)	6.3	6.4	
Exchange rate (local currency units per $)	1.8	2.0	
Exports of goods and services (% of GDP)	8.2	10.4	40.4
Imports of goods and services (% of GDP)	37.1	43.9	36.4
Business environment			
Ease of doing business (ranking 1-178; 1=best)	..	47	
Time to start a business (days)	..	32	53
Procedures to start a business (number)	..	4	10
Firing cost (weeks of wages)	..	..	50.2
Closing a business (years to resolve insolvency)	..	2.7	3.3
Total tax rate (% of profit)	..	25.0	45.8
Highest marginal tax rate, corporate (%)	..	..	
Business entry rate (new registrations as % of total)	..	..	7.6
Enterprise surveys			
Time dealing with gov't officials (% of management time)	..	..	
Firms expected to give gifts in meetings w/tax officials (%)	..	..	
Firms using banks to finance investments (% of firms)	..	..	
Delay in obtaining an electrical connection (days)	..	..	
ISO certification ownership (% of firms)	..	..	
Private sector investment			
Invest. in infrastructure w/private participation ($ millions)	7	10	38,154
Private foreign direct investment, net (% of GDP)	3.2	–0.7	3.0
Gross fixed capital formation (% of GDP)	18.5	16.7	33.5
Gross fixed private capital formation (% of GDP)	..	..	10.9
Finance and banking			
Government cash surplus or deficit (% of GDP)	..	..	–0.9
Government debt (% of GDP)	..	..	..
Deposit money banks' assets (% of GDP)	55.1	58.9	87.8
Total financial system deposits (% of GDP)	40.3	45.9	43.1
Bank capital to asset ratio (%)	..	..	10.7
Bank nonperforming loans to total gross loans ratio (%)	..	..	4.0
Domestic credit to the private sector (% of GDP)	52.5	62.5	81.3
Real interest rate (%)	11.1	4.7	
Interest rate spread (percentage points)	6.0	5.5	7.2
Infrastructure			
Paved roads (% of total roads)	27.0	..	65.8
Electric power consumption (kWh per capita)	..	..	1,502
Power outages in a typical month (number)	..	..	
Fixed line and mobile subscribers (per 100 people)	10	44	60
Internet users (per 100 people)	2.4	3.1	11.4
Cost of telephone call to U.S. ($ per 3 minutes)	4.09	..	2.08

Trinidad and Tobago

High income

	Country data		High-income group
	2000	2006	2006
Economic and social context			
Population (millions)	1.3	1.3	1,031
Labor force (millions)	0.59	0.64	504
Unemployment rate (% of labor force)	12.1	8.0	6.2
GNI per capita, *World Bank Atlas* method ($)	5,170	12,500	36,608
GDP growth, 1995–2000 and 2000–06 (average annual %)	5.0	9.5	2.3
Agriculture value added (% of GDP)	1.4	0.6	1.5
Industry value added (% of GDP)	49.5	61.7	26.2
Manufacturing value added (% of GDP)	7.3	5.8	16.8
Services value added (% of GDP)	49.1	37.7	72.3
Inflation (annual % change in consumer price index)	3.6	8.3	
Exchange rate (local currency units per $)	6.3	6.3	
Exports of goods and services (% of GDP)	59.1	64.5	25.6
Imports of goods and services (% of GDP)	45.5	43.5	26.3
Business environment			
Ease of doing business (ranking 1-178; 1=best)	..	67	
Time to start a business (days)	..	43	22
Procedures to start a business (number)	..	9	7
Firing cost (weeks of wages)	..	67.0	34.9
Closing a business (years to resolve insolvency)	..	..	2.0
Total tax rate (% of profit)	..	33.1	41.5
Highest marginal tax rate, corporate (%)	35	25	
Business entry rate (new registrations as % of total)	..	..	10.1
Enterprise surveys			
Time dealing with gov't officials (% of management time)	..	..	
Firms expected to give gifts in meetings w/tax officials (%)	..	..	
Firms using banks to finance investments (% of firms)	..	..	
Delay in obtaining an electrical connection (days)	..	..	
ISO certification ownership (% of firms)	..	..	
Private sector investment			
Invest. in infrastructure w/private participation ($ millions)	120	229	849
Private foreign direct investment, net (% of GDP)	8.3	6.2	2.7
Gross fixed capital formation (% of GDP)	20.0	15.5	20.4
Gross fixed private capital formation (% of GDP)	14.3	19.4	..
Finance and banking			
Government cash surplus or deficit (% of GDP)	2.0	6.1	-1.3
Government debt (% of GDP)	..	..	47.6
Deposit money banks' assets (% of GDP)	35.4	32.7	99.7
Total financial system deposits (% of GDP)	48.1	39.1	
Bank capital to asset ratio (%)	..	..	6.2
Bank nonperforming loans to total gross loans ratio (%)	..	..	1.1
Domestic credit to the private sector (% of GDP)	41.0	34.3	162.0
Real interest rate (%)	3.2	3.1	
Interest rate spread (percentage points)	8.3	6.1	4.4
Infrastructure			
Paved roads (% of total roads)	51.1	..	90.9
Electric power consumption (kWh per capita)	3,891	5,038	9,760
Power outages in a typical month (number)	..	..	
Fixed line and mobile subscribers (per 100 people)	37	149	143
Internet users (per 100 people)	7.7	12.3	59.3
Cost of telephone call to U.S. ($ per 3 minutes)	2.47	2.19	0.77

Tunisia

Middle East & North Africa **Lower middle income**

	Country data		Lower middle-income group
	2000	2006	2006
Economic and social context			
Population (millions)	9.6	10.1	2,276
Labor force (millions)	3.3	3.9	1,209
Unemployment rate (% of labor force)	15.7	14.2	5.7
GNI per capita, World Bank Atlas method ($)	2,090	2,970	2,038
GDP growth, 1995–2000 and 2000–06 (average annual %)	5.5	4.6	7.6
Agriculture value added (% of GDP)	12.3	11.3	11.9
Industry value added (% of GDP)	28.6	28.4	43.5
Manufacturing value added (% of GDP)	18.2	17.4	26.7
Services value added (% of GDP)	59.1	60.3	44.6
Inflation (annual % change in consumer price index)	2.9	4.5	
Exchange rate (local currency units per $)	1.4	1.3	
Exports of goods and services (% of GDP)	44.5	54.4	40.4
Imports of goods and services (% of GDP)	48.2	54.3	36.4
Business environment			
Ease of doing business (ranking 1-178; 1=best)	..	88	
Time to start a business (days)	..	11	53
Procedures to start a business (number)	..	10	10
Firing cost (weeks of wages)	..	17.0	50.2
Closing a business (years to resolve insolvency)	..	1.3	3.3
Total tax rate (% of profit)	..	61.0	45.8
Highest marginal tax rate, corporate (%)	..	..	
Business entry rate (new registrations as % of total)	11.4	10.2	7.6
Enterprise surveys			
Time dealing with gov't officials (% of management time)	..	..	
Firms expected to give gifts in meetings w/tax officials (%)	..	..	
Firms using banks to finance investments (% of firms)	..	..	
Delay in obtaining an electrical connection (days)	..	..	
ISO certification ownership (% of firms)	..	..	
Private sector investment			
Invest. in infrastructure w/private participation ($ millions)	261	2,343	38,154
Private foreign direct investment, net (% of GDP)	3.9	10.8	3.0
Gross fixed capital formation (% of GDP)	26.0	23.2	33.5
Gross fixed private capital formation (% of GDP)	13.7	..	10.9
Finance and banking			
Government cash surplus or deficit (% of GDP)	-2.7	-2.8	-0.9
Government debt (% of GDP)	62.6	55.1	..
Deposit money banks' assets (% of GDP)	57.8	65.1	87.8
Total financial system deposits (% of GDP)	45.3	49.0	43.1
Bank capital to asset ratio (%)	7.5	7.7	10.7
Bank nonperforming loans to total gross loans ratio (%)	21.6	19.2	4.0
Domestic credit to the private sector (% of GDP)	66.3	65.0	81.3
Real interest rate (%)	..	..	
Interest rate spread (percentage points)	..	..	7.2
Infrastructure			
Paved roads (% of total roads)	68.4	65.8	65.8
Electric power consumption (kWh per capita)	991	1,194	1,502
Power outages in a typical month (number)	..	..	
Fixed line and mobile subscribers (per 100 people)	11	85	60
Internet users (per 100 people)	2.7	12.8	11.4
Cost of telephone call to U.S. ($ per 3 minutes)	2.25	..	2.08

Turkey

Europe & Central Asia   **Upper middle income**

	Country data		Upper middle-income group
	2000	2006	2006
Economic and social context			
Population (millions)	67.4	73.0	811
Labor force (millions)	23.7	27.4	374
Unemployment rate (% of labor force)	6.5	10.3	9.8
GNI per capita, World Bank Atlas method ($)	2,990	5,400	5,913
GDP growth, 1995–2000 and 2000–06 (average annual %)	3.4	5.6	3.9
Agriculture value added (% of GDP)	14.7	9.7	5.7
Industry value added (% of GDP)	24.3	26.8	32.4
Manufacturing value added (% of GDP)	20.0	22.2	19.4
Services value added (% of GDP)	61.0	63.5	62.0
Inflation (annual % change in consumer price index)	54.9	10.5	
Exchange rate (local currency units per $)	0.6	1.4	
Exports of goods and services (% of GDP)	24.0	28.2	32.7
Imports of goods and services (% of GDP)	31.5	35.9	30.3
Business environment			
Ease of doing business (ranking 1-178; 1=best)	..	57	
Time to start a business (days)	..	6	41
Procedures to start a business (number)	..	6	9
Firing cost (weeks of wages)	..	95.0	39.7
Closing a business (years to resolve insolvency)	..	3.3	2.9
Total tax rate (% of profit)	..	45.1	44.5
Highest marginal tax rate, corporate (%)	30	30	
Business entry rate (new registrations as % of total)	9.6	14.7	9.1
Enterprise surveys			
Time dealing with gov't officials (% of management time)	..	10.8	
Firms expected to give gifts in meetings w/tax officials (%)	43.7	20.1	
Firms using banks to finance investments (% of firms)	6.0	7.5	
Delay in obtaining an electrical connection (days)	4.6	6.1	
ISO certification ownership (% of firms)	..	12.6	
Private sector investment			
Invest. in infrastructure w/private participation ($ millions)	8,215	2,438	45,869
Private foreign direct investment, net (% of GDP)	0.5	5.0	3.5
Gross fixed capital formation (% of GDP)	22.4	21.0	19.9
Gross fixed private capital formation (% of GDP)	16.4	16.7	..
Finance and banking			
Government cash surplus or deficit (% of GDP)	..	2.5	..
Government debt (% of GDP)	..	67.8	..
Deposit money banks' assets (% of GDP)	32.6	42.2	52.9
Total financial system deposits (% of GDP)	28.5	34.3	41.4
Bank capital to asset ratio (%)	6.1	11.3	9.8
Bank nonperforming loans to total gross loans ratio (%)	9.2	3.2	3.2
Domestic credit to the private sector (% of GDP)	24.6	34.1	41.4
Real interest rate (%)	..	..	
Interest rate spread (percentage points)	..	..	5.9
Infrastructure			
Paved roads (% of total roads)	34.0	..	..
Electric power consumption (kWh per capita)	1,550	1,898	3,131
Power outages in a typical month (number)	..	..	
Fixed line and mobile subscribers (per 100 people)	51	98	88
Internet users (per 100 people)	3.7	16.8	22.2
Cost of telephone call to U.S. ($ per 3 minutes)	3.30	2.40	1.06

Turkmenistan

Europe & Central Asia   **Lower middle income**

	Country data		Lower middle-income group
	2000	2006	2006
Economic and social context			
Population (millions)	4.5	4.9	2,276
Labor force (millions)	1.9	2.3	1,209
Unemployment rate (% of labor force)	..	..	5.7
GNI per capita, *World Bank Atlas* method ($)	650	..	2,038
GDP growth, 1995–2000 and 2000–06 (average annual %)	4.0	..	7.6
Agriculture value added (% of GDP)	24.4	19.6	11.9
Industry value added (% of GDP)	44.4	40.1	43.5
Manufacturing value added (% of GDP)	10.6	21.7	26.7
Services value added (% of GDP)	31.2	40.3	44.6
Inflation (annual % change in consumer price index)	..	..	
Exchange rate (local currency units per $)	5,200.0	..	
Exports of goods and services (% of GDP)	95.5	72.2	40.4
Imports of goods and services (% of GDP)	80.9	54.1	36.4
Business environment			
Ease of doing business (ranking 1-178; 1=best)	..	..	
Time to start a business (days)	..	..	53
Procedures to start a business (number)	..	..	10
Firing cost (weeks of wages)	..	..	50.2
Closing a business (years to resolve insolvency)	..	..	3.3
Total tax rate (% of profit)	..	..	45.8
Highest marginal tax rate, corporate (%)	..	..	
Business entry rate (new registrations as % of total)	..	..	7.6
Enterprise surveys			
Time dealing with gov't officials (% of management time)	..	..	
Firms expected to give gifts in meetings w/tax officials (%)	..	..	
Firms using banks to finance investments (% of firms)	..	..	
Delay in obtaining an electrical connection (days)	..	..	
ISO certification ownership (% of firms)	..	..	
Private sector investment			
Invest. in infrastructure w/private participation ($ millions)	20	16	38,154
Private foreign direct investment, net (% of GDP)	4.3	7.0	3.0
Gross fixed capital formation (% of GDP)	34.7	22.9	33.5
Gross fixed private capital formation (% of GDP)	..	..	10.9
Finance and banking			
Government cash surplus or deficit (% of GDP)	..	..	-0.9
Government debt (% of GDP)	..	..	..
Deposit money banks' assets (% of GDP)	..	..	87.8
Total financial system deposits (% of GDP)	..	..	43.1
Bank capital to asset ratio (%)	..	..	10.7
Bank nonperforming loans to total gross loans ratio (%)	..	..	4.0
Domestic credit to the private sector (% of GDP)	2.0	..	81.3
Real interest rate (%)	..	..	
Interest rate spread (percentage points)	..	..	7.2
Infrastructure			
Paved roads (% of total roads)	81.2	..	65.8
Electric power consumption (kWh per capita)	1,698	1,731	1,502
Power outages in a typical month (number)	..	..	
Fixed line and mobile subscribers (per 100 people)	8	10	60
Internet users (per 100 people)	0.1	1.3	11.4
Cost of telephone call to U.S. ($ per 3 minutes)	..	..	2.08

Uganda

Sub-Saharan Africa   **Low income**

	Country data		Low-income group
	2000	2006	2006
Economic and social context			
Population (millions)	24.7	29.9	2,420
Labor force (millions)	10.5	12.6	995
Unemployment rate (% of labor force)	..	3.2	..
GNI per capita, *World Bank Atlas* method ($)	260	300	649
GDP growth, 1995–2000 and 2000–06 (average annual %)	6.4	5.6	6.5
Agriculture value added (% of GDP)	37.3	32.3	20.4
Industry value added (% of GDP)	20.3	18.4	27.7
Manufacturing value added (% of GDP)	9.8	9.1	15.8
Services value added (% of GDP)	42.4	49.2	51.9
Inflation (annual % change in consumer price index)	2.8	6.8	
Exchange rate (local currency units per $)	1,644.5	1,831.5	
Exports of goods and services (% of GDP)	11.2	14.9	26.7
Imports of goods and services (% of GDP)	23.0	29.5	30.1
Business environment			
Ease of doing business (ranking 1-178; 1=best)	..	118	
Time to start a business (days)	..	28	54
Procedures to start a business (number)	..	18	10
Firing cost (weeks of wages)	..	13.0	62.6
Closing a business (years to resolve insolvency)	..	2.2	3.8
Total tax rate (% of profit)	..	32.3	67.4
Highest marginal tax rate, corporate (%)	30	30	
Business entry rate (new registrations as % of total)	..	*9.0*	*6.4*
Enterprise surveys			
Time dealing with gov't officials (% of management time)	..	5.2	
Firms expected to give gifts in meetings w/tax officials (%)	..	14.5	
Firms using banks to finance investments (% of firms)	..	7.7	
Delay in obtaining an electrical connection (days)	..	33.0	
ISO certification ownership (% of firms)	..	15.5	
Private sector investment			
Invest. in infrastructure w/private participation ($ millions)	57	416	29,785
Private foreign direct investment, net (% of GDP)	2.7	4.2	2.6
Gross fixed capital formation (% of GDP)	19.6	23.2	26.7
Gross fixed private capital formation (% of GDP)	13.3	18.7	19.6
Finance and banking			
Government cash surplus or deficit (% of GDP)	–2.0	–2.0	–2.6
Government debt (% of GDP)	44.9	..	..
Deposit money banks' assets (% of GDP)	9.7	13.3	50.5
Total financial system deposits (% of GDP)	10.7	14.0	44.6
Bank capital to asset ratio (%)	9.8	9.7	..
Bank nonperforming loans to total gross loans ratio (%)	9.8	2.8	..
Domestic credit to the private sector (% of GDP)	6.5	7.9	38.3
Real interest rate (%)	18.4	10.7	
Interest rate spread (percentage points)	13.1	9.6	*11.3*
Infrastructure			
Paved roads (% of total roads)	..	23.0	..
Electric power consumption (kWh per capita)	..	..	391
Power outages in a typical month (number)	..	11.0	
Fixed line and mobile subscribers (per 100 people)	1	7	17
Internet users (per 100 people)	0.2	2.5	*4.2*
Cost of telephone call to U.S. ($ per 3 minutes)	*3.63*	*3.21*	*1.99*

Ukraine

Lower middle income

	Country data		Lower middle-income group
	2000	2006	2006

Economic and social context

Population (millions)	49.2	46.8	2,276
Labor force (millions)	23.0	22.5	1,209
Unemployment rate (% of labor force)	11.6	7.2	5.7
GNI per capita, *World Bank Atlas* method ($)	700	1,940	2,038
GDP growth, 1995–2000 and 2000–06 (average annual %)	–1.9	7.8	7.6
Agriculture value added (% of GDP)	17.1	8.7	11.9
Industry value added (% of GDP)	36.3	34.6	43.5
Manufacturing value added (% of GDP)	19.2	20.7	26.7
Services value added (% of GDP)	46.6	56.7	44.6
Inflation (annual % change in consumer price index)	28.2	9.1	
Exchange rate (local currency units per $)	5.4	5.0	
Exports of goods and services (% of GDP)	62.4	47.2	40.4
Imports of goods and services (% of GDP)	57.4	50.1	36.4

Business environment

Ease of doing business (ranking 1-178; 1=best)	..	139	
Time to start a business (days)	..	27	53
Procedures to start a business (number)	..	10	10
Firing cost (weeks of wages)	..	13.0	50.2
Closing a business (years to resolve insolvency)	..	2.9	3.3
Total tax rate (% of profit)	..	57.3	45.8
Highest marginal tax rate, corporate (%)	30	25	
Business entry rate (new registrations as % of total)	6.7	6.1	7.6
Enterprise surveys			
Time dealing with gov't officials (% of management time)	..	8.1	
Firms expected to give gifts in meetings w/tax officials (%)	54.6	44.0	
Firms using banks to finance investments (% of firms)	4.5	14.7	
Delay in obtaining an electrical connection (days)	36.8	30.4	
ISO certification ownership (% of firms)	..	10.8	

Private sector investment

Invest. in infrastructure w/private participation ($ millions)	206	865	38,154
Private foreign direct investment, net (% of GDP)	1.9	5.3	3.0
Gross fixed capital formation (% of GDP)	19.7	24.0	33.5
Gross fixed private capital formation (% of GDP)	17.3	21.7	10.9

Finance and banking

Government cash surplus or deficit (% of GDP)	–0.6	–1.0	–0.9
Government debt (% of GDP)	45.3	..	..
Deposit money banks' assets (% of GDP)	10.7	37.2	87.8
Total financial system deposits (% of GDP)	9.3	29.1	43.1
Bank capital to asset ratio (%)	16.2	12.1	10.7
Bank nonperforming loans to total gross loans ratio (%)	29.6	17.8	4.0
Domestic credit to the private sector (% of GDP)	11.2	44.9	81.3
Real interest rate (%)	15.0	1.3	
Interest rate spread (percentage points)	27.8	7.6	7.2

Infrastructure

Paved roads (% of total roads)	96.7	97.4	65.8
Electric power consumption (kWh per capita)	2,773	3,246	1,502
Power outages in a typical month (number)	..	..	
Fixed line and mobile subscribers (per 100 people)	23	131	60
Internet users (per 100 people)	0.7	11.9	11.4
Cost of telephone call to U.S. ($ per 3 minutes)	..	1.65	2.08

United Arab Emirates

	Country data		High-income group
	2000	2006	2006
Economic and social context			
Population (millions)	3.2	4.2	1,031
Labor force (millions)	1.9	2.7	504
Unemployment rate (% of labor force)	2.3	..	6.2
GNI per capita, *World Bank Atlas* method ($)	19,270	26,210	36,608
GDP growth, 1995–2000 and 2000–06 (average annual %)	5.1	8.2	2.3
Agriculture value added (% of GDP)	3.5	2.3	1.5
Industry value added (% of GDP)	55.7	55.7	26.2
Manufacturing value added (% of GDP)	13.5	14.1	16.8
Services value added (% of GDP)	40.8	42.0	72.3
Inflation (annual % change in consumer price index)	..	..	
Exchange rate (local currency units per $)	3.7	3.7	
Exports of goods and services (% of GDP)	73.3	94.3	25.6
Imports of goods and services (% of GDP)	55.3	76.3	26.3
Business environment			
Ease of doing business (ranking 1-178; 1=best)	..	68	
Time to start a business (days)	..	62	22
Procedures to start a business (number)	..	11	7
Firing cost (weeks of wages)	..	84.0	34.9
Closing a business (years to resolve insolvency)	..	5.1	2.0
Total tax rate (% of profit)	..	14.4	41.5
Highest marginal tax rate, corporate (%)	20	..	
Business entry rate (new registrations as % of total)	..	..	10.1
Enterprise surveys			
Time dealing with gov't officials (% of management time)	..	..	
Firms expected to give gifts in meetings w/tax officials (%)	..	..	
Firms using banks to finance investments (% of firms)	..	..	
Delay in obtaining an electrical connection (days)	..	..	
ISO certification ownership (% of firms)	..	..	
Private sector investment			
Invest. in infrastructure w/private participation ($ millions)	..	..	849
Private foreign direct investment, net (% of GDP)	..	..	2.7
Gross fixed capital formation (% of GDP)	22.1	22.8	20.4
Gross fixed private capital formation (% of GDP)	9.5	11.4	..
Finance and banking			
Government cash surplus or deficit (% of GDP)	0.1	..	-1.3
Government debt (% of GDP)	..	..	47.6
Deposit money banks' assets (% of GDP)	..	..	99.7
Total financial system deposits (% of GDP)	..	..	..
Bank capital to asset ratio (%)	12.9	12.6	6.2
Bank nonperforming loans to total gross loans ratio (%)	12.7	6.3	1.1
Domestic credit to the private sector (% of GDP)	46.2	60.9	162.0
Real interest rate (%)	-9.9	..	
Interest rate spread (percentage points)	3.5	..	4.4
Infrastructure			
Paved roads (% of total roads)	100.0	..	90.9
Electric power consumption (kWh per capita)	11,886	13,708	9,760
Power outages in a typical month (number)	..	..	
Fixed line and mobile subscribers (per 100 people)	75	161	143
Internet users (per 100 people)	23.6	40.2	59.3
Cost of telephone call to U.S. ($ per 3 minutes)	3.51	1.73	0.77

United Kingdom

	Country data		High-income group
	2000	2006	2006
Economic and social context			
Population (millions)	59.7	60.6	1,031
Labor force (millions)	30.2	30.8	504
Unemployment rate (% of labor force)	5.5	4.6	6.2
GNI per capita, *World Bank Atlas* method ($)	24,970	40,560	36,608
GDP growth, 1995–2000 and 2000–06 (average annual %)	3.2	2.5	2.3
Agriculture value added (% of GDP)	1.0	0.9	1.5
Industry value added (% of GDP)	28.2	24.1	26.2
Manufacturing value added (% of GDP)	17.9	13.6	16.8
Services value added (% of GDP)	70.7	75.0	72.3
Inflation (annual % change in consumer price index)	2.9	3.2	
Exchange rate (local currency units per $)	0.7	0.5	
Exports of goods and services (% of GDP)	28.1	28.7	25.6
Imports of goods and services (% of GDP)	30.1	32.9	26.3
Business environment			
Ease of doing business (ranking 1-178; 1=best)	..	6	
Time to start a business (days)	..	13	22
Procedures to start a business (number)	..	6	7
Firing cost (weeks of wages)	..	22.0	34.9
Closing a business (years to resolve insolvency)	..	1.0	2.0
Total tax rate (% of profit)	..	35.7	41.5
Highest marginal tax rate, corporate (%)	30	30	
Business entry rate (new registrations as % of total)	13.6	15.4	10.1
Enterprise surveys			
Time dealing with gov't officials (% of management time)	..	..	
Firms expected to give gifts in meetings w/tax officials (%)	..	..	
Firms using banks to finance investments (% of firms)	..	..	
Delay in obtaining an electrical connection (days)	..	..	
ISO certification ownership (% of firms)	..	..	
Private sector investment			
Invest. in infrastructure w/private participation ($ millions)	..	..	849
Private foreign direct investment, net (% of GDP)	8.5	5.9	2.7
Gross fixed capital formation (% of GDP)	16.9	17.3	20.4
Gross fixed private capital formation (% of GDP)	..	..	..
Finance and banking			
Government cash surplus or deficit (% of GDP)	1.7	-2.8	-1.3
Government debt (% of GDP)	48.8	49.9	47.6
Deposit money banks' assets (% of GDP)	122.7	162.6	99.7
Total financial system deposits (% of GDP)	..	..	..
Bank capital to asset ratio (%)	6.5	8.9	6.2
Bank nonperforming loans to total gross loans ratio (%)	2.5	0.9	1.1
Domestic credit to the private sector (% of GDP)	132.5	175.8	162.0
Real interest rate (%)	4.6	2.2	
Interest rate spread (percentage points)	2.7	..	4.4
Infrastructure			
Paved roads (% of total roads)	100.0	100.0	90.9
Electric power consumption (kWh per capita)	6,027	6,253	9,760
Power outages in a typical month (number)	..	..	
Fixed line and mobile subscribers (per 100 people)	132	171	143
Internet users (per 100 people)	26.4	55.4	59.3
Cost of telephone call to U.S. ($ per 3 minutes)	1.07	0.77	0.77

United States

	Country data		High-income group
	2000	2006	2006
Economic and social context			
Population (millions)	282.2	299.4	1,031
Labor force (millions)	147.8	157.0	504
Unemployment rate (% of labor force)	4.0	5.1	6.2
GNI per capita, *World Bank Atlas* method ($)	34,400	44,710	36,608
GDP growth, 1995-2000 and 2000-06 (average annual %)	4.2	2.6	2.3
Agriculture value added (% of GDP)	1.2	1.2	1.5
Industry value added (% of GDP)	24.2	22.8	26.2
Manufacturing value added (% of GDP)	17.0	14.4	16.8
Services value added (% of GDP)	74.6	76.0	72.3
Inflation (annual % change in consumer price index)	3.4	3.2	
Exchange rate (local currency units per $)	1.0	1.0	
Exports of goods and services (% of GDP)	11.2	10.5	25.6
Imports of goods and services (% of GDP)	15.1	16.3	26.3
Business environment			
Ease of doing business (ranking 1-178; 1=best)	..	3	
Time to start a business (days)	..	6	22
Procedures to start a business (number)	..	6	7
Firing cost (weeks of wages)	..	..	34.9
Closing a business (years to resolve insolvency)	..	1.5	2.0
Total tax rate (% of profit)	..	46.2	41.5
Highest marginal tax rate, corporate (%)	35	35	
Business entry rate (new registrations as % of total)	..	13.1	10.1
Enterprise surveys			
Time dealing with gov't officials (% of management time)	..	..	
Firms expected to give gifts in meetings w/tax officials (%)	..	..	
Firms using banks to finance investments (% of firms)	..	..	
Delay in obtaining an electrical connection (days)	..	..	
ISO certification ownership (% of firms)	..	..	
Private sector investment			
Invest. in infrastructure w/private participation ($ millions)	..	..	849
Private foreign direct investment, net (% of GDP)	3.3	1.4	2.7
Gross fixed capital formation (% of GDP)	19.9	19.1	20.4
Gross fixed private capital formation (% of GDP)	..	..	..
Finance and banking			
Government cash surplus or deficit (% of GDP)	0.5	-2.0	-1.3
Government debt (% of GDP)	33.0	46.9	47.6
Deposit money banks' assets (% of GDP)	55.9	62.9	99.7
Total financial system deposits (% of GDP)	63.7	69.6	..
Bank capital to asset ratio (%)	8.5	10.5	6.2
Bank nonperforming loans to total gross loans ratio (%)	1.1	0.8	1.1
Domestic credit to the private sector (% of GDP)	170.7	201.1	162.0
Real interest rate (%)	6.9	4.6	
Interest rate spread (percentage points)	..	..	4.4
Infrastructure			
Paved roads (% of total roads)	58.8	65.3	90.9
Electric power consumption (kWh per capita)	13,668	13,648	9,760
Power outages in a typical month (number)	..	..	
Fixed line and mobile subscribers (per 100 people)	107	135	143
Internet users (per 100 people)	43.9	69.5	59.3
Cost of telephone call to U.S. ($ per 3 minutes)	..	..	0.77

Uruguay

Latin America & Caribbean   **Upper middle income**

	Country data		Upper middle-income group
	2000	2006	2006
Economic and social context			
Population (millions)	3.3	3.3	811
Labor force (millions)	1.6	1.7	374
Unemployment rate (% of labor force)	13.6	12.2	9.8
GNI per capita, *World Bank Atlas* method ($)	6,220	5,310	5,913
GDP growth, 1995–2000 and 2000–06 (average annual %)	2.2	2.3	3.9
Agriculture value added (% of GDP)	6.2	9.2	5.7
Industry value added (% of GDP)	27.2	32.4	32.4
Manufacturing value added (% of GDP)	16.9	23.2	19.4
Services value added (% of GDP)	66.6	58.4	62.0
Inflation (annual % change in consumer price index)	4.8	6.4	
Exchange rate (local currency units per $)	12.1	24.1	
Exports of goods and services (% of GDP)	19.3	29.9	32.7
Imports of goods and services (% of GDP)	21.0	30.3	30.3
Business environment			
Ease of doing business (ranking 1-178; 1=best)	..	98	
Time to start a business (days)	..	44	41
Procedures to start a business (number)	..	11	9
Firing cost (weeks of wages)	..	31.0	39.7
Closing a business (years to resolve insolvency)	..	2.1	2.9
Total tax rate (% of profit)	..	40.7	44.5
Highest marginal tax rate, corporate (%)	30	30	
Business entry rate (new registrations as % of total)	..	..	9.1
Enterprise surveys			
Time dealing with gov't officials (% of management time)	..	7.0	
Firms expected to give gifts in meetings w/tax officials (%)	..	0.6	
Firms using banks to finance investments (% of firms)	..	6.9	
Delay in obtaining an electrical connection (days)	..	38.6	
ISO certification ownership (% of firms)	..	6.8	
Private sector investment			
Invest. in infrastructure w/private participation ($ millions)	681	30	45,869
Private foreign direct investment, net (% of GDP)	1.3	7.0	3.5
Gross fixed capital formation (% of GDP)	13.2	16.0	19.9
Gross fixed private capital formation (% of GDP)	9.9	13.1	..
Finance and banking			
Government cash surplus or deficit (% of GDP)	-3.4	-0.9	..
Government debt (% of GDP)	45.8	70.0	..
Deposit money banks' assets (% of GDP)	54.7	31.8	52.9
Total financial system deposits (% of GDP)	44.0	42.8	41.4
Bank capital to asset ratio (%)	7.2	9.8	9.8
Bank nonperforming loans to total gross loans ratio (%)	12.4	1.9	3.2
Domestic credit to the private sector (% of GDP)	51.2	26.2	41.4
Real interest rate (%)	40.5	2.3	
Interest rate spread (percentage points)	27.8	7.4	5.9
Infrastructure			
Paved roads (% of total roads)	90.0	10.0	..
Electric power consumption (kWh per capita)	1,990	2,007	3,131
Power outages in a typical month (number)	..	0.5	
Fixed line and mobile subscribers (per 100 people)	41	100	88
Internet users (per 100 people)	10.6	22.8	22.2
Cost of telephone call to U.S. ($ per 3 minutes)	4.88	0.52	1.06

Uzbekistan

Europe & Central Asia   **Low income**

	Country data		Low-income group
	2000	2006	2006
Economic and social context			
Population (millions)	24.7	26.5	2,420
Labor force (millions)	9.8	11.6	995
Unemployment rate (% of labor force)	..	..	..
GNI per capita, *World Bank Atlas* method ($)	630	610	649
GDP growth, 1995–2000 and 2000–06 (average annual %)	4.1	5.7	6.5
Agriculture value added (% of GDP)	34.4	26.1	20.4
Industry value added (% of GDP)	23.1	27.4	27.7
Manufacturing value added (% of GDP)	9.4	10.8	15.8
Services value added (% of GDP)	42.5	46.5	51.9
Inflation (annual % change in consumer price index)	..	..	
Exchange rate (local currency units per $)	236.6	..	
Exports of goods and services (% of GDP)	24.6	37.5	26.7
Imports of goods and services (% of GDP)	21.5	25.9	30.1
Business environment			
Ease of doing business (ranking 1-178; 1=best)	..	138	
Time to start a business (days)	..	15	54
Procedures to start a business (number)	..	7	10
Firing cost (weeks of wages)	..	22.0	62.6
Closing a business (years to resolve insolvency)	..	4.0	3.8
Total tax rate (% of profit)	..	96.3	67.4
Highest marginal tax rate, corporate (%)	26	12	
Business entry rate (new registrations as % of total)	..	..	6.4
Enterprise surveys			
Time dealing with gov't officials (% of management time)	..	2.5	
Firms expected to give gifts in meetings w/tax officials (%)	50.0	60.4	
Firms using banks to finance investments (% of firms)	1.2	3.3	
Delay in obtaining an electrical connection (days)	21.0	8.6	
ISO certification ownership (% of firms)	..	8.7	
Private sector investment			
Invest. in infrastructure w/private participation ($ millions)	26	100	29,785
Private foreign direct investment, net (% of GDP)	0.5	1.0	2.6
Gross fixed capital formation (% of GDP)	24.0	21.5	26.7
Gross fixed private capital formation (% of GDP)	15.5	18.0	19.6
Finance and banking			
Government cash surplus or deficit (% of GDP)	..	..	-2.6
Government debt (% of GDP)	..	..	
Deposit money banks' assets (% of GDP)	..	..	50.5
Total financial system deposits (% of GDP)	..	..	44.6
Bank capital to asset ratio (%)	..	..	
Bank nonperforming loans to total gross loans ratio (%)	..	..	..
Domestic credit to the private sector (% of GDP)	..	..	38.3
Real interest rate (%)	..	..	
Interest rate spread (percentage points)	..	..	11.3
Infrastructure			
Paved roads (% of total roads)	87.3	..	..
Electric power consumption (kWh per capita)	1,780	1,659	391
Power outages in a typical month (number)	..	..	
Fixed line and mobile subscribers (per 100 people)	7	10	17
Internet users (per 100 people)	0.5	6.4	4.2
Cost of telephone call to U.S. ($ per 3 minutes)	13.95	..	1.99

Vanuatu

Lower middle income

	Country data		Lower middle-income group
	2000	2006	2006
Economic and social context			
Population (millions)	0.19	0.22	2,276
Labor force (millions)	0.09	0.11	1,209
Unemployment rate (% of labor force)	..		5.7
GNI per capita, *World Bank Atlas* method ($)	1,250	1,690	2,038
GDP growth, 1995–2000 and 2000–06 (average annual %)	1.4	2.0	7.6
Agriculture value added (% of GDP)	15.6	15.6	11.9
Industry value added (% of GDP)	9.3	9.2	43.5
Manufacturing value added (% of GDP)	4.4	3.4	26.7
Services value added (% of GDP)	75.1	81.7	44.6
Inflation (annual % change in consumer price index)	2.5	1.9	
Exchange rate (local currency units per $)	137.6	110.6	
Exports of goods and services (% of GDP)	43.6	39.8	40.4
Imports of goods and services (% of GDP)	56.5	60.5	36.4
Business environment			
Ease of doing business (ranking 1-178; 1=best)	..	62	
Time to start a business (days)	..	39	53
Procedures to start a business (number)	..	8	10
Firing cost (weeks of wages)	..	56.0	50.2
Closing a business (years to resolve insolvency)	..	2.6	3.3
Total tax rate (% of profit)	..	8.4	45.8
Highest marginal tax rate, corporate (%)	..	..	
Business entry rate (new registrations as % of total)	..	..	7.6
Enterprise surveys			
Time dealing with gov't officials (% of management time)	..	..	
Firms expected to give gifts in meetings w/tax officials (%)	..	..	
Firms using banks to finance investments (% of firms)	..	..	
Delay in obtaining an electrical connection (days)	..	..	
ISO certification ownership (% of firms)	..	..	
Private sector investment			
Invest. in infrastructure w/private participation ($ millions)	6	..	38,154
Private foreign direct investment, net (% of GDP)	8.3	11.2	3.0
Gross fixed capital formation (% of GDP)	20.2	20.5	33.5
Gross fixed private capital formation (% of GDP)	..	..	10.9
Finance and banking			
Government cash surplus or deficit (% of GDP)	–0.8	..	–0.9
Government debt (% of GDP)	29.2	..	..
Deposit money banks' assets (% of GDP)	..	..	87.8
Total financial system deposits (% of GDP)	..	..	43.1
Bank capital to asset ratio (%)	..	..	10.7
Bank nonperforming loans to total gross loans ratio (%)	..	..	4.0
Domestic credit to the private sector (% of GDP)	34.8	47.5	81.3
Real interest rate (%)	8.6	8.2	
Interest rate spread (percentage points)	8.6	6.3	7.2
Infrastructure			
Paved roads (% of total roads)	23.9	..	65.8
Electric power consumption (kWh per capita)	..	..	1,502
Power outages in a typical month (number)	..	..	
Fixed line and mobile subscribers (per 100 people)	4	9	60
Internet users (per 100 people)	2.1	3.5	11.4
Cost of telephone call to U.S. ($ per 3 minutes)	7.45	..	2.08

Venezuela, RB

Latin America & Caribbean   **Upper middle income**

	Country data		Upper middle-income group
	2000	**2006**	**2006**
Economic and social context			
Population (millions)	24.3	27.0	811
Labor force (millions)	10.5	13.3	374
Unemployment rate (% of labor force)	13.9	15.0	9.8
GNI per capita, *World Bank Atlas* method ($)	4,100	6,070	5,913
GDP growth, 1995–2000 and 2000–06 (average annual %)	0.6	3.4	3.9
Agriculture value added (% of GDP)	4.2	4.0	5.7
Industry value added (% of GDP)	49.7	55.5	32.4
Manufacturing value added (% of GDP)	19.8	17.9	19.4
Services value added (% of GDP)	46.1	40.5	62.0
Inflation (annual % change in consumer price index)	16.2	13.7	
Exchange rate (local currency units per $)	680.0	2,147.0	
Exports of goods and services (% of GDP)	29.7	36.6	32.7
Imports of goods and services (% of GDP)	18.1	21.0	30.3
Business environment			
Ease of doing business (ranking 1-178; 1=best)	..	172	
Time to start a business (days)	..	141	41
Procedures to start a business (number)	..	16	9
Firing cost (weeks of wages)	..	47.3	39.7
Closing a business (years to resolve insolvency)	..	4.0	2.9
Total tax rate (% of profit)	..	53.3	44.5
Highest marginal tax rate, corporate (%)	34	34	
Business entry rate (new registrations as % of total)	..	..	9.1
Enterprise surveys			
Time dealing with gov't officials (% of management time)	..	33.6	
Firms expected to give gifts in meetings w/tax officials (%)	..	2.6	
Firms using banks to finance investments (% of firms)	..	35.7	
Delay in obtaining an electrical connection (days)	..	25.4	
ISO certification ownership (% of firms)	..	12.5	
Private sector investment			
Invest. in infrastructure w/private participation ($ millions)	774	1,091	45,869
Private foreign direct investment, net (% of GDP)	4.0	–0.3	3.5
Gross fixed capital formation (% of GDP)	21.0	22.5	19.9
Gross fixed private capital formation (% of GDP)	..	..	..
Finance and banking			
Government cash surplus or deficit (% of GDP)	–1.2	2.2	..
Government debt (% of GDP)	..	..	..
Deposit money banks' assets (% of GDP)	11.9	11.9	52.9
Total financial system deposits (% of GDP)	15.0	15.2	41.4
Bank capital to asset ratio (%)	13.0	9.8	9.8
Bank nonperforming loans to total gross loans ratio (%)	6.6	1.1	3.2
Domestic credit to the private sector (% of GDP)	12.5	17.1	41.4
Real interest rate (%)	–3.3	–1.2	
Interest rate spread (percentage points)	8.9	5.2	5.9
Infrastructure			
Paved roads (% of total roads)	33.6	..	..
Electric power consumption (kWh per capita)	2,654	2,848	3,131
Power outages in a typical month (number)	..	3.6	
Fixed line and mobile subscribers (per 100 people)	33	85	88
Internet users (per 100 people)	3.4	15.3	22.2
Cost of telephone call to U.S. ($ per 3 minutes)	0.78	0.84	1.06

Vietnam

East Asia & Pacific **Low income**

	Country data		Low-income group
	2000	**2006**	**2006**
Economic and social context			
Population (millions)	77.6	84.1	2,420
Labor force (millions)	39.2	44.8	995
Unemployment rate (% of labor force)	2.3	2.1	..
GNI per capita, *World Bank Atlas* method ($)	390	700	649
GDP growth, 1995–2000 and 2000–06 (average annual %)	6.7	7.6	6.5
Agriculture value added (% of GDP)	24.5	20.4	20.4
Industry value added (% of GDP)	36.7	41.6	27.7
Manufacturing value added (% of GDP)	18.6	21.3	15.8
Services value added (% of GDP)	38.7	38.1	51.9
Inflation (annual % change in consumer price index)	-1.7	7.7	
Exchange rate (local currency units per $)	14,167.8	15,994.3	
Exports of goods and services (% of GDP)	55.0	73.5	26.7
Imports of goods and services (% of GDP)	57.5	76.8	30.1
Business environment			
Ease of doing business (ranking 1-178; 1=best)	..	91	
Time to start a business (days)	..	50	54
Procedures to start a business (number)	..	11	10
Firing cost (weeks of wages)	..	87.0	62.6
Closing a business (years to resolve insolvency)	..	5.0	3.8
Total tax rate (% of profit)	..	41.1	67.4
Highest marginal tax rate, corporate (%)	32	28	
Business entry rate (new registrations as % of total)	..	..	6.4
Enterprise surveys			
Time dealing with gov't officials (% of management time)	..	3.1	
Firms expected to give gifts in meetings w/tax officials (%)	..	78.7	
Firms using banks to finance investments (% of firms)	..	29.2	
Delay in obtaining an electrical connection (days)	..	12.4	
ISO certification ownership (% of firms)	..	11.4	
Private sector investment			
Invest. in infrastructure w/private participation ($ millions)	150	260	29,785
Private foreign direct investment, net (% of GDP)	4.2	3.8	2.6
Gross fixed capital formation (% of GDP)	27.6	32.8	26.7
Gross fixed private capital formation (% of GDP)	..	..	19.6
Finance and banking			
Government cash surplus or deficit (% of GDP)	..	..	-2.6
Government debt (% of GDP)	..	..	..
Deposit money banks' assets (% of GDP)	32.0	71.5	50.5
Total financial system deposits (% of GDP)	7.4	12.6	44.6
Bank capital to asset ratio (%)	..	..	..
Bank nonperforming loans to total gross loans ratio (%)	..	..	..
Domestic credit to the private sector (% of GDP)	35.3	71.3	38.3
Real interest rate (%)	6.9	3.6	
Interest rate spread (percentage points)	6.9	3.5	11.3
Infrastructure			
Paved roads (% of total roads)	25.1	..	..
Electric power consumption (kWh per capita)	295	573	391
Power outages in a typical month (number)	..	..	
Fixed line and mobile subscribers (per 100 people)	4	31	17
Internet users (per 100 people)	0.3	17.5	4.2
Cost of telephone call to U.S. ($ per 3 minutes)	9.29	1.95	1.99

Virgin Islands (U.S.)

	Country data		High-income group
	2000	2006	2006
Economic and social context			
Population (millions)	0.11	0.11	1,031
Labor force (millions)	0.05	0.05	504
Unemployment rate (% of labor force)	..	..	6.2
GNI per capita, *World Bank Atlas* method ($)	..	..	36,608
GDP growth, 1995–2000 and 2000–06 (average annual %)	..	..	2.3
Agriculture value added (% of GDP)	..	..	1.5
Industry value added (% of GDP)	..	..	26.2
Manufacturing value added (% of GDP)	..	..	16.8
Services value added (% of GDP)	..	..	72.3
Inflation (annual % change in consumer price index)	..	..	
Exchange rate (local currency units per $)	1.0	1.0	
Exports of goods and services (% of GDP)	..	..	25.6
Imports of goods and services (% of GDP)	..	..	26.3
Business environment			
Ease of doing business (ranking 1-178; 1=best)	..	..	
Time to start a business (days)	..	..	22
Procedures to start a business (number)	..	..	7
Firing cost (weeks of wages)	..	..	34.9
Closing a business (years to resolve insolvency)	..	..	2.0
Total tax rate (% of profit)	..	..	41.5
Highest marginal tax rate, corporate (%)	..	..	
Business entry rate (new registrations as % of total)	..	..	10.1
Enterprise surveys			
Time dealing with gov't officials (% of management time)	..	..	
Firms expected to give gifts in meetings w/tax officials (%)	..	..	
Firms using banks to finance investments (% of firms)	..	..	
Delay in obtaining an electrical connection (days)	..	..	
ISO certification ownership (% of firms)	..	..	
Private sector investment			
Invest. in infrastructure w/private participation ($ millions)	..	..	849
Private foreign direct investment, net (% of GDP)	..	..	2.7
Gross fixed capital formation (% of GDP)	..	..	20.4
Gross fixed private capital formation (% of GDP)	..	..	..
Finance and banking			
Government cash surplus or deficit (% of GDP)	..	..	-1.3
Government debt (% of GDP)	..	..	47.6
Deposit money banks' assets (% of GDP)	..	..	99.7
Total financial system deposits (% of GDP)	..	..	..
Bank capital to asset ratio (%)	..	..	6.2
Bank nonperforming loans to total gross loans ratio (%)	..	..	1.1
Domestic credit to the private sector (% of GDP)	..	..	162.0
Real interest rate (%)	..	..	
Interest rate spread (percentage points)	..	..	4.4
Infrastructure			
Paved roads (% of total roads)	..	..	90.9
Electric power consumption (kWh per capita)	..	..	9,760
Power outages in a typical month (number)	..	..	
Fixed line and mobile subscribers (per 100 people)	95	140	143
Internet users (per 100 people)	13.8	27.6	59.3
Cost of telephone call to U.S. ($ per 3 minutes)	0.87	..	0.77

Zambia

	Country data		Low-income group
	2000	2006	2006
Economic and social context			
Population (millions)	10.5	11.7	2,420
Labor force (millions)	4.5	5.0	995
Unemployment rate (% of labor force)	12.0	..	..
GNI per capita, *World Bank Atlas* method ($)	300	630	649
GDP growth, 1995–2000 and 2000–06 (average annual %)	2.2	5.0	6.5
Agriculture value added (% of GDP)	22.3	21.8	20.4
Industry value added (% of GDP)	25.3	32.9	27.7
Manufacturing value added (% of GDP)	11.4	11.1	15.8
Services value added (% of GDP)	52.4	45.3	51.9
Inflation (annual % change in consumer price index)	26.0	9.0	
Exchange rate (local currency units per $)	3,110.8	3,603.1	
Exports of goods and services (% of GDP)	27.1	38.2	26.7
Imports of goods and services (% of GDP)	41.5	29.6	30.1
Business environment			
Ease of doing business (ranking 1-178; 1=best)	..	116	
Time to start a business (days)	..	33	54
Procedures to start a business (number)	..	6	10
Firing cost (weeks of wages)	..	178.0	62.6
Closing a business (years to resolve insolvency)	..	2.7	3.8
Total tax rate (% of profit)	..	16.1	67.4
Highest marginal tax rate, corporate (%)	35	35	
Business entry rate (new registrations as % of total)	..	5.2	6.4
Enterprise surveys			
Time dealing with gov't officials (% of management time)	13.0	..	
Firms expected to give gifts in meetings w/tax officials (%)	..	5.4	
Firms using banks to finance investments (% of firms)	17.4	10.1	
Delay in obtaining an electrical connection (days)	142.4	93.2	
ISO certification ownership (% of firms)	5.8	..	
Private sector investment			
Invest. in infrastructure w/private participation ($ millions)	27	238	29,785
Private foreign direct investment, net (% of GDP)	3.8	5.4	2.6
Gross fixed capital formation (% of GDP)	16.0	23.0	26.7
Gross fixed private capital formation (% of GDP)	6.0	19.0	19.6
Finance and banking			
Government cash surplus or deficit (% of GDP)	1.8	-2.8	-2.6
Government debt (% of GDP)	176.2	..	
Deposit money banks' assets (% of GDP)	12.4	13.9	50.5
Total financial system deposits (% of GDP)	16.3	15.4	44.6
Bank capital to asset ratio (%)	..	..	..
Bank nonperforming loans to total gross loans ratio (%)	23.6	10.8	..
Domestic credit to the private sector (% of GDP)	8.6	9.7	38.3
Real interest rate (%)	6.7	9.8	
Interest rate spread (percentage points)	18.6	12.8	11.3
Infrastructure			
Paved roads (% of total roads)	22.0	..	..
Electric power consumption (kWh per capita)	595	721	391
Power outages in a typical month (number)	..	4.2	
Fixed line and mobile subscribers (per 100 people)	2	15	17
Internet users (per 100 people)	0.2	4.3	4.2
Cost of telephone call to U.S. ($ per 3 minutes)	2.57	1.41	1.99

Zimbabwe

Sub-Saharan Africa   **Low income**

	Country data		Low-income group
	2000	2006	2006
Economic and social context			
Population (millions)	12.7	13.2	2,420
Labor force (millions)	5.4	6.0	995
Unemployment rate (% of labor force)	6.0	..	..
GNI per capita, *World Bank Atlas* method ($)	450	340	649
GDP growth, 1995-2000 and 2000-06 (average annual %)	0.7	-5.7	6.5
Agriculture value added (% of GDP)	18.5	19.1	20.4
Industry value added (% of GDP)	25.0	23.9	27.7
Manufacturing value added (% of GDP)	15.8	13.5	15.8
Services value added (% of GDP)	56.5	57.0	51.9
Inflation (annual % change in consumer price index)	55.9	1,096.7	
Exchange rate (local currency units per $)	0.0	164.4	
Exports of goods and services (% of GDP)	35.9	56.8	26.7
Imports of goods and services (% of GDP)	36.2	73.0	30.1
Business environment			
Ease of doing business (ranking 1-178; 1=best)	..	152	
Time to start a business (days)	..	96	54
Procedures to start a business (number)	..	10	10
Firing cost (weeks of wages)	..	446.0	62.6
Closing a business (years to resolve insolvency)	..	3.3	3.8
Total tax rate (% of profit)	..	53.0	67.4
Highest marginal tax rate, corporate (%)	30	30	
Business entry rate (new registrations as % of total)	..	..	6.4
Enterprise surveys			
Time dealing with gov't officials (% of management time)	..	..	
Firms expected to give gifts in meetings w/tax officials (%)	..	..	
Firms using banks to finance investments (% of firms)	..	..	
Delay in obtaining an electrical connection (days)	..	..	
ISO certification ownership (% of firms)	..	..	
Private sector investment			
Invest. in infrastructure w/private participation ($ millions)	8	20	29,785
Private foreign direct investment, net (% of GDP)	0.3	3.0	2.6
Gross fixed capital formation (% of GDP)	11.8	21.0	26.7
Gross fixed private capital formation (% of GDP)	11.1	19.5	19.6
Finance and banking			
Government cash surplus or deficit (% of GDP)	-5.2	..	-2.6
Government debt (% of GDP)	58.1	..	
Deposit money banks' assets (% of GDP)	24.3	15.9	50.5
Total financial system deposits (% of GDP)	28.3	18.4	44.6
Bank capital to asset ratio (%)	9.4	12.1	..
Bank nonperforming loans to total gross loans ratio (%)	19.6	23.2	..
Domestic credit to the private sector (% of GDP)	24.5	26.6	38.3
Real interest rate (%)	7.7	-0.7	
Interest rate spread (percentage points)	18.0	293.1	11.3
Infrastructure			
Paved roads (% of total roads)	19.0	..	..
Electric power consumption (kWh per capita)	843	953	391
Power outages in a typical month (number)	..	..	
Fixed line and mobile subscribers (per 100 people)	4	9	17
Internet users (per 100 people)	0.4	9.2	4.2
Cost of telephone call to U.S. ($ per 3 minutes)	4.36	..	1.99

Glossary

Agriculture value added is the net output of agriculture (International Standard Industrial Classification divisions 1–5, including forestry and fishing) after totaling outputs and subtracting intermediate inputs. (World Bank and Organisation for Economic Co-operation and Development)

Bank capital to asset ratio is the ratio of bank capital and reserves to total assets. Capital and reserves include funds contributed by owners, retained earnings, general and special reserves, provisions, and valuation adjustments. Capital includes tier 1 capital (paid-up shares and common stock), which is a common feature in all countries' banking systems, and total regulatory capital, which includes several specified types of subordinated debt instruments that need not be repaid if the funds are required to maintain minimum capital levels (these comprise tier 2 and tier 3 capital). Total assets include all nonfinancial and financial assets. (International Monetary Fund)

Bank nonperforming loans to total gross loans ratio is the value of nonperforming loans divided by the total value of the loan portfolio (including nonperforming loans before the deduction of specific loan loss provisions). The loan amount recorded as nonperforming should be the gross value of the loan as recorded on the balance sheet, not just the amount that is overdue. (International Monetary Fund)

Business entry rate is the number of firms newly registered in 2005 as a percentage of total registered firms. Total firms registered includes all limited liability corporations. (World Bank Group Entrepreneurship Survey)

Closing a business is the number of years from the time of filing for insolvency in court until resolution of distressed assets. Data listed for 2006 are for June 2007. (World Bank)

Cost of telephone call to U.S. is the cost of a three-minute, peak rate, fixed-line call from the country to the United States. (International Telecommunication Union)

Delay in obtaining an electrical connection is the average wait, in days, to obtain an electrical connection from the day an establishment applies for it to the day it receives the service. (World Bank)

Deposit money banks' assets are claims on the domestic real nonfinancial sector by deposit money banks. (International Monetary Fund)

Domestic credit to the private sector is financial resources provided to the private sector—such as through loans, purchases of nonequity securities, and trade credits and other accounts receivable—that establish a claim for repayment. For some countries these claims include credit to public enterprises. (International Monetary Fund, World Bank, and Organisation for Economic Co-operation and Development)

Glossary

Ease of doing business index ranks economies from 1 to 178, with 1 being the best. A high ranking means that a country's regulatory environment is conducive to business operation. The index ranks the simple average of a country's percentile rankings on 10 topics covered in *Doing Business 2008*. The ranking on each topic is the simple average of the percentile rankings on its component indicators. Data listed for 2006 are for June 2007. (World Bank)

Electric power consumption is the production of power plants and combined heat and power plants minus transmission, distribution, and transformation losses and own use by heat and power plants. (International Energy Agency)

Exchange rate is the exchange rate determined by national authorities or the rate determined in the legally sanctioned exchange market. It is calculated as an annual average based on monthly averages (local currency units relative to the U.S. dollar). (International Monetary Fund)

Exports of goods and services are the value of all goods and other market services provided to the rest of the world. They include the value of merchandise, freight, insurance, transport, travel, royalties, license fees, and other services, such as communication, construction, financial, information, business, personal, and government services. They exclude compensation of employees and investment income (formerly called factor services) as well as transfer payments. (World Bank and Organisation for Economic Co-operation and Development)

Firing cost is the cost of advance notice requirements, severance payments, and penalties due when terminating a redundant worker, expressed in weekly wages. One month is recorded as 4 1/3 weeks. Data listed for 2006 are for June 2007. (World Bank)

Firms expected to give gifts in meetings with tax officials are the percentage of firms that report that a gift or informal payment is expected or requested during a meeting with tax officials. (World Bank)

Firms using banks to finance investments are the percentage of firms using banks to finance purchases of fixed assets. (World Bank)

Fixed line and mobile subscribers are telephone mainlines connecting subscribers' equipment to the public switched telephone network and users of portable telephones subscribing to an automatic public mobile telephone service using cellular technology that provides access to the public switched telephone network. (International Telecommunication Union)

GDP growth is the annual percentage growth rate of gross domestic product (GDP) at market prices based on constant local currency. Aggregates are based on constant 2000 U.S. dollars. GDP is the sum of gross value added by all resident producers in the economy plus any product taxes and minus any subsidies not included in the value of the products. It is calculated without deducting for depreciation of fabricated assets or for depletion and degradation of natural resources. (World Bank and Organisation for Economic Co-operation and Development)

GNI per capita, *World Bank Atlas* method, is gross national income (GNI) converted to U.S. dollars using the *World Bank Atlas* method, divided by the midyear population. GNI is the sum of value added by all resident producers plus any product taxes (less subsidies) not included in the valuation of output plus net receipts of primary income (compensation of employees and property income) from abroad. GNI, calculated in national currency, is usually converted to U.S. dollars at official exchange rates for comparisons across economies. To smooth fluctuations in prices and exchange rates, the *World Bank Atlas* method is used; it averages the exchange rate for a given year and the two preceding years, adjusted for differences in rates of inflation between the country and the euro zone, Japan, the United Kingdom, and the United States. (World Bank)

Government cash surplus or deficit is revenue (including grants) minus expense and net acquisition of nonfinancial assets. (International Monetary Fund, World Bank, and Organisation for Economic Co-operation and Development)

Government debt is the entire stock of direct government fixed-term contractual obligations to others outstanding on a particular date. It includes domestic and foreign liabilities such as loans, currency and money deposits, and securities other than shares. It is the gross amount of government liabilities reduced by the amount of equity and financial derivatives held by the government. Because debt is a stock rather than a flow, it is measured as of a given date, usually the last day of the fiscal year. (International Monetary Fund, World Bank, and Organisation for Economic Co-operation and Development)

Gross fixed capital formation includes land improvements (fences, ditches, drains, and so on); plant, machinery, and equipment purchases; and the construction of roads, railways, and the like, including schools, offices, hospitals, private residential dwellings, and commercial and industrial buildings. According to the 1993 System of National Accounts, net acquisition of valuables is also considered capital formation. (World Bank and Organisation for Economic Co-operation and Development)

Gross fixed private capital formation is gross outlays by the private sector (including private nonprofit organizations) on additions to its fixed domestic assets. (World Bank and Organisation for Economic Co-operation and Development)

Highest marginal tax rate, corporate, is the highest rate shown on the national level schedule of tax rates applied to the annual taxable income of corporations. (PricewaterhouseCoopers)

Glossary

Imports of goods and services are the value of all goods and other market services received from the rest of the world. They include the value of merchandise, freight, insurance, transport, travel, royalties, license fees, and other services, such as communication, construction, financial, information, business, personal, and government services. They exclude compensation of employees and investment income (formerly called factor services) as well as transfer payments. (World Bank and Organisation for Economic Co-operation and Development)

Industry value added is the net output of industry (International Standard Industrial Classification divisions 10–45, including mining, manufacturing, construction, electricity, water, and gas) after totaling outputs and subtracting intermediate inputs. (World Bank and Organisation for Economic Co-operation and Development)

Inflation is the annual percentage change in the cost to the average consumer of acquiring a basket of goods and services that may be fixed or changed at specified intervals, such as yearly. The Laspeyres formula is generally used. (International Monetary Fund)

Interest rate spread is the interest rate charged by banks on loans to prime customers minus the interest rate paid by commercial or similar banks for demand, time, or savings deposits. (International Monetary Fund)

Internet users are people with access to the worldwide network. (International Telecommunication Union)

Investment in infrastructure with private participation is the value of infrastructure projects in telecommunications, energy (electricity and natural gas transmission and distribution), transport, and water and sanitation that have reached financial closure and directly or indirectly serve the public, including operation and management contracts with major capital expenditure, greenfield projects (in which a private entity or public-private joint venture builds and operates a new facility), and divestitures. Incinerators, movable assets, standalone solid waste projects, and small projects such as windmills are excluded. (World Bank)

ISO certification ownership is the percentage of firms that have earned a quality certification recognized by the International Organization for Standardization (ISO). (World Bank)

Labor force is all people who supply labor for the production of goods and services during a specified period, according to the International Labour Organization definition of the economically active population. It includes both the employed and the unemployed. While national practices vary in the treatment of such groups as the armed forces and seasonal or part-time workers, in general the labor force includes the armed forces, the unemployed, and first-time job-seekers and excludes homemakers and other unpaid caregivers and workers in the informal sector. (International Labour Organization and World Bank)

Manufacturing value added is the net output of industries belonging to International Standard Industrial Classification divisions 15–37 after totaling outputs and subtracting intermediate inputs. (World Bank and Organisation for Economic Co-operation and Development)

Paved roads are roads surfaced with concrete, cobblestones, or crushed stone (macadam) and hydrocarbon binder or bituminized agents. (International Road Federation)

Population is based on the de facto definition of population, which counts all residents regardless of legal status or citizenship—except for refugees not permanently settled in the country of asylum, who are generally considered part of the population of their country of origin. Data are midyear estimates. (World Bank)

Power outages in a typical month are the average number of power outages that establishments experience in a typical month. (World Bank)

Private foreign direct investment, net, is net inflows of private investment to acquire a lasting management interest (10 percent or more of voting stock) in an enterprise operating in an economy other than that of the investor. It is the sum of equity capital, reinvestment of earnings, other long-term capital, and short-term capital, as shown in the balance of payments. (International Monetary Fund, World Bank, and Organisation for Economic Co-operation and Development)

Procedures to start a business are the number of procedures required to start a business, including interactions to obtain necessary permits and licenses and to complete all inscriptions, verifications, and notifications to start operations. Data are for businesses with specific characteristics of ownership, size, and type of production. Data listed for 2006 are for June 2007. (World Bank)

Real interest rate is the lending interest rate adjusted for inflation as measured by the GDP deflator. (International Monetary Fund and World Bank)

Services value added is the net output of services (International Standard Industrial Classification divisions 50–99) after totaling outputs and subtracting intermediate inputs. (World Bank and Organisation for Economic Co-operation and Development)

Time dealing with government officials is the percentage of management time in a given week spent on requirements imposed by government regulations (taxes, customs, labor regulations, licensing, and registration). (World Bank)

Glossary

Time to start a business is the number of calendar days needed to complete the required procedures for legally operating a business. If a procedure can be expedited at additional cost, the fastest procedure, independent of cost, is chosen. Data listed for 2006 are for June 2007. (World Bank)

Total financial system deposits are the demand, time, and saving deposits in deposit money banks and other financial institutions. (International Monetary Fund)

Total tax rate is the total amount of taxes payable by the business (except for labor taxes) after accounting for deductions and exemptions as a percentage of profit. For further details on the method used for assessing the total tax payable, see the World Bank's *Doing Business 2008*. Data listed for 2006 are for June 2007. (World Bank)

Unemployment rate is the share of the labor force without work but available for and seeking employment. Definitions of *labor force* and *unemployment* differ by country. (International Labour Organization)

West Bank and Gaza

Middle East & North Africa			Lower middle income

	Country data		Lower middle-income group
	2000	**2006**	**2006**
Economic and social context			
Population (millions)	3.0	3.8	2,276
Labor force (millions)	0.62	0.80	1,209
Unemployment rate (% of labor force)	14.1	26.8	5.7
GNI per capita, *World Bank Atlas* method ($)	1,580	*1,230*	2,038
GDP growth, 1995–2000 and 2000–06 (average annual %)	7.4	0.2	7.6
Agriculture value added (% of GDP)	..	..	11.9
Industry value added (% of GDP)	..	..	43.5
Manufacturing value added (% of GDP)	..	..	26.7
Services value added (% of GDP)	..	..	44.6
Inflation (annual % change in consumer price index)	3.0	3.5	
Exchange rate (local currency units per $)	..		
Exports of goods and services (% of GDP)	16.0	15.7	40.4
Imports of goods and services (% of GDP)	71.2	69.7	36.4
Business environment			
Ease of doing business (ranking 1-178; 1=best)	..	117	
Time to start a business (days)	..	92	53
Procedures to start a business (number)	..	12	10
Firing cost (weeks of wages)	..	91.0	50.2
Closing a business (years to resolve insolvency)	..	..	3.3
Total tax rate (% of profit)	..	17.1	45.8
Highest marginal tax rate, corporate (%)	..	..	
Business entry rate (new registrations as % of total)	..	..	7.6
Enterprise surveys			
Time dealing with gov't officials (% of management time)	..	5.7	
Firms expected to give gifts in meetings w/tax officials (%)	..	2.7	
Firms using banks to finance investments (% of firms)	..	4.2	
Delay in obtaining an electrical connection (days)	..	37.1	
ISO certification ownership (% of firms)	..	18.2	
Private sector investment			
Invest. in infrastructure w/private participation ($ millions)	237	23	38,154
Private foreign direct investment, net (% of GDP)	..	..	3.0
Gross fixed capital formation (% of GDP)	32.7	26.9	33.5
Gross fixed private capital formation (% of GDP)	..	..	10.9
Finance and banking			
Government cash surplus or deficit (% of GDP)	..	..	-0.9
Government debt (% of GDP)	..	..	..
Deposit money banks' assets (% of GDP)	..	..	87.8
Total financial system deposits (% of GDP)	..	..	43.1
Bank capital to asset ratio (%)	..	..	10.7
Bank nonperforming loans to total gross loans ratio (%)	..	..	4.0
Domestic credit to the private sector (% of GDP)	5.5	8.0	81.3
Real interest rate (%)	10.5	8.0	
Interest rate spread (percentage points)	6.9	4.8	7.2
Infrastructure			
Paved roads (% of total roads)	*100.0*	*100.0*	65.8
Electric power consumption (kWh per capita)	..	..	*1,502*
Power outages in a typical month (number)	..	3.3	
Fixed line and mobile subscribers (per 100 people)	15	31	60
Internet users (per 100 people)	1.2	7.0	11.4
Cost of telephone call to U.S. ($ per 3 minutes)	*1.11*	*1.17*	*2.08*

Yemen, Rep.

Middle East & North Africa   **Low income**

	Country data		Low-income group
	2000	**2006**	**2006**
Economic and social context			
Population (millions)	18.2	21.7	2,420
Labor force (millions)	4.9	6.3	995
Unemployment rate (% of labor force)	11.5	..	..
GNI per capita, *World Bank Atlas* method ($)	400	760	649
GDP growth, 1995–2000 and 2000–06 (average annual %)	5.6	3.9	6.5
Agriculture value added (% of GDP)	10.3	14.3	20.4
Industry value added (% of GDP)	46.5	40.3	27.7
Manufacturing value added (% of GDP)	5.2	4.7	15.8
Services value added (% of GDP)	43.2	45.4	51.9
Inflation (annual % change in consumer price index)	4.6	20.8	
Exchange rate (local currency units per $)	161.7	197.0	
Exports of goods and services (% of GDP)	42.3	38.0	26.7
Imports of goods and services (% of GDP)	36.6	41.4	30.1
Business environment			
Ease of doing business (ranking 1-178; 1=best)	..	113	
Time to start a business (days)	..	63	54
Procedures to start a business (number)	..	12	10
Firing cost (weeks of wages)	..	17.0	62.6
Closing a business (years to resolve insolvency)	..	3.0	3.8
Total tax rate (% of profit)	..	41.4	67.4
Highest marginal tax rate, corporate (%)	..	..	
Business entry rate (new registrations as % of total)	..	8.4	6.4
Enterprise surveys			
Time dealing with gov't officials (% of management time)	..	..	
Firms expected to give gifts in meetings w/tax officials (%)	..	..	
Firms using banks to finance investments (% of firms)	..	..	
Delay in obtaining an electrical connection (days)	..	..	
ISO certification ownership (% of firms)	..	..	
Private sector investment			
Invest. in infrastructure w/private participation ($ millions)	20	287	29,785
Private foreign direct investment, net (% of GDP)	0.1	5.9	2.6
Gross fixed capital formation (% of GDP)	18.6	23.1	26.7
Gross fixed private capital formation (% of GDP)	13.2	13.4	19.6
Finance and banking			
Government cash surplus or deficit (% of GDP)	-2.3	..	-2.6
Government debt (% of GDP)	..	..	
Deposit money banks' assets (% of GDP)	8.6	12.0	50.5
Total financial system deposits (% of GDP)	17.4	18.7	44.6
Bank capital to asset ratio (%)	..	..	..
Bank nonperforming loans to total gross loans ratio (%)	..	..	..
Domestic credit to the private sector (% of GDP)	5.0	6.9	38.3
Real interest rate (%)	-4.9	4.1	
Interest rate spread (percentage points)	5.5	5.0	11.3
Infrastructure			
Paved roads (% of total roads)	15.5	8.7	..
Electric power consumption (kWh per capita)	136	174	391
Power outages in a typical month (number)	..	..	
Fixed line and mobile subscribers (per 100 people)	2	14	17
Internet users (per 100 people)	0.1	1.2	4.2
Cost of telephone call to U.S. ($ per 3 minutes)	4.45	2.39	1.99